Queering International Law

AF695036

This ground-breaking collection reflects the growing momentum of interest in the international legal community in meshing the insights of queer legal theory with those critical theories that have a much longer genealogy – notably postcolonial and feminist analyses. Beyond the push in the human rights field to ensure respect for the rights of people with diverse sexual orientations and gender identities, queer legal theory provides a means to examine the structural assumptions and conceptual architecture that underpin the normative framework and operation of international law, highlighting bias and blind spots and offering fresh perspectives and practical innovations.

The contributors to the book use queer legal theory to critically analyse the basic tenets and operations of international law, with many surprising, thought-provoking and instructive results. The volume will be of interest to many scholars, students and researchers in international law, international relations, cultural studies, gender studies, queer studies and postcolonial studies.

Dianne Otto held the Francine V McNiff Chair in Human Rights Law at the University of Melbourne Law School, Australia, 2013–2016. She is currently a Professorial Fellow at Melbourne Law School.

Routledge Research in International Law

For a full list of titles in this series, visit https://www.routledge.com/Routledge-Research-in-International-Law/book-series/INTNLLAW

Available:

Universal Jurisdiction in International Criminal Law
The Debate and the Battle for Hegemony
Aisling O'Sullivan

The Right to Democracy in International Law
Between Procedure, Substance and the Philosophy of John Rawls
Khalifa A. Alfadhel

The Rule of Law in the United Nations Security Council Decision-Making Process
Turning the Focus Inwards
Sherif Elgebeily

Sovereignty Conflicts and International Law and Politics
A Distributive Justice Issue
Jorge E. Núñez

Queering International Law
Possibilities, Alliances, Complicities, Risks
Dianne Otto

Prosecuting Juvenile Piracy Suspects
The International Legal Framework
Milena Sterio

Forthcoming titles in this series include:

Technology and the Law on the Use of Force
New Security Challenges in the Twenty First Century
Jackson Maogoto

International Law and the Rights of those Displaced by Armed Conflict
Elena Katselli Proukaki

International Criminal Law and Sexual Violence against Women
The Interpretation of Gender in the Contemporary International Criminal Trial
Daniela Nadj

Fighting and Victimhood in International Criminal Law
Joanna Nicholson

Queering International Law

Possibilities, Alliances, Complicities, Risks

Edited by Dianne Otto

Routledge
Taylor & Francis Group
LONDON AND NEW YORK

First published 2018 by Routledge

2 Park Square, Milton Park, Abingdon, Oxfordshire OX14 4RN
52 Vanderbilt Avenue, New York, NY 10017

Routledge is an imprint of the Taylor & Francis Group, an informa business

First issued in paperback 2019

Copyright © 2018 selection and editorial matter, Dianne Otto; individual chapters, the contributors

The right of Dianne Otto to be identified as the author of the editorial material, and of the authors for their individual chapters, has been asserted in accordance with sections 77 and 78 of the Copyright, Designs and Patents Act 1988.

All rights reserved. No part of this book may be reprinted or reproduced or utilised in any form or by any electronic, mechanical, or other means, now known or hereafter invented, including photocopying and recording, or in any information storage or retrieval system, without permission in writing from the publishers.

Notice:
Product or corporate names may be trademarks or registered trademarks, and are used only for identification and explanation without intent to infringe.

British Library Cataloguing in Publication Data
A catalogue record for this book is available from the British Library

Library of Congress Cataloging in Publication Data
Names: Otto, Dianne, editor.
Title: Queering international law : possibilities, alliances, complicities, risks / Edited by Dianne Otto.
Description: New York : Routledge, 2017. |
Series: Routledge research in international law | Includes bibliographical references and index.
Identifiers: LCCN 2017012346 | ISBN 9781138289918 (hbk) | ISBN 9781315266787 (ebk)
Subjects: LCSH: Gays—Legal status, laws, etc. | Human rights. | Homosexuality—Law and legislation. | Gender identity—Law and legislation. | International law. | Sex and law. | Heterosexism.
Classification: LCC K3242.3. Q45 2017 | DDC 342.08/7—dc23
LC record available at https://lccn.loc.gov/2017012346

ISBN: 978-1-138-28991-8 (hbk)
ISBN: 978-0-367-88637-0 (pbk)

Typeset in Galliard
by Keystroke, Neville Lodge, Tettenhall, Wolverhampton

For
Professor Thomas Frank,
who mentored me and shared my hopefulness
and
Joan Nestle, my partner,
without whom I would lose hope.

Contents

List of figures

Notes on contributors

Doris Buss is Professor of Law in the Department of Law and Legal Studies at Carleton University. Her research explores the socio-legal dimensions of law and human rights, women's rights, the gender of armed conflict and its aftermath, and feminist theory.

Maria Elander is Lecturer in Criminology and Law at La Trobe Law School, La Trobe University. Her research is in the broader field of international criminal justice, and engages with theories in cultural and feminist legal studies, often with a focus on the Khmer Rouge Tribunal/ECCC.

Bina Fernandez is Senior Lecturer in Development Studies at the University of Melbourne. Major research awards include an Australian Research Council DECRA Fellowship (2015–17), a British Academy Small Grant in 2010, the UNDP Human Development Fellowship in 2005 and a Radhakrishnan Chevening Award in 2001–3.

Aeyal Gross is Professor of Law at Tel Aviv University. He is also a Visiting Reader at SOAS, the University of London. He holds an LLB from Tel Aviv University and SJD from Harvard Law School. He is a board member of the Association for Civil Rights in Israel.

Vanja Hamzić is Senior Lecturer in Legal History and Legal Anthropology at SOAS, the University of London. His research primarily revolves around human subjectivity formation and insurrectionary vernacular knowledge. He also explores various Islamic legal traditions and their intersections with Marxist social, political and economic thought.

Ratna Kapur is currently Visiting Professor of Law at Queen Mary University of London. She is also Professor of Law at Jindal Global Law School. She has taught and published extensively on issues of human rights, postcolonial theory and feminist legal theory. Her current work seeks to critically analyse the relationship between human rights and freedom.

Dianne Otto held the Francine V McNiff Chair in Human Rights Law at Melbourne Law School (2013–16). Her research engages feminist, queer and postcolonial perspectives in international human rights law, the UN Security

Council's peacekeeping, the technologies of global 'crisis governance', social and economic rights, people's tribunals and other NGO initiatives.

Tamsin Phillipa Paige is Research Associate with the Research Unit on Military Law and Ethics at Adelaide Law School, as a part of her PhD Candidature with the University of Adelaide. She holds an LLB from the University of Technology Sydney and an MPhil from the Australian National University, while in a previous life she was a pastry chef.

Rahul Rao is Senior Lecturer in Politics at SOAS, the University of London. He has a law degree from the National Law School of India University and a doctorate in international relations from the University of Oxford.

Blair Rutherford is Professor of Anthropology in the Department of Sociology and Anthropology at Carleton University. He has been researching the gendered and raced cultural politics of livelihoods in sub-Saharan Africa since the early 1990s.

Nan Seuffert is Director of the Legal Intersections Research Centre at the University of Wollongong School of Law. She teaches and researches in the areas of critical legal theory, law and history, law and literature, race, gender, sexuality and the law, contract and securities regulation.

Anniken Sørlie is PhD Candidate at the Department of Public and International Law, the University of Oslo, and participates in the research project 'gender identity and sexual orientation in international and national (Norwegian) law'. Her PhD critically reflects on laws and regulations that impact the lives of transgender people in Norway.

Monika Zalnieriute is a scholar and activist working in the area of Internet policy and queer rights online. She is a Post-Doctoral Fellow at the Melbourne Law School and is a co-founder of SapfoFest – the first queer festival in Lithuania. Monika engages actively with academic, activist and policy-making circles.

Acknowledgements

Thanks are due to all the contributors to this volume for their enthusiastic commitment to our collaborative exploration of new scholarly, disciplinary and activist frontiers. I am grateful for all the thinking and writing time they devoted to the project and for their generous responsiveness to feedback and suggestions for revision. It has been a great pleasure to work with all of them.

Gratitude is also due to my indefatigable research assistant, Mimi Oorloff, whose magnificent copy-editing skills got the manuscript over the line and kept me from anxious collapse. I very much appreciate the grant from the Melbourne Law School (MLS) Research Support Fund which made Mimi's employment possible.

The collection originated with a celebratory legal theory workshop of the same name, *Queering International Law: Possibilities, Alliances, Complicities, Risks*, which I convened at Melbourne Law School (MLS), 14 to 15 December 2015. Hosted by the Institute for International Law and the Humanities (IILAH), the second in its annual legal theory workshop series *Provocations*, the workshop was funded by IILAH, MLS Office for Research International Collaboration Fund, MLS Dean's Discretionary Fund and those many participants who found funds to cover the balance of their travel expenses. The workshop was beautifully organised by IILAH Administrator Vesna Stefanovski with her usual close attention to people and to detail. Christopher Pidgley, the new IILAH Administrator, took up the project in its final stages. Both of them helped to make the workshop an unforgettable intellectual, collegial and gastronomic experience.

I gratefully acknowledge the contributions of all those who participated in the workshop. In particular, I thank those who presented papers for discussion which do not appear in this collection: Neo Sinoxolo Musangi, Philipp Kastner, Elisabeth Roy Trudel and Ralph Wilde. I also thank those who prepared commentaries on the papers presented: Maddee Clarke, Debolina Dutta, Maria Elander, Laura Grenfell, Fleur Johns, Christina Kenny, Dave McDonald, Wayne Morgan, Claire Opperman, Sundhya Pahuja, Oishik Sircar and Marc Trabsky. My gratitude to several others who made important contributions to the workshop in various ways: Joan Nestle, Yasmin Tambiah, Maddy Chiam, Mark McMillan and Kristen Walker.

Additional generosities that made this book possible were the permissions for the use of images granted by Ebba Backlund of Cancerfonden (the Swedish Cancer Society) and Agnes Hellström, President of the Swedish Peace and Arbitration Society. Finally, thanks to Rob Gibson, Katie Carpenter and Olivia Manley at Routledge, Taylor & Francis, for believing in this project and working with me to make it happen.

Introduction

Embracing queer curiosity

Dianne Otto

> Curiosity is always transgressive, always a sign of the rejection of the known as inadequate, incorrect, even uninteresting.[1]

What kind of questioning does an invitation to 'queer' international law call for? In putting this collection together, I have understood 'queering' international law as both a scholarly and an activist project, inspired by a hope for change that is far more ambitious than LGBTI normative inclusion, as important as that is. Like feminist and postcolonial structural critiques of the discipline, the terminology of queer signals a curiosity about the conceptual and analytical underpinnings of international law's adjudication of the normal. A queer analysis cannot be answered by granting equal rights, although this may constitute a partial response. Queering international law presents a fundamental challenge to the usual way of framing international legal problems and crafting solutions. The terminology of queer also signals a concern with pleasure, which may require 'taking a break'[2] from the politics of heteronormative injury, in order to celebrate human sexuality and gender expression in all its diversity and fluidity, beyond the dualistic confines of heterosexuality/homosexuality and male/female.

Whether or not the analytics of sexuality alone provide an adequate foundation for queer theory is a matter of some debate. In my view, while sexuality has its own biopolitical forms and governmental modes, its analytics are deeply intertwined with other systems of hierarchy, including those of sex/gender, class, race, indigeneity and (dis)ability. They are all vectors of power that are constituted in relation to each other. This understanding is more or less shared by the other contributors to this collection. By paying close attention to the imperial histories that accompany the operation of sexual and gender norms in the neoliberal present, the extraordinary power these norms have to shore up the status quo and

1 Barbara M Benedict, *Curiosity: A Cultural History of Early Modern Inquiry* (University of Chicago Press, 2001) 2.
2 Janet Halley, *Split Decisions: How and Why to Take a Break from Feminism* (Princeton University Press, 2006).

create fear and panic in the face of the shifting contours of the 'abnormal' – Muslims, sex workers, migrants, asylum seekers, feminist and SOGI rights activists – is revealed. By changing meanings, unsettling taxonomies and inverting conventions, it is my hope that queer curiosity can open new ways to imagine a more peaceful, equitable and inclusionary world, and offer fresh means and methods to work towards its realisation.

In the crisis-saturated international community of today, new ways of framing and applying international law are desperately needed. We need an international legal framework that can build solidarity rather than foster division, promote redistributive values rather than private enrichment, challenge the entrenched inequalities of the quotidian rather than normalising and exploiting them, advance positive peace rather than militarism, and ensure environmental sustainability rather than degradation. The critical insights of queer theory can offer new insights into how international law works to reinforce unequal relations of power, resources and knowledge, and how this might be resisted. It promises to enrich our understanding of the conceptual and practical limits of the discipline and help us to imagine the liberatory possibilities that emerge from challenging these limits. Just as feminist curiosity exposed international law's gendered framework, and postcolonial curiosity its European underpinnings, queer curiosity makes visible its [hetero]sexual ordering that is so taken for granted that it is considered 'natural'.

In fact, curiosity has a decidedly queer genealogy. At least since Eve's desire for forbidden knowledge, curiosity has been linked to the Old Testament account of man's [sic] fall into sin and death, which was connected, through Eve, with lust, pride and the pursuit of improper knowledge (more than God allows).[3] In keeping with this tradition of treating curiosity as a dangerous inclination, iconographer Cesare Ripa portrayed curiosity as a wild, feminine force, operating without regard to law and order, in his 1611 guide to moral emblems.[4]

Ripa's commentary describes his representation in the following way:

> She has abundance of Ears and Frogs on her Robe; her Hair stands up on end; Wings on her Shoulders; her Arms lifted up; she thrusts out her Head in a prying Posture. The Ears denote the *Itch* of knowing more than concerns her. The Frogs are Emblems of *Inquisitiveness*, by reason of their goggle-Eyes. The other things denote her running up and down, to hear, and to see, as some do after News.[5]

Just as the transgressiveness of queer thinking is often maligned today, Ripa associates curiosity with deviant expressions of gender, uncontrollable sexual

3 Peter Harrison, 'Curiosity, Forbidden Knowledge, and the Reformation of Natural Philosophy in Early Modern England' (2001) 92 *Isis* 265, 267.

4 Cesare Ripa, *ICONOLOGIA or Moral Emblems* (Benj Motte, 1709) figure 80 <https://archive.org/details/iconologiaormora00ripa>.

5 Ibid (emphasis in the original).

Figure 1 Curiosity, Cesare Ripa, 1611

desires and interest in myriad forms of knowledge considered disruptive and dangerous to the status quo.

Yet, even as curiosity moved from vice to virtue over the course of the seventeenth century and into the eighteenth, its rehabilitation was tied up with the emergence and celebration of scientific knowledge, which imposed a new set of limits on thinking in the guise of specific procedures of rationality associated with empiricism and objectivity.[6] This highly disciplined form of curiosity was lauded as a means to seek knowledge for public benefit and social advancement.[7] Scientific inquiry left a vast realm of curiosities outside proper knowledge, and many of those who asked improper questions were pathologised by the new sciences as mad, or criminalised as a danger to society. According to Michel Foucault's genealogy, nineteenth-century European scientific (medico-juridical) thought produced the figure of 'the homosexual' as a species who, along with other perverts, became 'a type of life' that was observed, analysed, categorised, re-educated and constrained.[8] He identified three other focal points for the production of sexual knowledge in the West, which emerged around the same time – the hysterical woman, the masturbating child and the 'Malthusian couple' who were willing to take 'responsible' control of their reproductive potential.[9] Thus, science made possible a vast expansion of the biopolitical reach of the state and its laws into more intimate, private areas of life.

Theories of evolution were also complicit in producing the new species of the sexual deviant, underscoring its racialised dimensions. Thus, outside the West, the degenerate (undeveloped) sexual practices of the totality of colonised people were imagined and produced by Europeans as needing civilisation, providing justification for colonialism.[10] At the same time, the metropole's understanding of its own enlightened bourgeois sexuality was shaped in contradistinction to the racialised imperial accounts of the uncontrollable libidinal energies of 'savages'.[11] These developments in science helped to institute and normalise hierarchies of sexual difference globally, in the name of universal progress and enlightenment.

Thus, curiosity took on a paradoxical quality, representing both 'value and valuelessness'.[12] Curiosity was lauded if it served elite interests as the 'trademark of progress itself',[13] by fostering increased consumption[14] and legitimating imperial exploitation.[15] At the same time, those whose curiosity cast them as freaks, including rebellious women, uncivilised natives, effete Orientals, sex workers, transsexuals, pirates and other queer figures, were vilified. Yet curiosity's paradoxical character has also meant there is the propensity for curiosity's taboo subjects to become valued and, in various ways, commodified and co-opted to

6 Benedict, above n 1, 25–8.
7 Harrison, above n 3, 280.
8 Michel Foucault, *The History of Sexuality: An Introduction* (Robert Hurley trans, Vintage, first published 1976, 1990 edn) vol 1, 101.
9 Ibid 104–5.
10 Neville Hoad, 'Arrested Development or the Queerness of Savages: Resisting Evolutionary Narratives of Difference' (2000) 3 *Postcolonial Studies* 133, 134.
11 Ann Laura Stoler, *Race and the Education of Desire: Foucault's History of Sexuality and the Colonial Order of Things* (Duke University Press, 1995) 6–7.
12 Benedict, above n 1, 3.
13 Ibid 1.
14 Ibid 37–8.
15 Ibid 251.

serve imperial ends.[16] Israel's portrayal of itself as a gay-friendly tourist destination even as it continues to build its illegal wall is just one example of turning queerness into a neoliberal imperial commodity.[17] Yet there have also always been efforts by the outcasts to subvert these dualistic geographies of value by (re)asserting their humanity and struggling for change. The reclamation of the derogatory language of queer as a positive assertion of transgressive sexual practices, identities and politics is one such effort to expose and subvert the inequitable conventional orderings of life and law.

Cynthia Enloe regards curiosity as an important characteristic of feminist epistemology.[18] The primary target of Enloe's curiosity is militarism and her technique is to start by 'taking women's [everyday] lives seriously',[19] thereby problematising the public/private dichotomy, politicising the personal and making visible masculinist forms of power that are so normalised they are no longer noticed. She draws attention to the Star Wars inspired weaponry-shaped pasta in a can of Heinz tomato and noodle soup, and latex condoms patterned as army camouflage, to illustrate that militarism has become an accepted part of everyday life.[20] In her view, the transgressive nature of feminist curiosity lies in its power to question and destabilise received gendered norms and settled grounds of analysis, together with the willingness to admit surprise and to think afresh.[21] Like queer theory, feminist analysis is thus not confined to seeking equal rights, but treats gender analytically, as 'a primary way of signifying relations of power',[22] which intersects with other articulations of power like race, class and nation.

More recently, Cynthia Weber employs 'queer intellectual curiosity' as an international relations method.[23] Her curiosity 'refuses to take for granted the personal-to-international institutional arrangements', taking readers on a journey of discovery that reveals what happens to our understanding of international politics when the variable of sexuality is included in mappings of its relations of power. Cynthia searches for, and finds, proliferating figurations of 'the homosexual' in international affairs, and examines the work these figures do to invest the modern state with authority and legitimacy. She shows how these figurations

16 Ibid 246–7.

17 Aeyal Gross, 'The Politics of LGBT Rights in Israel and beyond: Nationality, Normativity, and Queer Politics' (2015) 46 *Columbia Human Rights Law Review* 81.

18 Cynthia Enloe, *The Curious Feminist: Searching for Women in a New Age of Empire* (University of California Press, 2004).

19 Cynthia Enloe, 'A Conversation with Cynthia Enloe on Curiosity, Confidence, and Feminist Questions' (2014) 38(2) *Fletcher Forum of World Affairs* 13, 14.

20 Cynthia Enloe, *Maneuvers: The International Politics of Militarizing Women's Lives* (University of California Press, 2000) 1–2.

21 Cynthia Enloe, 'The Surprised Feminist' (2000) 25 *Signs: Journal of Women in Culture and Society* 1023, 1025.

22 Joan Wallach Scott, 'Gender: A Useful Category of Historical Analysis' in *Gender and the Politics of History* (Columbia University Press, revised edn, 1999) 28–50.

23 Cynthia Weber, *Queer International Relations: Sovereignty, Sexuality and the Will to Knowledge* (Oxford University Press, 2016) 19.

also do work beyond the state to sexualise the formal and informal ways that international relations are arranged.

In a similar way, this collection seeks to engage curiosity transgressively, to show how sexuality works as a fundamental organising principle in international law. By uncovering some of the manifold ways that tropes of sexual and gender deviance have helped to institute, legitimate, authorise and sustain a neoliberal international legal order that is socially and economically unjust, dependent on violence and environmentally unsustainable, a powerful case is made for fostering more conversations between queer theory and activism, and international law. Queer curiosity brings to the mix of emancipatory (improper) curiosities, and the critical analysis they foster, a particular concern with conventions of sexuality and the part they play in signifying hierarchical relations of power – not only in their attachment to material bodies, but to structures of understanding that constitute the norms and practices of international law.

I want to particularly emphasise that the contributors to this collection do not think of queer theory as autonomous from, or as surpassing, feminist analysis.[24] There is a strong feminist tradition of support for sexual freedom that has coexisted, not always easily, with feminist concern with sexual violence and exploitation.[25] There is also a long-standing feminist critique of 'compulsory heterosexuality',[26] and insistence that 'sex/gender' is a performative, social construct rather than biologically based.[27] In many respects, queer theory expands the feminist project by drawing attention to the demonisation of all sexual and gender minorities, which includes others, as well as women.

Yet the paradoxes of curiosity are ever present. Enloe describes the risk of producing consequences that have unintended effects, as presenting us with 'puzzles'.[28] I will draw attention to just four of them here, which haunt many of the discussions in the chapters that follow:

How can discrimination and violence experienced by queer individuals and communities be addressed *without* reaffirming the regulatory power of the nation-state to confer rights and responsibilities through its technologies of gay marriage, gay consumerism and gay patriotism, which domesticate queer desires and de-radicalise queer politics?

24 Judith Butler, 'Against Proper Objects: Introduction' (1994) 6(2–3) *Differences: A Journal of Feminist Cultural Studies* 1.

25 See, eg, Carole S Vance (ed), *Pleasure and Danger: Exploring Female Sexuality* (Routledge and Kegan Paul, 1984); Dianne Otto, 'Between Pleasure and Danger: Lesbian Human Rights' (2014) (6) *European Human Rights Law Review* 618.

26 Adrienne Rich, 'Compulsory Heterosexuality and Lesbian Existence' (1980) 5 *Signs: Journal of Women in Culture and Society* 631.

27 Margaret Davies, 'Taking the Inside Out: Sex and Gender in the Legal Subject' in Ngaire Naffine and Rosemary J Owens (eds), *Sexing the Subject of Law* (Sweet & Maxwell, 1997) 25.

28 Enloe, above n 20, 299.

How can appeals be made to international human rights law to make precarious queer lives more liveable *without* legitimising the heteronormative imperial heritage of the normative framework of international law?

How can queer activists work in transnational coalitions to support challenges to the homophobic laws and practices of states *without* the treatment of 'the homosexual' serving as a new measure of 'civilisation'?

How can queer social and cultural change be promoted (and enjoyed) *without* assimilation into the pink economies of neoliberalism which run counter to queer visions of redistributional and egalitarian economics?

Antecedents

This collection did not just 'fall from the sky'. Acknowledging some of its antecedents is to honour those who had the courage to lay the groundwork for this and other challenging exchanges between queer scholars/activists and the discipline of international law. The earliest interventions were in the field of international human rights law. If we go back to 1948, the adoption of the Universal Declaration of Human Rights ('UDHR') by the UN General Assembly declared a new global era in which states would strive to ensure that *everyone* enjoyed human rights and fundamental freedoms.[29] This was a hopeful moment, when the member states of the United Nations affirmed the full humanity of every human being, recognising everyone's intrinsic value and dignity. Yet there were many gaps in the coverage of the UDHR. While these gaps reflect the conceptions of humanity that prevailed at that time, I still find it bewildering that homosexuals were not protected explicitly in the UDHR because of their internment in Nazi concentration camps during the Second World War, where many thousands of them died.[30] Indeed, this omission, and the support of the Allies for the continued criminalisation of homosexuality in post-war Germany,[31] confounds every sense of inherent human dignity, at least from the perspective of today. Instead, the UDHR, and the other international human rights instruments that followed in its wake, confined sexuality to heterosexual marriage and, even then, only by way of obscure references to the right to 'found a family'.[32] There was no reference to sexual freedom or to reproductive rights.

29 Universal Declaration of Human Rights, GA Res 217A (III), UN GAOR, 3rd sess, 183rd plen mtg, UN Doc A/810 (10 December 1948) ('UDHR').

30 See, eg, Geoffrey J Giles, 'The Institutionalization of Homosexual Panic in the Third Reich' in Robert Gellately and Nathan Stoltzfus (eds), *Social Outsiders in Nazi Germany* (Princeton University Press, 2001) 233, 243, 249–50.

31 Nicole LaViolette and Sandra Whitworth, 'No Safe Haven: Sexuality as a Universal Human Right and Gay and Lesbian Activism in International Politics' (1994) 23 *Millennium: Journal of International Studies* 563, 567.

32 See, eg, UDHR, UN Doc A/810, art 16(1); International Covenant on Civil and Political Rights, opened for signature 16 December 1966, 999 UNTS 171 (entered into force 23 March 1976) art 23(2).

It was not until 1982 that the Human Rights Committee, which monitors the International Covenant on Civil and Political Rights ('ICCPR'), in its first decision dealing with lesbians and gay men, found that the Finnish government was justified in limiting the freedom of expression of positive views about homosexuality on radio and television programmes, in order to protect public morals.[33] A report on the legal and social problems of sexual minorities, commissioned in 1983 by the UN Sub-Commission on Prevention of Discrimination and Protection of Minorities,[34] usually a very progressive body, relied heavily on 'stereotypes and misinformation' and claimed disparagingly that same-sex relationships never last[35] – even though we were 35 years into the new era of universal human rights and freedoms. Finally, it was an Australian case, brought by gay Tasmanian Nicholas Toonen, which led the Human Rights Committee to find, in 1994, that anti-sodomy laws were a violation of the right to privacy, as protected by article 17 of the ICCPR.[36]

A sign of the move from a focus on human rights to a broader queer interest in international legal circles was the American Society of International Law's first panel on 'Queering International Law' held at its 2007 Annual Meeting.[37] In 2008, the European Society of International Law hosted an Agora entitled 'Sexuality and Gender in International Law' at its Biennial Conference[38] and, in 2011, a Queer Legal Theory Workshop was organised at the School of Oriental and African Studies (SOAS) in London, which included a panel focused on international law.[39] This collection brings together a number of scholars who played key roles in these developments, as well as young scholars who are eager to bring new insights and enthusiasm to this growing field.

Early in 2015, I invited a number of academics working with queer, feminist and postcolonial theories and practices in international law and related disciplines

33 Human Rights Committee, Report of the Human Rights Committee, 37th sess, Supp No 40, UN Doc A/37/40 (22 September 1982) annex XIV, 165 [10.3]–[11].

34 Jean Fernand-Laurent, Study on Legal and Social Problems of Sexual Minorities, UN ESCOR, UN Doc E/CN.4/Sub.2/1988/31(13 June 1988).

35 Douglas Sanders, 'Getting Lesbian and Gay Issues on the International Human Rights Agenda' (1996) 18 *Human Rights Quarterly* 67, 88.

36 Human Rights Committee, Communication No 488/1992, 50th sess, UN Doc CCPR/C/50/D/488/1992 (31 March 1994) ('*Toonen v Australia*').

37 'Queering International Law' (2007) 101 *American Society of International Law Proceedings* 119–32: Ralph Wilde (chair), Dianne Otto, Doris E Buss, Amr Shalakany and Aeyal Gross (presenters).

38 Agora, 'Sexuality and Gender in International Law' (European Society of International Law 3rd Biennial Conference, Heidelberg, Germany, 4–6 September 2008): Dianne Otto (chair), Aeyal Gross, Marjolein van den Brink, Zoe Pearson and Sari Kouvo (presenters) <http://www.esil-sedi.eu/sites/default/files/Heidelberg%20Programme.pdf>.

39 'Queer Perspectives on Law: Sharing Reflections' (SOAS Spring Queer Legal Theory Workshop, 13 May 2011). Co-organisers: Aeyal Gross and Dianne Otto, hosted by the Centre for the Study of Colonialism, Empire and International Law (CCEIL) and the SOAS Centre for Gender Studies <https://www.soas.ac.uk/cceil/events/13may2011-queer-perspectives-on-law-sharing-reflections.html>.

to contribute to this collection. Scholars from Australia, Canada, India, Israel, Kenya, Norway and the United Kingdom agreed to participate. They presented early drafts of their chapters at a two-day legal theory workshop, hosted by the Institute for International Law and the Humanities (IILAH) at Melbourne Law School, 14 to 15 December 2015. The workshop participants rose to the challenge of locating their analyses in the interstices of queer, feminist and postcolonial theory and activism, fostering alliances and borrowings from across theoretical and disciplinary boundaries, while promoting a better understanding of the complicities and compromises that engagement with power, in the form of international law, may extract.

The structure of this collection

The four themes in the title of this collection gesture towards some of the paradoxes facing queer engagement with international law: complicities, possibilities, alliances and risks. The chapters have been grouped around these themes. Together, these themes reflect an observation made by Foucault, 'that nothing is an evil in itself, but everything is dangerous'.[40] I take him to mean that there is no guarantee that any particular scholarly or activist strategy for change (resistance) will be 'successful', but that there is nevertheless always the possibility of transformation. That queer efforts to challenge the normal practices and operations of international law and politics will face many dangers is therefore part of the journey – to be desired rather than feared. Most of the chapters overlap several of the themes, oscillating between optimism and despair. Ultimately, their final placement in this volume is as much due to my own queer idiosyncrasies as to the author's choice of orientation.

Complicities: Sexuality, coloniality and governance

The first group of chapters explore the theme of colonial and governmental queer complicities in three quite disparate contexts: British efforts to play a leading role in the removal of anti-sodomy laws which it had imposed on its colonies; global attempts to regulate the mining of precious and rare minerals; and the neoliberal model of Internet governance. In Rahul Rao's examination of the emerging discourse of 'atonement' among British elites for the legacy of anti-sodomy laws in Commonwealth countries, the neo-colonial complexities are highlighted and the important question as to why atonement seems more contemplable for the sexual injustices of colonialism than for its racial crimes is raised. In the second chapter, Doris Buss and Blair Rutherford argue that the artisanal and small-scale miner is cast as a queer figure, a mining 'outlaw', used to

40 Colin Gordon, 'Governmental Rationality: An Introduction' in Graham Burchell, Colin Gordon and Peter Miller (eds), *The Foucault Effect: Studies in Governmentality* (University of Chicago Press, 1991) 1, 46.

bolster the global regulation of 'industrial' mining as the norm. They show how sexuality continues to operate as one axis along which unequal global legal relations are constituted (despite efforts elsewhere at atonement). Monika Zalnieriute, in the third chapter, draws attention to how the Information-Industrial-Complex, dominated by the United States and several of its major corporations, has come to control Internet governance, enabling repression of the rights of queer people in the global North and South, even as it claims to be supporting Internet freedom. All three chapters pinpoint the continuing utility of tropes of sexual excess and perversion for extending neoliberal global governance, despite appearances of sexual liberality.

Possibilities: Rethinking violence, war and law

The queer possibilities of international law's commitment to the peaceful resolution of international disputes and to promoting transitional justice are explored in this section. In Chapter 4, Vanja Hamzić analyses the paradox of international law's continuous evolution towards evermore-diverse forms of juridical violence through the frame of the UN Security Council's first-ever meeting on the persecution of 'LGBT Syrians and Iraqis' by the so-called Islamic State in 2015. He argues that the meeting produced some 'productive voids' which allow for the theorising of the absence of international law, and thus the absence of juridical violence. The Security Council is also the focus of Tamsin Phillipa Paige's chapter, which explores some of the heteronormative assumptions that inform the Council's determinations of when it can legitimately authorise violence in response to a threat to the peace. She argues that these assumptions serve to legitimate the culture of impunity that attends wartime sexual violence. In Chapter 6, Maria Elander picks up on the theme of impunity in the context of testimonies of sexual and gender-based violence at the Extraordinary Chambers in the Courts of Cambodia. Engaging with the testimonies of transgender activist Sou Southeavy, she raises questions about whose testimony is accorded space and what is heard. The possibilities of productive voids, and of taking seriously the violence endured by sexual outsiders, offer new footholds for queer engagements with (or without) international law.

Alliances: Making queer lives matter

The third section questions the costs of alliances made in the advocacy of LGBTI human rights. In Chapter 7, Ratna Kapur argues that rights advocacy has become embedded within a security discourse which has taken the radicality out of queer, rather than resulting in the queering of international human rights. She argues that there are abundant possibilities for queer radicality outside the parameters of the liberal imaginary. This is followed by Aeyal Gross's examination of 'global gay governance', emerging through LGBT advocacy in international economic and human rights institutions. He argues the importance of a cost-benefit analysis that assesses the promise of making queer lives matter against the risk of co-option by global institutions for their own purposes. Finally, Anniken Sørlie's chapter shows how, despite legislative efforts in many countries to remove the requirement of sterilisation before a change in legal gender is allowed, parenting laws continue to reconstitute transgender people as 'other' to the norm of heterosexual biological kinship. These costs are among the dangers that Foucault warns about. The challenge is to find ways to hold on to queer aspirations for transformative change, while struggling to maximise sexual and gender freedoms in the present.

Risks: Troubling statehood, sovereignty and its borders

The last section turns to the nation-state, bringing to light the figurations of sexual and gender perversity operating at its formative moments in international law, and in its contemporary anxieties about border protection. In Chapter 10, Bina Fernandez examines queer struggles for reform of immigration and asylum laws, which, in order to make applicants legible to the state, have led to the construction of LGBTI identities in specifically classed, raced, gendered and imperial ways. She suggests a re-alignment of queer migrant activism with a 'no borders' politics in order to hold on to queer radicality. Nan Seuffert's chapter takes us back to the sixteenth-century work of Francisco de Vittoria, which argued that the Spanish invasion of Mesoamerica could be justified on the basis of universal natural law duties of friendship and hospitality. By unpacking the allegory of Sodom and Gomorrah in his work, she points to the sedimentation of discourses of sexuality in international law at its inception. My final chapter argues that national heteronormative allegiances help to justify militarism and carceral states, and thus the urgent need to value the myriad other assemblages of human kinship and loyalty. Some thoughts are offered as to how queer kinship systems might reshape border protection strategies and shift military resources into ensuring that all lives matter.

Queering international law means taking a break from the accepted methods of getting things done. The goal is to open new ways of seeing international legal problems and expose the limitations of international law's normal responses to them. Queer curiosity looks to the shifting constellations of non-normative subject positions, which are not only sexually marked, but also distinguished by reference to race, class, gender and other vectors of power. Moving against the grain of identitarian and disciplinary separations, the queer contributors to this collection seek to open up the possibilities of emancipatory alliances and more complex and mobile understandings of power, both within and beyond the law. It is hoped that asking queer questions will lead to solutions that ensure, rather than threaten, the proliferation of diverse practices of freedom and pleasure, and help to fundamentally change the way in which things have been normally done in international law.

Part I

Complicities: Sexuality, coloniality and governance

1 A tale of two atonements

*Rahul Rao**

The claim that homosexuality is a Western 'import' is frequently used to discredit demands for the decriminalisation of queer sex in many non-Western societies. A common response to this argument has been the rejoinder that the criminalisation of same-sex sexualities was a Western colonial legal intervention – that is, it is institutionalised homophobia that is the Western import. This is especially true of territories once ruled by the British.[1] French colonies were largely spared an anti-sodomy law because most were annexed after it had been dropped from the Napoleonic Code in 1806. This code also influenced France's European neighbours and their colonies.[2] One study notes that 'the Commonwealth includes 42 (53.8%) of the 78 states which continue to criminalise same-sex sexual behaviour, and only 12 (10.6%) of 113 where it is legal', before concluding that 'the criminalisation of same-sex sexual behaviour by the British Empire, and associated colonial culture, have had a lasting negative impact'.[3] Michael Kirby, former Justice of the High Court of Australia, speaks of sexual minorities being 'kept in legal chains by the enduring penal code provisions of the British Empire'.[4]

* Thanks are due to Grietje Baars, Maria Elander, Gina Heathcote, Jordan Osserman, Dianne Otto, Robbie Shilliam, Akshi Singh and all participants at the 'Queering International Law' workshop held at Melbourne Law School in December 2015. I take full responsibility for the views expressed here.

1 Alok Gupta, 'This Alien Legacy: The Origins of "Sodomy" Laws in British Colonialism' (Research Report, Human Rights Watch, 17 December 2008); Enze Han and Joseph O'Mahoney, 'British Colonialism and the Criminalization of Homosexuality' (2014) 27 *Cambridge Review of International Affairs* 268.

2 Michael Kirby, 'The Sodomy Offence: England's Least Lovely Criminal Law Export?' in Corinne Lennox and Matthew Waites (eds), *Human Rights, Sexual Orientation and Gender Identity in the Commonwealth: Struggles for Decriminalisation and Change* (Institute of Commonwealth Studies, 2013) 61, 64.

3 Corinne Lennox and Matthew Waites, 'Human Rights, Sexual Orientation and Gender Identity in the Commonwealth: From History and Law to Developing Activism and Transnational Dialogues' in Corinne Lennox and Matthew Waites (eds), *Human Rights, Sexual Orientation and Gender Identity in the Commonwealth: Struggles for Decriminalisation and Change* (Institute of Commonwealth Studies, 2013) 1, 24. At the time of this writing, the number of states criminalising sodomy stands at 75.

4 Kirby, above n 2, 75.

In the lead-up to the 2011 Commonwealth Heads of Government Meeting (CHOGM) in Perth, he remarked that 'it's just a dear little legacy of the British Empire. It's a very special British problem'.[5] British lesbian, gay, bisexual and transgender (LGBT) activist Peter Tatchell went further by declaring that these provisions 'are not authentic national laws that were freely legislated by the indigenous populations'.[6]

The reminder that anti-sodomy laws are an inheritance from British colonialism has shaded into an argument for Britain to play a leading role in their removal, particularly in the institutional arena of the Commonwealth. In anticipation of the 2011 CHOGM, Tatchell called on then British Prime Minister David Cameron to apologise for Britain's imposition of the sodomy law on its colonies.[7] Under pressure from activists, Cameron responded with an ill-advised comment suggesting that British aid would be linked to respect for LGBT rights in recipient countries.[8] Confronted with the spectre of a novel form of conditionality camouflaged as a civilising mission, leaders in Tanzania,[9] Uganda,[10] Ghana[11] and elsewhere reacted with hostility. More significantly, a number of African queer activists publicly criticised Cameron's statement, warning that the refusal of aid on sexual rights grounds would trigger the scapegoating of queers in these countries, reinforce perceptions of the 'Westernness' of homosexuality and further entrench power disparities between donor and recipient countries.[12] Two things became apparent in this moment: first, that British elites seemed unusually receptive to the suggestion that they ought to recognise anti-sodomy laws in the Commonwealth as an unfortunate legacy of British colonialism, with such recognition entailing a responsibility on their part to agitate against such laws; but second, that the ways in which they sought to assume this responsibility left them open, ironically, to charges of neo-colonialism.

In this chapter, I try to do three things. First, I offer an account of an emerging discourse of 'atonement' among British elites for the anti-sodomy laws in

5 Simon Lauder, 'Commonwealth Leaders to Be Confronted on Homophobia', *ABC News* (online), 18 October 2011 <http://www.abc.net.au/am/content/2011/s3341950.htm>.

6 Peter Tatchell, 'David Cameron Urged: Apologise for Anti-Gay Laws Imposed by UK' on *Peter Tatchell Foundation* (27 October 2011) <http://www.petertatchellfoundation.org/commonwealth/david-cameron-urged-apologise-anti-gay-laws-imposed-uk>.

7 Ibid.

8 BBC News, 'Transcript Philip Hammond Interview', *The Andrew Marr Show*, 30 October 2011 (David Cameron) <http://news.bbc.co.uk/1/hi/programmes/andrew_marr_show/9627898.stm>.

9 Richard Mbuthia, 'Tanzania: Africa, Want Aid? Recognise Gay Rights!', *Tanzania Daily News* (online), 26 December 2011 <http://allafrica.com/stories/201112271071.html>.

10 'Uganda Fury at David Cameron Aid Threat over Gay Rights', *BBC News* (online), 31 October 2011 <http://www.bbc.co.uk/news/world-africa-15524013>.

11 'Ghana Refuses to Grant Gays' Rights Despite Aid Threat', *BBC News* (online), 2 November 2011 <http://www.bbc.co.uk/news/world-africa-15558769>.

12 'Statement on British "Aid Cut" Threats to African Countries That Violate LBGTI rights', *Pambazuka News* (online), 27 October 2011 <http://www.pambazuka.org/activism/statement-british-aid-cut-threats-african-countries-violate-lbgti-rights>.

Commonwealth countries that are seen to be a legacy of British colonialism. Second, drawing on political theoretic, literary and psychoanalytic resources, I develop a critique of the forms in which this atonement is expressed, arguing that it is underpinned by a desire to avoid engaging with guilt. Third, I contrast this 'imperious' atonement with a more equivocal discourse of atonement expressed in relation to the question of slavery. In doing so, my aim is not so much to make a case for atonement for the treatment of sodomites or slaves under colonial rule – a task that is beyond the scope of this chapter – as to think through why atonement seems to be more contemplable for the sexual injustices of colonialism than for its racial crimes. In doing so, I hope to say something about the relative discursive power wielded by claims to sexual and racial justice respectively in contemporary British society.

Responsibility and atonement for anti-sodomy laws in the Commonwealth

The notion that Britain bears a historic responsibility for extant anti-sodomy laws in Commonwealth countries and that moral and political obligations follow from this recognition was articulated most explicitly in a debate on the 'Treatment of Homosexual Men and Women in the Developing World' in the House of Lords in October 2012. Observing the proceedings from the public gallery, Mark Gevisser suggested that the most remarkable thing about the debate might have been that it was not a debate at all: speakers from across the political spectrum seemed to share a consensus that the United Kingdom should protect and advance LGBT rights globally.[13]

Opening the debate, the Conservative peer Lord Lexden, official historian of the Conservative Party since 2009, sought to underscore the provenance of laws criminalising sexual minorities. In a strikingly romanticised view of pre-colonial history and a correspondingly damning indictment of colonialism (all the more remarkable for coming from a Tory historian), he noted that '[t]he love that had freely spoken its name and found expression in . . . native cultures became, in the definition of their new British-imported law, an unnatural offence'.[14] Another Conservative peer, Lord Black of Brentwood, elaborated: 'It is important to explain why the UK, with this House in the vanguard, should care . . . we caused this problem. That so many people around the globe still suffer from legal discrimination is one toxic legacy of empire. It is our duty to help sort that out'.[15] He would encounter little disagreement from Lord Smith of Finsbury, formerly

13 Mark Gevisser, 'Human Rights vs. Homophobia: Who is Winning Africa's Cultural Wars' on *Open Society Initiative for Southern Africa* (20 June 2013) <http://www.osisa.org/openspace/regional/human-rights-vs-homophobia-who-winning-africas-cultural-wars>.

14 UK, *Parliamentary Debates*, House of Lords, 25 October 2012, vol 740, col 378.

15 Ibid col 389.

of the Labour Party and one of the first British MPs to come out as gay and HIV positive:

> The continued existence of discrimination, violence and criminalisation in so many Commonwealth countries is particularly shaming. There is a bitter irony . . . in that most laws in these countries have been inherited from us. I believe that that gives us a special responsibility to do whatever we can to help to change things.[16]

The repeated references to 'special responsibility' struck Gevisser as a contemporary form of '"white man's burden": because Britain had brought homophobia to the developing world, it was Britain's responsibility to take it away'. While admiring the noble intentions of the speakers, Gevisser wondered 'whether those brave Peers had learned much from the colonial experience: they were still adopting the missionary position'.[17]

The discourse of British responsibility for anti-sodomy laws is also audible in civil society. The singer Elton John recently remarked in an interview to CNBC, 'these are old laws from the British Commonwealth and they need to be changed . . . the Queen could do that with one wave of her hand'.[18] While blithe assertions of this kind are laughable, more serious and credible voices have been urging the British state to advocate for the repeal of anti-sodomy laws globally. Two new London-based organisations – Kaleidoscope Trust and Human Dignity Trust (HDT) – have been at the forefront of this effort. Besides lobbying government, HDT's core mission is to provide 'technical legal assistance' in the form of funding and/or advice to lawyers and activists working to challenge the criminalisation of homosexuality through courts. The Trust claims the support of a global network of local human rights lawyers as well as large multinational law firms. Indeed, its raison d'être lies in bridging these otherwise separate worlds, leveraging the resources of the latter (who commit to working for the Trust pro bono) to bolster the advocacy efforts of the former. To date, HDT has supported litigation in Belize, Jamaica, Northern Cyprus, Singapore and the European Union.[19]

Notwithstanding its avowed intention to match Northern resources and expertise with Southern needs, HDT's modus operandi has attracted criticism. Soon after its formation, Trinidad and Tobago activist Colin Robinson described its approach as 'unproductive', arguing that the Trust had 'muscled into a carefully

16 Ibid col 391.

17 Gevisser, above n 13.

18 Sean Mandell, 'Elton John: The Queen Could Change Anti-Gay Laws in the Commonwealth "With One Wave of Her Hand" – Watch', *Towleroad* (online), 5 November 2015 <http://www.towleroad.com/2015/11/elton-john-the-queen-could-change-anti-gay-laws-in-the-commonwealth-with-one-wave-of-her-hand-watch/>.

19 Human Dignity Trust, 'Legal Cases Challenging the Criminalisation of Homosexuality Supported by the Human Dignity Trust' (2016) <http://www.humandignitytrust.org/pages/OUR%20WORK/Cases>.

planned constitutional suit by local and regional actors in Belize, daringly spun in the media as the Trust's global campaign kick-off'.[20] Indeed, HDT CEO Jonathan Cooper, QC, seemed to reinforce this image in early publicity for the organisation. Speaking to *The Guardian*'s Zoe Williams, Cooper explained:

> 'I email our legal panel, asking: anyone have any experience of litigating in Belize? Someone comes back and says yeah, we'll represent you in this legal challenge. They bring in as their counsel [former UK attorney general] Lord Goldsmith, and the former attorney general of Belize, Godfrey Smith. We turn up as the international community, with a legitimate interest in the outcome of this case, but we do change the nature of the struggle because we have approached it on the basis that it's a major legal challenge. That is our intention'. They're not going to know what's hit them, [Williams] observe[s]. 'You almost feel sorry for the judge!' Cooper replies, delighted. . . . 'We will fundraise, and there is something rather charming that you can say to somebody: "If you give us £50,000, I can more or less guarantee that you will have decriminalised homosexuality in Tonga." And actually, you know, that's great.'[21]

Let us bracket, for a moment, the hubris of the claim of legal standing as framed in this way: 'we turn up as the international community'. In contrast to Cooper's focus on international legal intervention, Robinson emphasises local solutions that do not rely solely on law reform and that are led by Southern organisations. In his words:

> The chorus coming from the powers who gave us the sodomy laws in the first place has shifted to singing morality in a different key, often appealing more to righteousness than to shared values. And they have outshouted those of us working within our own nations to build ownership for a vision of postcolonial justice, national pride and liberty that includes sexual autonomy. . . . Global North advocates wanting the same changes often believe they have the answers but get in the way by taking the reins too often rather than following our lead. It is essential that those who genuinely support our equality listen to us, get behind where we are going, and push in the same directions.[22]

It is conceivable that this early critique had considerable, even if unacknowledged, impact on how HDT functions. Today, the organisation's publicity strongly endorses the principle of local ownership. Its public events in London have tended

20 Colin Robinson, 'Decolonising Sexual Citizenship: Who Will Effect Change in the South of the Commonwealth?' (Discussion Paper, Commonwealth Advisory Bureau, April 2012).

21 Zoe Williams, 'Gay Rights: A World of Inequality', *The Guardian* (online), 14 September 2011 <http://www.theguardian.com/world/2011/sep/13/gay-rights-world-of-inequality>.

22 Robinson, above n 20, 6.

to be organised around the visits of the Southern activists whom the Trust spends much of its time supporting. Nonetheless, the claim of a British duty to work towards the repeal of anti-sodomy laws for which it bears historic responsibility remains a prominent theme in its advocacy. The Trust has recently begun lobbying for the creation of the position of a UK Special Envoy to work towards ending LGBT persecution globally, in imitation of the analogous position established by the US State Department in 2015. In a briefing paper outlining the rationale for such a post, the Trust underscores its belief in the need for international intervention with the claim that 'history shows that a helping hand from outside is needed to initiate the domestic protection of LGBT people'. This observation is followed up by the claim that 'the UK, in particular, has the means and obligation to advocate for the repeal of criminalising and persecutory laws'. Unsurprisingly, the question of 'obligation' is tied to Britain's historic role in introducing anti-sodomy laws in its colonies. The task of the proposed Special Envoy is framed as being necessary 'to help correct a historical wrong – not to impose an alien foreign agenda'.[23] The success of HDT's advocacy is evident in the fact that a number of these themes are reflected in the April 2016 report of an All Party Parliamentary Group (APPG) on Global LGBT Rights. The product of testimony from a range of different stakeholders, this report is more nuanced on the implications of the colonial provenance of anti-sodomy laws, noting that while this 'offers a justification for British action to address the persecution faced by LGBT people . . . the same colonial history that impels action can also lead to accusations of neo-colonialism when that action fails to take into account local contexts'.[24] The report recommends the identification of a single authority responsible for the coordination of international LGBT advocacy across government departments, but remains agnostic on the question of what form this authority should take.

Buried in the discourse of a putative British 'responsibility' for anti-sodomy laws in the Commonwealth is a deeper misunderstanding of the very notion of responsibility. Certainly, reminders that such laws are a legacy of colonialism are appropriate insofar as they point to the origin of these laws. Yet we cannot fully account for their persistence without paying attention to their appropriation and resignification by postcolonial states. Former colonies have taken ownership of sodomy laws in a variety of ways: some have decriminalised sodomy or are in the process of doing so (Canada, Australia, New Zealand, Hong Kong, Bahamas, Cyprus, South Africa, Vanuatu, Fiji, Belize); others have widened the ambit of anti-sodomy laws to criminalise sex between women (Malaysia, Sri Lanka, Malawi), enhance already existing punishments (Uganda), or introduce new offences

23 'Should the UK Government Appoint a Special Envoy to Work towards Ending the Persecution of the LGBT Community across the Globe?' (Discussion Paper, Human Dignity Trust, 3 July 2015) 5–6 <http://www.humandignitytrust.org/uploaded/Library/Other_Material/Special_Envoy_Six_Reasons_-_3_July_2015_FINAL.pdf>.

24 'The UK's Stance on International Breaches of LGBT Rights' (Report, All Party Parliamentary Group on Global LGBT Rights, April 2016) 12–13 <http://www.appglgbt.org/#!publications/cghg>.

(Nigeria); and still others have introduced anti-sodomy legislation after decolonisation (Cameroon, Benin, Senegal). To put the point more generally, if swathes of colonial law remain in force in the postcolony, this is a function of the commonality of interest shared by colonial and postcolonial governments alike in 'seeing like a state'.[25] Equally, postcolonial states might find new uses for old laws. Whatever the motivation, we must read the persistence of colonial law in the postcolony not simply as a sign of neglect by the postcolonial state, but as expressive of conscious policy.

Western activists responding to postcolonial anti-sodomy laws find themselves having to strike a difficult balance between two opposite and equally problematic tendencies: first, the 'homonationalist' tendency to construct the Orient as a backward space of homophobia needing intervention from an enlightened Occident;[26] second, what might be called a 'homoromanticist' tendency to view the Orient as blameless for its contemporary predicaments, these being attributed solely to the interventions of Occidental modernity. Indeed, the difficulty of avoiding these antithetical extremes can be seen in the way some activists have ricocheted between both positions. Thus, Kirby's 2011 statement about anti-sodomy laws being a 'dear little legacy of the British Empire'[27] stands in contrast to a stroppier observation in 2015: 'It is pathetic to blame this on British colonial administrators. Most Commonwealth countries have been independent for 50 years and the responsibility is theirs alone.'[28] Kirby's contradictions exemplify the dilemma of Western activists who, in seeking to avoid homonationalism and homoromanticism, find themselves flirting with both.

Antithetical as these tendencies seem, we ought to view them as complementary facets of Orientalism – one in which the Orient is denigrated for its backwardness, and the other in which it is overvalued for its noble savagery.[29] While recognising that both tendencies are problematic, it is the second of these that I am examining here. In attributing postcolonial anti-sodomy laws largely to colonial imposition, contemporary metropolitan 'atonement' discourses evacuate the agency of postcolonial states in preserving such laws, protecting them from challenge, and putting them to new use. Joel Nana, a prominent Cameroonian LGBT activist, framed the problem eloquently:

> If we truly believe that Africans are human, we should also be able to understand that they can make their own decisions. These decisions may be

25 James C Scott, *Seeing Like a State: How Certain Schemes to Improve the Human Condition Have Failed* (Yale University Press, 1998).

26 Jasbir K Puar, *Terrorist Assemblages: Homonationalism in Queer Times* (Duke University Press, 2007).

27 Lauder, above n 5.

28 'Human Dignity Trust Launches Criminalisation in the Commonwealth 2015 Report', *Human Dignity Trust* (online), 22 November 2015 <http://www.humandignitytrust.org/pages/NEWS/News?NewsArticleID=470>.

29 Edward Said, *Orientalism* (Penguin, 1979).

> influenced by the need to protect or to violate rights, for real or perceived personal or collective good, but they remain African decisions. They are owned and defended. Denying them the agency that allows them to do that is similar to stripping them of their humanity.[30]

Failing to give 'credit' for homophobia where it is due, metropolitan 'atonement' effectively delivers insult in the same breath as it offers apology. To understand how attempts to atone can get it so wrong, we need to think more deeply about the effect of atonement. How can atonement for imperialism end up looking so imperious?

Imperious atonement

In his novel *Atonement*, Ian McEwan – always a reliable guide to the affective lives of the British upper classes – offers a finely drawn portrait of the anatomy of atonement. The details of the plot need not concern us here. Suffice it to say that the young protagonist, Briony Tallis, driven by a potent mix of ambition, passion and jealousy, is led to commit an act for which she will later feel the need to atone. Convinced of her destiny as a writer, Briony weaves a series of events that she has watched from afar into a narrative of lust, betrayal and violation, akin to the dark fairy tales that her precocious 13-year-old imagination favours. Placed in the position of sole witness, her 'vile excitement' and self-importance lead her to level an allegation that will prove unfounded, but will forever alter the lives of the other protagonists. As the consequences of her actions slowly become apparent to her, Briony is wracked with guilt and shame. Distancing herself from family and abandoning plans to go to university, she embraces the arduous life of a nurse in the London of the Second World War, in penance for her act of falsehood. Her offer to recant her incriminating testimony is received with scepticism, her every expression of atonement compromised by the self-interest of wanting to clear a conscience whose weight she can no longer bear. Towards the end of the novel, we realise that these scenarios of atonement have only ever been played out in Briony's mind. Coming too late to make any difference in the lives that she has so drastically altered, it is the novel itself – it turns out that we have been reading *Briony's* novel – that is the act, or better still, the speech act of atonement. This places us, as readers, in the difficult position of having nothing but the (more than occasionally self-justifying) narrative offered by the wrongdoer as our sole account of events. As Briony herself wonders on the penultimate page of her self-flagellating meditation: '[H]ow can a novelist achieve atonement when, with her absolute power of deciding outcomes, she is also God?'[31]

Understanding atonement not merely as an act of contrition, but as an affective voyage that navigates the treacherous shoals of guilt, shame, resentment, self-pity,

30 Quoted in Gevisser, above n 13.
31 Ian McEwan, *Atonement* (Vintage, 2002) 371.

ambition and self-interest, across gradients of power, might take us some way towards appreciating how atonement can seem very far from an exercise in humility. Because atonement purports to establish a new relationship between actors, we might further unpack it by drawing on the object relations theory of psychoanalyst Melanie Klein. Julia Gallagher has argued that Klein is particularly useful for an understanding of morality in international relations because relationships are central to her thought and practice.[32] Object relations theory explains the development of the psyche during early childhood through an account of how people relate to objects – both real objects in the world around them, and the internal objects that they build unconsciously to reflect and help them to make sense of the world. As Gallagher explains, the child experiences external objects through projection, and mentally internalises these objects which then constitute her personality, thereby shaping further encounters with, and internalisations of, external objects. In doing so, the child is both author of, and subject to, her internal objects, which are built on both positive and negative interactions with the world. If at first the positive and the negative seem separable, with 'good' objects fostering security and well-being and 'bad' objects bringing frustration and pain, it is in the child's shocked realisation that both good and bad are personified in the same object – the mother – that the reparative impulse is born as an attempt to attenuate the hateful feelings that the child experiences for the mother whom she also loves.[33] As Will Kaufman explains, for Klein, this reparative impulse is at the heart of psychic health, enabling a move from the destructive, psychotic, immature stage – the 'paranoid-schizoid position' – to the mature, integrated stage that she calls the 'depressive position'.[34] It is the experience of pain and guilt in the depressive position that fuels the reparative urge.

And yet guilt provides only a starting point, and a particularly fraught one at that, for the reparative drive which can itself take different trajectories. Even sympathetic commentators have criticised as introverted Klein's thinking about reparation, which focuses more on making reparation to one's injured internal objects than to external ones. For C Fred Alford, this kind of reparation is 'morally untrustworthy, as likely to be satisfied by painting a picture about the terrible deeds one has done as by making amends to actual victims'.[35] This might also be why Derek Hook is suspicious of reactions to guilt, which, despite the gestures of reparation that may flow from them, are often fundamentally self-serving in being motivated primarily by the need to alleviate the atoner's psychic discomfort. Hook

32 Julia Gallagher, 'Can Melanie Klein Help Us Understand Morality in IR? Suggestions for a Psychoanalytic Interpretation of Why and How States Do Good' (2009) 38 *Millennium: Journal of International Studies* 295.

33 Ibid 298–302, 304.

34 Will Kaufman, 'On the Psychology of Slavery Reparation: A Kleinian Reading' (2007) 4 *Atlantic Studies* 267, 269.

35 C Fred Alford, *Psychology and the Natural Law of Reparation* (Cambridge University Press, 2006) 6 quoted in ibid 270.

questions whether a reparative act that is more concerned with salving one's own pain can constitute a genuinely ethical act.[36]

Klein herself recognised that a subject overwhelmed by guilt may choose to deny or refuse it rather than acknowledge and work through it, provoking gestures of what she called 'manic reparation'. As Hanna Segal explains:

> Manic reparation is a defence in that its aim is to repair the object in such a way that guilt and loss are never experienced. An essential feature of manic reparation is that it has to be done without acknowledgement of guilt. . . . The object in relation to which reparation is done must never be experienced as having been damaged by oneself. . . . The object must be felt as inferior, dependent and, at depth, contemptible. There can be no true love or esteem for the object or objects that are being repaired, as this would threaten the return of true depressive feelings.[37]

From this, Kaufman extracts what he sees as the hallmarks of manic reparation, namely a sense of 'control' over the object of reparation, a sense of 'triumph' through which the object's true value is diminished in relation to oneself and a sense of 'contempt' for the object.[38]

Much of this is strikingly visible in the British discourse of 'atonement' for Commonwealth anti-sodomy laws. This might sound paradoxical because, on the face of it, the discourse *does* acknowledge guilt in astonishingly categorical terms. Yet the guilt is easily displaced onto a historic self, demarcated from the contemporary self by the temporal rupture of decolonisation and of Britain's own decriminalisation of sodomy by the 1967 Sexual Offences Act. This means that, protestations of guilt notwithstanding, the object in relation to which reparation is done is not experienced as having been damaged by a recognisable self. British decriminalisation, albeit too late to benefit what were by then former colonies, fuels the sense of triumph and superiority vis-à-vis the object (we have progressed, they have stagnated). The zealous assumption of British 'responsibility' for anti-sodomy laws in the Commonwealth, blind to the postcolonial agency that perpetuates these laws, effectively constructs the objects of reparation as passive, inferior and in need of a 'helping hand'. Cameron's incipient articulation of 'gay conditionality' reasserts a desire for control and betrays the delusions of omnipotence that are a hallmark of manic reparation. One suspects that this rare expression of 'atonement' for colonialism at the highest levels of British government has been forthcoming only because it is thought to furnish the requisite standing for a moral crusade in which Britain can assert leadership.

36 Derek Hook, 'White Privilege, Psychoanalytic Ethics, and the Limitations of Political Silence' (2011) 30 *South African Journal of Philosophy* 494, 497.

37 Hanna Segal, *Introduction to the Work of Melanie Klein* (Karnac Books, 1988) 95–6 quoted in Kaufman, above n 34, 271.

38 Kaufman, above n 34, 271.

Equivocal atonement

Anti-sodomy laws were but one manifestation of colonialism and their persistence only one of its many toxic legacies. So one might expect the shame and outrage expressed in relation to them to be magnified with respect to colonialism *in toto*. This is not the case. To illustrate this claim, I juxtapose 'atonement' for anti-sodomy laws with a more fractious discourse on the question of Britain's historic responsibility for slavery. These discourses are not easily comparable. Atonement, such as it is, for anti-sodomy laws is a relatively recent discourse that has emerged out of a small circle of largely British LGBT activists. Discussions about responsibility for, and the legacies of, slavery have been geographically more widespread and historically more long-running, acquiring particular intensity most recently in 2007 on the 200th anniversary of the abolition of slavery. These discussions have taken place across continents at virtually every level of society from grassroots movements to intergovernmental negotiations. To render these incomparable discourses comparable, I mirror the argument offered above with an analysis of the ways in which 'atonement' for slavery was expressed in one institutional arena: the British Parliament.

In March 2007, the House of Commons commemorated the bicentenary of the abolition of the slave trade in a wide-ranging debate. Many contributors to the debate were unsparing in their descriptions of the 'trade' and in acknowledging the extent to which Britain had benefited from it, naming the royal family, the Church of England, the City and indeed Members of Parliament themselves as beneficiaries of the £20 million compensation that was paid to slave owners when the trade was abolished in 1807.[39] Notwithstanding this candour, the debate is shot through with discursive moves that seek to mitigate Britain's culpability for slavery.

The two most common arguments in the service of mitigation were offered at the outset by then Labour Deputy Prime Minister John Prescott, who opened the debate by citing the lyrics of a slave chain re-enactment that he had reportedly seen Ghanaian children perform: 'Not every black man was innocent. Not every white man was guilty.'[40] A number of speakers sought to substantiate the first point by drawing attention to the involvement of Arab and African slave raiders in the trade, with one member describing slavery as 'a darker chapter in the development of every world civilisation'.[41] Alongside this de-exceptionalisation of the European slave trade came an assertion of British virtue prominent in the very framing of the debate as a commemoration of abolition rather than of the trade itself. Thus, Prescott opened the debate by seizing what he described as 'an historic moment for the United Kingdom, which led the world in legislating

39 See, eg, the contributions of Chris Bryant, Vince Cable, Diane Abbott, Dawn Butler, Jeremy Corbyn and Claire Curtis-Thomas.

40 UK, *Parliamentary Debates*, House of Commons, 20 March 2007, vol 458, col 689.

41 Ibid cols 763, 704, 741–2. See also UK, *Parliamentary Debates*, House of Lords, 10 May 2007, vol 691, cols 1556–9.

against the vile trade in the slavery of human beings'.[42] Conservative MP William Hague, biographer of abolitionist William Wilberforce, described abolition as 'a moral benchmark of which other civilised societies rightly took note'.[43] Another Conservative, Malcolm Moss, ruled out an apology for the slave trade, asserting triumphantly that 'it was our country that produced the moral giants of their time'.[44] Obscuring the fact that one out of every two enslaved Africans shipped across the Atlantic was transported in British ships, the debate was effectively an exercise in 'remembering the abolition, forgetting the "trade"'.[45]

Underpinning the anxiety to mitigate blame for the slave trade were concerns about the demand for an apology by the British state to descendants of slaves in its former colonies, principally in the Caribbean – a gesture that many in the British establishment fear could potentially strengthen the case for reparations. Certainly, such anxieties lurked beneath then Prime Minister Tony Blair's expression of 'deep sorrow', rather than categorical apology, on the eve of the bicentenary.[46] (More recently, Cameron reiterated this position while on a trip to Jamaica, ruling out the possibility of Britain making reparations to its former Caribbean colonies and urging these countries to 'move on' from such demands.)[47] Speakers across party lines in the Commons expressed support for Blair, avoiding – in some cases explicitly refusing – apology, while offering expressions of 'sincere regret', 'profound regret' and 'acknowledgement' instead.[48] Only one MP, Liberal Democrat Malcolm Bruce, spoke of the need to 'apologise unreservedly and show shame for our actions', but even he quickly rowed back with the disclaimer that 'the world cannot go on trading apologies instead of delivering leadership and action that move things forward and create change'.[49]

The imperative to 'move things forward' became a key temporal trope in the debate that obviated a reckoning with the past. For many speakers, the inexorably forward movement of time provided a cue to speak about the present and future rather than the past, so that large swathes of a debate that was supposed to be about the slave trade and its abolition segued into a discussion about contemporary human trafficking. When one member, Conservative Anthony Steen, was rebuked by the Speaker for straying too far from the topic of the debate, he protested –

42 UK, *Parliamentary Debates*, House of Commons, 20 March 2007, vol 458, col 687.

43 Ibid col 696.

44 Ibid col 742.

45 Emma Waterton, 'Humiliated Silence: Multiculturalism, Blame, and the Trope of "Moving On"' (2010) 8 *Museum and Society* 128, 131.

46 'Blair "Sorrow" over Slave Trade', *BBC News* (online), 27 November 2006 <http://news.bbc.co.uk/2/hi/6185176.stm>.

47 'David Cameron Rules Out Slavery Reparation during Jamaica Visit', *BBC News* (online), 30 September 2015 <http://www.bbc.com/news/uk-34401412>.

48 UK, *Parliamentary Debates*, House of Commons, 20 March 2007, vol 458, cols 710, 741–2, 773.

49 Ibid col 750. In a later debate in the House of Lords, only the black peer Lord Morris of Handsworth endorsed the imperative of apology, see UK, *Parliamentary Debates*, House of Lords, 10 May 2007, vol 691, col 1555.

quite rightly[50] – that 'at least 50 per cent. of hon. Members' speeches have concentrated on human trafficking and the new forms of slavery'.[51] Pressing as these issues are, their discussion had the effect of dimming the spotlight that the debate was meant to have shone on British institutions and their culpability for the slave trade. For one thing, the geography of contemporary human trafficking is different from that of the Middle Passage, in that the old slave-owning powers have become the countries of destination, refuge and potential rescue of trafficked persons rather than the most proximate agents of their enslavement. Those agents are now located elsewhere – in Russia and Eastern Europe, Asia and sub-Saharan Africa. In addition, the discussion of contemporary slavery focused almost entirely on sexual slavery, as if to insinuate that 'race slaves' are a thing of the past, while 'sex slaves' are a problem for the present. Such a framing, even if unintentional, obscures the sexual slavery that was an inescapable element of plantation life, as well as the racialisation of contemporary human sex trafficking.

Many of the speeches suggested that time was the great obstacle to the offering of an apology. Some argued that morality is historically contingent: acts considered crimes against humanity today were not morally wrong at the time they were committed, making their retrospective condemnation anachronistic.[52] In insisting on viewing slave owners as 'men of their time', the objection on grounds of anachronism takes a rather flattened view of the past, failing to recognise the ways in which time is always already split. One could go as far back as the writings of the sixteenth-century Spanish theologian Bartolomé de las Casas to find influential critiques of European conquest, genocide and slavery emerging almost contemporaneously with the advent of these practices.[53] More importantly, slaves, and former slaves such as Olaudah Equiano, themselves articulated powerful and eloquent objections to their enslavement.[54] To speak of slave owners as 'men of their time' is effectively to place the voices of slaves living in the same time, *out* of time, and thereby out of humanity itself.

The more widely articulated temporal objection to apology underscored a putative lack of connection between those who committed morally heinous acts and those being called upon to apologise on their behalf. Liberal Democrat Vince Cable opined that 'in any sensible ethical system, one cannot apologise for things that happened 10 generations ago'.[55] For Conservative Tobias Ellwood, the lack

50 See, eg, UK, *Parliamentary Debates*, House of Commons, 20 March 2007, vol 458, cols 710, 714, 718, 728, 766.

51 Ibid col 728.

52 Ibid cols 741–2.

53 Bartolomé de las Casas, *A Brief Account of the Destruction of the Indies* (Project Gutenberg, first published 1542, 2007 edn) <http://www.gutenberg.org/cache/epub/20321/pg20321-images.html>.

54 Olaudah Equiano, *The Interesting Narrative of the Life of Olaudah Equiano, or Gustavus Vassa, the African Written by Himself* (Project Gutenberg, first published 1789, 2005 edn) <http://www.gutenberg.org/files/15399/15399-h/15399-h.htm>.

55 UK, *Parliamentary Debates*, House of Commons, 20 March 2007, vol 458, cols 710, 773, 779.

of any 'direct connection' between today's leaders and their predecessors made an apology unfeasible.[56] Introducing temporal rupture in the narrative of the nation, such statements sever the past from the present, allowing the contemporary nation to disclaim responsibility for the actions of its prior iterations. Remarking on this tendency, Emma Waterton notes that 'paradoxically, while there is a strongly-held view that one cannot feel guilty about those things you did not commit, there is no such injunction against feeling pride in a temporally distant group's achievements'.[57] Indeed, as we have seen, much of the debate featured precisely such expressions of pride in the past as exemplified by figures like Wilberforce and others associated with the abolitionist movement. Moreover, as the recent Brexit discourse demonstrates, far from declining with the passage of time, pride in the past is continually renewed and recycled, with nostalgia for empire enjoying a resurgence at the time of this writing because it seems to reassure an anxious populace that Britain can thrive when unencumbered by continental entanglements.[58]

Writing against the disavowal of responsibility for the actions of prior generations, Janna Thompson has argued for a view of the state as an intergenerational agent that transcends individuals and generations and that can take decisions, act and assume responsibility in its own right. Indeed, without such a conception of intergenerational responsibility, it would be impossible for present citizens to enter into commitments that bind future generations. As Thompson explains:

> Present citizens have a moral entitlement to impose . . . obligations on future citizens only if they have reason to believe that in making such commitments they are operating in the framework of a practice that requires them to take responsibility for the commitments made by past citizens and the injustices that they have committed. Those who think that they are entitled to impose demands on future people must be prepared to assume the responsibilities intrinsic to a transgenerational polity.[59]

Perhaps unsurprisingly, black MPs had less difficulty making connections with the past, pointing to numerous present-day accumulations of wealth that had been built on profits from the slave trade, and drawing lines of continuity between slavery and the conditions in which communities descended from slaves lived today. Labour MP Diane Abbott, the first black woman to be elected to the Commons, wondered 'whether the extraordinary brutality of the slave plantation experience in the West Indies mark[ed] Caribbean life today', noting that Jamaica,

56 Ibid col 762.

57 Waterton, above n 45, 133.

58 Nadine El-Enany, 'Brexit as Nostalgia for Empire' on *Critical Legal Thinking* (19 June 2016) <http://criticallegalthinking.com/2016/06/19/brexit-nostalgia-empire/>.

59 Janna Thompson, 'Apology, Justice, and Respect: A Critical Defense of Political Apology' in Mark Gibney, Rhoda E Howard-Hassmann, Jean-Marc Coicaud and Niklaus Steiner (eds), *The Age of Apology: Facing Up to the Past* (University of Pennsylvania Press, 2008) 31, 39.

the country of her parents, had the highest murder rate in the world.[60] Her colleague Dawn Butler referred specifically to the legacy of slavery, defining 'legacy' as 'what has been passed to the present' and remarking, in a poetic turn of phrase, that 'those enslaved gave their tomorrows for our todays'.[61] Speeches by Abbott (and Jeremy Corbyn) were also instrumental in offsetting the 'Wilberforcemania'[62] of some members with the crucial reminder that slavery was brought to an end, in no small measure, by the agency of slaves themselves in insurrections such as the Haitian Revolution and countless lesser-known rebellions.[63]

While clearly seeking to force a more meaningful reckoning with the legacy of slavery, what is striking about the interventions by black MPs is that they too seemed deeply cautious about broaching the subject of apology and/or reparations. Having wondered about links between past and present, Abbott backpedalled – 'I do not want to stretch the thought too far'[64] – and while raising the subject of reparations, Butler did so only in respect of the indemnity that Haiti had been forced to pay France for its freedom;[65] indeed, when speaking of the future, she could countenance only 'emotional and spiritual reparation to repair minds'.[66] David Lammy, MP for Tottenham and then Culture Minister, pleaded that he 'did not want to get into a blame fest' and commended Blair for having 'gone further than any other leader of any western democracy' in his expression of sorrow for the country's slave-trading past.[67]

It is difficult, looking simply at the record of the 2007 debate, to fully grasp why black British politicians, with rare exceptions (Lammy's predecessor Bernie Grant being one), have been so pusillanimous in their approach to the question of apology and reparations. Those who are descendants of slave ancestors but also present-day representatives of the state that did more than any other to enable the slave trade, find themselves caught in the uncomfortable double bind that Homi K Bhabha theorises as the liminal, hybrid space of the colonised native elite.[68] One cannot underestimate the pressures of hostile white constituents, or the incentives for disciplined parliamentary behaviour offered by the prospect of career advancement. It should be pointed out, however, that a figure like Abbott

60 UK, *Parliamentary Debates*, House of Commons, 20 March 2007, vol 458, col 704. See also the opening speech by Baroness Howells in UK, *Parliamentary Debates*, House of Lords, 10 May 2007, vol 691, col 1542.
61 UK, *Parliamentary Debates*, House of Commons, 20 March 2007, vol 458, col 719.
62 Verene A Shepherd, 'Slavery, Shame and Pride: Debates over the Marking of the Bicentennial of the Abolition of the British Trans-Atlantic Trade in Africans in 2007' (2010) 56(1–2) *Caribbean Quarterly* 1, 13.
63 UK, *Parliamentary Debates*, House of Commons, 20 March 2007, vol 458, cols 698, 714, 706.
64 Ibid col 704.
65 Ibid col 706.
66 Ibid col 721.
67 'Blair "Sorrow" over Slave Trade', above n 46.
68 Homi K Bhabha, *The Location of Culture* (Routledge, 1994).

has forged an alternative parliamentary career for herself precisely by defying the Blairite line on most issues. So why not on this one? One answer may lie in an intervention that Abbott made in the midst of Butler's speech:

> Does my hon. Friend agree that it is important for young black people to learn about the black involvement in this country's history, and about the reality of the slave trade? Does she accept that they have to understand that they are not merely the passive recipients of charity from the majority community and that they can be the architects of their own fate?[69]

We can hear in Abbott's intervention an anxiety that the demand for *too much* atonement from white Britain might obviate the agency and responsibility that black people, in her view, ought to exercise in relation to their own futures.

In coming to grips with the reticence of black British politicians to endorse the notion of apology and/or reparations for slavery, we must also consider the less edifying possibility of the instrumentalisation of black faces by a white establishment to legitimate a stance of denial and disavowal. When the United States famously withdrew from the 2001 Durban Conference Against Racism, Racial Discrimination, Xenophobia and Related Intolerance in protest against the equation of Zionism with racism, but also because of the appearance of the demand for slavery reparations on the conference agenda, its objections were articulated by then Secretary of State Colin Powell and National Security Advisor Condoleezza Rice, both African Americans. Following US withdrawal, it was left to Britain and other Western European countries to lead the opposition to this demand. The British delegation was led by the black Labour politician Baroness Valerie Amos (now Director of SOAS, University of London, where I am employed). Hilary Beckles – historian, advocate for reparations and head of the delegation from Barbados – recalls Amos's contribution to the conference:

> Amos was adamant that slavery and slave trading were not crimes because the British Parliament, and its colonial machinery, had made them legal. Despite two hundred years of black resistance and rebellion, she insisted that the slave system was legal because the British Parliament deemed it to be so. Aware that national law does not legalize crimes against humanity, she did not retreat in the face of overwhelming historical arguments.[70]

Resting on a strictly positivist interpretation of international law, Amos's position seemed – to her Caribbean counterparts – unwilling to entertain the moral responsibilities that Britain owed, as a duty of justice rather than charity, to the countries that were ravaged by its slave trade and that, left undischarged,

69 UK, *Parliamentary Debates*, House of Commons, 20 March 2007, vol 458, col 720.

70 Hilary McD Beckles, *Britain's Black Debt: Reparations for Caribbean Slavery and Native Genocide* (University of West Indies Press, 2013) 195.

undermined the prospects for a moral global economy.[71] Reading the 2007 British parliamentary debates, Beckles concludes bitterly that 'it was a shameful sight to see and hear descendants of enslaved blacks singing the Blair song in and out of Parliament. What was clear . . . was that the black group in the British Parliament did not support, even moderately, the notion of reparations as reconciliation.'[72] Beckles's indictment brings to mind the odious image of black minstrel performance at the behest of white directors, leaving us with an image, quite literally, of the white state making anti-black arguments in blackface.

(Why) is sex sexier than race?

In December 2013, the computer pioneer and Second World War codebreaker Alan Turing was granted a posthumous royal pardon for a 1952 conviction for gross indecency.[73] Turing had been arrested for having sex with a 19-year-old man and was given a choice between chemical castration and a sentence of imprisonment. He chose the former, but was dead within two years as a result of what was described, not without controversy, as suicide. The 2013 pardon was the result of a campaign launched by a coalition of computer scientists, historians and LGBT activists who were determined to honour Turing's memory for his contribution to the war effort and to science. It followed a 2009 apology from the then Prime Minister Gordon Brown, who said 'on behalf of the British government, and all those who live freely thanks to Alan's work, I am very proud to say: we're sorry. You deserved so much better.'[74] While a number of factors distinguish the apology to Turing from the non-apology for slavery, the former reinforces the impression that the British state appears more willing to atone for past sexual injustices in which it was complicit than for its racial crimes. So, it is worth considering whether the differences between these contexts are morally significant. In what follows, I want to make a distinction between factors that appear to distinguish these contexts but that, on closer scrutiny, ought not to; and factors that do indeed distinguish them in ways that might illuminate why atonement is more forthcoming in some contexts than others.

First, let us consider the question of time. In contrast to arguments disavowing responsibility for slavery on grounds of a lack of connection between slave owners and present-day representatives of the state, in the Turing case the evident lack of connection between the authorities who had zealously enforced an unjust law against him and present-day representatives of the state did not seem to affect the

71 Max du Plessis, 'Historical Injustice and International Law: An Exploratory Discussion of Reparation for Slavery' (2003) 25 *Human Rights Quarterly* 624.

72 Beckles, above n 70, 197.

73 'Royal Pardon for Codebreaker Alan Turing', *BBC News* (online), 24 December 2013 <http://www.bbc.com/news/technology-25495315>.

74 Gordon Brown, 'I'm Proud to Say Sorry to a Real War Hero', *The Telegraph* (online), 10 September 2009 <http://www.telegraph.co.uk/news/politics/gordon-brown/6170112/Gordon-Brown-Im-proud-to-say-sorry-to-a-real-war-hero.html>.

ability or willingness of the latter to take responsibility for the actions of their predecessors. Here, 'direct connection' was established by the continuous corporate personality of the state rather than by an affinity between the individuals who committed the injustice and those who apologised for it. Moreover, the question of moral anachronism was never raised insofar as the Turing case was concerned, even though it might justifiably have been: after all, Turing was retrospectively pardoned for an act that had been considered criminal at the time of its commission under a duly constituted law whose procedural status as law had never been contested then or since. If anything, the enormously popular Turing pardon demonstrated a public appetite for morally anachronistic gestures in the service of justice and, perhaps more importantly, as an affirmation of the contemporary values of the political community. So much for the dogs that might have barked, but did not.

This leaves a different kind of temporal claim, namely that the Turing case was more amenable to apology because of the shorter lapse of time between the commission of the injustice and the demand for apology. Like the Turing case, Britain's 'responsibility' for anti-sodomy laws in its former colonies can be dated, at the latest, to the moment of decolonisation in the mid twentieth century, roughly a century and a half after the end of slavery. But the significance of the putative temporal difference between these contexts can be challenged in two ways. First, we can ask, empirically, whether slavery ended when we think it did. Here, the choice of 1807 as marking the end of slavery in British commemorations becomes suspect when we recall that the possession of slaves was not outlawed in the British Empire until 1834 (and in the Spanish colonies until the 1880s). When Beckles reminds us that former slave-owning families such as the Lascelles of Harewood retained their sugar plantations in Barbados until as recently as 1975, it becomes easier to appreciate how slavery can remain part of 'living memory'[75] in the Caribbean and how the shame associated with it can continue to infuse the post-Emancipation present.[76] Writing in a US context, Angela Davis has drawn lines of continuity between the political economy of slavery and the contemporary 'prison-industrial complex', unsettling the received wisdom about the achievement of emancipation and civil rights.[77] Second, even accepting that slavery ended well before the prosecution of sodomy did, we can ask the conceptual question of whether the passage of time should attenuate the case for atonement. It may be supposed that a shorter lapse of time makes the case for apology more compelling because the injury is fresh in the minds of victims (if still alive) and/or their descendants, or because they have had less time and opportunity to adjust to its consequences. Yet to accept this argument would impose an arbitrary limitation on the period within which acknowledgements for historic injustice ought to be made. Moreover, it would overlook the fact that it is precisely in circumstances of

75 Beckles, above n 70, 16, 168–9.
76 Shepherd, above n 62.
77 Angela Davis, *The Prison Industrial Complex* (AK Press, 1999).

gross power disparities between perpetrator and victim that injustices tend to remain unacknowledged for long periods.

This brings us to a second possible distinction between the Turing apology and the slavery non-apology, namely money. The only criticism of the Turing pardon was that it had not been extended to the nearly 50,000 men who had been convicted under the same law. The fact that some of these men were still alive and might have become entitled to compensation as a result of such a move may have weighed on the minds of those who operationalised the royal prerogative of mercy. In the context of reckoning with the legacies of slavery, the demand for reparations, not to mention the presumed scale of such reparations were they to be meaningful, seems to exercise a chilling effect on even non-monetary expressions of atonement for slavery, because of the feared link between words and money. It seems clear that atonement is more easily contemplable in contexts in which it is seen to have no serious material repercussions.

Third, we cannot ignore Turing's exceptional status as a white man of genius committed to the defence of the state through his efforts to break the Nazi Enigma code, in understanding why the demand for apology on his behalf was successful. I suggest that atonement in the British establishment for anti-sodomy laws in the colonies is informed by the awareness that such laws also punished people within or near that establishment – elite white men like Oscar Wilde and Turing. At a reception in the Chamber of the Speaker of the House of Commons marking the formation of the APPG on Global LGBT Rights in 2015, I listened as MPs expressed grateful incredulity at the possibility of doing such work in an institution where poignantly remembered (unnamed) senior colleagues had been unable to be 'out', let alone take public positions on LGBT issues, in the not very distant past.[78] That white elites also suffer(ed) as queers allows an elision between 'queer' and 'whiteness', spurring atonement for anti-sodomy laws in a way that is not forthcoming with regard to slavery.

Picture the atonement discourses for anti-sodomy laws and slavery as two triangles. The former is an inverted triangle, standing on its apex: a small group of civil society voices who have generated an astonishingly contrite discourse for this particular legacy of colonialism at the highest levels of British politics. The latter is a triangle standing on its base: an enormous, transnational, multi-generational grassroots movement advanced by pan-Africanist voices in civil society and some state institutions in the Caribbean, black America, sub-Saharan Africa and Western Europe, that struggles to have its arguments taken seriously by the governments of former slave-owning powers. Since 2014, British Afro-Caribbean people have marked Emancipation Day (1 August) by walking from Brixton to Westminster in London to reiterate the demand for reparation in commemorative marches that are comparable in their size and vivacity with the

78 Participant observation, UK, House of Commons, 21 July 2015.

most raucous Gay Pride marches, but with only a fraction of the coverage in mainstream media.[79]

My argument should not be taken to imply that Britain has more adequately reckoned with the sexual injustices that are a legacy of its colonial rule. If anything, this chapter has been a study in two styles of atonement, both of which are problematic. If imperious atonement assumes too much responsibility for the state of the contemporary world, equivocal atonement does not assume enough. If imperious atonement hovers uncertainly between the extremes of viewing the postcolony as sole author or non-author of its fate, equivocal atonement seems keener to apportion blame for the heinous outcomes that it is called to account for. Time, which is equivocal atonement's great alibi for inaction, poses fewer problems in imperious atonement's manic quest to rewrite its legacy. Both styles of atonement offer ways of managing a difficult past without changing too much about oneself or the world.

79 Rastafari Movement UK, *Reparations March 2014* (15 October 2014) YouTube <https://www.youtube.com/watch?v=vjqxkC9Gr04>.

2 'Dangerous desires'

Illegality, sexuality and the global governance of artisanal mining

*Doris Buss and Blair Rutherford**

The mining of precious and rare minerals has recently become the subject of increased international attention and regulation. Starting in the 2000s, and with the sharp rise in commodity prices, a new surge in international and transnational efforts unfolded to regulate mining in the global South, particularly on the African continent. Those initiatives have spawned an array of voluntary frameworks, global norms and standards, regional agreements, new national mining codes and mining policies, all in the service of opening up, and 'better regulating', mining economies. Collectively, these developments are part of a new global governance regime on the extractive sector.

Sexuality is more relevant to this emerging regime than suggested by this rather dry summary. Mining for precious minerals, particularly in the Western imaginary, conjures images of risk and reward: the allure of found wealth – gold nuggets or diamonds extracted from the earth's secret interiors that can make a poor man rich; combined with danger – the unregulated frontiers where mines and enterprises collapse, and wily salesmen and women rob the poor of their pittances. These tropes of desire and danger[1] are centrally implicated in the global claims made about the need for particular types of mining regulation. In this chapter,

* Our analysis draws in part from our involvement in two projects on the gendered dynamics of artisanal and small-scale mining (ASM) in six countries on the African continent: Democratic Republic of the Congo, Rwanda and Uganda (funded through *Growth and Economic Opportunities for Women*, International Development Research Centre, Canada, Department for International Development, UK, William and Flora Hewlett Foundation), in one project; Kenya, Mozambique and Sierra Leone in the other (funded by the Government of Canada's Social Sciences and Humanities Research Council, Insight Grant, awarded 2014, No 435-2014-1630). These projects are conducted with colleagues in Africa and Canada. We thank all our colleagues for enriching our understanding of ASM and particularly Jennifer Hinton who read and commented on earlier versions of this chapter and has generally been a patient and wise guide for us in this research. Our thanks also to Dianne Otto for her encouragement and patience.

1 Roseann Cohen, for example, refers to depictions of artisanal and small-scale gold mining in Colombia in terms of 'dangerous desires': Roseann Cohen, 'Extractive Desires: The Moral Control of Female Sexuality at Colombia's Gold Mining Frontier' (2014) 19 *Journal of Latin American and Caribbean Anthropology* 260, 260.

we read the emerging global governance regime on mining in terms of the 'evolutionary tropes' of development discourses that cohere through raced, gendered and sexualised meanings.[2] Law, and particularly the determination of who has law and who needs it, is a key mechanism through which hierarchical conceptions of order are racially and sexually inflected.[3]

Our focus is more particularly on a form of mining that, until recently, was largely overlooked by researchers and policy makers; artisanal and small-scale mining (ASM). With limited or no mechanisation, ASM is a rudimentary type of mining which provides a livelihood for tens of millions of people worldwide and which is now increasingly embraced by international actors as an important poverty-alleviation activity.[4] Operating in a contradictory legal space, ASM has historically been minimised, criminalised or ignored in formal legal structures otherwise oriented towards 'industrialised' mining.

The artisanal gold miner in dominant legal and policy approaches, we argue, is a queer figure; a mining 'outlaw', whose excesses and underdeveloped form are often referenced in official accounts of ASM's dangers. In these figurations, ASM helps to bolster 'industrial' mining as the norm against which ASM is the perversion. Sexuality is operable here, not so much in terms of sexual practices (or, at least, this is not directly our focus), but as providing one of the discursive structures[5] through which constructs of disorder and order cohere. Reading the regulation of mining through sexuality as episteme[6] highlights the productive power of discourses on mining's dangers; the kinds of legal, regulatory order that emerge as necessary against the disorders attributed to ASM. Sexuality is not the only context in which the artisanal miner is figured, but in this chapter we highlight it as one axis along which 'uneven global legal relations' are constituted.[7]

The chapter begins with an introduction to the emerging global regime on governing the extractives sector that is premised on state and corporate transparency and self-exposure and a dialectic between law and disorder. In the

2 Neville Hoad, 'Arrested Development or the Queerness of Savages: Resisting Evolutionary Narratives of Difference' (2000) 3 *Postcolonial Studies* 133, 133. See also Cynthia Weber, *Queer International Relations: Sovereignty, Sexuality and the Will to Knowledge* (Oxford University Press, 2016); Roderick A Ferguson, 'Of Our Normative Strivings: African American Studies and the Histories of Sexuality' (2005) 23(3–4) *Social Text* 85.

3 Teemu Ruskola, *Legal Orientalism: China, the United States, and Modern Law* (Harvard University Press, 2013) 5.

4 Jennifer J Hinton, 'Communities and Small-Scale Mining: An Integrated Review for Development Planning' (Report, Communities and Small-Scale Mining Initiative, World Bank Group, December 2005); Gavin Hilson, 'Small-Scale Mining, Poverty and Economic Development in Sub-Saharan Africa: An Overview' (2009) 34(1–2) *Resources Policy* 1.

5 Gayle S Rubin, 'Thinking Sex: Notes for a Radical Theory of the Politics of Sexuality' in Henry Abelove, Michèle Aina Barale and David M Halperin (eds), *The Lesbian and Gay Studies Reader* (Routledge, 1993) 3.

6 Michel Foucault, 'Politics and the Study of Discourse' in Graham Burchell, Colin Gordon and Peter Miller (eds), *The Foucault Effect: Studies in Governmentality* (University of Chicago Press, 1991) 53, 55 quoted in Ferguson, above n 2, 87.

7 Teemu Ruskola, 'Raping like a State' (2010) 57 *UCLA Law Review* 1477, 1527.

second section, we explore the sexualised dimensions of disorder as they are articulated in relation to the 'numerous negatives'[8] often imputed to ASM. Sexual metaphors, and moralising discourses of ASM's sexual excesses, we argue in the third section, have helped to rationalise the global governance of ASM. Focusing specifically on the global regulation of 'conflict minerals', we explore the ways in which foundational dichotomies between private/public, secrecy/disclosure and excess/restraint resonate with sexualised meanings that serve, ultimately, to construct an idealised, self-regulating global subject. The focus of global regulation of mineral extraction comes to rest on the conditions for self-managed restraint of both artisanal miners and a global class of consuming subjects.

The global governance of mining

International and national policy makers, agencies and donors have, over the last decade or more, unrolled various initiatives to reform resource extraction on the African continent in order to address the twin concerns of armed conflict/criminality and endemic poverty. These initiatives include establishing global standards and monitoring mechanisms to improve mining governance within mineral-rich states of the global South, such as the Extractive Industries Transparency Initiative (EITI),[9] regimes aimed at encouraging changes in corporate behaviour in the extractives sector, such as the Organisation for Economic Cooperation and Development (OECD) *Due Diligence Guidelines for Responsible Supply Chains of Minerals from Conflict-Affected and High-Risk Areas*,[10] as well as more regional mechanisms to identify shared approaches and priorities, such as the African Mining Vision and the efforts of the International Conference of the Great Lakes Region (ICGLR).[11] Alongside and in relation to these initiatives are further efforts supporting revisions of national mining codes.

8 Gavin Hilson and Angélique Gatsinzi, 'A Rocky Road Ahead? Critical Reflections on the Futures of Small-Scale Mining in sub-Saharan Africa' (2014) 62(A) *Futures* 1, 4; for discussion see Chris Huggins, Doris Buss and Blair Rutherford, 'A "Cartography of Concern": Place-Making Practices and Gender in the Artisanal Mining Sector in Africa' (2016) 74 *Geoforum* 182.

9 Which is described on its website as a 'global standard to promote the open and accountable management of natural resources', in text emblazoned on a photograph of a room of African men sitting in a large press conference: 'Who We Are', Extractive Industries Transparency Initiative (EITI) <https://eiti.org/about/who-we-are>.

10 The website for the Organisation for Economic Cooperation and Development (OECD) describes the Guidelines as providing 'detailed recommendations to help companies respect human rights and avoid contributing to conflict through their mineral purchasing decisions and practices': OECD, 'OECD Due Diligence Guidance for Responsible Supply Chains of Minerals from Conflict-Affected and High-Risk Areas', <http://www.oecd.org/corporate/mne/mining.htm>.

11 A 12-member body of state governments in Africa's Great Lakes region formed to promote regional stability and which has undertaken significant work to increase and harmonise legal regimes on mining in the region: International Conference on the Great Lakes Region <http://www.icglr.org/index.php/en>.

Bonnie Campbell characterises these as unfolding in 'generations' as changing conceptions of the state's role in regulating the sector drive variations in legal frameworks.[12] The 1990s saw upwards of 30 African countries reform their mining codes,[13] and the 2000s witnessed yet another wave of mining law reform which Hany Besada and Philip Martin have suggested constitutes a fourth generation,[14] unfolding alongside the transnational regimes of the EITI and others.

Concerns about the so-called 'resource curse' loom large in these efforts. The term is a catch-all phrase referring to the failure of states to economically benefit and develop despite the presence of valuable natural resources such as oil, gas and minerals. The 'curse' is that valuable minerals can undermine local economies or encourage corruption and oligarchy in states, fostering, in turn, the conditions for armed conflict.[15] Country examples given of the resource curse tend to be exclusively African – Nigeria, Democratic Republic of the Congo (DRC), Angola, and the list goes on.[16]

While a number of scholars are critical of the phrase 'resource curse' and its reductionist approach to the complex political economies of resource extraction,[17] the general concerns behind the term are influential in international approaches to resource governance. The resulting myriad of regimes and programmes at national, international and regional levels are targeting not just mining codes and policies, but also state structures, from taxation to land registration, deemed necessary for 'improved governance capacity'. Regional reforms are also unfolding to encourage consistency across national standards, for example in the Great Lakes region,[18] and global initiatives that work through private sector (corporations), civil society, donor and recipient country collaborations on extractive industries are increasingly influential.[19] The extractives governance regime thus encompasses a diffuse, multi-sited, multi-scalar set of institutions, relations, ideas/consciousness,

12 Bonnie Campbell (ed), 'Regulating Mining in Africa: For Whose Benefit?' (Discussion Paper No 26, Nordiska Afrikainstitutet, 2004).

13 James Otto, Craig Andrews, Fred Cawood et al, 'Mining Royalties: A Global Study of Their Impact on Investors, Government and Civil Society' (Report, Directions in Development: Energy and Mining, World Bank, 2006) xvi.

14 Hany Besada and Philip Martin, 'Mining Codes in Africa: Emergence of a "Fourth" Generation?' (2015) 28 *Cambridge Review of International Affairs* 263.

15 See, eg, Jeffrey D Sachs and Andrew M Warner, 'The Curse of Natural Resources' (2001) 45(4–6) *European Economic Review* 827.

16 See, eg, Terra Lawson-Remer and Joshua Greenstein, 'Beating the Resource Curse in Africa: A Global Effort', *Council on Foreign Relations* (August 2012) <http://www.cfr.org/africa-sub-saharan/beating-resource-curse-africa-global-effort/p28780>.

17 Kuntala Lahiri-Dutt, '"May God Give Us Chaos, So That We Can Plunder": A Critique of "Resource Curse" and Conflict Theories' (2006) 49(3) *Development* 14.

18 The International Conference on the Great Lakes Region has undertaken significant work, including through the Lusaka Declaration to increase and harmonise legal regimes on mining: above n 11.

19 See, eg, above n 9.

flows and locales that are better described as an 'assemblage'[20] rather than a single system. The legal disciplinary categories of international, national or comparative do not fully capture the (legal) orders entailed within this regime. While some aspects of this governance regime could be comprised of, and give rise to, plural legal orders, this too has conceptual limits because of the complex flows and normative orderings that are not necessarily 'legal' or law-like.[21]

Our focus is on ASM as a site of, and embedded within, various, multi-scalar governance relations. This focus on governance, rather than specific legal orders, is informed by work of international relations and African studies scholars who have begun to explore the global dimensions of governmentality; the different and dispersed processes, institutions, agencies and subjects through which management of conduct is enacted.[22] Such an approach allows for an emphasis on complex governance techniques, effects and ideological claims, without, at the same time, reifying the contours (boundedness) of the state and its non-state corollaries – civil society and private sector actors. It also opens up for consideration a greater variety of relations and 'micro-centres'[23] of control where legal meaning is created, and legal actors figured, in relation to the global governance of resource extraction.

Finally, we read this emerging regime of resource governance as another example of what John and Jean Comaroff have referred to as a 'dialectic of law and disorder'[24] where 'legal fetish'[25] unfolds in a '*pas-de-deux*' with preoccupations with criminality and disorder.[26] Law, and the need for more and different kinds of law, is a driving force in efforts to govern mining, which is consistently placed in relation to claims about 'disorder' and 'lawlessness' associated with resource governance that are mostly, but not entirely, located on the African continent. We explore this dialectical relationship and, particularly, the ways in which allegations about sexual excess, and the use of sexual metaphors, buttress depictions of disorder and criminality against which the demands for legality are constructed.

20 Aihwa Ong and Stephen J Collier (eds), *Global Assemblages: Technology, Politics, and Ethics as Anthropological Problems* (Wiley-Blackwell, 2008).

21 The question of 'global law' and its relation to spatially demarcated, plural legal order is outside the scope of this chapter. See, eg, Hans Lindahl, 'A-Legality: Postnationalism and the Question of Legal Boundaries' (2010) 73 *Modern Law Review* 30.

22 See, eg, James Ferguson and Akhil Gupta, 'Spatializing States: Toward an Ethnography of Neoliberal Governmentality' (2002) 29 *American Ethnologist* 981; William Walters, 'Some Critical Notes on "Governance"' (2004) 73(1) *Studies in Political Economy* 27; James Ferguson, *Global Shadows: Africa in the Neoliberal World Order* (Duke University Press, 2006); Sally Engle Merry, 'New Legal Realism and the Ethnography of Transnational Law' (2006) 31 *Law & Social Inquiry* 975.

23 Ann Laura Stoler, *Race and the Education of Desire: Foucault's History of Sexuality and the Colonial Order of Things* (Duke University Press, 1995) 190.

24 John L Comaroff and Jean Comaroff, 'Law and Disorder in the Postcolony: An Introduction' in Jean Comaroff and John L Comaroff (eds), *Law and Disorder in the Postcolony* (University of Chicago Press, 2000) 1.

25 Ibid 22–35.

26 Ibid 5.

Desires and dangers in artisanal and small-scale mining (ASM)

Paradoxically, ASM is both central and marginal to current efforts at promoting better governance of the mining sector. It relies on the low-cost labour of millions of people, for whom it is an important, if dangerous and unreliable, livelihood when other sectors such as agriculture are diminishing because of neoliberal economic policies, armed conflict and climate change, for example. Indeed, the World Bank estimates that 100 million people worldwide work in, or rely on, ASM.[27]

Despite the large numbers of people engaged in ASM and related livelihoods, it has been widely disparaged by policy makers. As a low yield form of mining compared to 'industrial mining', which routinely takes place without or in 'violation' of licences or property rights, ASM is often positioned as an impediment to developing the large-scale mining sector in Africa. It is routinely depicted in terms of 'numerous negatives', including environmental degradation, illegality and criminality, exploitation and occupational hazards, prostitution, marriage breakdown, sexual liberty, disease and drug-use.[28] The various harms attributed to ASM historically have led to contradictory legal and policy responses.

In the 1980s and into the 1990s, mining laws and policies on the continent were directed at 'opening up' African countries to entry by international mining companies for large-scale extraction. In this period, donors and international agencies, like the World Bank, worked with state governments to develop or revise domestic mining laws to attract 'greater foreign investment through decreased regulation, liberalised social and labour policies, and more private sector-friendly ownership and taxation schemes'.[29] These revisions tended to ignore or criminalise ASM, with legal regimes providing no route for artisanal miners to operate legally, effectively mandating their permanent informality and illegality. Efforts that did unfold to 'formalise' the sector, such as through requirements for licences, were ill-suited and poorly implemented.[30] Licensing regimes, including many that operate today, may require travel to a capital city, the cost of which is beyond most artisanal miners, and/or involve application forms requiring good literacy skills or access to notaries. Further, some of the definitions of legal artisanal mining specify conditions – such as the maximum depth of a mine shaft – inconsistent with actual practices. Thus, ASM has become something of an open secret:[31] nominally illegal, even criminal, often passively tolerated, with occasional expensive

27 World Bank, 'Artisanal and Small-Scale Mining' (21 November 2013) <http://www.worldbank.org/en/topic/extractiveindustries/brief/artisanal-and-small-scale-mining>.

28 For a discussion, see Hilson and Gatsinzi, above n 8, 4.

29 Besada and Martin, above n 14; Campbell, above n 12.

30 Gavin Hilson and James McQuilken, 'Four Decades of Support for Artisanal and Small-Scale Mining in Sub-Saharan Africa: A Critical Review' (2014) 1 *Extractive Industries and Society* 104.

31 Ibid 112.

police or military crack-downs or requests for payments to forestall such enforcements of 'the law', while widely practised and seen at the grassroots level as a legitimate livelihood option.

Starting in the 2000s, international concerns about ongoing armed conflict and human rights abuses in the DRC and neighbouring countries introduced a new dynamic. At that time, sexual violence became a key theme in international concerns about the wars in eastern DRC, which was described as the 'rape capital' of the world, and the 'worst place' to be a woman.[32] International policy makers also began to investigate the role of multinational companies operating in the region, the role of 'illegal exploitation and trade of natural resources and financing of armed groups'.[33]

These efforts led, in turn, to the development of new laws and policies aimed at regulating the trade in 'conflict minerals', laws that were often justified by reference to concerns about sexual violence and related human rights abuse. Section 1502 of the 2010 US Dodd-Frank Act[34] is the leading example. Under this highly influential yet hastily implemented law, US-registered corporations are required to monitor and report on where and from whom they buy minerals used in their products, with the aim of reducing armed conflict and (sexual) violence in the region by ensuring that the mineral supply chain, from the eastern DRC mine site to the electronic gadgets purchased in the global North, is certified as 'conflict free'.[35]

At the root of these concerns about conflict minerals is ASM. After decades of state decay, followed by years of armed conflict, ASM is an important form

32 The origin of the description of DRC as 'rape capital' is not clear. Press reports from 2007 quote John Homes, a 'top UN humanitarian official', as saying that rape in DRC has become 'almost a cultural phenomenon' and in intensity and frequency 'worse than anywhere else in the world': Stephanie McCrummen, 'Prevalence of Rape in E. Congo Described as Worst in World', *Washington Post Foreign Service* (online) (9 September 2007) <http://www.washingtonpost.com/wp-dyn/content/article/2007/09/08/AR2007090801194.html>. 'Rape capital' is used by media outlets in 2007–8 but becomes a frequent reference by 2010 when Margot Wallström, Special Representative of the UN Secretary-General on Sexual Violence in Conflict, wrote that eastern DRC 'has been labelled the rape capital of the world': Margot Wallström, '"Conflict Minerals" Finance Gang Rape in Africa', *The Guardian* (online) (15 August 2010) <https://www.theguardian.com/commentisfree/2010/aug/14/conflict-minerals-finance-gang-rape>. Human Rights Watch, in its 2009 World Report chapter on DRC, wrote, '[i]n a region already labelled "the worst place in the world to be a woman"': 'Democratic Republic of Congo (DRC): Events of 2009' (Report, Human Rights Watch) <https://www.hrw.org/world-report/2010/country-chapters/democratic-republic-congo>.

33 Vuyelwa Kuuya, 'The Illegal Exploitation of Natural Resources and Other Forms of Wealth in the Democratic Republic of Congo', *Business & Human Rights Resource Centre* (1 November 2008) <https://business-humanrights.org/en/doc-the-illegal-exploitation-of-natural-resources-and-other-forms-of-wealth-in-the-democratic-republic-of-congo>.

34 Dodd-Frank Wall Street Reform and Consumer Protection Act, Pub L No 111-203, 124 Stat 1375 (2010) ('Dodd-Frank Act').

35 See also Doris Buss, 'Sexual Violence, Conflict Minerals, and the "Economies of Appearance"' (unpublished manuscript).

of mining in eastern DRC and neighbouring areas, and the source of livelihoods for many. As a conflict-driven livelihood of last resort, ASM is also enmeshed in coercive authority structures implicating state and non-state militias.[36] The legal and regulatory response to 'conflict minerals', such as section 1502, were de facto directed at ASM, linking it with armed conflict, violence and criminal, 'black market' economies. The dominant policy response, as we write in late 2016, is the insistence on 'formalising' the artisanal sector, to minimise the conditions seen as giving rise to criminality, illegality and the 'black market' global trade in minerals.

Formalisation is a development strategy that endeavours to bring the informal economies of ASM into the mainstream through a mix of legal recognition, enabling institutional structures and financial supports and incentives.[37] Emphasis is placed on granting some kind of legal right to artisanal miners from which related benefits are hoped to flow: strengthening access to capital to invest in better, safer technology, resisting predation by rent-seeking officials/land owners, accessing training and improving use of technology and, ultimately, improving mining efficiency and environmental protection.[38] The resulting approaches to formalisation are often highly legalistic, requiring changes to an array of laws and institutions, and the establishment of technical regimes for monitoring and inspection.[39]

In Africa's Great Lakes region, concerns about ASM's link to black market mineral trade and armed conflict have resulted in a globalised regime of monitoring and regulation that is even more technical and legalistic. Requirements established by section 1502 of the Dodd-Frank Act mean that corporations must report on the origin of designated minerals, gold and tin, tantalum and tungsten (referred to as '3TGs') used in their products, leading in turn to an array of initiatives to both formalise ASM and the mineral trade, but also monitor and certify – as 'conflict free' – 3TGs from the region and along each stage of the global supply chain. The costs of complying with section 1502 are estimated at US $3–4 billion initially and between US $200 and 600 million annually thereafter.[40]

36 Louise Arimatsu and Hemi Mistry, 'Conflict Minerals: The Search for a Normative Framework' (International Law Programme Paper No 2012/01, Chatham House, September 2012).

37 Laura Barreto, 'Analysis for Stakeholders on Formalization in the Artisanal and Small-Scale Gold Mining Sector Based on Experiences in Latin America, Africa, and Asia' (Report, UN Environment Programme, September 2011); 'Analysis of Formalization Approaches in the Artisanal and Small-Scale Gold Mining Sector Based on Experiences in Ecuador, Mongolia, Peru, Tanzania and Uganda' (Report, UN Environment Programme, June 2012).

38 Barreto, above n 37.

39 Such as, for example, Mozambique's Natural Resources and Environment Protection Force, an environmental 'police force' to ensure ASM is conducted in compliance with the law: Buss's field notes, Maputo, Mozambique, July 2016 and Rutherford's field notes, Manica district, Mozambique, 2016.

40 *National Association of Manufacturers v Securities and Exchange Commission* (DC Cir, No 13-5252, 18 August 2015) 15.

Sexuality and gender in ASM

The 'numerous negatives' of ASM against which the fetishism of legalisation currently unfolds are clearly imbricated in – and make reference to and perpetuate – colonial, raced, gendered and sexualised discourses through which highly unequal, idealised conceptions of order are constructed. Our focus is on the operation of just one of these – sexuality, often in combination with gender – as a vector along which some constructs of ASM's 'numerous negatives' cohere. In highlighting sexuality, we recognise that it is not always the principal matrix through which meaning is constructed and social life ordered. Yet, following Michel Foucault,[41] Anne McClintock[42] and Ann Laura Stoler,[43] we attend to sexuality as an important vector along which contemporary discourses of self and other, order and criminality, are both constituted and inflected with racial and colonial meanings in contemporary forms of global governance.

Sexuality operates in multiple ways in the complex social, political and economic relations that structure ASM sites. Hard rock and, in particular, underground artisanal mining sites are, at one level, saturated with sexual and gendered imagery. Livelihood practices are also entangled in gendered and sexualised norms and performances that combine in ways central to the organisation of women's and men's roles in, and access to, mining-related livelihoods.

The digging and exploitation of mine 'shafts', the term that is common in some sub-Saharan countries, such as Kenya, is the privileged activity on a mine site that also gives rise to an array of livelihoods, from crushing, sifting and washing ore, to the manufacture and sale of food, alcohol and domestic and sexual services. In many artisanal gold-mining areas, there are strict gendered norms and taboos against women going into the shafts where the ore is dug and extracted. The shafts are hot, humid, tight enclosures, and worked almost entirely by groups of men. They are spaces constructed in terms of desire and danger.

Other than the buyers of gold, the men who work, own or control the shaft generally gain the greatest financial rewards on the mine site. The other mining activities – stone crushing, washing and panning – are more accessible to women, but can be financially more risky and less lucrative. Shafts are generally owned by men and getting (into) a shaft is a good prospect for making money.[44]

In some mine sites, the edict against women in the shafts is framed in terms of magic or luck; women will 'chase away' the gold; they bring bad luck. Sometimes this prohibition is tied specifically to women's menstrual cycle as the source of

41 Michel Foucault, *The History of Sexuality: An Introduction* (Robert Hurley trans, Vintage, first published 1976, 1990 edn) vol 1.

42 Anne McClintock, *Imperial Leather: Race, Gender, and Sexuality in the Colonial Contest* (Routledge, 1995).

43 Stoler, above n 23, 190–5. See also Weber, above n 2.

44 This section and the following discussion rely on field notes of the authors and colleagues generated in the course of visits in 2015 and 2016 to selected ASM gold sites in Kenya, Mozambique, DRC, Rwanda, Sierra Leone and Uganda.

pollution and curse. Some men in an artisanal tin-mining area in Western Uganda noted its similarity to a restriction against women entering tomato gardens during their menstrual cycle for fear their presence would lead to the drying up of the plants. If women enter the mines at any time, according to these men, menstruating or not, the tin will disappear. In other regions, such as western Kenya's Migori gold belt, women are said to be 'weak' or not sufficiently courageous to be in the shafts. Alternatively, women are excluded from shafts for their own safety precisely because shafts are dark, small places where miners work in close proximity with each other often wearing limited clothes given the high temperatures in the shafts. Hence, the argument goes, sexual violence would be inevitable if women were in the shafts. Relations between men who share these tight enclosures, in states of undress, are generally not remarked upon. Modesty and respectability were also emphasised by women and men in ASM sites in eastern DRC, as only immediate family members should see men in such a state of undress. As one woman involved in gold mining in Ituri province, DRC, exclaimed, 'In the digging area, men dress badly! It is not good to see the body of a man who is not your husband! We are African!'[45]

The concerns of illicit sexual liaisons were particularly marked for married women. A married woman working with men in mining activities without the presence of a husband is rare, for the fear expressed by many men is that she would could be 'wooed' by one of the men and have sex with him. In Tonkolili district, Sierra Leone, migrant men digging in alluvial gold mines said they would only hire a married woman to cook food for them after gaining permission from her husband; otherwise, hiring a married woman would arouse her husband's suspicions and could lead to conflict. In the Ituri gold mines, it was common for sites to have a person called 'mother chief', who was married to the man who is the 'camp commander'. Among other duties, she is in charge of regulating the morals of women working and living in the mining area. For instance, she identifies those who are the 'free women' (*femmes libre* — those never married) and those who are married. This is sartorially symbolised with the camp rule encouraging married women to wear two '*pagnes*' (cloth wraps) and the free and/or single women using one *pagne*, a skirt and/or pants. People interpret the extra wrap worn by married women to signify that they are 'taken' (controlled) by a husband, while the other women are potentially 'available' for relationships with men.[46]

Thus, mine sites are places in which sexuality and sexual relations unfold within specific cultural contexts and practices. Katja Werthmann, in her study of artisanal gold mining in Burkina Faso, for example, found that some young women are drawn to gold mining because of the economic opportunities available,

45 Field notes, University of Kisangani and the Associates for Research and Education for Development, 2015.

46 Ibid.

as well as the freedom to exercise sexual autonomy;[47] a finding resonant with a larger history of African women moving to towns or even missions to try to escape patriarchal (or matriarchal) controls over their sexuality and lives.[48] Similarly, ASM sites may hold out the possibility of (limited) forms of sexual self-expression, although they remain structured by gendered power relations, which subject women (and men) to forms of exploitation and danger, as well as pleasure.

In the organisational dynamics of the ASM site, the length of the shaft matters. The deeper and thus riskier the shaft becomes, the harder life is for everyone in the mine area. Deep shafts can encounter more flooding and require more technology and money in order to access the gold. Accidents are often fatal and may result in officials closing a mine, usually temporarily, but often with an enormous impact on the many men and women who rely on it for their daily livelihoods. Characterisations of masculinity in terms of courage and strength take on a particular resonance within an artisanal mining site where all other livelihoods are reliant upon the men successfully exploiting the shaft.

There is a distinct homosociality and, at times, sexualised hypermasculinity among the men in these ASM sites. In Mozambique's Manica district, miners, diggers and shaft owners commonly expressed both a masculine camaraderie and competitiveness. Men who worked in some of the activities of the mines, but did not enter the shafts, were commonly depicted in feminised terms as scared or weak, while school-aged boys who did odd jobs around the mines were considered to be miners (and men) in training, learning the ropes of mining. Men worked together in teams, but there was also competition among them that could lead to fights or accusations of cheating. At the same time, when a cave-in occurred, loud whistles called men from other pits and shafts to come and try to dig out the affected men. In such events, women were said to provide 'supportive roles', bringing food and drink to the frantically digging men.[49]

In Katanga, south-east DRC, Jeroen Cuvelier describes the masculine dimensions of an ASM 'mining sub-culture which has its own moral economy' and includes an embrace of *kivoyou*, or 'deviant lifestyle', comprised of profligate spending, 'swearing, wearing eccentric or expensive clothes, cross-dressing, drinking excessively, being disrespectful towards senior members of society and speaking *hindubill* – a kind of tongue-in-cheek, "underworld" slang'.[50] Mining is

47 Katja Werthmann, 'Working in a Boom-Town: Female Perspectives on Gold-Mining in Burkina Faso' (2009) 34 *Resources Policy* 18.

48 See, eg, Teresa A Barnes, *'We Women Worked So Hard': Gender, Urbanization, and Social Reproduction in Colonial Harare, Zimbabwe, 1930–1956* (Heinemann, 1999); Dorothy L Hodgson and Sheryl A McCurdy (eds), *'Wicked' Women and the Reconfiguration of Gender in Africa* (Heinemann, 2001); Blair Rutherford, *Farm Labor Struggles in Zimbabwe: The Ground of Politics* (Indiana University Press, 2017).

49 Rutherford field notes, above n 39.

50 Jeroen Cuvelier, 'Money, Migration and Masculinity among Artisanal Miners in Katanga (DR Congo)' (2016) *Review of African Political Economy* 7.

seen as an important process for developing one's masculinity, and in which attention to the male body, and the camaraderie among men, were key features. Cuvelier's research suggests that these norms of masculinity are a departure from earlier identities. As T Dunbar Moodie's pathbreaking work on sexuality among male South African industrial gold miners in pre-apartheid and apartheid South Africa reminds us, these forms of masculinity – including the roles of 'mine wives' – can shift and need to be placed in the wider cultural politics and political economy of particular locales in specific historical conjunctures.[51]

While there is not space in this chapter to do justice to the operation of gender and sexuality in structuring ASM sites, the examples above point to some important features. First, they indicate that sexuality and sexualisation of mining practices is an important, albeit complex, part of the organisation of ASM sites. Second, sexuality is woven into gendered norms and behaviours that structure how women and men pursue mining-related livelihoods and that may, in turn, condition forms of physical and economic vulnerability. And, third, these gendered and sexed relations vary over time in relation to the changing dynamics of mining, its geology and location in a larger political economy of resource extraction. Yet, while gender and sexuality are complex, multihued vectors of ASM practices and identities, the dominant portrayals of ASM in terms of its 'numerous negatives' tend to a highly reductionist account of gender and sexuality in terms of dangerous masculinity and vulnerable femininity.

Gender, sexuality and the constructs of ASM's dangers

A recurring theme in the moralising discourses on ASM's 'numerous negatives' is its threat to 'normal' sexuality. The sexualisation of ASM sites takes place both through the insistent characterisations of them as disordered and disorderly, and more directly, as linked to prostitution, sexual promiscuity and family break-up, along with child labour, alcoholism, disease and environmental destruction. In one of the few published studies on gender and gold mining in Kenya's western region,[52] the authors note the high rates of venereal and sexually transmitted diseases and the connection with 'prostitutes' who

> took advantage of the miners at Kilingili, Chavakali, Mbale and other neighboring towns where a majority especially the young miners went for entertainment and to socialize in the evenings and weekends. Drunkenness

51 T Dunbar Moodie, 'Migrancy and Male Sexuality on the South African Gold Mines' (1988) 14 *Journal of Southern African Studies* 228.

52 Media coverage is also scant, but here too both prostitution and child labour have been the focus of international news stories: 'Gold Mining Beats School Any Day', *IRIN* (online) (9 February 2012) <https://www.irinnews.org/report/94822/kenya-gold-mining-beats-school-any-day>; 'Tackling Underage Sex Work in Nyanza's Gold Mines', *IRIN* (online) (7 February 2012) <https://www.irinnews.org/fr/node/251581>.

> was also another problem . . . [leading] men into cheap and unprotected sex, and depletion of hard earned family incomes.[53]

A study of *galamsay*, artisanal miners in Ghana, similarly asserted that

> the growth in population of people from different backgrounds . . . has increased active social life, resulting in prostitution and sexual promiscuity, and as a result the increased spreading of communicable diseases such as syphilis, gonorrhea and AIDS. There are also cases of drug abuse among small-scale gold miners. This is especially prevalent among illegal operators.[54]

In each of these examples, the negatives of ASM are consistently linked to the social and sexual life of the mines; sexually transmitted disease alongside drunkenness and prostitution that feeds from profligacy. Gendered characterisations of these sexual wrongs, in which those who work in the mine sites are simultaneously risky and at risk, are also important, with men depicted as either dupes or dissolutes and women as both predators and victims.[55]

The preoccupation with the sexual dimensions of ASM's negatives continues in the more recent focus on conflict minerals and their linkage to sexual violence in eastern DRC. While sexual violence and sexualised forms of exploitation in ASM *are* important and serious, the predominant concerns about the sexual in depictions of ASM's negatives does not capture the complex social and economic dynamics that structure sexual activity, as discussed above. It also tends towards policy prescriptions that emphasise abolition or prohibition, which may undermine women's already precarious economic roles within mining sites, as Dianne Otto has noted in the context of sexual prohibitions in peacekeeping.[56] In contemporary, official discourse, ASM is now positioned as in need of reform and aid, but this sits alongside historical policy approaches closer to abolition.

53 Maurice Amutabi and Mary Lutta-Mukhebi, 'Gender and Mining in Kenya: The Case of Mukibira Mines in Vihiga District' (2001) 1(2) *Jenda: A Journal of Culture and Women Studies* 1, 16.

54 P A Eshun, 'Sustainable Small-Scale Gold Mining in Ghana: Setting and Strategies for Sustainability' in B R Marker, M G Petterson and F McEvoy (eds), *Sustainable Minerals Operations in the Developing World* (Geological Society, 2005) 61.

55 Cohen, above n 1. Feminist geographer, Kuntala Lahiri-Dutt, notes that in policy context, women are almost invariably depicted as negatively impacted by ASM, and usually in the form of prostitution: Kuntala Lahiri-Dutt, 'Digging Women: Towards a New Agenda for Feminist Critiques of Mining' (2012) 19 *Journal of Feminist Geography* 193.

56 Dianne Otto, 'The Sexual Tensions of UN Peace Support Operations: A Plea for "Sexual Positivity"' (2007) 18 *Finnish Yearbook of International Law* 33. See also Mats Utas, 'Victimcy, Girlfriending, Soldiering: Tactic Agency in a Young Woman's Social Navigation of the Liberian War Zone' (2005) 78 *Anthropological Quarterly* 403.

Legal fetish and 'consumer appetites'

So far in this chapter, we have explored how sexual and gendered metaphors and norms, found in policy-level discourses as well as the social lives of artisanal mines, construct the sexual order of mining and its regulation. Overwhelmingly, ASM is constructed (by those on the outside) in terms of numerous, sexualised negatives, while sexualised and gendered tropes are mobilised by those within mining communities to structure hierarchical and unequal economic practices. In this last section, we move from sexual metaphors to the operation of binaries – of publicity and secrecy, excess and restraint – through which sexual meanings are dispersed.[57]

Stoler provides a powerful case for reading colonialism through a matrix of race, empire and sexuality, a move that requires going beyond a 'neat story of colonizers pitted against the colonized'.[58] 'Colonial discourses of desires', she writes, 'were also productive of, and produced in, a social field that was always specific about class and gender locations'.[59] For Stoler, 'discourses of sexuality' operated to define social and political orders through which membership, rights and recognition, both within and outside of 'Europe', were indexed along racial, class and sexualised vectors.[60] Attending to the ways in which sexual morality becomes imbricated in discourses on, for example, citizenship or legality, can reveal how certain values, like 'self-restraint, self-discipline [or] managed sexuality', become woven into the 'truths' of, in Stoler's case, European identity.[61]

Deconstructing binaries, and their indexing of values, is one mechanism for considering the epistemological force of sexuality. Eve Kosofsky Sedgwick suggests that homosexual/heterosexual may be one 'master' binary that is entangled in the 'filaments of other important definitional nexuses',[62] which she lists as 'secrecy/disclosure, knowledge/ignorance, private/public, [and] masculine/feminine' to name a few. Stoler, in the quote above, draws our attention to the significance of 'self-restraint' and 'self-discipline' in colonial constructs of self and other. In the following discussion, we examine how similar binaries are deployed in current policy discourses on mining governance and through which order and disorder take on sexualised meanings, shaping, in turn, their normative force.

Earlier, we explored the ways in which ASM sites are constructed through overlapping normative orders and discourses in which gendered and sexualised conceptions of risk pervade, influencing the policy frameworks premised on the sexualised dis/orders of artisanal mining. In response, policy prescriptions directed at regulating ASM sites overwhelmingly embrace 'formalisation', in which legal

57 Ferguson, above n 2, 85.
58 Stoler, above n 23, 199.
59 Ibid 178.
60 Ibid 7–10.
61 Ibid 177–8. See also McClintock, above n 42.
62 Eve Kosofsky Sedgwick, *Epistemology of the Closet* (University of California Press, first published 1990, 2008 edn) 11.

regulation of mining activity, through licences, mining associations such as cooperatives and designated mining areas, is presumed to provide the order needed for economic development. These policy prescriptions are embedded in development programmes aimed at specific national mining contexts and within emerging global regulatory regimes seeking to end elite predation, armed conflict and sexual violence. In these contexts, law and legalisation, and the order they will initiate, are celebrated as the route to economic and social development.

The presumptions about the need for law, and the sources for legal guidance, are normative moves by which global legal subjects (the undeveloped and lawless versus the developed and law-abiding) are constituted.[63] While the emphasis on the legal in the regulation of extractives certainly demarks a duality between the global North, as the source of law/legal knowledge, and the global South and Africa in particular, as unruly and in need of law, this binary, when read through sexualised meanings, is more nuanced.

On one level, the sexualisation of the wrongs of ASM tends to characterise African states, and mining sites specifically, as lawless spaces. But discourses on the globalised threats posed by African mining construct dangerous sexual excess as something found not just in the (African) mine site, but also within the global North. The concerns about conflict and sexual violence linked to mining in the Great Lakes region have led to a view that global legal regulation is needed also to keep in check excess desires *for* African minerals.

As mentioned earlier, section 1502 of the Dodd-Frank Act is one of the most significant and catalysing developments in the globalised regime for mining regulation. Among its notable features is its focus on requiring corporations to review and report on their global supply chains. Section 1502 does not prevent corporations from buying 'conflict minerals'. It merely requires that corporations research the origins of the minerals used in their products and disclose on corporate websites and in annual reports whether or not products are 'DRC conflict free'. This is, in effect, a rather soft and seemingly bland regulatory device that compels a form of corporate self-knowledge (where its minerals come from) and public revelation (by way of websites and annual reports). In this respect, section 1502 buttresses other extractives sector governance initiatives, like the OECD's *Due Diligence Guidelines for Responsible Supply Chains*,[64] and also state-directed mechanisms, like the EITI, that operate primarily through ideals of 'transparency' that are, in turn, secured, through corporate or state self-disclosure.

Underlying these transparency regimes is a characterisation of social and political problems and their resolution 'through a dynamic of concealment and disclosure, through a primary opposition between what is hidden and what

63 Ruskola, above n 3.

64 OECD, 'OECD Due Diligence Guidance for Responsible Supply Chains of Minerals from Conflict-Affected and High-Risk Areas: Second Edition' (2013) <http://www.oecd.org/corporate/mne/mining.htm>.

is revealed'.[65] Section 1502, for example, and the extensive governance regime it has initiated, implicitly constructs 'the problem' of sexual violence and armed conflict in central Africa in terms of an equation about lack of knowledge (even secrecy) about mineral origins and the transformative potential of 'making known'; drawing on the weight given to transparency as a marker of rational modernity starting in the last half of the twentieth century.[66] The logic of section 1502 goes something like this: transnational corporations do not know (refuse to know?) the source of their minerals and thus contribute (knowingly?) to armed conflict in DRC. Making those corporations discover and then make public the origins of their minerals will generate public demand in the North for supply chain improvements.[67]

Privacy (secrecy) versus publicity (disclosure) is a foundational binary through which sexualised (and gendered) orders have been constituted within the Western imaginary.[68] In the context of conflict minerals, this binary also operates with sexualised meanings, particularly in terms of the connotations of excessive 'appetites' (for Africa's commodities) that are to be managed through a new legal order predicated on transparency and self-restraint.

One of the key advocacy organisations promoting adherence to section 1502 is the US-based Enough Project. Headed by Washington and Hollywood-insider, John Prendergast, Enough released a campaign drive in the late 2000s for increased US response to 'conflict minerals'. A 2009 advocacy video and lobbying brochure begins with this statement by Prendergast:

> The time has come to expose a sinister reality: Our insatiable demand for electronics products such as cell phones and laptops is helping fuel waves of sexual violence in a place that most of us will never go, affecting people most of us will never meet. The Democratic Republic of the Congo is the scene of the deadliest conflict globally since World War II. There are few other conflicts in the world where the link between our consumer appetites and mass human suffering is so direct.[69]

65 Jodi Dean, *Publicity's Secret: How Technoculture Capitalizes on Democracy* (Cornell University Press, 2002).

66 Harry G West and Todd Sanders (eds), *Transparency and Conspiracy: Ethnographies of Suspicion in the New World Order* (Duke University Press, 2003).

67 For a recent illustration of this logic, in which corporations that rely on cobalt for making their products (such as the vast majority of those involved in computer and cellphone manufacture) are urged to demand that cobalt be included with the 3TGs as a 'conflict mineral', see Katherine Martinko, 'What You Should Know about the Cobalt in Your Smartphone', *Treehugger* (21 October 2016) <http://www.treehugger.com/corporate-responsibility/what-you-should-know-about-cobalt-your-smartphone.html>.

68 Sedgwick, above n 62; Davina Cooper, *Challenging Diversity: Rethinking Equality and the Value of Difference* (Cambridge University Press, 2004) ch 5.

69 John Prendergast, 'Can You Hear Congo Now? Cell Phones, Conflict Minerals, and the Worst Sexual Violence in the World', *Enough* (1 April 2009) <http://www.enoughproject.org/publications/can-you-hear-congo-now-cell-phones-conflict-minerals-and-worst-sexual-violence-world>.

In the language of Enough, the appetites for minerals are found among 'us' (those in the United States and other countries of the global North), and our consumption of consumer electronics that are tied through a 'complex chain of events' to 'widespread sexual violence in Congo'. But while 'we' are part of the problem, our complicity may be 'unconscious' and, thus, can be redressed by 'consciously becom[ing] part of the solution'; using 'our considerable market muscle to demand evidence from companies such as Apple, Nokia, Hewlett Packard, and Nintendo that their products do not contain conflict minerals'.[70] In this formulation, Enough locates our base desires in the unconscious and maps a route forward through a conscious commitment to consumer activism and restraint. The answer is not to deny ourselves the electronics we desire, but to manage those desires and the sources of our fulfillment.

Campaigns such as this, and the emerging regime for regulating conflict minerals, can thus be read as doing more than simply (re)coding a foundational binary between (civilised) global North and (unruly) Africa. It is also a process, drawing on Stoler again, by which the 'truth' of Northern identity is 'lodged in self-restraint, self-discipline, in a managed sexuality that was susceptible and not always under control'.[71] The recognition that just as '"the colonized" were driven by an insatiable instinct, certain Europeans were as well'[72] serves, ultimately, to rationalise a regulatory regime premised on the control of 'insatiable demands', the management of which indexes the making of a good global society, marked as such by its putative role in protecting African women. Underpinning this characterisation of conflict minerals, and equally the resource curse, is a conception of 'the problem' as one of excess and secrecy. Mining itself, and the global consumption of minerals (and electronics) are not the problem, or at least, they are not the problem when managed appropriately, including through exposing the actions of Western companies in propping up African militias which are inflicting sexual violence against African women.

Conclusion

Sexuality is an important vector along which ideas, expectations and understandings of mining in Africa are unfolding as a matter of global governance. While mining, sexual regulation and colonial intervention in the continent have a long history, contemporary discourses, and their preoccupations with the intricately technical practices of good governance, can appear quite distant from the intimate realms of the sexual. The increasing interest in mining, and mining-related regulation as a tool for development in Africa, with its focus on the technical dimensions of corporate and state 'transparency', may also make it harder to see mining in relation to sexual practice and sexualised meanings. Placing sexuality at the

70 Ibid.
71 Stoler, above n 23, 177–8.
72 Ibid.

centre of the analysis opens up important questions about how sexualised connotations of disorder operate to normalise particular forms of globally orchestrated mining regulation.

We suggest that the emerging regime for governing the extractives sector needs to be viewed in terms of the implicit binaries it re-encodes between restraint and excess, public and private, disclosure and secrecy. These binaries, when read in terms of sexualised meanings, reinforce ideas of the forms (and authors) of good politics and good governance premised on self-revelation and disclosure, and self-managed restraint. These qualities, while echoing some key tenants of neo-liberalism, also serve to validate a global order in which resource extraction, when 'properly' managed and conducted, is beyond question. Indeed, against the aberrancy of artisanal mining, large-scale mining becomes the unstated norm.

Finally, we have sought to illustrate the importance of attending to the multiple sites where ideas of normative order, including legality, are constituted. The global regulation of mineral extraction unfolds at multiple scales, from the norms and practices found in individual artisanal and small-scale mines, to the discourses on mining and governance that occur in national, regional and internationalised policy sites. Legal order, we suggest, is constituted, at least in part, by and through the sexualised ordering of meanings and practices at these multiple scales.

3 The anatomy of neoliberal Internet governance

A queer critical political economy perspective

*Monika Zalnieriute**

This chapter moves beyond narratives of the liberatory role of the Internet and digital technologies for queer communities by examining the current neoliberal model of Internet governance from a queer critical economy perspective. In particular, it discusses how the neoliberal model has been used to repress and limit the rights of queer people (among others) and how such repressions have been justified. I start by outlining the celebrated dominant narrative of the liberatory potential of the Internet for various oppressed and marginalised groups such as queer people, women, ethnic and racial minorities, before introducing the emerging counter-narrative, which suggests that these evolving technologies enable new modes of control and suppression that can be exercised by way of the communication mediums themselves. In the second part, I discuss the anatomy of the neoliberal model of Internet governance and introduce the concept of the Information-Industrial-Complex (IIC) and its significance in the political economy of the Internet. I explain how the IIC has enabled powerful state and non-state actors to repress the rights of queer people both in the global South and North. The third part focuses on the ways in which the repression of queer rights on the Internet, as well as the structurally unjust system of Internet governance, built around the needs of the IIC, is maintained and justified. The prevailing narratives for justifying and sustaining the current Internet governance model are juxtaposed to those deployed in other areas of international politics and law, such as 'pinkwashing', to achieve strategic geopolitical ends and maintain the (im)balances of global power and economy. The chapter concludes that such similarities are unsurprising, given that the Internet is a socio-technical system, which is not simply a neutral technology (like is often mistakenly assumed), but rather reflects normative political bargains and continuing battles for power and resources. In the fast-changing and complex reality of the information economy, the 'struggle for new rights'[1] – both offline and online – for queer communities

* I dedicate this chapter to Sandra Amanka, for all the love and comradeship in my life. I would also like to express my gratitude to Dianne Otto for the invaluable comments and suggestions for the earlier drafts of this chapter. All errors, as usual, remain my own.

1 Clifford Bob (ed), *The International Struggle for New Human Rights* (University of Pennsylvania Press, 2009).

around the globe inevitably has to continue. This chapter aims to reveal the power disparities involved in information exchange and debunk the justifications that support such disparities in order to better understand the state of the art and open the way for new strategies of queer resistance.

Competing narratives about the Internet and queer communities

It is difficult to deny that information and communication technologies have revolutionised the ways in which individuals, communities and societies communicate, exchange information and participate in democratic processes.[2] While the so-called information age brings novel opportunities for various marginalised communities to effect social change, it also conveys new modes for oppression and control that can be exercised through the communication mediums. Two dominant and perhaps interdependent narratives can be ascertained on the implications of digital technologies for queer political engagement and the advancement of queer communities – the dominant celebratory narrative and the emerging disquieting counter-narrative.

The celebrated dominant narrative

The liberatory narrative maintains that the Internet is a critical space for communities and individuals whose voices are often marginalised, negated and discriminated against in everyday life.[3] For such communities, the Internet is understood as a vital 'public platform' that overcomes the significant barriers to access presented by traditional media and political representation.[4] For queers, the Internet is often argued to provide an invaluable medium for transcending geographic boundaries and reducing isolation, providing access to safe virtual communities and connecting members to education, information about queer identity and civic engagement.[5] In addition to providing access to crucial information resources, the Internet for queer communities is also portrayed as an especially vital space for democratic deliberation.[6] This is particularly so for

2 See, eg, Natasha Primo, 'Gender Issues in the Information Society' (Report, UNESCO, 2003).

3 'I Want Respect and Equality – Racial Discrimination: National Consultations: Racism and Civil Society' (Report, Australian Human Rights Commission, 2001) <https://www.humanrights.gov.au/i-want-respect-and-equality-racial-discrimination-national-consultations-racism-and-civil-society#forward>.

4 Jac sm Kee (ed), '://EROTICS: Sex, Rights and the Internet' (Research Study, Association for Progressive Communications, 2011) 1.

5 Natalie T J Tindall and Richard D Waters, *Coming out of the Closet: Exploring LGBT Issues in Strategic Communication with Theory and Research* (Peter Lang, 2013).

6 Rebecca Walker, *Lesbian Deliberation: The Constitution of Community in Online Lesbian Forums* (PhD thesis, University of Wollongong, 2010) <http://ro.uow.edu.au/cgi/viewcontent.cgi?article=4637&context=theses>.

younger generations who are much more ready to engage in activism via social networks than their older peers.[7] Political awareness of younger members of the LGBT communities thus often comes from their engagement with online discussion forums and social platforms.[8] In tandem with these democratising conceptions of the Internet, empirical data suggests that queer communities were among the earliest adopters of digital technology, relying on the Internet to a much greater extent than the general population to combat social isolation, marginalisation and lack of access to health, economic and legal information, especially in rural areas.[9]

The narrative of celebration is based on popular conceptions of the Internet as an inherently democratising and liberating medium because it facilitates information exchange. These conceptions stem from Jürgen Habermas's 'theory of communicative action',[10] as well as Manuel Castells's 'rising network society',[11] which generally depict the Internet as a key facilitative space for the exercise of fundamental rights and freedoms, providing access to critical information, the building of knowledge, the expression of thoughts and beliefs, and the formation of networks and communities, and for mobilising for change.[12] Such conceptions have also gained traction among mainstream, international political institutions, with the former UN Special Rapporteur for Freedom of Expression pronouncing that 'the Internet . . . facilitates the realization of a range of human rights'.[13] However, these liberatory claims have also been co-opted for geopolitical and commercial purposes which form the central core of the (in)famous US 'Internet Freedom' agenda.[14] The agenda, as will be discussed later in this chapter, has been

7 Jac sm Kee and Jan Moolman, 'Sexuality and Women's Rights' in *Global Information Society Watch 2011: Internet Rights and Democratization* (Report, Association for Progressive Communications, 2011) 46 <https://www.giswatch.org/sites/default/files/gisw_-_sexuality_and_womens_rights.pdf>.

8 'Out Online: The Experiences of Lesbian, Gay, Bisexual and Transgender Youth on the Internet' (Report, GLSEN, 2013) <http://www.glsen.org/sites/default/files/Out%20Online%20FINAL.pdf>.

9 Mary L Gray, *Out in the Country: Youth, Media, and Queer Visibility in Rural America* (New York University Press, 2009); Jessie Daniels and Mary L Gray, 'A Vision for Inclusion: An LGBT Broadband Future' (Research Paper, LGBT Technology Partnership, April 2014) <http://academicworks.cuny.edu/cgi/viewcontent.cgi?article=1213&context=gc_pubs>.

10 Jürgen Habermas, *The Theory of Communicative Action* (Thomas McCarthy trans, Beacon Press, 1984) vols 1, 2.

11 Manuel Castells, *The Rise of the Network Society: The Information Age: Economy, Society, and Culture* (Wiley, 2nd edn, 2009) vol 1.

12 sm Kee (ed), above n 4; 'Going Visible: Women's Rights on the Internet' (Thematic Consultation, Association for Progressive Communications, October 2012) <https://www.apc.org/en/node/15912>.

13 Frank La Rue, Report of the Special Rapporteur on the Promotion and Protection of the Right to Freedom of Opinion and Expression, UN GAOR, 17th sess, Agenda Item 3, UN Doc A/HRC/17/27 (16 May 2011) 7.

14 US Bureau of Democracy, Human Rights, and Labor, 'Internet Freedom', <http://www.humanrights.gov/issues/internet-freedom/>.

the main ideological construct, crafted by the US State Department and US technology giants, supporting and legitimating the current model of US private-sector-dominated Internet governance.[15]

The emerging counter-narrative

While the Internet has indeed boosted freedom of communication and participatory democracy as professed by the liberatory narrative, it has also been progressively subjected to increased surveillance and monitoring techniques, as well as content regulation, in both liberal democracies and authoritarian regimes around the globe. Examples of limitations on queer expression and exercise of fundamental rights online are numerous. The most worrying ones are death penalties for accessing LGBT content online in countries such as Sudan, Saudi Arabia, Yemen, Mauritania, Somalia and Iran.[16] More modest restrictions range from explicit blanket bans of queer expression online, such as the Russian anti-gay propaganda law,[17] to covert Internet filtering mechanisms, like the Internet filters in public schools in the United States and other countries.[18] They also include 'real name' policies of Internet platforms, such as Facebook,[19] and controversial decisions by the Internet Corporation for Assigned Names and Numbers (ICANN), such as not approving an LGBT community application for the *.lgbt* and *.gay* top level domain name.[20] The LGBT community application intended to create an explicit LGBT community space on the Internet by ending community domain names with *.lgbt* or *.gay*, such as, for example, www.mentalhealth.lgbt. However, ICANN did not consider the LGBT community to be 'community enough' and the community application was not given priority over the commercial interests.[21] In addition to these intentional restrictions, scholars and activists have

15 Shawn M Powers and Michael Jablonski, *The Real Cyber War: The Political Economy of Internet Freedom* (University of Illinois Press, 2015).
16 Daniels and Gray, above n 9.
17 *For the Purpose of Protecting Children from Information Advocating for a Denial of Traditional Family Values 2013* (Russian Federation).
18 American Civil Liberties Union, 'ACLU "Don't Filter Me" Initiative Finds Schools in Four More States Unconstitutionally Censoring LGBT Websites' (11 April 2011) <https://www.aclu.org/news/aclu-dont-filter-me-initiative-finds-schools-four-more-states-unconstitutionally-censoring-lgbt>.
19 Andrew Griffin, 'Facebook to Tweak "Real Name" Policy after Backlash from LGBT Groups and Native Americans', *The Independent* (online) (2 November 2015) <http://www.independent.co.uk/life-style/gadgets-and-tech/news/facebook-to-tweak-real-name-policy-after-backlash-from-lgbt-groups-and-native-americans-a6717061.html>; Powers and Jablonski, above n 15.
20 Monika Zalnieriute and Thomas Schneider, 'ICANN's Procedures and Policies in the Light of Human Rights, Fundamental Freedoms and Democratic Values' (Report, Council of Europe, 2014) 15–35.
21 See Eve Salomon and Kinanya Pijl, 'Applications to ICANN for Community-Based New Generic Top Level Domains (gTLDs): Opportunities and Challenges from a Human Rights

also noted how the Internet is transforming the way in which queer individuals experience violence and social exclusion.[22] For example, online threats, stalking, bullying and sexual harassment are just a part of the online aggression faced by queer communities,[23] and it is a challenge to find meaningful ways to respond to such threats. To a much greater extent than is often assumed, such restrictions present a daily struggle for queer communities to connect with like-minded peers, raise awareness, conduct advocacy work and even access critical health information online.

Contrary to the popular belief that Internet filtering and censorship is only demanded and imposed by authoritarian governments, limitations on queer content online are also imposed by democratic governments, as well as by private actors and social media platforms themselves. Critical information for queer communities is often inaccessible due to the Internet censorship policies in many countries, ranging from a blanket ban on LGBT-related content in some countries to Internet filters installed in public library networks and public schools.[24] It is true that queer communities encounter extra hurdles in the countries with *explicitly* discriminatory national legislation, affecting their rights to free speech online, such as the Russian anti-LGBT censorship laws already mentioned.[25] Similar legislation also exists in Lithuania,[26] despite being a member state of the European Union. This makes providing positive information to young LGBT people a real challenge, especially through school-based Internet access. It is unclear to what extent access to queer community websites is limited by public schools and public libraries in other EU member states, or in the global North more generally. This issue urgently requires empirical research. The limited research which has been conducted in the United States suggests that the Internet filtering of queer content, including critical health-related information (and even words such as 'breast cancer'),[27] may be prevalent in Western liberal democracies.[28]

Even in countries with strong free speech reputations, such as the United States, Internet censorship is hardly a minor issue. For example, the American

Perspective' (Report No DGI(2016)17, Council of Europe, 2016) <https://rm.coe.int/CoERMPublicCommonSearchServices/DisplayDCTMContent?documentId=09000016806b5a14>; David Goldstein, 'ICANN Controversially Rejects .GAY Community Application Again', *DomainPulse* (4 February 2016) <http://www.domainpulse.com/2016/02/04/icann-rejects-gay-community-application/>.

22 Gray, above n 9.

23 'Out Online', above n 8.

24 sm Kee (ed), above n 4.

25 Susie Armitage, 'Russia's Main Online Support Group for LGBT Teens May Soon Be Blocked', *BuzzFeed News* (6 April 2015) <http://www.buzzfeed.com/susiearmitage/russias-main-online-support-group-for-lgbt-teens-may-soon-be>.

26 See, eg, Law on the Protection of Minors against the Detrimental Effect of Public Information 2002 (Lithuania), No IX-1067 (as last amended on 22 December 2009, No XI-594).

27 Daniels and Gray, above n 9.

28 See Kevicha Echols and Melissa Ditmore, 'Restricted Access to Information: Youth and Sexuality' in sm Kee (ed), above n 4.

Civil Liberties Union's (ACLU) 'Don't Filter Me' project revealed Internet filters on school computers that are unconstitutionally blocking access to hundreds of LGBT websites, including sites that contain vital resources on subjects like bullying and student gay-straight alliances.[29] Disturbingly, the ACLU research suggests that the filters do not block access to comparable anti-LGBT websites that address the same topics with negative connotations.[30] Most worryingly, the research revealed that most schools were not aware that their filters were blocking not only sexually explicit websites, but were also configured to block LGBT websites.[31]

Furthermore, the rise of large-scale data collection and algorithm-driven analysis targeting sensitive information poses many threats for LGBT communities, who are especially vulnerable to privacy intrusion due to their often hostile social, political and even legal environments.[32] Much publicly available data, such as Facebook friend information or individual music playlists on YouTube, are incredibly effective at inferring individual sexual preferences with high levels of accuracy.[33] The accuracy of the online trail of information we leave is argued to be higher than predictions by our human friends about our personal sexuality and gender preferences.[34] If widely traded advertising information 'correctly discriminates between homosexual and heterosexual men in 88% of cases',[35] then most Internet users should assume that all of the companies advertising to them can predict their sexual orientation with a high degree of accuracy – and are incentivised to do so in order to sell them products. Issues may go well beyond simple product advertising, and can potentially include different treatment in, for example, health and life insurance policies,[36] as well as in so-called 'predictive policing' (prevention of crime before it happens).[37] Such ready access to personal information can get even more complicated with the 'real name' policies of social platforms, such as

29 ACLU, above n 18.

30 *Parents, Families, and Friends of Lesbian and Gays, Inc v Camdenton R-III School District* (Mo Dist Ct Cent Div, No 2:11-cv-04212, 15 February 2012) 5.

31 ACLU, 'Don't Filter Me' (Final Report, 2012) 5 <https://www.aclu.org/files/assets/dont_filter_me-2012-1001-v04.pdf>.

32 EU Agency for Fundamental Rights, 'EU LGBT Survey: European Union Lesbian, Gay, Bisexual and Transgender Survey' (Report, 2013) 14 <http://fra.europa.eu/sites/default/files/eu-lgbt-survey-results-at-a-glance_en.pdf>.

33 Michal Kosinski, David Stillwell and Thore Graepel, 'Private Traits and Attributes Are Predictable from Digital Records of Human Behavior' (2013) 110 *Proceedings of the National Academy of Sciences* 5802.

34 Wu Youyou, Michal Kosinski and David Stillwell, 'Computer-Based Personality Judgments Are More Accurate than Those Made by Humans' (2015) 112 *Proceedings of the National Academy of Sciences* 1036.

35 Kosinski et al, above n 33.

36 Angela Daly, 'The Law and Ethics of "Self Quantified" Health Information: An Australian Perspective' (2015) 5 *International Data Privacy Law* 144.

37 Zeynep Tufekci, 'Engineering the Public: Big Data, Surveillance and Computational Politics' (2014) 19 *First Monday* <http://firstmonday.org/ojs/index.php/fm/article/view/4901>.

Facebook,[38] which may place queer people in danger of physical assaults in certain parts of the world.

The global scope of restrictions

Thus, it becomes clear that the centrality of the Internet as a communication tool has also led to new approaches to surveillance, both commercial and non-commercial, and novel ways to restrict queer and sexual expression online. While it is true that many restrictive measures are domestically applied, such as Internet filters in public schools, there are also many restrictions that are global in scope, such as the Facebook censorship mechanisms and real name policies. This contrasts sharply with the popular belief that such restrictions are mainly targeting particular people (individual queer and LGBT activists, for example) or specific groups (LGBT organisations and queer collectives), and only in specific countries (extremely conservative and hostile to human rights and freedoms), where non-conforming sexual expression and behaviour are criminalised. In fact, empirical research suggests that these limitations on queer and sexual expression and rights advocacy online are often imposed at the global level.

So the important challenge becomes to understand how and why such global restrictions work. Where and with whom is such centralised capacity located? It is often claimed by various liberal institutions in the West, including the US White House, that the Internet is not controlled by any single entity or organisation, but it is rather a 'network of networks' where information just flows freely.[39] We are led to believe that it is only repressive governments that misuse the Internet, like 'shutting it down' during the Egyptian and Syrian uprisings or conducting 'denial-of-service attacks' (making websites inaccessible) on undesirable political or human rights organisations.[40] It is claimed that such things do not happen in the West. Instead, Western governments, as well as Google and Facebook, are portrayed as defenders of Internet 'freedom': they are the ones fighting for freedom of expression in China and Russia. Recall, for example, Google leaving China because the Chinese government asked for its cooperation with Internet censorship.[41] So how can it be that these very same private actors and governments filter and censor queer and sexual expression online? How does it work? Why do other governments, and private and civil society actors, accept such arrangements

38 Griffin, above n 19.

39 This is a famous construct of the Internet Freedom Agenda, see, eg, Internet Association, 'Protecting Internet Freedom', <https://internetassociation.org/policy-platform/protecting-internet-freedom/>.

40 See Laura DeNardis and Andrea M Hackl, 'Internet Control Points as LGBT Rights Mediation' (2016) 19 *Information, Communication & Society* 753.

41 See, eg, how Google is presented as a very anti-censorship human rights defender, Kaveh Waddell, 'Why Google Quit China – and Why It's Heading Back', *The Atlantic* (online) (19 January 2016) <http://www.theatlantic.com/technology/archive/2016/01/why-google-quit-china-and-why-its-heading-back/424482/>.

whereby some actors can exercise centralised global control over what is popularly regarded as an 'ungovernable' medium free from governmental authority and regulation?

In the next section, I will explore these questions by zooming in to the anatomy of the Internet governance model, and describing how its main proponent – the IIC – has succeeded in establishing a hegemonic neoliberal communications system. I hope to prompt readers to critically re-assess their perceptions of the liberatory role of the Internet for queers (among others) and of altruistic corporate claims about the freedom offered by the Internet for everyone, by having a closer look at the political economy of the Internet and information flows, as well as the techno-imperial and neo-colonial nature of the current Internet governance regime.

The dominance of the US Information-Industrial-Complex (IIC)

In short, the answer to the questions above is simple: the global scope of restrictions on queer and sexual expression is possible because of the nature of the technical structures and design of the Internet.[42] The Internet infrastructure, ranging from the Domain Name System (DNS) to algorithmic governance by Internet platforms, is increasingly co-opted by various public and private actors to impose restrictions on the exercise of fundamental rights in the digital sphere.[43] However, neither I nor you could impose such restrictions because we lack access to this infrastructure. So the more nuanced question arises: who has access and can exercise control over the Internet infrastructure? While various actors in the international sphere influence and shape 'permissible' online content and decide on the boundaries of human rights online, it is dominated by the US government and a few US-based information technology giants.[44] The interdependent relationships between these actors has been described as the IIC.[45] In this section I will start by describing this complex, then discuss how it operates at both domestic and international levels, and conclude by arguing that human rights standards online are being set by the IIC.

The emergence of US dominance

The dominance of the global information and communications sphere by the United States, and a handful of multinational corporations, has been widely

42 Laura DeNardis, *The Global War for Internet Governance* (Yale University Press, 2014).

43 Laura DeNardis, 'Hidden Levers of Internet Control: An Infrastructure-Based Theory of Internet Governance' (2012) 15 *Information, Communication & Society* 720.

44 Ben Wagner, *Global Free Expression – Governing the Boundaries of Internet Content* (Springer, 2016).

45 Powers and Jablonski, above n 15.

identified and studied by international communications scholars.[46] To explain the initial emergence of US dominance in this field in the second half of the twentieth century, political-economist Herbert Schiller provided a critical account of how US public resources were used to support a privatised communications system driven by commercial interests, as opposed to civic and democratic values, and how the US government promoted and protected the interests of US communications and media firms domestically and internationally.[47] To understand these processes and dynamics, Schiller developed the concept of the 'military-industrial-communications-complex' to expose and analyse the relationships between the US Department of Defense and communications corporations.[48] He detailed how the Department of Defense 'channeled enormous funds from its astronomical budget into research and development on new information and communication technologies', and how public resources were used to support the growth of these 'later-to-be-privatized' information communication technologies, such as computer electronics, satellites and the future infrastructure of the Internet.[49] Although the global communications landscape has since been completely transformed by digital technologies and the Internet, Schiller's concept of the military-industrial-communications-complex, as well as his broader theory of US empire and cultural imperialism, continues to have enduring conceptual, descriptive and analytical relevance in the twenty-first century, as demonstrated by important critical scholarship exploring the political economy of communications.[50]

The contemporary situation, in the so-called Information or Digital Economy, is essentially the same. The older media corporations have been replaced by the information technology giants, such as Google, Apple, Facebook, Verisign and GoDaddy, and the mutually beneficial and interdependent relationships between the US government and information technology corporations are well established. Grounding their work on Schiller's insights, Shawn M Powers and Michael Jablonski explain how the dynamics of the IIC have catalysed the rapid growth of information and communication technologies within the global economy, while firmly embedding US strategic interests and companies at the heart of the current neoliberal regime.[51] Maintaining this central strategic position

46 Daya Kishan Thussu, *International Communication: Continuity and Change* (Bloomsbury Academic, 2nd edn, 2006).

47 Herbert I Schiller, *Mass Communications and American Empire* (Westview Press, 2nd edn, 1992) 63–75.

48 Ibid.

49 Ibid 5.

50 Les Levidow and Kevin Robins, *Cyborg Worlds: The Military Information Society* (Free Association Books, 1989); Richard Maxwell, *Herbert Schiller* (Rowman & Littlefield, 2003); Vincent Mosco, *The Political Economy of Communication: Rethinking and Renewal* (Sage, 1996); Dan Schiller, 'The Militarization of US Communications' in Janet Wasko, Graham Murdock and Helen Sousa (eds), *The Handbook of Political Economy of Communications* (Wiley-Blackwell, 2014) 262.

51 Powers and Jablonski, above n 15, 47.

necessitates action and support from the US government, both domestically and internationally.

The domestic level: Continuous support and subsidisation

Just as Schiller described the continuous subsidisation of private communications companies back in the 1960s and 1970s, the contemporary IIC is also supported by the enormous amounts of US government money allocated to these technology giants and the many procurement contracts it awards to them. It is useful to recall that the invention and early deployment of the Internet in the 1950s and 1960s was funded by the US government, particularly the Department of Defense, until the commercialisation of the Internet in 1995.[52] However, commercialisation did not mean that the US government became uninvolved. For instance, in 2015, US $171 million were awarded to a Silicon Valley consortium ($75 million by the Pentagon and $96 million by universities and local governments) to support research and development into wearable technology (clothing or accessories incorporating digital technologies, such as activity trackers).[53] As earlier, these same companies are often contractors of the Department of Defense.[54] As pointed out by Tanner Mirrlees, the billions of dollars acquired by these companies from the Department of Defense undermines the neoliberal claim that private and corporate wealth is accrued because free markets are separated from public expenditure.[55]

Against this background, the extent to which the US government and agencies, such as the US National Security Agency (NSA), have direct (unconstitutional and illegal) access to the infrastructure of information technology giants is not very surprising. As revealed by Edward Snowden back in 2013, the NSA was secretly and directly tapping into user data collected by all the major US technology giants, such as Apple, Google, Facebook and Microsoft.[56] These companies allowed the NSA to directly collect the personal data of their customers and never informed the public of such governmental access.

52 Barry M Leiner, Vinton G Cerf, David D Clark et al, 'A Brief History of the Internet' (1997) e-OTI: OnTheInternet <http://www.isoc.org/oti/printversions/0797prleiner.html>.

53 W J Hennigan, 'Secretary of Defense Unveils $75-Million Investment in Silicon Valley Venture', *Los Angeles Times* (online) (28 August 2015) <http://www.latimes.com/business/la-fi-pentagon-cyber-20150829-story.html>.

54 See InsideGov, 'Research Government Contracts', <http://government-contracts.insidegov.com/>.

55 Tanner Mirrlees, 'US Empire and Communications Today: Revisiting Herbert I Schiller' (2015) 3(2) *Political Economy of Communication* 3, 16.

56 Glenn Greenwald and Ewen MacAskill, 'NSA Prism Program Taps in to User Data of Apple, Google and Others', *The Guardian* (online) (8 June 2013) <https://www.theguardian.com/world/2013/jun/06/us-tech-giants-nsa-data>.

The international level: The Internet freedom agenda

In addition to domestic subsidisation, internationally the US government enthusiastically promotes the so-called 'Internet Freedom' agenda, which favours large US information technology giants and US economic interests. This is particularly apparent with regard to globally 'normalised' strong legal protections for intellectual property rights, advertising-based consumerism and the commodification of information and personal data.[57] To maintain the global dominance of the IIC, the US government opposes, and so far has effectively prevented, the establishment of any international organisation and the drafting of any multilateral treaty that would regulate the management of critical Internet resources, such as domain names. Second, it aggressively promotes the 'free flow of information doctrine' and the global free trade regime, intellectual property enforcement and other policies that suit its interests and favour the IIC.

The dominance of the neoliberal US model of Internet governance is reflected in the current international arrangements over Internet infrastructure and critical resources. These arrangements present a unique challenge in international law and international relations, as the Internet is the only communications medium that lacks a binding international treaty, or intergovernmental organisation, to oversee its operation. In part, this situation reflects the early cyber-libertarian perception of the Internet as a 'network of networks' – an 'ungovernable' communications medium compared to previous technologies, such as radio, television, print media and the telephony.[58] While cyber-libertarian ideas have since been overshadowed by more realist accounts of Internet control,[59] the dominant paradigm, still promoted by the IIC, is that because 'the Internet is different from other networks, its governance must also be different than that of other networks'.[60] Therefore, instead of being internationally regulated by states, the Internet infrastructure and resources are governed under the so-called 'multistakeholder' model.[61] In 2005, the UN-sponsored World Summit on the Information Society defined Internet governance as 'the development and application by governments, the private sector and civil society, in their respective roles, of shared principles, norms, rules, decision-making procedures, and programmes that

57 Powers and Jablonski, above n 15.

58 See, eg, Leiner et al, above n 52.

59 Jack Goldsmith and Tim Wu, *Who Controls the Internet?: Illusions of a Borderless World* (Oxford University Press, 2008).

60 See, eg, Don MacLean, *Internet Governance: A Grand Collaboration: An Edited Collection of Papers Contributed to the United Nations ICT Task Force Global Forum on Internet Governance, New York, March 25–26, 2004* (UN Publications, 2004).

61 Laura DeNardis and Mark Raymond, 'Thinking Clearly about Multistakeholder Internet Governance' (paper presented at the Eighth Annual GigaNet Symposium, Bali, Indonesia, 21 October 2013) <http://www.phibetaiota.net/wp-content/uploads/2013/11/Multistakeholder-Internet-Governance.pdf>.

shape the evolution and use of the Internet'.[62] As such, 'multistakeholderism' has been successfully promoted as a better, 'unique and novel alternative' to the outdated conventional governance models of international law.

Multistakeholderism is supported by the two main Internet governance institutions – the ICANN (mentioned above) and the Internet Engineering Task Force (IETF). These organisations are respectively responsible for the global coordination of the DNS and the development of Internet standards and protocols. They both operate as non-profit corporations registered in the United States, but claim to be global and open for any interested stakeholders to participate, and maintain that they develop policies or Internet standards based on consensus. It is hardly surprising that those 'interested' stakeholders are largely private for-profit corporations from the IIC, whose business models are built around the Internet, such as Internet platforms and search engines like Google, Amazon, Facebook and e-Bay, Internet service providers like Telstra and Verisign, and domain name registrars like GoDaddy. Nevertheless, it is claimed that '[c]ivil society organizations and governments participate alongside these stakeholders in contributing to the development of technical policies'.[63] Therefore, Internet governance is often depicted 'not [as] the product of an institutional hierarchy, but rather, [as emerging] from the decentralized, bottom-up coordination of tens of thousands of mostly private-sector entities across the globe'.[64] Multistakeholderism is portrayed as the only suitable and logical model for the Internet (it has to be assumed because of its 'distinct' and 'decentralised' nature), and public regulation is presented as unviable (because governments are incapable of understanding the operation and nature of the Internet). Recent efforts by the Obama Administration to move the supervisory role of the National Telecommunications Agency over ICANN and DNS to an 'international multistakeholder community' were welcomed because it had avoided 'a governmental or intergovernmental solution'.[65] However, the clear dominance of a few US-based information technology giants, as well as the central role played by the US government in Internet governance, undermines all these claims. Power is clearly centralised in the US IIC rather than dispersed among multiple stakeholders.[66]

While the underlying logic of the multistakeholder model of Internet governance theoretically implies that no other international organisations should interfere with matters related to the Internet, the US government, the main facilitator and

62 Tunis Agenda for the Information Society, UN Doc WSIS-05/TUNIS/DOC/6(Rev. 1)-E (18 November 2005) <http://www.itu.int/net/wsis/docs2/tunis/off/6rev1.html>.

63 See, eg, Jonathan Masters, 'What is Internet Governance?', *Council on Foreign Relations* (23 April 2014) <http://www.cfr.org/internet-policy/internet-governance/p32843>.

64 Ibid.

65 See, David McCabe, 'Obama Administration Approves Transition of Internet Domain System', *The Hill* (online) (9 June 2016) <http://thehill.com/policy/technology/282860-commerce-approves-domain-name-transition>.

66 Powers and Jablonski, above n 15.

promoter of the multistakeholder model, applies this idea selectively to suit its interests. For example, while the UN and the International Telecommunications Union should not, under the multistakeholder framework, interfere with Internet policy and governance; according to the United States, the World Intellectual Property Organization's treaties should be applied to the Internet.[67] Similarly, the United States and its allies, such as the European Union and Australia, argue that the World Trade Organization (WTO) is capable of adopting certain decisions regarding the Internet.[68] Indeed, the WTO is one of the core platforms through which the United States maintains its control via the 'free flow of information doctrine', which was promoted by the US State Department in the GATT, GATS and TRIPS negotiations.[69] The doctrine is a crucial element in the neoliberal model of Internet governance and the digital economy because it allows US corporations to collect and monetise the personal data of individuals from around the world, without paying any taxes on such activities. If 'data is the new oil', as it is often proclaimed,[70] the fact that the new oil is not taxed should attract some critical thinking, at least by those who do not benefit from these arrangements. However, the free flow of information doctrine has been so successfully ingrained that it is now taken for granted by states and Internet users alike.

Given the unprecedented global dominance of many of the US information technology giants, such as Google and Facebook, the United States and its corporate actors have an incomparable advantage in exporting their rules and social norms, and normalising them as 'universal' principles of the Internet. For example, data protection and privacy are not part of the 'universal' values of Internet Freedom, while robust intellectual property protection and gambling bans are not only argued to be viable and doable, but are strictly enforced. 'Information colonialism', 'techno-imperialism' and similar terms are used to describe the dominance of the IIC internationally and the means by which it maintains and extends its control over economic and policy matters.[71]

67 See Catherine Saez, 'US Defender of Internet Freedom, Keen on Protecting IP Rights', *Intellectual Property Watch* (8 March 2013) <http://www.ip-watch.org/2013/03/08/us-as-defender-of-internet-freedom-keen-on-protecting-ip-rights>.

68 See Communication from the European Union and the United States: Contribution to the Work Programme on Electronic Commerce, WTO Doc S/C/W/338 (13 July 2011); Communication from Australia: Suggestions on ICT principles, WTO Doc S/C/W/349 (26 September 2012).

69 Herbert I Schiller, *Culture Inc: The Corporate Takeover of Public Expression* (Oxford University Press, 1991) 118; Herbert I Schiller, *Mass Communications and American Empire* (Westview Press, 2nd edn, 1992) 93.

70 See, eg, Jonathan Vanian, 'Why Data Is the New Oil', *Fortune* (online) (11 July 2016) <http://fortune.com/2016/07/11/data-oil-brainstorm-tech/>.

71 Sharon J McLennan, 'Techno-Optimism or Information Imperialism: Paradoxes in Online Networking, Social Media and Development' (2016) 22 *Information Technology for Development* 380.

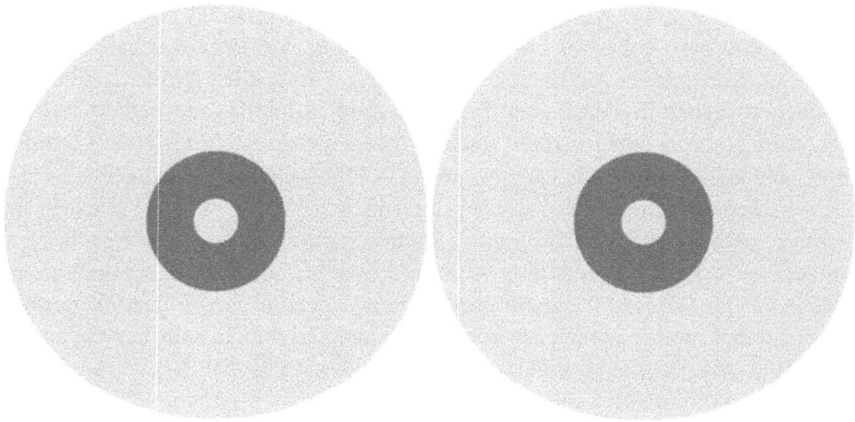

Figure 3.1 'Offensive' animated breast cancer awareness image removed by Facebook (restored after public outcry, with apology from Facebook)

Privatised human rights governance: De facto global standards set by the Information-Industrial-Complex

Since a large part of the Internet architecture and infrastructure is coordinated and owned by private actors, such as Internet intermediaries, this ownership enables them to directly set de facto global standards for human rights online, including the rights of queer, LGBT and other communities. Recent examples of Facebook removing animated videos promoting breast cancer awareness,[72] the iconic photograph of a girl fleeing a Napalm attack during the Vietnam War in 1972 (restored after a huge protest on social media)[73] and a number of pictures of mothers breastfeeding their children[74] indicate that it is very often private Internet platforms that own virtual Internet infrastructure, who set global free speech standards online about, for example, which parts of bodies can be displayed (not allowing for female nudity and nipples in particular).

These standards are set through Facebook's content moderation and standard contractual policies, to which users must agree in order to be able to use the service. Similarly, Internet intermediaries decide on the permissible levels of personal data protection and privacy, and sometimes even physical security for queer individuals, as is demonstrated by Facebook's 'real name' policies, not allowing individuals to use pseudonyms or non-legal names on its platform, and thus subjecting certain groups, such as transgender people, to the danger of

72 'Facebook Apologises for Removing Breast Cancer Awareness Video', *BBC* (online) (20 October 2016) <http://www.bbc.com/news/world-europe-37721193>.

73 'Facebook U-Turn over "Napalm Girl" Photograph', *BBC* (online) (9 September 2016) <http://www.bbc.com/news/technology-37318040>.

74 Facebook vs Breastfeeding Alliance <https://www.facebook.com/the.ban.on.breastfeeding/>.

physical violence in hostile environments.[75] Likewise, actual decision-making about the level of protection of the right to privacy and whether one has a 'right to be forgotten' – to have their personal data removed from the Google search engine – are made internally by the sub-contractors of Internet giants – and the guidelines and criteria for such decisions are largely unknown to the public. As such, the basic tools of accountability and governance – public and legal transparency and pressure – are very limited,[76] with private corporate actors holding the most power over queer expression and sexual freedom online.

In effect, this leads to privatised human rights governance, whereby private actors establish the boundaries of human rights online, such as freedom of expression and privacy protection, in accordance with their business models.[77] The opportunities for queer and other non-mainstream sexual and gender communities to effectively communicate, raise awareness, provide access to critical information and knowledge about legal rights, health and community resources – as promised by the liberatory narrative of Internet Freedom – are in reality often deliberately limited by various public and private actors. As discussed, the actors that exercise most control over the freedom of expression of queer communities on the Internet are not only the 'usual suspects' touted by the Western media, such as the governments of Russia, China and Iran. On the contrary, the most powerful actors are part of the IIC, which is at the very heart of the neoliberal model of multistakeholder Internet governance and the Internet Freedom agenda. While this agenda claims that information should move freely online, there are numerous examples of the architectural and technical features of the Internet being employed by IIC actors to restrict rights of queer communities to freedom of expression and association, privacy, security and self-autonomy. It is precisely the Internet infrastructure – both virtual and physical – that enables those in control to prevent the exercise of fundamental human rights in the digital environment, usually without users being aware that this is happening. Particular features of the Internet's architecture and infrastructure, such as Internet protocols and domain names, as well as algorithms and the standard contractual clauses of Internet intermediaries, enable them to restrict the fundamental rights of queer and LGBT communities, defeating even constitutional protections of free speech, privacy, equality and non-discrimination, as well as avoiding obligations imposed by international human rights law.

75 Griffin, above n 19.

76 Catherine Buni and Soraya Chemaly, 'The Secret Rules of the Internet', *The Verge* (13 April 2016) <http://www.theverge.com/2016/4/13/11387934/internet-moderator-history-youtube-facebook-reddit-censorship-free-speech>.

77 Ben Wagner, 'Algorithmic Regulation and the Global Default: Shifting Norms in Internet Technology' (2016) 10(1) *Etikk i praksis – Nordic Journal of Applied Ethics* 5; Emily Taylor, 'The Privatization of Human Rights: Illusions of Consent, Automation and Neutrality' (Paper No 24, Global Commission on Internet Governance, January 2016) 24 <https://ourinternet-files.s3.amazonaws.com/publications/no24_web_2.pdf>.

Justifications: Panics of sexual immorality, security and repressive capture

This brings me to another important question: what justifications are put forward by actors – both public and private – for limiting queer expression and other rights online? In this part, I also examine the prevailing narratives for justifying and sustaining the dominance of the US IIC over Internet policy. I examine, in turn, the justifications proffered for Internet censorship and mass surveillance, and how the arguments of human rights defenders have been co-opted to serve the 'Internet Freedom' agenda. I conclude by drawing links between these justifications and those deployed in other areas of international politics and law.

Justifying Internet censorship: Sexual and gender panics

Internet censorship and filtering policies, and restrictions on queer and LGBT expression online, are often justified as protecting cultural and religious 'values', which in effect preserve mainstream heteronormative gender and sexual norms, roles and stereotypes. As suggested by Human Rights Watch, 'traditional values are often deployed as an excuse to undermine human rights'.[78] Indeed, back in 2012, the UN Human Rights Council agreed that 'traditions shall not be invoked to justify harmful practices violating universal human rights norms and standards', thereby acknowledging that 'tradition' is often invoked to justify human rights violations and condemning the practice.[79] A number of other human rights NGOs have noted that for women, as well as many marginalised groups, 'traditional values' are regularly invoked to restrict the enjoyment of human rights because, from a conservative viewpoint or the perspective of those in authority, they challenge mainstream norms.[80]

The Internet censorship and filtering policies are often built around so-called sexual and moral panics, which mobilise public fears and anxieties about the 'dangers' of sexual content and interaction. As argued by Dianne Otto, sexual and gender panics play a critical role in what she describes as 'crisis governance' in international law.[81] These panics, according to Otto, help to 'divert attention from

78 See Graeme Reid, 'The Trouble with Tradition: When "Values" Trample over Rights' (2013) Human Rights Watch <https://www.hrw.org/world-report/2013/country-chapters/africa>.

79 Resolution Adopted by the Human Rights Council 16/3: Promoting Human Rights and Fundamental Freedoms through a Better Understanding of Traditional Values of Humankind, GA Res 16/3, UN GAOR, 16th sess, Agenda Item 3, UN Doc A/HRC/RES/16/3 (8 April 2011).

80 See Joint Written Statement Addressed to the Advisory Committee Stemming from Human Rights Council Resolutions: Promoting Human Rights and Fundamental Freedoms through a Better Understanding of Traditional Values of Humankind, UN GAOR, 7th sess, Agenda Item 3(a)(viii), UN Doc HRC/AC/7/NGO/1 (8–12 August 2011).

81 Dianne Otto, 'Decoding Crisis in International Law: A Queer Feminist Perspective' in Barbara Stark (ed), *International Law and Its Discontents: Confronting Crises* (Cambridge University Press, 2015) 115.

larger injustices perpetrated in the name of the emergency, while also enabling the adoption of ever more personally invasive laws and regulations that states would otherwise not be able to justify'.[82] As documented by many free speech scholars and advocates, the protection of children is a particularly sensitive issue, with panicked concerns about child pornography, the protection of children from sexual predators and, increasingly, from access to any explicit sexual information, are manipulated to justify the enormous, ever-expanding Internet filtering apparatus.[83] The so-called 'censorship creep'[84] often results in filtering out crucial health-related information in public spaces, such as libraries and schools, and basic information about gender and sexuality that many young people simply wish to become informed about. A recent example, already mentioned, was the filtering out of the term 'breast cancer', as well as removing cancer awareness videos on social platforms, even when animation was used rather than actual human breasts, for being 'offensive' or 'indecent' and therefore inappropriate for children. The result is that such information is filtered out for people around the world.[85] Facebook has also routinely removed pictures of mothers breastfeeding their children.[86] Other photos have reportedly been removed, including one of a mammogram and another of a technician who tattoos nipples and areolas for breast cancer survivors.[87]

Policy debates around the development of these censorship mechanisms, or terms of services by social platforms, seldom include the perspectives of those who are deemed to need that 'special protection' – be they children or young people, or (as it would seem from Facebook's policies) people around the world who are 'sensitive' to nudity, and female breasts and nipples in particular. Interestingly, it is only female breasts and nipples that are considered 'indecent' or 'offensive', leading to some strategic self-censorship by some breast cancer campaigners, who release videos and photographs with male – rather than female – breasts to avoid removal by Facebook.[88] Thus, it is not simply nudity which is considered 'offensive', but rather *female* nudity, leading to questions not only of censorship by private actors, but also discriminatory censorship based on

82 Ibid 117.

83 See, eg, Sonia Corrêa, Horacio Sívori and Bruno Zilli, 'Internet Regulation and Sexual Politics in Brazil' (2012) 55 *Development* 213.

84 Laurie Penny, 'David Cameron's Internet Porn Filter Is the Start of Censorship Creep', *The Guardian* (online) (3 January 2014) <https://www.theguardian.com/commentisfree/2014/jan/03/david-cameron-internet-porn-filter-censorship-creep>.

85 'Facebook Apologises for Removing Breast Cancer Awareness Video', above n 72.

86 Facebook vs Breastfeeding Alliance, above n 74.

87 Carol Off, 'Facebook Bans Technician Who Tattoos Nipples and Areolas for Breast Cancer Survivors', *CBC Radio* (online) (11 October 2016) <http://www.cbc.ca/radio/asithappens/as-it-happens-tuesday-edition-1.3800033/facebook-bans-technician-who-tattoos-nipples-and-areolas-for-breast-cancer-survivors-1.3800040>.

88 Amar Toor, 'Facebook Still Has a Nipple Problem', *The Verge* (12 October 2016) <http://www.theverge.com/2016/10/12/13241486/facebook-censorship-breast-cancer-nipple-mammogram>.

sex and gender. As stressed by cancer awareness campaigners, it is 'incomprehensible and strange how one can perceive medical information as offensive'.[89] In the end, while queer and LGBT young people and children are supposedly the intended 'beneficiaries' of this censorship along with all other children, they are denied agency in the design and the effects of these protectionist policies. What is needed then is a more proactive approach from queer communities and activists to make sure that their voices are heard in debates and decision-making around technology design. Currently, these debates are dominated by white rich males from Silicon Valley and those who direct the global Internet governance institutions, such as the ICANN and the IETF.

It would be naive to think that sexual and moral panics are mobilised only in countries where sexual and gender freedom is not respected, even criminalised, because numerous examples of censorship of queer and LGBT content online suggest that such filtering is just as prevalent in Western liberal democracies as it is in conservative Eastern European, African, Asian and Middle Eastern countries.

Justifying mass surveillance: Security and terrorism panics

In Internet policy, many otherwise unjustifiable restrictions on the exercise of fundamental rights and freedoms have been imposed in the name of panics about national and transnational 'security' and the 'prevention of terrorism'. These restrictions have led, in the eyes of Internet activists, to a 'digital decay of human rights',[90] which has enabled private and public actors to overcome democratic safeguards and the rule of law by adopting numerous private ad hoc measures and memorandums of understanding between public actors and private technology companies. Examples of unlimited personal data collection and illegal mass-surveillance practices requiring cooperation by governments and technology companies are prevalent and numerous, as revealed by Snowden in 2013.[91] Whenever public information about these Internet mass-surveillance programmes and restrictions on fundamental freedoms becomes available, they are first of all justified on the grounds of national security and prevention of terrorism.[92] And if the public still remains unconvinced of the proportionality and necessity of such blanket mass-data collection practices, they are then defended by Western

89 'Facebook Apologises for Removing Breast Cancer Awareness Video', above n 72.

90 'Human Rights and Privatised Law Enforcement: Abandoning Rights – Abandoning Democracy – Abandoning Law' (Report, European Digital Rights Association, 25 February 2014) <https://edri.org/wp-content/uploads/2014/02/EDRi_HumanRights_and_PrivLaw_web.pdf>.

91 Zygmunt Bauman, Didier Bigo, Paulo Esteves et al, 'After Snowden: Rethinking the Impact of Surveillance' (2014) 8 *International Political Sociology* 121.

92 The terrorism prevention paradigm is also used by governments to demand cooperation for private actors: see, eg, Nicholas Watt and Patrick Wintour, 'Facebook and Twitter Have "Social Responsibility" to Help Fight Terrorism, Says David Cameron', *The Guardian* (online) (16 January 2015) <https://www.theguardian.com/world/2015/jan/16/cameron-interrupt-terrorists-cybersecurity-cyberattack-threat>.

governments and technology giants as a lesser (even negligible) evil than the mass-surveillance programmes conducted by repressive governments like Russia and China.[93] This kind of defence is also indirectly offered by many academics working explicitly within the Internet governance field, who often repeat very similar narratives of legitimation, portraying the IIC as a great defender of human rights, which simply happened ('allegedly') to conduct secret mass-surveillance programmes.[94]

Justifying the 'Internet Freedom' agenda: Panics of repressive capture

Sadly, the goals, ideas and language of human rights defenders have also been co-opted by governmental and corporate powers to justify and sustain the structures that favour their strategic and commercial interests. Advocates for the human rights of LGBT people have inadvertently been drawn into the service of 'crisis governance' and exploited for geopolitical ends in international politics.[95] A good illustration is 'pinkwashing' – the way in which many Western states, especially the United States, the United Kingdom and Israel, have used their pro-gay laws and policies to draw xenophobic comparisons between the sexual freedoms (superiority) of the West and the 'unfreedoms' of many non-Western (uncivilised) states.[96]

Similarly, the 'Internet Freedom' agenda heavily promotes the view that non-Western countries, particularly China and Russia, cannot be trusted to respect human rights online.[97] Some, if not most, forms of Internet privacy and free speech advocacy, as well as feminist and queer digital rights advocates, have inadvertently supported the 'Internet Freedom' paradigm by drawing similar xenophobic comparisons between the digital and Internet freedoms (superiority) of the West and the '*un*freedoms' of many non-Western ('evil' authoritarian) traditions, aligning particularly well with the neoliberal model of Internet governance, dominated by the United States. The difference, in this case, is that the primary

93 Matthias Schulze, 'Patterns of Surveillance Legitimization: The German Discourse on the NSA Scandal' (2015) 13 *Surveillance & Society* 197.

94 Francesca Musiani, D L Cogburn, L DeNardis et al (eds), *The Turn to Infrastructure in Internet Governance* (Palgrave Macmillan, 2015).

95 Daphne Rousseau, 'LGBT Campaigners Say Israel "Pinkwashing" to Distract from Palestinian Occupation', *Yahoo! News* (online) (4 June 2016) <https://www.yahoo.com/news/lgbt-campaigners-israel-pinkwashing-distract-palestinian-occupation-183337145.html>.

96 See Jasbir K Puar, *Terrorist Assemblages: Homonationalism in Queer Times* (Duke University Press, 2007); Sarah Schulman, *Israel/Palestine and the Queer International* (Duke University Press, 2012); Aeyal Gross, ch 8, this volume, 'Homoglobalism: The emergence of global gay governance'.

97 See, eg, Leigh Munsil, 'Cruz: Obama Proposal Puts Internet Freedom in Hands of Russia, China', *The Blaze* (online) (24 June 2016) <http://www.theblaze.com/stories/2016/06/24/cruz-obama-proposal-puts-internet-freedom-in-hands-of-russia-china/>.

'uncivilised others' are the governments of China and Russia, rather than those of Muslim nations.[98]

It would be naive to think that digital rights and Internet policy are like a binary in which digital rights are fully protected in the West, and fully undermined by repressive governments outside the West. However, it is precisely this binary that is touted by the 'Internet Freedom' paradigm: that increased censorship and intensified mass surveillance by undemocratic and repressive governments is the only (and a very threatening!) alternative to the current US-dominated neoliberal model. This framing of the danger and imminence of Internet 'capture' by repressive governments is the response to any criticism of the current model, which is praised as a 'global Internet multistakeholder community'.[99]

In summary, all of these justifications are heavily reliant on paradigms of fear and panic. They have enabled various states – both authoritarian and liberal – to restrict queer expression and rights online, in the name of defending freedoms against threats from 'outsiders'. Similar narratives have also very effectively enabled the IIC to maintain its dominance over Internet policy, content and infrastructure.

Conclusion

And so the IIC techno-empire thrives, and is especially strong because it owns large parts of the Internet infrastructure, on which global economic, political and social structures are dependent in the twenty-first century. A basic understanding of the anatomy of Internet governance is necessary to inform queer human rights advocacy in contemporary international law and politics, because of its power to shape the social and economic relations of our time. In this chapter, I have briefly outlined the neoliberal model of the Internet governance, showing how it reflects the economic and geopolitical interests of Western, particularly US, power. In doing so, I have challenged the dominant narratives of 'Internet Freedom' promoted by the US government and its corporate technology allies. I have sought to debunk the popular belief that online queer expression and advocacy of LGBT human rights is limited only in the global South. Internet restrictions on queer expression are also imposed in the global North, by both liberal governments and multinational technology giants, who are often portrayed as champions of human rights and freedoms online.

Real-life examples discussed in this chapter demonstrate that such a belief, which is prevalent among queer communities and activists, is not only naive, but deeply problematic. At its worst, the belief that human rights on the Internet, as well as gender and sexuality freedoms, are respected and protected by the West reflects

98 Ibid.

99 The US government has initially advocated 'a private-sector-led' Internet governance model; however, gradually the term was replaced with a 'multistakeholder model'. See Milton L Mueller, *Networks and States: The Global Politics of Internet Governance* (MIT Press, 2010).

xenophobic, neo-imperial assumptions about the lack of civility of states outside Western liberal democracies. Conveniently, the global spread of 'sodomy' laws through the 'civilising mission' of the British colonial empire is forgotten.[100] Similarly, the Internet Freedom agenda downplays the West's mass surveillance and Internet filtering programmes, if they come to light, as marginal and incomparable to the restrictions on freedom imposed by states like Russia and China. Indeed, they might be incomparable, but for very different reasons than it is often assumed. Whereas China, just like many other governments, does engage in Internet filtering and surveillance activities, the scope of such activities is usually confined to the territory of China, which is separated from the rest of the world by the 'Great Firewall of China'.[101] In contrast, Western-imposed restrictions on the exercise of fundamental rights and freedoms online, including queer expression and human rights advocacy, are often global in scope because it is the US government and US corporations who exercise the greatest control over Internet infrastructure and the multistakeholder neoliberal model of Internet governance.

With no meaningful opposition to the global standard setting and continuing expansion of the IIC, the 'global default'[102] position of the Internet enables US technology giants to shape and influence queer, sexual and other content online, without the knowledge of Internet users. When discriminatory online restrictions on queer rights come to light, they are usually justified by manufacturing panics about sexual morality and protection of children. Similarly, the threat of the 'repressive capture' of the Internet by illiberal states is used by the IIC to maintain its dominance over Internet policy, content and infrastructure. Similarities between these narratives of fear and those employed in other areas of international law and politics are unsurprising, given the socio-technical nature of the Internet. Indeed, the Internet is not simply a neutral technology, as often mistakenly assumed, but rather reflects domestic and global normative political bargains and continuing geo-political battles for power and resources. In the fast-changing and complex reality of the global information economy, the struggle for visibility and human rights – both offline and online – for queer communities around the globe has to continue.

100 See Enze Han and Joseph O'Mahoney, 'British Colonialism and the Criminalization of Homosexuality' (2014) 27 *Cambridge Review of International Affairs* 268.

101 The term was coined in Geremie R Barme and Sang Ye, 'The Great Firewall of China', *Wired* (6 January 1997) <https://www.wired.com/1997/06/china-3/>.

102 Wagner, above n 77.

Part II

Possibilities: Rethinking violence, war and law

4 International law as violence

Competing absences of the other

Vanja Hamzić

Always mistrust the law.[1]

Law and violence are an old couple and analytical forays into their affairs have produced a welter of disparate diagnoses, most of which, however, agree that this relationship is an unhealthy but necessary 'fact of life'. As with many children in abusive families, we are cautioned that any alternative to enduring this relationship in our lives would be catastrophic and that we 'better shape up' for a long journey ahead and, indeed, 'better understand' that all this is for our own good.[2] For instance, in *Law's Violence*, Austin Sarat and Thomas Kearns conclude 'that violence, as a fact and a metaphor, is integral to the constitution of modern law, and that law is a creature of both literal violence, and of imaginings and threats of force, disorder, and pain'.[3] Without either literal or abstract violence, we are told, there can be no law. But law *is*, or rather *ought* to be, because it also holds a promise that it can contain and control the violence *it* deems brute and excessive, the very violence of the world outside law. The imperfection immanent to law's violent taming of extralegal violence is law's *driving force*, an anomaly built into the system to ensure its preservation. For Sarat and Kearns, '[v]iolence stands as the limit of law, as a reminder of both law's continuing necessity and its ever-present failing. Without

1 An *ancien régime* saying, recorded in Nicole Castan, 'The Arbitration of Disputes under the *Ancien Régime*' in John Bossy (ed), *Disputes and Settlements: Law and Human Relations in the West* (Cambridge University Press, first published 1983, 2003 edn) 219, 224.

2 The allusion to 'You're the One That I Want' from *Grease* (1978) is not accidental.

3 Austin Sarat and Thomas R Kearns, 'Introduction' in Austin Sarat and Thomas R Kearns (eds), *Law's Violence* (University of Michigan Press, 1995) 1. As for the evidence of 'modern' law's inevitable coupling with violence, Sarat and Kearns provide an eclectic list of seminal works, including Thomas Hobbes, *Leviathan* (C B MacPherson (ed), Penguin Books, first published 1651, 1981 edn); Hans Kelsen, *General Theory of Law and State* (A Wedberg trans, Russell & Russell, 1961); Norberto Bobbio, 'Law and Force' (1965) 49 *Monist* 321; Walter Benjamin, 'Critique of Violence' in Walter Benjamin, *Reflections: Essays, Aphorisms, Autobiographical Writings* (Peter Demetz (ed), Edmund Jepchott trans, Schocken Books, first published 1978, 1986 edn), 277–300; Peter Fitzpatrick, 'Violence and Legal Subjection' (unpublished typescript, 1991).

violence, law is unnecessary, yet, in its presence, law . . . may be impossible'.[4] The couplet of law and violence is thus forever entangled in a double bind: a distressing existential drama that both threatens and makes the relationship possible.

But, although apparently interdependent, law and violence are not in an equal relationship. Whether it is described as a product of social and economic relations or, more alarmingly, as biologically predetermined (as 'inherent heritage')[5] in humans and other animals, violence is thought to pre-date law and exist both within and without law's life-worlds. In contrast, law is *constituted* by violence, because violence 'provides the occasion and method for founding legal orders, it gives law (as the regulator of force and coercion) a reason for being, and it provides a means through which the law acts'.[6] This aetiological connection is, however, typically denied by law and contrasted with law's seemingly nobler originative myths – such as those of justice, peace and security – which are also projected as law's ultimate ends. It is *non-violence*, then, in which law claims to inhere and in which it wants to rest. Except that, as ever, law's claims are deceptive.

Samera Esmeir has demonstrated in her analysis of the recent wars in Iraq how law's operations for global peace, security and non-violence 'are themselves productive of their own violence'[7] and how wars can be 'carried out *for* the law'.[8] Thus, the violence of non-violence mediated through law reaffirms law's subordinate relationship with violence, a relationship in which violence is not only law's raison d'être but its *magistra vitae*, too – the ultimate heuristic device for contemplating law's past, present and future.

International law is particularly notorious for its continuous evolution towards evermore-diverse forms of juridical violence. From the falsehood of imperial pacifism that characterised the early-twentieth-century efforts to juridify war,[9] through the perils of the multiple turns to 'pragmatism' and quasi-proportionality with regard to legally sanctioned uses of force,[10] to the infinitude[11] of contemporary warfare – international law's spectacles of violence seem to proliferate at an

4 Sarat and Kearns, above n 3, 2.

5 For a recent example of biological determinism in legal scholarship, see István T Kristó-Nagy, 'Violence, Our Inherent Heritage' in Robert Gleave and István T Kristó-Nagy (eds), *Violence in Islamic Thought from the Qur'ān to the Mongols* (Edinburgh University Press, 2015) 2–17.

6 Sarat and Kearns, above n 3, 4.

7 Samera Esmeir, 'The Violence of Non-Violence: Law and War in Iraq' (2007) 34 *Journal of Law and Society* 99, 102.

8 Ibid 103 (emphasis in the original).

9 Gerry Simpson, *Law, War and Crime: War Crimes Trials and the Reinvention of International Law* (Polity Press, 2007) 140–56. For Simpson, the Treaty of Versailles (1919) provided a revolutionary legal interpretation of war and crime and laid the ground for a criminalisation of war at the Nuremberg trials (1945–6).

10 For an illuminating analysis of the law on the use of force, see Gina Heathcote, 'Feminist Perspectives on the Law on the Use of Force' in Marc Weller (ed), *The Oxford Handbook of the Use of Force in International Law* (Oxford University Press, 2015) 114.

11 The 'war on terror' and 'cyber warfare' being but some of the most recent expressions of global warring that defy the neat distinction between the *ius ad bellum* and the *ius in bello*, as they, indeed, defy the distinction between 'war' and 'peace' as such.

unprecedented pace. Is it, then, too preposterous to ask what insights could be obtained if international law is posited no longer as a discipline and practice intrinsically committed to regulation of violence, but as violence *itself*?

If it is presumed that *all* law *is* violence, then the time-honoured analytical dyad of 'law and violence' no longer makes sense. Law's violence becomes the very essence of law and law's violence against both literal and abstract forms of extralegal violence can be seen as law's intrinsic survival strategy – something law *does* in order to *be*, in order to distinguish itself from an otherwise indistinguishable multitude of violent acts. Law's *difference* from such acts is then merely circumstantial and contingent, owed to particular societal conditions that rule *over* it, rather than vice versa (thus exposing the fallacy of the rule of law). Such law is not exceptional, not worth preserving at any cost; it can and perhaps should wither away.[12]

If all law is violence, then international law is perfectly suited for global violent pursuits. It is well entrenched and institutionalised and it provides multiple fora of engagement, each violent in its own right and with respect to a specific set of conditions that govern, or purport to govern, human lives and relations. This chapter considers *one* such forum – the UN Security Council – which has evolved over time into perhaps the most potent symbol of legally sanctioned state violence in international relations, not least because of its botched attempts to curb wars and punish war crimes. The Council is also, as Dianne Otto avers, *the* 'seat of power of the world's superpower(s), whose permanent members are also the world's largest arms dealers'.[13] Initially envisaged as pursuing military actions in its own right, instead of merely 'advising' states on such matters, and even 'having armed forces continuously available to it',[14] the Council has gradually moved towards juridical, rather than literal, forms of violence. Those are epitomised in the establishment of its ad hoc war crimes tribunals, which followed the Yugoslav and Rwandan conflicts in the 1990s, and subsequently in its resolutions on counter-terrorism. The oxymoronic formulae on which the Council has relied in these operations, such as its insistence on international legal *enforcement* of global peace, justice and security, reveal all too plainly the violent nature of such purportedly *non-violent* acts. As Jacques Derrida suggests, '[t]he word *enforceability* reminds us that there is no such thing as law that doesn't imply in itself, a priori,

12 The bold claim that all law will wither away (in the advent of a true communist society) is, of course, a staple of Marxist jurisprudence. See, eg, China Miéville, *Between Equal Rights: A Marxist Theory of International Law* (Brill, 2005).

13 Dianne Otto, 'Beyond Stories of Victory and Danger: Resisting Feminism's Amenability to Serving Security Council Politics' in Gina Heathcote and Dianne Otto (eds), *Rethinking Peacekeeping, Gender Equality and Collective Security* (Palgrave Macmillan, 2014) 157, 159.

14 Vaughan Lowe, Adam Roberts, Jennifer Welsh and Dominik Zaum, 'Introduction' in Vaughan Lowe et al (eds), *The United Nations Security Council and War: The Evolution of Thought and Practice since 1945* (Oxford University Press, 2008) 1, 12.

. . . the possibility of being "enforced", applied by force'.[15] The Council's repeated vows to 'kill insecurity for security' and to 'defeat violence for peace'[16] should therefore be understood literally – as acts of juridical aggression, as international law's own war on war.

The discussion on the intrinsic violence of the Council's dealings in international law, which in turn reveals the intrinsic violence of international law, is framed in this chapter in relation to a single recent event: the 'first-ever' Security Council meeting on the persecution of 'LGBT Syrians and Iraqis' by the so-called 'Islamic State' (hereinafter ISIS),[17] which took place on 24 August 2015.[18] I argue that, while 'dealing with' but also perpetrating and perpetuating multiple forms of violence, this event, at the same time, reveals some *productive voids*, especially with regard to the dominant framing of the subjectivities and subjects of the international legal discourse and intervention. Such voids, I propose, allow for theorising the *absence* of international law and, in turn, the absence of the subject of juridical violence.

On the pages that follow, I revisit, first, certain *loci classici* of critical theory's discussions on violence, so as to assess their relevance for my premise that all law *is* violence. I inquire, in particular, whether the diverse categories of violence, as devised by critical theorists, make sense in law's life-worlds and, if not, *what is to be done*.[19] I turn, then, to international law's (intrinsic) violence as espoused in the Security Council's engagements with ISIS – that newly begotten *hostis humani generis*[20] – as well as with ISIS's potential 'perfect alterity' in the image of 'LGBT Syrians and Iraqis'. I conclude that this conceptual meeting of two unlikely actants

15 Jacques Derrida, 'Force of Law: The "Mystical Foundation of Authority"' (1990) 11 *Cardozo Law Review* 919, 925 (emphasis in the original).

16 Esmeir, above n 7, 103.

17 The acronym 'ISIS' denotes the so-called 'Islamic State of Iraq and Syria', which is also known as 'ISIL' (substituting the word 'Syria' with 'the Levant'), *Da'ish* or *Daesh* (the Arabic equivalents of 'ISIL'/'ISIS'), or simply 'Islamic State' (IS). Although this terrorist organisation hardly needs any introduction, it is worth noting that, on 29 June 2014, ISIS proclaimed itself to be an Islamic state (*al-dawla al-islamīya*) and *global* caliphate (*khilāfa*). By the end of 2015, ISIS was thought to control territory inhabited by *c* 10 million people in Syria and Iraq, while its affiliates control small areas of Afghanistan, Libya and Nigeria. In the sea of less-than-mediocre literature on ISIS, only two journalistic accounts currently stand out – Abdel Bari Atwan's *Islamic State: The Digital Caliphate* (Saqi, 2015) and Patrick Cockburn's *The Rise of Islamic State: ISIS and the New Sunni Revolution* (Verso, 2015).

18 See Michelle Nichols, 'UN Security Council to Meet on Islamic State Gay Attacks', *Reuters* (online) (13 August 2015) <http://uk.reuters.com/article/2015/08/13/uk-mideast-crisis-islamic-state-gay-idUKKCN0QI26I20150813>.

19 To echo Lenin's 'What Is to Be Done', which, coincidentally, although relating to a different context, asks an important additional question: 'what is there in common between economism and terrorism?' See Vladimir Ilyich Lenin, 'What Is to Be Done?' in Vladimir Ilyich Lenin, *Essential Works of Lenin: 'What Is to Be Done?' and Other Writings* (BN Publishing, 2009) 53, 108.

20 *Hostis humani generis* ('enemy of humankind') is a legal term-of-art denoting an entity (for instance, a pirate ship) operating outside the bounds of the law (traditionally admiralty law and nowadays public international law) and outside the jurisdiction of national law.

(or 'personalities') of international law – one deemed *quintessentially* evil and the other *quintessentially* good – is not an ordinary event. Rather, it probes the very foundations of law's violence and signals an existential crisis amid the global operations of international law – thus revealing an *alegal* space for critique and contemplation or, simply, for a life imagined beyond law.

Towards a critique of law as violence

Out of an array of critical engagements on the political Left with violence as a social phenomenon, two analytical encounters are almost proverbial for their depth and the number of productive responses they were able to elicit. First is Walter Benjamin's notoriously dense 'Critique of Violence', published in 1921.[21] Second is Jean-Paul Sartre's controversial 'Preface' to the 1961 edition of Frantz Fanon's *The Wretched of the Earth*.[22] Both texts have proven difficult to *render* into English, not least because the words *Recht* and *droit* in German and French respectively denote both 'law' and 'right' (a trait shared across many Germanic, Romanesque and Slavic languages), while the German word *Gewalt* means not only 'violence', but also, as Derrida carefully noted, 'legitimate power, authority, public force'.[23] The failures and misfortunes of translation – taken as a linguistic, philosophical and cultural labour – thus befall, in particular, Benjamin's text.[24]

At the same time, Benjamin's text has been described as 'at once "mystical" . . . and hypercritical' – a 'text which, in certain respects, can be read as neo-messianic Jewish mysticism (mystique) grafted onto post-Sorelian neo-Marxism (or [the] reverse)'.[25] It might be this Benjaminian 'mystical critique' that propelled Slavoj Žižek to compose his 2008 book on violence out of 'six sideways glances', rather than 'confronting violence directly'.[26] In so doing, Žižek is careful not to *succumb* to the mystique of violence itself. 'My underlying premise', he writes, 'is that there is something inherently mystifying in a direct confrontation with [violence]: the overpowering horror of violent acts and empathy with the victims inexorably function as a lure which prevents us from thinking.'[27] The same, perhaps, could be said of the *lure* of law (with the noun 'lure' echoing uncannily the word 'rule') in its messianic mode – the law that solemnly resolves that *justice be done.*

21 Walter Benjamin, 'Zur Kritik der Gewalt' (1921) 47 *Archiv für Sozialwissenschaft und Sozialpolitik* 809. For an English translation, see Benjamin, above n 3, 277–300.

22 Jean-Paul Sartre, 'Préface' in Frantz Fanon, *Les damnés de la terre* (François Maspero, 1961) 17. For an English translation, see Jean-Paul Sartre, 'Preface' in Frantz Fanon, *The Wretched of the Earth* (R Philcox trans, Grove Press, 2004) xliii.

23 Derrida, above n 15, 927.

24 Ibid.

25 Ibid 979.

26 Slavoj Žižek, *Violence: Six Sideways Reflections* (Profile Books, 2008) 3. The sixth of these reflections directly concerns Benjamin's 'Critique of Violence'.

27 Ibid.

Benjamin's approach to the lure of both law and violence is to bring these terms-of-art (that is, 'law' as *Recht* and 'violence' as *Gewalt*) into a symbiotic relationship in which their interdependence becomes the key for their dialectical *difference* as well as their metaphysical *unity*.[28] This symbiosis is achieved through a series of distinctions. Benjamin distinguishes, for example, between 'lawmaking violence' (*rechtsetzende Gewalt*) and 'law-preserving violence' (*rechtserhaltende Gewalt*) to account for two different ways in which violence is memorialised and built into the (legal) system and, crucially, to move beyond the impasse contained in the distinction between 'natural' and 'positive' law. 'Among all the forms of violence permitted by both natural law and positive law', Benjamin suggests, 'there is not one that is free of the gravely problematic nature . . . of all legal violence'.[29] To explain this nature, he erects yet another pair of oppositions – that of 'mythic violence' (*mytische Gewalt*) and 'divine violence' (*göttliche Gewalt*) – the former denoting the very *lure* of law, its mystifying powers to keep us forever entrapped in its vicious circle, while the latter suggests a path to liberation from that circle. 'Divine violence', in that sense, is quite literally a *deus ex machina*: a type of violence, such as 'the proletarian general strike [that] sets itself the sole task of destroying state power',[30] which will ultimately open 'again all the eternal forms'.[31] Benjamin's 'divine violence' is, thus, revolutionary in that it serves no means other than that of liberating us from the intrinsic injustice of law;[32] it reminds us of the *possibility* of a life outside law and juridical violence.

While a lawless life for Benjamin is a possibility, it is not a life without violence. Whether 'divine violence' is conceived as a temporary occurrence or, indeed, a road to a new form of 'sovereignty',[33] it can only set us free from one pervasive form of violence – that of law *as such*. Absent a revolution, even that is but a distant dream. So, what is to be done?

Sartre's answer, in his 'Preface' to Fanon's *The Wretched of the Earth*, seemed to be to embrace, even celebrate, the insurgent violence of the oppressed, since such violence, 'like Achilles' spear, can heal the wounds it has inflicted'.[34] Sartre's call to arms, as it were, was primarily intended to wake the 'Europeans'[35] to Third World de-colonial struggle. Still, the would-be self-soothing properties of violence in his reference to Achilles's spear elicited a barrage of criticism. For instance, in her essay *On Violence*, Hannah Arendt dismisses this reference as utter nonsense: '[i]f this were true', she writes, 'revenge would be the cure-all for most of our

28 Thus bringing together dialectical materialism and Abrahamic metaphysics, the latter of which can be observed, for example, in the Ṣūfī concept of *waḥdat al-wujūd* (Unity of Existence).
29 Benjamin, above n 3, 293.
30 Ibid 291.
31 Ibid 300.
32 Cf Žižek, above n 26, 169.
33 After all, Benjamin concludes his analysis with the assertion that '[d]ivine violence . . . may be called sovereign violence'; Benjamin, above n 3, 300.
34 Sartre, above n 22, lxii.
35 Ibid xlviii.

ills'.[36] Against this zero-sum exchange, Judith Butler's analysis centres on the specific context in which Sartre wrote this text:

> Sartre's portrayal of insurgent violence is meant to provide insight into the person who lives under [colonial] oppression. As such, it serves as a reconstruction of an induced psychological state. It also reads as a fully instrumental rationalization for violence and thus as a normative claim. Indeed, the violent acts by which decolonization is achieved are also those by which *man 'recreates himself'*. Sartre is describing a psychopolitical reality, but he is also offering, we might say, a new humanism to confound the old, one that requires, under these social conditions, violence to materialize.[37]

Butler's analysis situates Sartre within *his* own existential drama, especially with regard to his self-avowed existential humanism and its normative limits. In this struggle, Sartre's affirmation of the violence of the colonised is at the same time an affirmation of 'the masculine [as] the presumptive norm of humanization'.[38] It is this gender-biased humanist normativity bent on violence that Butler primarily objects to and proposes, instead, that we seek a *touch* 'and form of yielding that establishes a relation to a "you"', that is, to 'a pronoun that is open-ended precisely on the question of gender'.[39] For Butler, then, this would be a search for an insurrectionary human *beyond* the constraints of humanism, and, indeed, an emancipatory quest *beyond* violence:

> If there is a relation between this 'you' whom I seek to know, whose gender cannot be determined, whose nationality cannot be presumed, and who compels me to relinquish violence, then this mode of address articulates a wish not just for a nonviolent future for the human, but for a new conception of the human where some manner of touch other than violence is the precondition of that making.[40]

Butler's presumptive 'you', then, is a 'you' still-untainted by law, gender roles and other forms of violence – the 'you' whose ways of being in the world invite *me* to explore the act of *touch* as an expression of infinite possibilities.[41]

36 Hannah Arendt, *On Violence* (Harcourt, 1970) 20.

37 Judith Butler, 'Violence, Nonviolence: Sartre on Fanon' in *Senses of the Subject* (Fordham University Press, 2015) 171, 186–7 (emphasis added).

38 Ibid 197.

39 Ibid.

40 Ibid.

41 See generally Eve Kosofsky Sedgwick, *Touching Feeling: Affect, Pedagogy, Performativity* (Duke University Press, 2003); Luce Irigaray, 'Toward a Divine in the Feminine' in Gillian Howie and J'annine Jobling (eds), *Women and the Divine: Touching Transcendence* (Palgrave Macmillan, 2009) 13.

The life-worlds of Butler's 'you' stand in opposition to law's life-worlds. The former entail conceptual and affective journeys into the human beyond violence. The latter are the worlds of radical violence that enliven but ultimately defeat the human. For violence cannot be cured by law; law can only beget more violence. As such, law cannot *be* other-than-violence.

The Security Council 'meets' to mete out the evil and the good

But, how can non-violence-other-than-violence[42] and other-than-legal ways to approach conflict and suffering ever be convincing in a world such as ours? Even if it is presumed that global 'peace', 'justice' and 'security' are all concepts steeped in violence – literal (subjective), symbolic and systemic[43] – can their oppositional pairs – global war, injustice and insecurity – ever be contained by anything other than sheer force, including the force of law?

Writing from Paris the day after the 13 November 2015 terrorist attacks, Judith Butler recalled, once again, the strange 'metrics of grievability' that render some human lives infinitely more grievable than others,[44] and warned that '*this* [the Paris attacks] will take some *time* to think through'.[45] This echoes Žižek's earlier discussed concern with the *lure* of violence/law, with its compulsive urge to 'intervene', to be 'drawn in' and, in doing so, to succumb to a 'hypocritical sentiment of moral outrage'.[46] This affective response only reinforces the presumed inevitability of violence/law. Instead of doing first and thinking later, is there a *time* to do the opposite? If so, the key question should be: what is it that law/violence *does* to contain and eradicate those *most direct* and most appalling forms of violence deemed extralegal?

When, on 24 August 2015, the Security Council convened its Arria-Formula meeting[47] on ISIS and its persecution of 'LGBT Syrians and Iraqis', it did so,

42 Cf Esmeir, above n 7. Esmeir's focus is, decidedly, on violent aspects of non-violence. One would, however, hope that there are also some aspects of non-violence that remain non-violent.

43 To borrow Žižek's classification of direct and visible, linguistic and formative, and economic and political forms of violence, respectively; Žižek, above n 26, 1.

44 'Mourning [here in Paris] seems fully restricted within the national frame. The nearly 50 dead in Beirut from the day before are barely mentioned, and neither are the 111 in Palestine killed in the last weeks alone, or the scores in Ankara', Judith Butler, 'Mourning Becomes the Law', *Instituto 25M Democracia* (14 November 2015) <https://instituto25m.info/mourning-becomes-the-law-judith-butler-from-paris/>.

45 Emphasis in the original. For '[i]t is difficult to think when one is appalled': ibid. For her enlightening exploration of post-9/11 America, see Judith Butler, *Precarious Life: The Powers of Mourning and Violence* (Verso, 2006). For her critique of state violence and the media-induced 'metrics of grievability', see Judith Butler, *Frames of War: When is Life Grievable?* (Verso, 2010).

46 Žižek, above n 26, 5.

47 So named after a Venezuelan diplomat who introduced the format in 1992 to allow for 'very informal, confidential gatherings which enable Security Council members to have a frank and

apparently, to *make history*. 'This will be a historic meeting', proclaimed US Ambassador to the UN Samantha Power: '[i]t will be the first Security Council meeting on LGBT rights'.[48] While LGBT rights are no stranger to the international legal system, they have been, indeed, absent from the Council's agenda, not least because at least one of its permanent members, Russia, opposes their existence *tout court*. Meanwhile, the Council's dealings with other 'comparable' issues – most notably its agenda on women, peace and security – have been less than impressive.[49] The agenda that was hoped (by some feminists involved in its original drafting) to play an important role 'in disrupting the gendered assumptions of collective security discourse, principally by (re)presenting women as vital participants in conflict resolution and peace-building',[50] quickly proved to be the very opposite. Four of the Council's seven follow-up resolutions 'focus[ed] solely on women as victims of sexual violence'.[51] So, what exactly, if anything, was *historic* about the 'secretive' and 'informal' Council's Arria-Formula meeting on ISIS and LGBT rights?

First, some facts. The meeting was organised by the United States and Chile, whose ambassadors delivered prepared remarks, along with UN Deputy Secretary-General Jan Eliasson and International Gay and Lesbian Human Rights Commission (since renamed OutRight Action International) Executive Director Jessica Stern. Of the 15 Security Council members, 13 were present and nine delivered remarks as well. Although in attendance, representatives from China, Russia, Nigeria and Malaysia (predictably) did not speak.[52]

The meeting was also addressed by a representative of one Muslim-majority country, who 'delivered generally supportive remarks', a representative of one Muslim human rights organisation, 'reaffirming the need to address abuses committed against all marginalized persons impacted by the conflict, including

private exchange of views . . . with persons whom the inviting member or members of the Council . . . believe it would be beneficial to hear and/or to whom they may wish to convey a message': UN Secretariat, 'Working Methods Handbook: Background Note on the "Arria-Formula" Meetings of the Security Council Members' (Informal Non-Paper, UN Security Council, 25 October 2002) <http://www.un.org/en/sc/about/methods/bgarriaformula.shtml>.

48 Reported in Scott Long, 'The UN Security Council Debates Gays and ISIS: Why This is a Bad Idea' on Scott Long, *A Paper Bird* (23 August 2015) <http://paper-bird.net/2015/08/23/the-un-security-council-terrible-idea/>. This entry provides an illuminating analysis of the Arria-Formula event in question and should be read in conjunction with other posts on the matter available at the same blog.

49 As inaugurated by SC Res 1325, UN Doc S/RES/1325 (31 October 2000). For a critical appraisal of feminist engagements with the Security Council, see Otto, above n 13, 157–72.

50 Dianne Otto and Gina Heathcote, 'Rethinking Peacekeeping, Gender Equality and Collective Security: An Introduction' in Dianne Otto and Gina Heathcote (eds), *Rethinking Peacekeeping, Gender Equality and Collective Security* (Palgrave Macmillan, 2014) 1, 2.

51 Ibid 2–3.

52 See Michael K Lavers, 'Islamic State Focus of UN Security Council's First LGBT Meeting', *Washington Blade* (online) (24 August 2015) <http://www.washingtonblade.com/2015/08/24/islamic-state-focus-of-u-n-security-councils-first-lgbt-meeting/>.

LGBTI persons', and an anonymous 'Iraqi gay man' who spoke to the Council via telephone.[53]

Finally, the Council heard 'Subhi Nahas, a gay man from the Syrian city of Idleb who received refugee status . . . and now lives in San Francisco'.[54] He 'spoke during the briefing on behalf of the Organization for Refuge, Asylum and Migration'.[55] 'I have witnessed with my own eyes the annihilation of *civility* and *humanity* as I knew them', Nahas told the Council. 'For millions of Syrians both in and outside the country, time is running out. For my compatriots who do not conform to gender and sexual norms, the eleventh hour has already passed. They need your help now.'[56]

The US Ambassador Power, OutRight Executive Director Stern and Syrian witness Nahas briefed the press later in the day. Stern told reporters that ISIS has executed at least 30 men charged with 'sodomy'. 'It is the obligation of the international community to take action', she concluded.[57] Nahas told the press that he would support international military intervention in order to stop ISIS and end the war in Syria.[58]

Thus ended the 'historic' gathering. Its flimsy 'recognition' of 'LGBT Syrians and Iraqis' as victims of ISIS's rule of terror *coincided* with a new wave of public executions of those accused of committing the 'deeds of Lot's people' (*'amāl qawm Lūṭ*)[59] that ISIS perpetrated and duly reported in social media. Two days before the Council's Arria-Formula meeting, ISIS militants reportedly threw nine male citizens of the city of Mosul from the top of a high building, after a 'judge' of an 'Islamic court' set up by ISIS condemned those people to death for the 'deeds of Lot's people'.[60] An ISIS-orchestrated

53 As this paragraph draws on a confidential report, the relevant identities are concealed for their own protection.

54 Lavers, above n 52.

55 Ibid.

56 Ibid (emphasis added).

57 Ibid. For Stern's remarks delivered at the Arria-Formula meeting, see OutRight Action International, 'Jessica Stern's Remarks at Historic UN Briefing on LGBT People Focuses [sic] on Persecution and Killings in Iraq and Syria' (Media Release, 24 August 2015) <https://www.outrightinternational.org/content/jessica-sterns-remarks-historic-un-briefing-lgbt-people-focuses-persecution-and-killings>.

58 Lavers, above n 52.

59 So-described in ISIS propaganda in order to invoke the Qur'ānic rendition of the Biblical parable about the Prophet Lot (Lūṭ) and thus 'prove' that severe punishments of male same-sex sexual acts are not only commendable, but obligatory, in Islamic law. On the fallacy and danger of such claims, see Vanja Hamzić, *Sexual and Gender Diversity in the Muslim World: History, Law and Vernacular Knowledge* (I B Tauris, 2016) 90–1.

60 Scott Long, 'New Killings: ISIS Answers the UN Security Council' on Scott Long, *A Paper Bird* (25 August 2015) <http://paper-bird.net/2015/08/25/new-killings-isis-answers-the-un-security-council/>. In this post, Long suggests that this might be the largest number that ISIS has murdered at one time for 'sodomy', and provocatively concludes that '[i]t's hard not to suspect this wave of killing was a pre-emptive answer to [the] UN Security Council

execution for 'sodomy' was also reported only a couple of weeks after the Council's meeting.[61]

The Arria-Formula meeting took place within the context of other such 'informal' and 'secretive' conversations that the Council has recently organised on other atrocious acts committed by ISIS that are seemingly deemed condemnable but 'sensitive' – such as the sexual enslavement of women and girls and ISIS's targeted killing of Christian, Yazidi, Turkic and Kurdish groups. While the Council's resolutions have already affirmed the need to combat terrorism 'by *all* means, in accordance with . . . international law',[62] its attempts to 'raise awareness' on crimes that ISIS has committed against *particular* groups – based on their ethnic or, indeed, sexual and gender difference – are a tricky business. On the one hand, as evidenced by the silence (and one rather lukewarm response) of certain state representatives at the Arria-Formula meeting of 24 August 2015, recognising some of these groups' very *existence* might be a problem for some of the Council's members – let alone condemning such crimes publicly. Such 'recognition' might give those groups a type of 'presence' – indeed, a 'personality' – in international law and politics that could later be invoked to condemn violence (both literal and juridical) that many member states happily commit or condone against those or other comparable groups.[63] On the other hand, emphasising the plights of *particular* groups such as these is seemingly necessary for building a case for the referral of ISIS's crimes to the International Criminal Court.

But how could ISIS's violence be effectively singled out and *juridified* (criminalised) *without* involving other participants in the wars in Syria and Iraq? The International Criminal Court's jurisdiction over ISIS is as problematic as ISIS's stand in international law in general. As an international terrorist organisation with an ominous claim to statehood that is both territorial (currently

meeting on gays and ISIS – which was making headlines in both Western and Arab media fully nine days earlier'.

61 Scott Long, 'New ISIS Execution for "Sodomy": Attention, UN Security Council' on Scott Long, *A Paper Bird* (17 September 2015) <http://paper-bird.net/2015/09/17/new-isis-execution-attention-un-security-council/>.

62 SC Res 2199, UN Doc S/RES/2199 (12 February 2015) (emphasis added). The resolution condemns all forms of trade with terrorist organisations and authorises its member states' economic sanctions targeting such trade. At the time of writing this chapter, a Council resolution *specifically* authorising the use of force against ISIS is yet to be adopted, although Resolution 2249 calls upon the Council's member states 'that have the *capacity* to do so to take *all necessary measures*, in compliance with international law, . . . on the territory under the control of ISIL, . . . in Syria and Iraq, to redouble and coordinate their efforts to *prevent* and *suppress* terrorist acts committed specifically by ISIL, . . . and to *eradicate* the safe haven they have established over significant parts of Iraq and Syria': SC Res 2249, UN Doc S/RES/2249 (20 November 2015) (emphasis added). For the resolutions explicitly calling for a political solution to the Syrian crisis, see SC Res 2254, UN Doc S/RES/2254 (18 December 2015); SC Res 2268, UN Doc S/RES/2268 (26 February 2016).

63 The likelihood of such further developments is precisely what, I presume, the LGBT organisations involved in the dealings with the Security Council rely upon: the likelihood that, as I hope to demonstrate here, does not come without its own costs.

primarily in Iraq and Syria, its most-evident physical 'strongholds') and extraterritorial (with its claim to a global – both 'real' and 'virtual' – caliphate),[64] coupled with most extreme forms of violence, ISIS's 'personality' in international law is perhaps closest to that of the *hostis humani generis*, otherwise reserved for pirates and certain rogue states, such as Nazi Germany during the Second World War.[65] The crimes of ISIS in Syria and Iraq cannot be referred to the International Criminal Court by those states, as they have not ratified the Rome Statute.[66] But the Security Council could vote a referral of both of *these states*, rather than ISIS specifically (as a non-state actor), to the International Criminal Court, as it did with Libya in 2011.[67] However, the likelihood of that happening is slim. Since the Rome Statute is 'designed to prevent one-sided referrals',[68] a referral would open the Syrian regime to prosecution, possibly along with all Syrian rebel formations. This would hardly be welcomed by Russia and China – two of the Council's permanent members – given their support of the Assad regime. As for Iraq, its government and the various paramilitary formations would also find themselves prosecutable, something the remaining three permanent member states in the Security Council could find troublesome.[69]

With the deadlock in the Security Council yet again resembling the 'old' Cold War fault lines, what little remains other than literal violence of war is to resort to the equally déjà-vu rhetoric of 'compassion' and 'peace-building' in international relations and law. It is this role that the Council has most readily embraced, even if it involves, at times, 'sensitive' issues such as the situation of sexually diverse and gender-variant people in Muslim-majority states. There is, however, nothing

64 A case in point is ISIS's investment in the production of both material and phantasmagorical presence in the world. For an analysis of ISIS's 'Cyber Caliphate' division, the declaration of its 'cyber war' on the United States and its own rip-off video game as important elements of its global warfare, see generally Atwan, above n 17.

65 The regulation of piracy was the original 'trigger' of the recognition that individuals had 'personality' in international law. Pirates, however, were of necessity 'rogue' and beyond the reach of a single state, and as such the (conceptual) precursors to war criminals and international terrorists. All of them came to be characterised as a *hostis humani generis*; see Simpson, above n 9, 162. The 'pirate' or 'rogue' state, defying the mores of international relations, inherited this status.

66 The Rome Statute of the International Criminal Court, adopted on 17 July 1998, provides for the Court's direct jurisdiction over the states that have ratified this treaty. States that are party to the Rome Statute, however, could prosecute *their own* nationals for international terrorist activities and war crimes committed in Syria and Iraq, or they could refer them to the International Criminal Court, since the Court has *personal* jurisdiction over them. Rome Statute of the International Criminal Court, opened for signature 17 July 1998, 2187 UNTS 90 (entered into force 1 July 2002).

67 SC Res 1970, UN Doc S/RES/1970 (26 February 2011).

68 Kevin Jon Heller, 'John Bellinger's Op-Ed on ISIS and the ICC (Updated)', *Opinio Juris* (2 April 2015) <http://opiniojuris.org/2015/04/02/john-bellingers-curious-op-ed-on-isis-and-the-icc/>.

69 '[N]ot least because it would provide the ICC with a backdoor to prosecuting their nationals for aiding and abetting rebel crimes': ibid (emphasis altered).

'historic' in its Arria-Formula meeting on ISIS and 'LGBT Syrians and Iraqis'. The meeting conferred only a 'contextual' (victim-based) recognition upon such individuals – *violating*, at the same time, their right to belong to, or devise for themselves, any other categories of personhood.[70] In doing so, it made the lives of 'LGBT Syrians and Iraqis' *temporarily* grievable,[71] albeit only inasmuch as this designation could serve a 'higher' legal and moral purpose – the putative 'robust' protection of 'civility' and 'humanity' as 'we' know them, that is, as they are known and protected in international law and as they are to be recognised and protected in the global war on ISIS. That a world law should be protected by a world war against a world enemy is, of course, not a coincidence; it is the very nature of international law *as* violence, the very nature of 'consensus-building' involved in the difficult task of embedding ISIS into the politically polarised system of international crimes and punishments. Since the juridification of ISIS cannot be achieved without unravelling the threads of international power relations – the relations in which international law as violence remains deeply invested – the violence of ISIS, as opposed to the violence of states or other non-state combatants, has to be made *special*: it has to be recognised as not just *malum prohibitum* ('evil [as or because] prohibited') but *malum in se* ('evil in itself'). As with the other *hostes humani generis*, ISIS as 'evil incarnate' invites international law to intervene with extreme violence, to kill in order to let live. This is the law *as* morality *as* violence, the law of the peremptory norm, or indeed a commandment, that there is something 'divine', or perhaps 'natural' (as an existential imperative), in exterminating the enemy.[72]

But constructing a 'personality' of an archetypal evil requires that an equally exemplary good be summoned, too. It is only in the opposites of these legal and moral actants *par excellence* that violence as law (rather than law as violence), or perhaps violence as *the* Law, could ever hope to be cleansed ('justified').[73] The

70 There is an abundance of literature on the (epistemic) violence involved in the deployments – however 'strategic' – of the acronym 'LGBT' as a catch-all identitary episteme for sexually diverse and gender-variant human subjectivities across cultures, societies, geographies and times. For my own take on the matter, see Vanja Hamzić, 'Unlearning Human Rights and False Grand Dichotomies: Indonesian Archipelagic Selves beyond Sexual/Gender Universality' (2012) 4(1) *Jindal Global Law Review* 157.

71 Cf the 'metrics of grievability' in Butler, 'Mourning Becomes the Law', above n 44. Butler's critique centres on the differential metrics of grievability that render some lives less grievable than others. My contention is that this differentiation also has a temporal effect; the lives less grievable are also grieved for a shorter period of time.

72 It should, then, come as no surprise that the early ideas on how to establish a global legal and political system of 'collective security' came from the notorious Cardinal Richelieu of France in 1629 and were partially reflected in the 1648 Peace of Westphalia; see Andreas Osiander, *The States System of Europe 1640–1990: Peacemaking and the Conditions of International Stability* (Oxford University Press, 1994) 40–3. The 'divine' violence of the law as morality as violence should not be confused with Benjamin's 'divine' violence of the oppressed.

73 In order for law to 'accommodate and control violence without becoming a captive of its own violent instincts'; Austin Sarat and Thomas R Kearns, 'Making Peace with Violence: Robert Cover on Law and Legal Theory' in Austin Sarat and Thomas R Kearns (eds), *Law's Violence*

Council's beckoning towards 'LGBT Syrians and Iraqis' and other 'personalities' (women and girls, Christians and Yazidis, Kurds and Turkmens) was no doubt an effort to conjure up the good from across the political divide in order to make the evil of ISIS more palpable, more personal, more punishable. The good are summoned so that evil can be eradicated, so that the violence of such eradication can be done in the name of the good. The LGBT organisations and individuals involved in this purification ritual of international law should be aware of the circumstances in which their temporary, contingent and informal 'recognition' before the Security Council had become possible.

I have argued elsewhere[74] for *alegality* as an exploratory site of other-than-legal life-worlds, through which the ideological dyad of legal/illegal could be effectively challenged. It is perhaps in the same fashion that the problem of law as violence could be productively approached. The events such as the Security Council's Arria-Formula meeting of 24 August 2015 are *not ordinary* inasmuch as they signal the increasing need on the part of international law to justify its operations in absolute terms, as the battle between good and evil. As ever, the language of the apocalypse is the language of crisis and the crisis currently befalling international law might be quite existential in nature. It is the crisis of violence spilling everywhere, of violence that no longer seems containable even by most violent acts of law. In it, it is becoming abundantly clear to law's various *subjects* that law *is* just violence, too.

Could such realisation lead to an *alegal* space for critique and contemplation amid the warring world? Could such a space survive, as Žižek and Butler had hoped,[75] the mindless accusations of being seemingly inert, cowardly and dispassionate in a time of global crises, each more ominous than the last? If law is abandoned, even if only theoretically, as *the* repository of people's identities and hopes that, in turn, constitute law's subjects, it should be possible to imagine and be *in touch* with the self and the 'you' in the human who do not conform to the dominant subjectivities and subjects of international law and legal-*cum*-military interventions – the constraints of the LGBT identitary matrix being a case in point. Such alegal selves corresponding to alegal others – thus living (in) the void of law – could lead to novel experiences and interpretations of the absence of law's violence. This would require an *inverse* logic in our approach to the problem of violence: a logic that no longer summons law's violence to tame excessive forms of violence in the world, but seeks, instead, to abandon law's violence (and, with it, the law *as such*) first and foremost in our search for a less violent future.

(University of Michigan Press, 1995) 211, 213. The authors conclude, and I concur, that such purification cannot succeed – that law is of necessity 'jurispathic'.

74 Vanja Hamzić, 'Alegality: Outside and beyond the Legal Logic of Late Capitalism' in Honor Brabazon (ed), *Neoliberal Legality: Understanding the Role of Law in the Neoliberal Project* (Routledge, 2016) 192.

75 Cf Žižek, above n 26, 179–83; Butler, 'Mourning Becomes the Law', above n 44.

5 The maintenance of ~~international peace and security~~ heteronormativity

*Tamsin Phillipa Paige**

> We are not your kind of people.
> Speak a different language, we see through your lies.
> We are not your kind of people.
> Won't be cast as demons, creatures you despise.[1]

Violence is a peculiar thing; it intrigues some people, horrifies others, and yet others just become numb to it from too much exposure. At an international level, the UN Security Council is gatekeeper to the use of lawful and legitimate violence under its mandate to maintain international peace and security. Under Chapter VII of the UN Charter, the Council has the power to authorise the lawful use of force by states in response to a finding under article 39 of a 'threat to the peace', 'breach of the peace' or an 'act of aggression'. It also has the capacity to levy sanctions and other similarly coercive measures through this power. Such authorisations, along with the right to self-defence, are the only exceptions to the prohibition of the use of force explicitly recognised by the UN Charter. More recently, in the context of the Council's gender mainstreaming efforts through its 'Women, Peace and Security' agenda, the United Kingdom has suggested that systematic sexual violence, when employed as a tactic of war, should be considered a threat to the peace within the meaning of article 39, leading to authorisations of violence to combat the phenomena. However, the six resolutions adopted on the matter tell us that sexual violence as a 'tactic of war' does not constitute a threat to the peace, but they do not tell us why not.[2] In this chapter, my goal is to explore why the Permanent Five members of the Security Council (P5) have

* This chapter was written during my time as a Visiting Researcher with Nottingham International Law and Security Centre and as a Visiting Scholar at Columbia Law School (as an Endeavour Scholarship recipient).

1 Garbage (American-Scottish alternative rock band), 'Not Your Kind of People', released 14 May 2012.

2 SC Res 1820, UN Doc S/RES/1820 (19 June 2008) ('Resolution 1820'); SC Res 1882, UN Doc S/RES/1882 (4 August 2009); SC Res 1888, UN Doc S/RES/1888 (30 September 2009) ('Resolution 1888'); SC Res 1960, UN Doc S/RES/1960 (16 December 2010)

taken this position.[3] I will examine the justificatory discourse of the P5 found in public statements they have made about sexual violence in Council meetings.[4] I will not be conducting an examination of the resolutions themselves, as this has already been aptly done by others.[5] Rather, my analysis will study official statements made by each of the P5 in the course of adopting those resolutions. Before we proceed, it is worth noting that when considering the existence of a threat to the peace it has been well established that the Security Council possesses a discretion fettered only by the limits of *jus cogens* norms and the purposes and principles set out in Chapter I of the UN Charter.[6] Inger Österdahl offers a succinct description of the limits faced by the Council: 'Put in simple terms, the Security Council may basically decide or do anything it wishes and it will remain within the limits of the legal framework for its action.'[7]

As a queer woman, I am no stranger to violence. I have experienced it personally and witnessed it done to others; both physical violence and other, subtler forms of violence.[8] My interest in the conditions under which violence, particularly

('Resolution 1960'); SC Res 2106, UN Doc S/RES/2106 (24 June 2013); SC Res 2272, UN Doc S/RES/2272 (11 March 2016).

3 The focus on the P5 (China, France, Russia, the United Kingdom and the United States) rather than all members of the Security Council is done for two reasons. First, the time periods involved in the study mean that there is no consistency in the rotating members and thus their positions are relatively unhelpful. Second, the ability of the P5 to veto a resolution makes them somewhat more equal than others in the context of the Security Council, regardless of the myth of sovereign equality. Should all of the P5 agree on a resolution then it is most likely to pass.

4 By 'justificatory discourse' I mean the public statements made by a state in relation to how they justify their position on any given issue. See Ian Johnstone, 'Security Council Deliberations: The Power of the Better Argument' (2003) 14 *European Journal of International Law* 437.

5 See, eg, Karen Engle, 'The Grip of Sexual Violence: Reading UN Security Council Resolutions on Human Security' in Gina Heathcote and Dianne Otto (eds), *Rethinking Peacekeeping, Gender Equality and Collective Security* (Palgrave Macmillan, 2014) 23; Gina Heathcote, 'Naming and Shaming: Human Rights Accountability in Security Council Resolution 1960 (2010) on Women, Peace and Security' (2012) 4 *Journal of Human Rights Practice* 82; Dianne Otto, 'Power and Danger: Feminist Engagement with International Law through the UN Security Council' (2010) 32 *Australian Feminist Law Journal* 99.

6 Note by the President of the Security Council, UN SCOR, UN Doc S/23500 (31 January 1992); *Prosecutor v Dusko Tadic a/k/a 'Dule' (Decision on the Defence Motion for Interlocutory Appeal on Jurisdiction)* (International Criminal Tribunal for the Former Yugoslavia, Appeals Chamber 29, 2 October 1995); *Prosecutor v Joseph Kanyabashi (Decision on the Defence Motion on Jurisdiction)* (International Criminal Tribunal for Rwanda 29, Trial Chamber II, Case No ICTR-96-15-T, 18 June 1997); Daniel Pickard, 'When Does Crime Become a Threat to International Peace and Security?' (1998) 12 *Florida Journal of International Law* 1, 19–20.

7 Inger Österdahl, *Threat to the Peace: The Interpretation by the Security Council of Article 39 of the UN Charter* (Iustus, 1998) 98.

8 My most vivid memory of violence is not physical but verbal. When someone I had known my whole life found out I was queer they informed me that I was an abomination and a threat to the safety and wellbeing of all people, especially children. I was told this while their children were being looked after by someone who I knew to be a child sex offender. The absurdity of this incident is still not lost on me.

in the form of armed force, might be formally authorised comes from these experiences. I personally think the anticipation of impending violence is worse than the experience of violence itself, but that may not be the case for everyone. With my interest in the issue acknowledged, I begin by examining the justificatory discourse of the P5 on the relationship between sexual violence in war and the finding of a threat to the peace. I then discuss how the choice of language largely excludes all forms of sexual violence outside of a heteronormative, male perpetrator/female victim framework and explain why this is problematic, in spite of the good work being done to address sexual violence.[9] Although the question of whether sexual violence as a tactic of war could be considered a threat to the peace was a relatively settled matter by the end of 2010, the debate regarding the Security Council's involvement in combating wartime sexual violence has continued. Therefore, statements made at meetings since 2010 continue to provide insight into the heteronormative discourse of the P5 and will also be discussed.

P5 discussions of sexual violence as a 'tactic of war' and/or 'threat to the peace'

The topic of sexual violence as a tactic of war has received significant attention from the Security Council during the last decade, with official reports and meeting transcripts on this issue generating around 1,000 pages of text between 2008 and June 2016. There was pressure from a number of states for the Council to take action in relation to article 39 by recognising that the use of widespread and systematic sexual violence as a tool of war could constitute a threat to the peace. However, all six of the relevant resolutions were made under Chapter VI of the UN Charter,[10] which means they did not rely on an article 39 determination. Instead, the resolutions expressed concern about sexual violence as a tactic of war. In order to discover the diversity of positions taken by the P5 on the relationship between sexual violence as a tactic of war and as a threat to the peace, we must look beyond the resolutions. From 2008 to 2011, there was significant discussion of the relationship of sexual violence as a tactic of war and the concept of threat to the peace in the Security Council's debates on Women, Peace and Security.[11] Some of the debates in this time period relating to Children and Armed

9 The use of heteronormative language also serves to contribute to, and perpetuate, unhelpful and limiting gender stereotypes. See, eg, Heathcote, above n 5, 99–100; Dianne Otto, 'Queering Gender [Identity] in International Law' (2015) 33 *Nordic Journal of Human Rights* 299.

10 Resolution 1820, S/RES/1820; SC Res 1882, S/RES/1882 (2009); Resolution 1888, S/RES/1888; Resolution 1960, S/RES/1960; SC Res 2106, S/RES/2106 (2013); SC Res 2272, S/RES/2272 (2016).

11 Repertoire of the Practice of the Security Council, *16th Supplement 2008–2009 Part VII: Actions with Respect to Threats to the Peace, Breaches of the Peace, and Acts of Aggression (Chapter VII of the Charter)*, 454–5; Repertoire of the Practice of the Security Council,

Conflict also addressed this issue.[12] Between 2008 and 2010, the Secretary-General's reports on the issue of sexual violence as a tactic of war provided details of its occurrence in ten non-international armed conflicts already on the Council's agenda,[13] and in an additional three conflict settings.[14] Further, the Secretary-General recommended that the Council find this issue to be a threat to the peace,[15] highlighting the importance placed upon the issue by the UN Secretariat, which is responsible for most of the Security Council's fact-finding. That some members of the P5 ignored this recommendation also highlights the Secretariat's limited ability to influence Council decisions and outcomes. I turn now to a brief discussion of the context of the Security Council debates about the problem of sexual violence in war before examining the positions taken by each of the P5 on the question of whether it could constitute a threat to the peace.

Context of the debates

The issue of sexual violence as a tactic of war was first raised at the Security Council by the United Kingdom,[16] following a conference jointly organised by the UN Development Fund for Women (now known as UN Women), the UN Department of Peacekeeping Operations and the UK government. The conference was aimed at 'the prevention of widespread and systematic sexual violence in conflict and post-conflict contexts'.[17] The Security Council debate this prompted led eventually to the unanimous adoption of Resolution 1820,[18] the first Security Council resolution focused solely on the issue of sexual violence as a tactic of war, and the second of its Women, Peace and Security resolutions. Resolution 1820 included a provision requiring the Secretary-General to monitor data relating to occurrences of wartime sexual violence and report to the Security Council on

17th Supplement 2010–2011 Part VII: Actions with Respect to Threats to the Peace, Breaches of the Peace, and Acts of Aggression (Chapter VII of the Charter), 27–9.

12 SC 6114th Mtg, UN Doc S/PV.6114 (29 April 2009); SC 6114th Mtg, UN Doc S/PV.6114 (Resumption 1) (29 April 2009).

13 These conflicts were Afghanistan, Burundi, Central African Republic, Chad, Côte d'Ivoire, Democratic Republic of the Congo, Haiti, Iraq, Somalia and Sudan. UN Secretary-General, Children and Armed Conflict: Report of the Secretary-General, UN GAOR, 63rd sess, Agenda Item 60 (a), UN Doc A/63/785-S/2009/158 (26 March 2009) 17, 22, 24–6, 33, 36–7, 44–5, 55, 57, 66, 97, 104 ('Children and Armed Conflict').

14 These conflicts were Colombia, the Philippines and Uganda. Ibid 117, 126, 143.

15 UN Secretary-General, Report of the Secretary-General pursuant to Security Council Resolution 1820, UN SCOR, UN Doc S/2009/362 (20 August 2009) [56] ('SG Report Resolution 1820').

16 Karen Pierce, Letter Dated 16 June 2008 from the Charge D'affaires A.I. of the Permanent Mission of the United Kingdom of Great Britain and Northern Island to the United Nations Addressed to the President of the Security Council, UN SCOR, UN Doc S/2008/402 (18 June 2008).

17 Ibid 2.

18 Resolution 1820, S/RES/1820; SC 5916th Mtg, UN Doc S/PV.5916 (Resumption 1) (19 June 2008) 40.

progress of implementation of the Resolution.[19] The Resolution also called for, inter alia, an immediate cessation of the use of sexual violence as a tactic of war, parties to conflicts to take immediate steps to prevent its use and the Secretary-General to implement effective training for peacekeeping forces to prevent and respond to wartime sexual violence.[20] Soon after, the Secretary-General's 2008 annual report on *Women and Peace and Security* characterised sexual violence as a tactic of war and a systematic security concern that needed to be addressed.[21] The report emphasised the urgent need to prevent sexual violence in war,[22] but did not include a recommendation in relation to Chapter VII.

The problem of wartime sexual violence was also highlighted in the Secretary-General's 2009 annual report on *Children in Armed Conflict*.[23] While the report generally addressed issues surrounding the involvement of children in armed conflicts, it identified the use of sexual violence as a tactic of war in numerous ongoing conflicts.[24] The report also contained a section addressing issues of sexual violence in war as experienced by children, focusing on the particular vulnerability of children and the widespread under-reporting of sexual violence being perpetrated against children in armed conflict situations,[25] but it did not characterise the problem as a threat to the peace.

In 2009, the Secretary-General presented his first report pursuant to the implementation of Resolution 1820. The report made for difficult reading. It noted, inter alia, the use of sexual violence as a tactic of war in conjunction with genocide and ethnic cleansings,[26] the inadequacy of municipal law in states where wartime sexual violence is occurring and how this compounds impunity issues,[27] how the majority of amnesties in conjunction with peace negotiations undermine efforts to combat impunity,[28] the inadequacy of support systems for survivors of wartime sexual violence[29] and that sexual violence is a tactic used by both state and non-state actors in conflict.[30] Most importantly, for present purposes, the Secretary-General urged the Security Council to address the issue under Chapter VII as a threat to the peace.[31] While no specific recommendations

19 Resolution 1820, S/RES/1820 [15].
20 Ibid [2]–[3], [6]–[7], [9].
21 UN Secretary-General, Women and Peace and Security: Report of the Secretary-General, UN SCOR, UN Doc S/2008/622 (25 September 2008) [5]–[7].
22 Ibid [96]–[97].
23 Children and Armed Conflict, UN Doc A/63/785-S/2009/158.
24 The specific conflicts are detailed at above nn 13, 14.
25 Ibid 154–60; for a definition of children in the context of armed conflict see article 38 of the Convention on the Rights of the Child, opened for signature 20 November 1989, 1577 UNTS 3 (entered into force 2 September 1990).
26 SG Report Resolution 1820, UN Doc S/2009/362, [15]–[16].
27 Ibid [23].
28 Ibid [28].
29 Ibid [30].
30 Ibid [45].
31 Ibid [56].

were made about what sort of enforcement measures the Council should employ, it is clear that resolutions made under Chapter VII would be legally binding on all states – in contrast to the current non-binding Chapter VI resolutions. This would open the door to a wide range of sanctions and the possibility of the Security Council authorising the use of force in conflicts where sexual violence is used as a military tactic.

The 6302nd Security Council Meeting in April 2010 included oral briefings from the recently appointed Special Representative of the Secretary-General on Sexual Violence in Conflict,[32] Margot Wallström, who highlighted that:

> From the Trojan War to the nuclear age, rape has existed in symbiotic relationship with armed conflict. And yet, it is a relationship we are just beginning to understand. History has perpetuated the ancient myth of 'arms and the man', prioritizing the plight of soldiers on the front lines while relegating women to the sidelines.[33]

She also noted, 'our approach to rape in places where peace and order prevail no more equips us to address systematic rape as a war strategy than our approach to murder prepares us for genocide. . . . [T]he crimes are incomparable'.[34] In the oral briefings related to the passing of Resolution 1960, the third resolution on sexual violence, the Secretary-General noted, '[s]exual violence is one of the only crimes where the victims – and not the perpetrators – are left with stigma',[35] and '[h]istorically, sexual violence by soldiers was prosecuted with a view to restoring military discipline, rather than upholding women's rights'.[36] Notably, both the Secretary-General and Wallström present wartime sexual violence in heteronormative terms. They characterise all perpetrators as male direct participants to hostilities, and all victims as female civilians, even though, by their own evidence, wartime sexual violence occurs more broadly.[37] That the dynamic of male belligerent perpetrator/female civilian victim is the most common form of sexual violence in war is not in dispute. However, what would it have cost them to use more inclusive language so that other victims of sexual violence would not be silenced and excluded, and the violence they have suffered further compounded?

While adopting Resolution 1960 extended the Secretary-General's monitoring and reporting requirements, it also signalled the death knell for considerations of sexual violence being a threat to the peace.[38] At this time it became abundantly clear that Russia would veto any attempt to have sexual violence as a tactic of

32 This position was established in Resolution 1888, S/RES/1888 [4].
33 SC 6302nd Mtg, UN Doc S/PV.6302 (27 April 2010) 2.
34 Ibid.
35 SC 6453rd Mtg, UN Doc S/PV.6453 (16 December 2010) 3.
36 Ibid 5.
37 Children and Armed Conflict, UN Doc A/63/785-S/2009/158 [154]–[155].
38 For more details on the effect of Resolution 1960 see Heathcote, above n 5.

war defined in this way.[39] Pursuant to its Women, Peace and Security agenda, the Security Council has continued to debate its involvement in combating wartime sexual violence and the issue was also discussed in one meeting of the 'Protection of Civilians in Armed Conflict' thematic agenda.[40] Yet it was not until June 2013 that the presumption of male belligerent perpetrator/female civilian victim was broken. In the 6948th Security Council Meeting in April 2013, Zaninab Bangura, who had replaced Wallström as the Special Representative, noted that for over 20 years the United Nations has had evidence of widespread and systematic rape of women, girls and men as a tactic of war.[41] At the same time, Bangura observed, appropriately, that the vast majority of instances fit the dynamic of male perpetrator/female victim.[42] However, five years after adopting the first Council resolution devoted to addressing sexual violence, the inclusion of men as potential victims was an important step to more inclusive language and policies that will diminish the number of silenced victims and work against impunity for perpetrators.

The use of more inclusive language by the Secretary-General and other individuals briefing the Security Council has continued since then. In the 7160th Meeting, the Secretary-General noted that wartime sexual violence affected all facets of society, 'women and men, girls and boys'.[43] Similarly, when Helen Durham briefed the Council on behalf of the International Committee of the Red Cross in relation to the protection of civilians in armed conflict, she noted that '[w]hile also affecting men and boys during armed conflict, the impact of sexual violence on women and girls is disproportionately greater'.[44] Her statement makes it clear that women and girls are most often the victims, yet does not exclude the recognition that victims may also include men and boys. The use of this type of inclusive language is evident in all following briefings to the Security Council.[45] Yet there continues to be silence about the particular vulnerabilities of those in the LGBTIQA community who express non-stereotypical queer gender and sexual identities.

The justificatory discourse of the P5

The justificatory discourse of the P5 regarding the relationship between sexual violence as a tactic of war and the concept of threat to the peace ranged from: insistence that sexual violence as a tactic of war in and of itself constitutes a threat

39 See below for Russian meeting statements on sexual violence in armed conflict.
40 SC 7374th Mtg, UN Doc S/PV.7374 (30 January 2015).
41 SC 6984th Mtg, UN Doc S/PV.6984 (24 June 2013) 4.
42 Ibid.
43 SC 7160th Mtg, UN Doc S/PV.7160 (25 April 2014) 2.
44 SC 7374th Mtg, S/PV.7374 (2015) 5.
45 SC 7428th Mtg, UN Doc S/PV.7428 (15 April 2015) 2–5; SC 7704th Mtg, UN Doc S/PV.7704 (2 June 2016) 2–5.

to the peace[46] by the United Kingdom, implied support for the notion by France, non-commitment by the United States, and disagreement by Russia and China, albeit for different reasons. While the position of each of the P5 differed on the relationship between sexual violence as a tactic of war and the finding of a threat to the peace, the justificatory discourse used to substantiate and articulate their positions focused on two main issues. The arguments centred, first, on the relationship between violence against women in armed conflict and the Security Council's mandate to maintain international peace and security and, second, on the Council's role in women's equality politics generally. Further, all of the P5 used heteronormative language to articulate their position, which has only recently begun to see some change.

The United Kingdom made its position on this issue clear from the outset. In the debates preceding adoption of the first sexual violence resolution, Resolution 1820, the United Kingdom stated that 'widespread and systematic sexual violence can pose a threat to international peace and security',[47] and acts of sexual violence as a warfare tactic are 'such unacceptable abuses that [they] threaten international peace and security'.[48] Beyond this they countered the argument that conflict-related sexual violence has always existed and therefore does not warrant an extension to the understanding of threat to the peace:

> But some, of course, will say, what is new about this? After all, it is true that rape and sexual violence have been associated with conflict before records began to be kept. Three things have changed. First, sexual violence is now being used as a tool of warfare, rather than it being just a tragic by-product of conflict, and it is taking place on a much larger scale than we have seen before. Secondly, we now better understand how sexual violence damages the prospects of postconflict recovery. And, thirdly and perhaps most important, we have the means to tackle this problem within our reach.[49]

They argued that the Security Council needed to take a leadership role by proposing practical measures that can be taken by all parties to armed conflict to prevent such tactics and to ensure those who commit sexual violence in conflict are 'brought to justice'.[50]

The United Kingdom made it clear that sexual violence in armed conflict was not simply a women's equality issue, but an issue of international peace and

46 While the positions of the P5 regarding threat to the peace varied greatly, all states supported Security Council action on this issue generally; see Resolution 1820, S/RES/1820; SC Res 1882, S/RES/1882 (2009); Resolution 1888, S/RES/1888; Resolution 1960, S/RES/1960; SC Res 2106, S/RES/2106 (2013); SC Res 2272, S/RES/2272 (2016).
47 SC 5916th Mtg, S/PV.5916 (2008) 14.
48 SC 6453rd Mtg, S/PV.6453 (2010) 10–11.
49 SC 5916th Mtg, S/PV.5916 (2008) 14.
50 Ibid 15.

security.[51] They suggested a number of strategies. First, sexual violence monitoring and reporting mechanisms needed to be expanded to include children (with no mention of gender) in addition to women.[52] Second, that '[i]f we are serious about preventing and resolving conflict, then we need to be serious about addressing conflict-related sexual violence'.[53] The key to ending sexual violence as a tactic of war in the long term was to establish and develop the rule of law in areas of war and post-conflict recovery,[54] and to end impunity for perpetrators.[55] The United Kingdom's commitment to action was reiterated: 'this requires more than just warm words; it requires meaningful actions that will ultimately make a difference to the situation of women on the ground'.[56]

In advocating for a finding of threat to the peace in relation to sexual violence, the United Kingdom's arguments were unremittingly heteronormative. That the alternative to classification as a threat to the peace was to classify the problem as solely a women's issue, illustrates their heteronormative assumptions and also explains their decision to debate wartime sexual violence as a part of the Women, Peace and Security agenda. The issue is thereby narrowed by focusing solely on the most affected group, and the opportunity for all victims to be represented is lost. Even if this focus was a strategic decision, made to garner support for a finding of threat to the peace in relation to sexual violence as a tactic of war, it undermines the United Kingdom's calls for ending impunity. That use of inclusive language would not have undermined their position on threat to the peace can be seen in the post-2010 statements by the United Kingdom. After the question of whether sexual violence could constitute a 'threat to the peace' had been settled in 2010, the United Kingdom began to speak about wartime sexual violence in broader terms than simply female civilian victims, often using gender-inclusive language. In the 6722nd Security Council Meeting in February 2012, they urged an end to impunity for 'conflict-related sexual violence against women, men, girls, and boys'.[57] Later in the 7374th Meeting, in January 2015, they called for special provisions in humanitarian programming 'for vulnerable populations, such as the young, the disabled, the elderly and the lesbian, gay, bisexual, transgender and intersex communities',[58] while also acknowledging that female civilians are the largest group impacted by wartime sexual violence.[59]

France's position on the issue of sexual violence in armed conflict was clear in their opening statement in the debates preceding the adoption of Resolution 1820:

51 SC 6302nd Mtg, S/PV.6302 (2010) 7.
52 SC 6114th Mtg, S/PV.6114 (2009) 28.
53 SC 6180th Mtg, UN Doc S/PV.6180 (7 August 2009) 23.
54 Ibid.
55 SC 6114th Mtg, S/PV.6114 (2009) 28; SC 6195th Mtg, UN Doc S/PV.6195 (30 September 2009) 8; SC 6411th Mtg, UN Doc S/PV.6411 (26 October 2010) 23–4.
56 SC 6411th Mtg, S/PV.6411 (2010) 24.
57 SC 6722nd Mtg, UN Doc S/PV.6722 (23 February 2012) 16.
58 SC 7374th Mtg, S/PV.7374 (2015) 8.
59 Ibid.

'The history of men has long been the history of their violence. In that intermarriage of blood and history, the war of men has all too often also been the story of violence against women.'[60] The French continued to treat violence against women during war as a security issue, through the following debates. When discussing whether or not the Security Council should act specifically on sexual violence as a tactic of war, they argued that it should:

> Doubts have at times been raised: should a debate on the issue of sexual violence in armed conflict be included on the agenda of the Security Council, which debates issues of peace and war? For France, that debate has been decided. One cannot establish peace by remaining silent on the subject of rape and violence done to women.[61]

However, France only implied its support for the notion that wartime sexual violence could be the basis of a finding of a threat to the peace under article 39, through its statement of full support for the Secretary-General's recommendations in his report pursuant to Resolution 1820 (discussed above), which included the Security Council taking Chapter VII action on this issue;[62] support that was reiterated in April 2010.[63] In both the Women, Peace and Security and Children and Armed Conflict thematic agendas, France argued the key to ending sexual violence as a tactic of war was to end impunity,[64] proposing that the presence of sexual violence as a tactic of war be added to the criteria examined when the Council considers the imposition of sanctions under Chapter VII in response to a situation.[65] Beyond ending impunity, they suggested '[f]ocus needs to be placed on the prevention of sexual violence, in particular to ensure that such violence does not become a systematic tactic of warfare'.[66]

Like the United Kingdom, in all these discussions about whether wartime sexual violence could constitute a threat to the peace, France spoke only in heteronormative terms, assuming female victims and male perpetrators. Following the rejection of a threat to the peace approach in 2010, France continued to adhere to a heteronormative framework in its focus on ending impunity, with only one exception.[67] In the 7160th Meeting, France highlighted that '[w]omen, men and children are being sexually abused', while also observing that women

60 SC 5916th Mtg, S/PV.5916 (2008) 16.
61 Ibid.
62 SC 6180th Mtg, S/PV.6180 (2009) 8.
63 SC 6302nd Mtg, S/PV.6302 (2010) 15.
64 SC 5916th Mtg, S/PV.5916 (2008) 17; SC 6114th Mtg, S/PV.6114 (2009) 14; SC 6411th Mtg, S/PV.6411 (2010) 20.
65 SC 6453rd Mtg, S/PV.6453 (2010) 13.
66 SC 6302nd Mtg, S/PV.6302 (2010) 15.
67 SC 6722nd Mtg, S/PV.6722 (2012) 20–1; SC 6948th Mtg, UN Doc S/PV.6948 (17 April 2013) 17–18; SC 6984th Mtg, S/PV.6984 (2013) 12; SC 7374th Mtg, S/PV.7374 (2015) 15; SC 7428th Mtg, S/PV.7428 (2015) 8–9.

and girls are disproportionately impacted by sexual violence due to the risk of pregnancy.[68]

The US position has been clear and consistent. At the meeting discussing the adoption of Resolution 1820, they said '[w]hen women and girls are preyed upon and raped, the international community cannot be silent or inactive. It is our responsibility to be their advocates and their defenders.'[69] Further, '[the US is] proud that today we can respond to that lingering question with a resounding "yes". This world body now acknowledges that sexual violence in conflict zones is, indeed, a security concern'.[70] Later in December 2010, the United States declared, 'our shared responsibility for the maintenance of international peace and security includes a profound responsibility to safeguard the lives and security of women and girls, who make up at least half of humankind'.[71] This clarity about the Security Council's responsibility to address sexual violence in armed conflict as a security concern did not extend to the question of whether, when the issue was sufficiently grave, sexual violence would constitute a threat to the peace. At no point in the debates did the United States express a position on this question. Rather, they continued to use general language, for example, 'the fight to end sexual violence has yet to be universally recognised as central to securing international peace and security'.[72]

In the view of the United States, sexual violence as a tactic of war is a security issue (but not necessarily a threat to the peace) and is accompanied by the argument that the way to end sexual violence is through ending impunity.[73] Further, they have characterised amnesties as a 'troubling dynamic of men with guns forgiving other men with guns for crimes committed against women. If peace processes are to succeed and endure, they must avoid this pitfall'.[74] The United States has also addressed the issue in more complex terms, as needing cultural and social change:

> It is time for all of us to assume our responsibility to go beyond condemning this behaviour and take concrete steps to end it, to make it socially unacceptable, to recognize that it is not cultural; it is criminal. And the more we say that, over and over and over again, the more we will change attitudes

68 SC 7160th Mtg, S/PV.7160 (2014) 14–15.
69 SC 5916th Mtg, S/PV.5916 (2008) 4.
70 Ibid 3.
71 SC 6453rd Mtg, S/PV.6453 (2010) 25.
72 Ibid 24.
73 SC 6180th Mtg, S/PV.6180 (2009) 4–5; SC 6195th Mtg, S/PV.6195 (2009) 3; '[We are eager to work] to ensure a coordinated approach to addressing a series of critical issues, ending the cycle of impunity, helping national authorities strengthen the rule of law . . . providing assistance to victims and creating a framework to prevent emerging or recurring outbreaks of violence or to provide early warning if they cannot be staved off': SC 6302nd Mtg, S/PV.6302 (2010) 9; SC 6453rd Mtg, S/PV.6453 (2010) 25.
74 SC 6180th Mtg, S/PV.6180 (2009) 5.

> and create peer pressure and the conditions for the elimination of this violation.[75]

Once the question of whether sexual violence as a tactic of war might constitute a threat to the peace was off the agenda, the language used by the United States became extremely broad and inclusive. While the focus remained on female civilians as victims, the language was often gender neutral or inclusive of other types of victims. The United States stated, for example, when discussing the protection of civilians in armed conflict, that war 'does not discriminate on the basis of gender, [but] does disproportionately affect those who are marginalized, vulnerable or oppressed'.[76] Finally, at the 7704th Meeting, on 2 June 2016, the United States stressed the need for improved documentation of violations 'against marginalized groups of victims, including women and girls, men and boys, ethnic and religious minorities; and lesbian, gay, bisexual, transgender and intersex individuals'.[77] This inclusive language supports their goal of ending impunity for perpetrators by not silencing or excluding any victim category.

While Russia supported each of the six resolutions that dealt specifically with sexual violence as a tactic of war, taking the position that 'in conflict as in peacetime, sexual violence is a detestable crime that requires condemnation and strict sanctioning',[78] this support was given under protest. Russia repeatedly argued that singling out one particular type of violence against women and children, in isolation from other threats they faced in armed conflict, 'significantly reduces'[79] efforts to provide protection, end poverty and the inequalities that lead to conflict, and address gender inequality,[80] stating:

> The United Nations should, as a priority, respond to systematic mass violence against women and children. Equal attention should be given to all categories of such violence in conflicts. Of serious concern are cases in which women and children are killed or injured, including as a result of the indiscriminate or excessive use of force.[81]

Further, they argued since other UN agencies were addressing issues of sexual violence, the Security Council's role should be confined to the maintenance of international peace and security. Therefore, Council work on wartime sexual

75 SC 6195th Mtg, S/PV.6195 (2009) 4.
76 SC 7374th Mtg, S/PV.7374 (2015) 16.
77 SC 7704th Mtg, S/PV.7704 (2016) 10.
78 SC 5916th Mtg, S/PV.5916 (2008) 26.
79 SC 6005th Mtg, UN Doc S/PV.6005 (29 October 2008) 15.
80 Ibid 14–15; SC 5916th Mtg, S/PV.5916 (2008) 26; SC 6195th Mtg, S/PV.6195 (2009) 11; SC 6302nd Mtg, S/PV.6302 (2010) 16; SC 6411th Mtg, S/PV.6411 (2010) 28; SC 6453rd Mtg, S/PV.6453 (2010) 21.
81 SC 6005th Mtg, S/PV.6005 (2008) 15.

violence would be a 'hardly optimal'[82] use of resources. They asked, '[s]hould we really turn a blind eye to other grievous crimes against civilians, including women and children? In that connection, the Secretary-General's proposals [found in his report pursuant to Resolution 1820] merit careful study, perhaps in a broader context'.[83] Russia argued repeatedly that to address the issue in isolation failed to take into account the totality of protection issues during armed conflict.[84] It follows that Russia's position all along was that sexual violence as a tactic of war does not constitute a threat to the peace.[85]

The only instance where Russia's choice of language could perhaps be regarded as inclusive was in the 7374th Meeting in January 2015, when speaking on the topic of Protection of Civilians in Armed Conflict in relation to sexual violence. In this instance, they stated, '[w]omen and girls, as well as other categories of civilians, continue to be victims of various forms of violence'.[86] It is probably reading too much into this statement to treat it as an awkward attempt at inclusive language. Also, even though the subject matter of the debate was wartime sexual violence, Russia has consistently pointed out that sexual violence is only one of many horrors faced by civilians in conflict zones.[87]

The assumption of heteronormativity by Russia is hardly surprising. It reflects the hyper-masculine nationalist persona presented by the Russian President, Vladimir Putin. It is also not surprising given the institutionalised homophobia within Russia.[88] Yet this heteronormativity and adherence to gender stereotypes is arguably of little consequence. Russian assertions that wartime sexual violence is a symptom rather than a cause of war, and thus lies outside the Security Council's mandate, means their position has little impact upon the question of impunity and concerns about the silencing of certain victims, as all victims of wartime sexual violence are treated equally, in a sense, by being excluded from the mandate.

82 SC 5916th Mtg, S/PV.5916 (2008) 26.
83 SC 6180th Mtg, S/PV.6180 (2009) 14.
84 Ibid; SC 6195th Mtg, S/PV.6195 (2009) 11; SC 6302nd Mtg, S/PV.6302 (2010) 16; SC 6411th Mtg, S/PV.6411 (2010) 28; SC 6453rd Mtg, S/PV.6453 (2010) 21.
85 SC 6722nd Mtg, S/PV.6722 (2012) 15; SC 6948th Mtg, S/PV.6948 (2013) 20–1; SC 6984th Mtg, S/PV.6984 (2013) 25–6; SC 7160th Mtg, S/PV.7160 (2014) 20–1; SC 7374th Mtg, S/PV.7374 (2015) 10; SC 7428th Mtg, S/PV.7428 (2015) 17; SC 7704th Mtg, S/PV.7704 (2016) 21–2.
86 SC 7374th Mtg, S/PV.7374 (2015) 9.
87 SC 6984th Mtg, S/PV.6984 (2013) 25–6; SC 7160th Mtg, S/PV.7160 (2014) 21; SC 7428th Mtg, S/PV.7428 (2015) 17.
88 See, eg, Human Rights Committee, Communication No 1932/2010, 106th sess, UN Doc CCPR/C/106/D/1932/2010 (30 November 2012); Innokenty Grekov, 'Russia's Anti-Gay Law, Spelled Out in Plain English', *Policy.Mic* (8 August 2013) <http://mic.com/articles/58649/russia-s-anti-gay-law-spelled-out-in-plain-english#.67nRdKqKP>; Nora Fitzgerald and Vladimir Ruvinsky, 'The Fear of Being Gay in Russia: Putin's State Has Allowed Violence against the Russian LGBT Community to Spike', *Politico Magazine* (22 March 2015) <http://www.politico.com/magazine/story/2015/03/russia-putin-lgbt-violence-116202>.

Finally, China has taken the view that sexual violence is deeply related to war and thus within the Security Council's mandate for the maintenance of international peace and security.[89] At the first meeting on sexual violence, China acknowledged that '[i]n the many conflicts underway today, women continue to be the most direct victims, and violence against women remains an extremely grave concern'.[90] They have also consistently pointed out that sexual violence within armed conflict constitutes a violation of international law and urged all parties to conflicts to 'abide by international humanitarian law and international human rights law'.[91] However, given their interrelatedness, they argued wartime sexual violence should not be dealt with as an independent issue,[92] repeatedly stressing, 'Governments bear the primary responsibility for protecting women in their respective countries.'[93] In line with this view that sexual violence is a domestic issue, China argued, like Russia, the 'Security Council should focus on preventing and reducing instances of armed conflict, thereby decreasing the root causes of women's suffering'.[94]

Beyond this, China's position on violence against women was somewhat paradoxical. On the one hand, China welcomed 'concepts such as gender equality, the empowerment of women and the prevention of and fight against sexual violence',[95] regularly condemning 'all acts of violence against women in conflict situations, including sexual violence'.[96] On the other hand, China argued, like Russia, that the role of the Security Council was to deal with threats to international peace and security, and other UN organs are responsible where such a threat does not exist,[97] confirming that China does not see wartime sexual violence as a standalone issue of international security. They also stated in October 2008 that:

> Unable to protect their personal security, women can hardly take an effective part in peace processes or political life. We attach great importance to this question . . . As the organ that bears the primary responsibility for the

89 SC 5916th Mtg, S/PV.5916 (2008) 19; SC 6005th Mtg, S/PV.6005 (2008) 26.
90 SC 5916th Mtg, S/PV.5916 (2008) 19.
91 SC 6195th Mtg, S/PV.6195 (2009) 14; See also SC 5916th Mtg, S/PV.5916 (2008) 19; SC 6114th Mtg, S/PV.6114 (2009) 17; SC 6453rd Mtg, S/PV.6453 (2010) 18.
92 SC 5916th Mtg, S/PV.5916 (2008) 19; SC 6005th Mtg, S/PV.6005 (2008) 26.
93 SC 6180th Mtg, S/PV.6180 (2009) 21; see also SC 5916th Mtg, S/PV.5916 (2008) 20; SC 6114th Mtg, S/PV.6114 (2009) 18; SC 6195th Mtg, S/PV.6195 (2009) 14; SC 6302nd Mtg, S/PV.6302 (2010) 17; SC 6411th Mtg, S/PV.6411 (2010) 29; SC 6453rd Mtg, S/PV.6453 (2010) 18.
94 SC 6302nd Mtg, S/PV.6302 (2010) 17; See also SC 6005th Mtg, S/PV.6005 (2008) 26; SC 6114th Mtg, S/PV.6114 (2009) 17; SC 6180th Mtg, S/PV.6180 (2009) 20–1; SC 6411th Mtg, S/PV.6411 (2010) 29; SC 6453rd Mtg, S/PV.6453 (2010) 18.
95 SC 6180th Mtg, S/PV.6180 (2009) 20.
96 SC 6195th Mtg, S/PV.6195 (2009) 14; see also SC 5916th Mtg, S/PV.5916 (2008) 19; SC 6180th Mtg, S/PV.6180 (2009) 20; SC 6411th Mtg, S/PV.6411 (2010) 29; SC 6453rd Mtg, S/PV.6453 (2010) 18.
97 SC 6195th Mtg, S/PV.6195 (2009) 14; SC 6411th Mtg, S/PV.6411 (2010) 30; SC 6453rd Mtg, S/PV.6453 (2010) 18.

> maintenance of international peace and security, the Security Council should step up its efforts for the prevention and resolution of conflicts so that the root causes of women's suffering in war can be removed and their rights and interests protected to the greatest extent possible.[98]

While China may attach great importance to the question of gender equality, other statements call this into question. By insinuating that women are incapable of protecting themselves, China demonstrates a stereotyped view of women as victims who lack agency, and therefore need to be protected, in a more overt way than any other P5 state. Rather than understanding that women suffer oppression, sexual violence and exclusion from civil society as a result of social structures that systematically privilege men, their approach naturalises these structures, which perpetuate gender equality. China's heteronormative approach to wartime sexual violence continued through all the ensuing debates.[99]

Even though China's approach is very similar to Russia's, its impact was far more consequential for two reasons. First, Russia did not make direct statements of support for gender equality, whereas China made such statements frequently. By failing to translate this support into inclusive language and support for Security Council action that promotes gender equality, China's position is hypocritical. The harm in this position is its dishonesty in offering words of hope to oppressed people only to have those hopes dashed by a failure to act on such words. Second, where Russia rejected the Council's role without a specific argument regarding who was responsible for protecting victims, China made it clear that this was the domestic responsibility of victims' states. The effect is to exclude and silence Chinese victims of wartime sexual violence from the international security agenda. While all of the P5 use language that reinforces oppressive and heteronormative gender stereotypes, China's reliance on them was the most overt.

This section has laid bare the peculiar nature of violence. Here we have the same set of facts – widespread use of sexual violence in armed conflict, usually (but not always) targeting women – yet this violence elicits different responses from each P5 state, with the only common ground being the decision to frame those responses in a heteronormative manner. Russia and China declare it to be somebody else's problem – in Russia's case there are other international organisations better able to address sexual violence which they see as a symptom of armed conflict, and for China it is the domestic responsibility of the states in question. For the United Kingdom, it is a Chapter VII Security Council issue, and France notionally supports the United Kingdom. The United States agrees it is a security issue, but has not committed itself to the use of Chapter VII. These varied

98 SC 6005th Mtg, S/PV.6005 (2008) 26.

99 SC 6722nd Mtg, S/PV.6722 (2012) 23–4; SC 6948th Mtg, S/PV.6948 (2013) 11–12; SC 6984th Mtg, S/PV.6984 (2013) 21; SC 7160th Mtg, S/PV.7160 (2014) 11–12; SC 7374th Mtg, S/PV.7374 (2015) 11; SC 7428th Mtg, S/PV.7428 (2015) 20–1; SC 7704th Mtg, S/PV.7704 (2016) 14–15.

responses highlight the way in which language use impacts legal formation, interpretation and application, the truly fascinating nature of violence, and most importantly, the difficulties with thinking of, analysing and addressing the Security Council as a unified entity.

As a researcher who works almost exclusively on security issues, and extensively on the Security Council, I am firmly of the belief that Russia is correct about the nature of the issue of wartime sexual violence and the role of the Council. The Security Council is not the most appropriate international body to address sexual violence as it is a symptom of armed conflict, and the Council would serve victims better by working to resolve the conflict and allowing more competent organisations to address sexual violence. That said, the Council would better serve the victims of sexual violence by acknowledging it occurs in a broader framework than male perpetrator and female victim.

The problem with exclusionary language choices

It is well established that sexual violence as a tactic of war occurs in a manner beyond the dichotomy of male perpetrators/female victims, as predominantly discussed by the Security Council. In the years preceding these debates, there were a number of public demonstrations that sexual violence as a wartime tactic is not restricted to male perpetrators and female victims. Of particular note was the torture and abuse of Abu Ghraib prisoners of war who were subjected to sexual violence during interrogations by the US military.[100] The courts martial that took place as a result of these incidences,[101] as well as public statements made by officers involved,[102] demonstrated quite clearly that the sexual violence involved both male and female perpetrators, and male and female victims.[103] The investigation into this incident noted that sexual violence, conducted in conjunction with other abuses, was 'systematic'[104] in nature, and resulted from a broader tactical decision relating to interrogation of detainees for military intelligence.[105] Another widely publicised incident was the failure of Canadian Forces to stop sexual violence

100 Antonio M Taguba, 'Article 15-6 Investigation of the 800th Military Police Brigade' (Oversight Report, No AR 15-6, US Military, 27 May 2004) 16–17.

101 Thom Shanker, '6 G.I.'s in Iraq Are Charged with Abuse of Prisoners', *New York Times* (online) (21 March 2004) <http://www.nytimes.com/2004/03/21/international/middleeast/21IRAQ.html>; Associated Press, 'England Sentenced to 3 Years for Prison Abuse: Soldier Dishonorably Discharged for Abu Ghraib Scandal', *NBC News* (online) (28 September 2005) <http://www.nbcnews.com/id/9492624/ns/us_news-crime_and_courts/t/england-sentenced-years-prison-abuse/#.VJdMlF7AA>.

102 BBC Radio 4, 'Iraq Abuse "Ordered from the Top"', *BBC News* (online) (15 June 2004) <http://news.bbc.co.uk/1/hi/world/americas/3806713.stm>.

103 Taguba, above n 100, 16–20.

104 Ibid 16.

105 Ibid 18–20.

against boys in Afghanistan, committed by Afghan soldiers.[106] The redacted executive summary of the Board of Inquiry report, released on 19 April 2016, clears the Canadian Forces of any wrongdoing,[107] noting in particular that no ordering of Canadian Forces personnel to ignore sexual abuse committed by Afghan soldiers ever occurred.[108]

Despite strong evidence that sexual violence in war occurs outside of the framework of male perpetrators/female victims, the P5 have been unwilling to engage with the issue as a whole. By dealing almost exclusively with the most common type of wartime sexual violence, male belligerent perpetrator/female civilian victim, other forms of sexual violence have remained invisible, encouraging impunity for the perpetrators.[109] It could be argued that this was because the issue was discussed as a part of the Women, Peace and Security agenda; however, this is unconvincing for two reasons. First, it was also discussed in relation to children in armed conflict with evidence demonstrating the issue affected both boys and girls. Second, the choice to place the debates within this setting was an active decision that encouraged exclusion, rather than accidental.

There are a number of ways in which the P5's avoidance of discussing sexual violence in more inclusive ways might be explained. Acknowledging female perpetrators would undermine social and cultural constructions of women as innocents, inherently peaceful and incapable of committing such atrocities.[110] Where the sexual violence has a male victim, the reluctance can be explained by the prevalence of homophobia, which drives the belief that sexual violence feminises the victim and suggests they may be homosexual, rather than a victim of sexual violence.[111] The failure to engage with sexual violence involving those who cannot be classified as cisgendered can be understood as a direct result of the invisibility of individuals who do not neatly fit into the normalised gender binary and the fear of undermining heteronormative social structures.[112]

106 Rick Westhead, 'Don't Look, Don't Tell, Troops Told', *Toronto Star* (online) (16 June 2008) <https://www.thestar.com/news/2008/06/16/dont_look_dont_tell_troops_told.html>; Rick Westhead, 'Canadian Military Still Investigating Afghanistan Sex Assault Claim', *Toronto Star* (online) (4 July 2013) <http://www.thestar.com/news/world/2013/07/04/canadian_military_still_investigating_afghanistan_sex_assault_claim.html>.

107 National Defence and Canadian Armed Forces, Government of Canada, *Board of Inquiry – Allegation of Assault of a Civilian by Afghan National Security Forces and the Canadian Forces Response to Such Incidents* (2016) [1.30]–[1.44] <http://www.forces.gc.ca/en/about-reports-pubs-boards-inquiry/ptsd-exec-summary.page#summary>.

108 Ibid [1.41].

109 Helen Durham and Katie O'Byrne, 'The Dialogue of Difference: Gender Perspectives on International Humanitarian Law' (2010) 92(877) *International Review of the Red Cross* 31, 49.

110 Ibid 41–2.

111 Sandesh Sivakumaran, 'Male/Male Rape and the "Taint" of Homosexuality' (2005) 27 *Human Rights Quarterly* 1274, 1290; Durham and O'Byrne, above n 109, 48.

112 Laura J Shepherd and Laura Sjoberg, 'Trans- Bodies in/of War(s): Cisprivilege and Contemporary Security Strategy' (2012) 101 *Feminist Review* 5, 11; Dianne Otto,

Further, the domestic audience of each of the P5 may be an influencing factor. In the Western democracies of France, the United Kingdom and the United States, governments rely upon women's votes in election cycles, so there may be a fear that more inclusive language in relation to what many see as a 'women's issue' could alienate this block and endanger re-election.[113] For Russia, the failure to be more inclusive is clearly an extension of domestic institutionalised homophobia, where anti-gay laws and state violence against the LGBTIQA community is commonplace.[114] China's response may be accounted for by the continuing influence of Confucianism on Chinese law and society, particularly with regard to heteronormative gender roles and sexual morality.[115]

While these explanations may be true, they do not excuse the Security Council for perpetuating impunity in relation to sexual violence outside of a heteronormative framework. To engage in discussions of wartime sexual violence in a manner that addresses female perpetrators, male victims, and perpetrators and victims from the LGBTIQA community (in particular transgender people), in addition to the most common dynamic of male perpetrators/female victims, would help to end the impunity for sexual violence the P5 all profess to be concerned about. However, such a challenge to dominant heteronormative world views seems unlikely to happen any time soon, although hints of it can be seen in the more recent interventions by the United Kingdom and the United States. The Security Council is mandated to secure and maintain international peace and security. In choosing to use almost exclusively heteronormative language to debate an issue central to maintaining international peace and security, even if it does not warrant Chapter VII action, the Council has failed the world at large.

The analysis of the language used by the P5 when discussing the relationship between threat to the peace and sexual violence as a tactic of war reveals a number of things. First, it displays the wide variety of interpretations and focuses that are in play when discussing the issue of sexual violence which are not apparent when the resolutions are the only texts considered. Second, it reveals the policy decision of each of the P5 states to perpetuate gender binaries and the heteronormative stereotypes they rely upon. While this approach may have been successful in bringing the issue of wartime sexual violence to the foreground of international legal developments in the 1990s, the question for today is why this clearly

'Transnational Homo-Assemblages: Reading "Gender" in Counter-Terrorism Discourses' (2013) 4(2) *Jindal Global Law Review* 79, 82.

113 For examples of some mainstream feminism having issues with inclusion, see generally Otto, 'Queering Gender', above n 9, 306–9; Cleis Abeni, 'Feminist Germaine Greer Goes on Anti-Trans Rant over Caitlyn Jenner', *Advocate* (26 October 2015) <http://www.advocate.com/caitlyn-jenner/2015/10/26/feminist-germaine-greer-goes-anti-trans-rant-over-caitlyn-jenner>; Katie Ellis, 'Destroy the Joint, Sure, but Feminism Must Include Disability Politics', *The Conversation* (24 November 2014) <https://theconversation.com/destroy-the-joint-sure-but-feminism-must-include-disability-politics-51119>.

114 See, eg, at above n 88.

115 See, eg, Teemu Ruskola, 'Law, Sexual Morality, and Gender Equality in Qing and Communist China' (1994) 103 *Yale Law Journal* 2531.

exclusionary language continues to be used, despite not being supported by facts and despite its contribution to perpetuating impunity.

The evidence that the use of sexual violence as a tactic of war is more widespread than its most common form of male perpetrator/female victim is irrefutable and evidence to this effect was before the Security Council well before debating this issue. The possible reasons for their continued use of heteronormative language are ultimately not compelling. They serve only to legitimate cultures of impunity for sexual violence as a tactic of war, which can only create more harm in the long run. On the question of the relationship between sexual violence as a tactic of war and threats to the peace under Chapter VII, Russia makes the most compelling argument. Wartime sexual violence is one of many symptoms of war and for the Council to prioritise it as a Chapter VII trigger would distract from the many other devastating effects of war endured by civilians in conflict zones. Further, the Security Council can best combat wartime sexual violence by focusing on ending and preventing conflicts, just as the way to end violence against queer people is to change the structural inequalities, cultural beliefs and social practices that foster trans- and homo-phobia.

6 In spite

Testifying to sexual and gender-based violence during the Khmer Rouge period

*Maria Elander**

On 23 August 2016, Sou Sotheavy appeared before the Extraordinary Chambers in the Courts of Cambodia (ECCC) to give testimony. Before the bench, the parties and an auditorium filled with listeners, she spoke about her experience of being forced to marry during the Khmer Rouge regime. She told the Court how she had not known her spouse beforehand and how neither of them had been able to refuse the marriage. Sotheavy appeared as one of a handful of women and men to testify during the trial segment dedicated to the charge of the regulation of marriage as an 'other inhumane act' of crimes against humanity in the massive *Case 002* against the surviving leaders of the Communist Party of Kampuchea (CPK), colloquially known as the Khmer Rouge. While the testimony in itself is notable for the unusual charge of forced marriage as an international crime, Sotheavy's appearance further challenged stereotypes of victims of sexual and gender-based violence (SGBV). As a transgender woman, her experience of the marriage was as a person identifying as a woman, but forced to live as a man and marry a woman. Later she explained, 'forced marriage [for heterosexual persons] implies pain alone. However, for homosexual people . . . it became an impossible thing'.[1]

Testimonies are particular speech acts, a way of giving word to and bearing witness to an experience. Through testimony, experiences are given certain shape, guided by rituals, conventions and formal legal rules. Significantly, testimony requires someone who hears, someone who listens to the 'creation of knowledge *de novo*'.[2] If successful, testimony may turn an experience into knowledge, perhaps

* The research presented here stems in part from research conducted in Cambodia during June 2016, which was generously funded by the Faculty of Arts Special Studies Program Short at the University of Melbourne, ethics ID 1646468.1. I am also grateful to Khom Sakhan for translation and transcription, Amber Karanikolas for research assistance, the organisers and participants at the Feminist Experiences of Law Symposium in Melbourne where an earlier draft was presented, Dianne Otto for support and useful comments, and Sou Sotheavy for so generously sharing her story with me.

1 Interview with Sou Sotheavy (Phnom Penh, 4 June 2016).

2 Dori Laub, 'Bearing Witness, or the Vicissitudes of Listening' in Shoshana Felman and Dori Laub, *Testimony: Crises of Witnessing in Literature, Psychoanalysis and History* (Taylor & Francis, 2013) 57 (emphasis in original).

register an experience in law and history.[3] Testimonies occur at various places. Whether testimony can or should occur inside courtrooms has been fiercely debated.[4] With its demand for narrow factual details, often subjected to cross-examination, trial testimony in many ways runs counter to the workings of trauma. As a result, some have turned to alternative, non-judicial settings for the presentation of testimonies that can be given, listened to and registered without having to submit to legal evidentiary demands.[5] Testimonies may be disruptive. They may resist and challenge dominant narratives and trigger breaks in the understandings of a certain event. As Kali Tal puts it, 'bearing witness is an aggressive act . . . Its goal is change'.[6] On this basis, testimonies about experiences of SGBV are often presented 'in spite': in spite of silencing, in spite of cultures of shame and stigma. Those listening are interpellated as part of breaking the silence. By listening, they are part of registering and recognising this experience of sexual and gender-based harm.

It is within this context of testimony, and the questions about place, silence and the listener, that I examine the presentation of SGBV testimonies during the Khmer Rouge regime. In 2010, the ECCC decided not to charge the surviving leaders for the many rapes that had occurred in security centres, at worksites and in communes. The only charge explicitly presented as concerned with SGBV is the 'regulation of marriage' as a crime against humanity.[7] In order to hear testimonies about rape and sexual violence outside of marriage, civil society set up alternative, non-judicial hearings.[8] These have also been presented 'in spite': in spite of a court which failed to pay proper attention to the various forms of SGBV during the regime and in spite of cultures of silence. The non-judicial hearings are then places where experience of SGBV may be heard. Yet, as I argue, while these

3 The discussion about whether testimonies are beneficial for the person testifying or for societal reconciliation is not something I engage with here. Instead, see, eg, Fiona C Ross, 'On Having Voice and Being Heard: Some After-Effects of Testifying before the South African Truth and Reconciliation Commission' (2003) 3 *Anthropological Theory* 325.

4 See, eg, Marie-Bénédicte Dembour and Emily Haslam, 'Silencing Hearings? Victim-Witnesses at War Crimes Trials' (2004) 15 *European Journal of International Law* 151; John D Ciorciari and Anne Heindel, 'Trauma in the Courtroom' in Beth Van Schaack, Daryn Reicherter and Youk Chhang (eds), *Cambodia's Hidden Scars: Trauma Psychology in the Wake of the Khmer Rouge* (Documentation Center of Cambodia, 2011) 121.

5 I am thinking here both of tribunals that to some extent mimic legal hearings, often called Peoples' or Women's Tribunals, as well as hearings that are state organised, but not based on criminal law, such as truth and reconciliation hearings.

6 Kali Tal, *Worlds of Hurt: Reading the Literatures of Trauma* (Cambridge University Press, 1996) 7, quoted in Mona Lilja, *Gender in a Global/Local World: Resisting Gendered Norms: Civil Society, the Juridical and Political Space in Cambodia* (Ashgate, 2013) 70.

7 *Prosecutor v Chea (Closing Order)* (ECCC, Trial Chamber, Case No 002, 15 September 2010) ('*Case 002 Closing Order*'). I discuss the charge of the regulation of marriage in Maria Elander, 'Prosecuting the Khmer Rouge Marriages' (2016) 42 *Australian Feminist Law Journal* 163.

8 See below.

testimonies are framed as breaking silences and registering truths, the framing also leaves out some testimonies and experiences.

In this chapter, I describe two narratives on SGBV during the Khmer Rouge period that have emerged from survivor testimonies. One has been produced in the confines of the legal formality of the ECCC and the other in alternative non-judicial fora. While the criticism of trials for the way they limit testimony is well established, the alternative fora also establish limits to what can be told and heard through testimony. I start by describing the way in which SGBV during the Khmer Rouge regime has been dealt with in *Case 002*.[9] I then examine the responses by civil society and their production of an alternative narrative. I argue that while the testimonies organised by civil society are presented as acts of resistance against the silencing of SGBV by the ECCC, they are also acts of exclusion. To illustrate the exclusion, I turn to the testimonies by Sotheavy. Notably, her testimony cannot be heard in the alternative fora, but it is given space inside the courtroom.

Presenting sexual and gender-based violence at the ECCC

The ECCC is not known for having effectively dealt with SGBV during the Khmer Rouge period. This internationalised criminal court, operating within the Cambodian judicial system, but with certain international features such as substantive law, staffing and funding, began operating in 2006 after a long period of difficult negotiations.[10] To date, it has concluded one case, against the former head of notorious security centre S-21,[11] as well as the first part of *Case 002* against the surviving former leaders.[12] The trial hearings for the second part of *Case 002* are expected to finish by the end of 2016. The case as a whole covers the entire period over which the court has jurisdiction (17 April 1975 to 6 January 1979), and charges have been laid in relation to crimes including forced movement of population as a crime against humanity, genocide against the Cham and Vietnamese minorities, execution of soldiers of the former Khmer Republic and internal

9 It should be noted that the Khmer Rouge and the CPK are not synonyms. The 'Khmer Rouge' was a name accorded to the CPK by Prince Sihanouk. However, for purposes of brevity and simplicity, the two names will be used interchangeably here.

10 On the negotiations, see Tom Fawthrop and Helen Jarvis, *Getting Away with Genocide? Elusive Justice and the Khmer Rouge Tribunal* (University of New South Wales Press, 2005); David Scheffer, *All the Missing Souls, A Personal History of the War Crimes Tribunals* (Princeton University Press, 2012).

11 *Prosecutor v Eav (Judgement)* (ECCC, Trial Chamber, Case No 001, 26 July 2010).

12 There were initially four charged persons, but after Ieng Sary died in 2013 and Ieng Thirith was first found unfit for trial and then died in 2015, there are now two persons charged: Nuon Chea, former 'Brother no 2', and Khieu Samphan, former Head of State. In 2014, the two were found guilty of crimes against humanity and sentenced to life in prison, a conviction upheld on appeal. *Chea v Prosecutor (Appeal Judgement)* (ECCC, Supreme Court Chamber, Case No 002/01, 23 November 2016).

purges of 'traitors' – perceived political dissidents.[13] However, despite documented cases of SGBV in various contexts, the former leaders have only been charged with the regulation of marriage. The omission of a charge in relation to the many rapes at security centres, worksites and communes has been heavily criticised. For example, Margot Wallström, then UN Special Representative of the Secretary-General on Sexual Violence in Conflict, lamented: 'The Court, which was created to give justice to survivors, is faced with a pool of victims without recourse to justice – and the accountability and acknowledgment it brings – for the crimes they experienced as part of the general atrocities.'[14] So why were no charges brought against the leaders?

When investigations began in 2006 and 2007,[15] little attention was paid to SGBV. At the time, the dominant narrative held that rape and other forms of sexual violence had not been prevalent during the Khmer Rouge regime. The assumption was that the regime had promoted gender neutrality and that its moral codes had been so strict that if rape had occurred, both the perpetrator and victim would have been punished by death. As one historian put it, 'the KR . . . whatever their own sins, managed to keep [rape and violations against women] at an absolute minimum'.[16] Thus, faced with the massive task of investigating 'tens of thousands of criminal episodes',[17] SGBV was simply not high on the agenda of the ECCC investigators.[18]

The investigations into crimes committed by the senior leaders of the CPK took four years. During this period, research began to emerge that contradicted the belief that there had been few occurrences of rape or sexual violence. For example,

13 *Case 002 Closing Order* (ECCC, Trial Chamber, Case No 002, 15 September 2010).

14 Margot Wallström, 'The Forgotten Khmer Rouge Victims', *Phnom Penh Post* (online) (29 May 2012) <http://www.phnompenhpost.com/national/forgotten-khmer-rouge-victims>.

15 The ECCC follows the civil law system in which the prosecutors only conduct a preliminary investigation on the basis of which they then ask investigative judges to conduct an investigation. Because of its internationalised nature, there is one international and one national staff for each important post, ie co-prosecutors, co-investigative judges etc. The co-prosecutors began working in 2006 and the co-investigative judges opened their investigation in 2007.

16 Michael Vickery, 'Wrong on Gottesman', *Phnom Penh Post* (online) (28 January 2005) <http://www.phnompenhpost.com/national/wrong-gottesman>.

17 Global Brief, Interview with Andrew Cayley (9 September 2011) <http://globalbrief.ca/blog/2011/09/09/on-international-criminal-justice/>. Andrew Cayley was International Co-Prosecutor 2009–13.

18 Former Co-Prosecutor Andrew Cayley claims that the Office of the Prosecutor never 'ignored gender-based crimes' and that 'female victims were not forgotten', something former civil party lawyer Silke Studzinsky claims never translated into action. Andrew Cayley, 'KR's Female Victims Not Forgotten', *Phnom Penh Post* (Phnom Penh) (1 June 2012); Silke Studzinsky, 'Challenges to a Successful Prosecution of Sexualized and Gender-Based Crimes' (paper presented at the International Conference on Bangladesh Genocide and the Issue of Justice, Heidelberg, Germany, 4–5 July 2013) <http://www.civilparties.org/?page_id=48>.

based on interviews with some 2,100 people, academic Kasumi Nakagawa and the NGO, Cambodian Defenders Project (CDP), documented accounts of a range of experiences of SGBV, ranging from rape at security centres, to forced marriage, survival sex, sexual mutilation and forced nudity.[19] For Nakagawa, these accounts contradicted the dominant belief that if sexual violence had occurred at all, then all victims would have been killed. Instead, she found victims willing to speak about the crimes.[20] Meanwhile, ECCC civil party lawyer, Silke Studzinsky, met a large number of people who claimed to have suffered from SGVG during the regime. In 2008, one of them, Sou Sotheavy, lodged the first application at the ECCC to become a civil party.[21] Notably, this was in relation to gender-based crimes, not sexual violence.[22] Soon, there were hundreds of applicants.

The Closing Order[23] for *Case 002* against the surviving leaders was issued in 2010. And as noted above, this included a charge in relation to the regulation of marriage as a crime against humanity. The charge raises questions about what exactly the harm is that constitutes the offence. Is it possible to conceive of a gender-based crime that is not focused on rape or sexual violence?[24] In the Closing Order, the regulation of marriage appears as two charges: one of rape and one of other inhumane acts. But after the defence successfully challenged the legality of classifying rape as a constitutive underlying offence of crimes against humanity, arguing (controversially) that when the acts were committed in the 1970s, rape was not recognised in international law as a crime against humanity,[25] rape – within

19 The interviews were done in two phases, first with 1,500 persons, and second with 600. Nakagawa Kasumi, 'Gender-Based Violence During the Khmer Rouge Regime: Stories of Survivors from the Democratic Kampuchea (1975–1979)' (GBV Under the Khmer Rouge, 2nd edn, 2008) <http://gbvkr.org/wp-content/uploads/2013/02/Kasumi-GBV-Study-2007.pdf>.

20 Ibid 10.

21 At the ECCC, victims can apply to become civil parties. In the first case, this meant being party to the case, but in *Case 002* it means participating in the case. All civil parties are represented by a civil party lawyer.

22 Silke Studzinsky, 'First Civil Party Application before the Extraordinary Chambers in the Courts of Cambodia (ECCC) on Gender-Based Violence under the Khmer Rouge Regime' (Press Statement, 3 September 2008).

23 In accordance with the Internal Rules, the Closing Order 'sets out the identity of the Accused, a description of the material facts and their legal characterisation by the Co-Investigating Judges, including the relevant criminal provisions and the nature of the criminal responsibility'. Extraordinary Chambers in the Courts of Cambodia, *Internal Rules* (*Rev 9*) (adopted 16 January 2015) r 67(2).

24 Indeed, in a case at the Special Court for Sierra Leone, the Appeals Chamber held that forced marriage was there 'not predominantly a sexual crime': *Prosecutor v Brima* (*Judgment*) (Special Court for Sierra Leone, Appeals Chamber, Case No SCSL-2004-16-A, 22 February 2008).

25 Rape was enumerated in the Law on the Establishment of the ECCC as an underlying offence (art 5), but the legality was still successfully challenged. *Ieng Thirith Appeal against Closing Order* (ECCC, Pre-Trial Chamber, Case No 002, 18 October 2010) [61]; *Ieng Sary's Appeal against Closing Order* (ECCC, Pre-Trial Chamber, Case No 002, 25 October 2010) [218];

the context of the marriages – was reclassified as 'other inhumane acts'.[26] Even so, the factual description in the Closing Order includes descriptions of both the wedding ceremonies and the consummations of marriages, leaving significant traces of sexual violence. Much was left to be determined by the trial and the judgment.

Whereas the Closing Order made possible a hearing of the marriages during trial, no such thing occurred for the many documented rapes outside of marriage. This was not because the co-investigative judges did not believe rape had occurred, but because they struggled to see a link between these rapes and the surviving former leaders of the regime who were being charged. According to the co-investigative judges, 'Intimate relationships outside of marriage were considered to be against the collectivist approach of the CPK and therefore deemed "immoral" and associated with behaviours from the old regime.'[27] As justification for this view, the judges pointed to the existence of certain moral codes, which they translated as 'Do not take liberties with women' and 'We must not do anything detrimental to women'.[28] Furthermore, despite the fact that the status and position of the codes during the Khmer Rouge regime is disputed, the co-investigative judges considered them to reflect the official policy of the CPK. On that basis, they concluded the policy 'was to prevent its [rape's] occurrence and to punish the perpetrators. Despite the fact that this policy did not manage to prevent rape, it cannot be considered that rape was one of the crimes used by the CPK leaders.'[29] And so, no charges were brought against the leaders in relation to these rapes.

The omission of a charge of rape (outside of marriage) has been widely read as reinforcing the prevailing silence about SGBV during armed conflict. Despite the co-investigative judges' acceptance that rapes had occurred, their failure to see a link to the accused led many commentators to conclude that the occurrence of SGBV and its victims were again being silenced. In her criticism of the lack of attention to SGBV at the ECCC, Wallström warned:

> Unless the Court finds a way to address this issue, it will be perceived as implicitly re-enforcing the silence about conflict-related sexual violence, and not providing a counterbalance to the impunity that has prevailed.[30]

Decision on Appeals by Nuon Chea and Ieng Thirith against the Closing Order (ECCC Pre-Trial Chamber, Case No 002, 15 February 2011) [154].

26 *Decision on Appeals by Nuon Chea and Ieng Thirith against the Closing Order* (ECCC Pre-Trial Chamber, Case No 002, 15 February 2011) [154].

27 *Case 002 Closing Order* (ECCC, Trial Chamber, Case No 002, 15 September 2010) [191] (emphasis altered).

28 Ibid. See also de Langis for another reading of the moral codes: Theresa de Langis, '"This is Now the Most Important Trial in the World": A New Reading of Code #6, the Rule against Immoral Offenses under the Khmer Rouge Regime' (2014) 3 *Cambodia Law and Policy Journal* 61.

29 *Case 002 Closing Order* (ECCC, Trial Chamber, Case No 002, 15 September 2010) [1429].

30 Wallström, above n 14.

Thus, both the inclusion of the charge of forced marriage and the exclusion of the rapes outside of marriage are presented as in spite: The inclusion of marriages appears in spite of pressures of silencing, while the rapes outside marriage have been excluded in spite of documented occurrences. Consider the reading of the charges of forced marriages by Theresa de Langis. For her, they stand as

> the Court's best last chance to contribute to the ever-evolving body of law aimed at better responding to perpetually neglected sexual and other gender-based crimes in times of conflict and atrocity globally. Above all, by including forced marriage in Case 002/02, the ECCC will finally be in a position to explain to survivors – who have courageously broken decades-long silence despite the risk of social stigma and censure – how gender-based violence was a feature of the general mass violence of the catastrophic Khmer Rouge regime.[31]

Here, the charge of the regulation of marriage appears in spite of previous neglect both at the ECCC and elsewhere, and thereby becomes representative of SGBV in general. Meanwhile, the survivors are presented as having spoken in spite of cultures of silencing and stigma. And so, when the ECCC did not provide for a space to hear testimonies on rape outside of marriage, activists turned elsewhere.

Civil society efforts to hear sexual and gender-based violence

When the co-investigative judges failed to find a link between the defendants and the occurrence of rape and sexual violence outside of marriage, thereby not allowing the issue to go to trial, activists and NGOs in Cambodia stepped in to create other forums to hear testimonies. They also wanted to document the manifold forms that SGBV took during the regime. The NGOs produced alternative, non-judicial spaces in which survivors and witnesses have given testimony. As such, they have been important sites for knowledge production and possibly spaces which have enabled those giving testimony to narrate and give their own account of what happened. Without wanting to diminish the value of initiatives such as these, and definitely not wanting to lessen the testimonies presented, I believe the presentation and representation of the testimonies need to be examined for the way in which they were framed.

Consider the three Women's Hearings, organised by the CDP, with support provided to testifiers by the Transcultural Psychosocial Organisation Cambodia. The first hearing focused on Cambodian women's testimony about SGBV during the Khmer Rouge period, while the second took a broader approach by also including testimonies from women who had experienced SGBV during other conflicts in the Asia-Pacific region (Bangladesh, Timor Leste and Nepal).

31 Theresa de Langis, 'A Missed Opportunity, a Last Hope? Prosecuting Sexual Crimes under the Khmer Rouge Regime' (2014) 2 *Cambodia Law and Policy Journal* 39, 43.

The third hearing sought to establish an intergenerational link with the younger Cambodian generation. Each with slightly different foci, the three hearings followed similar formats: survivors and witnesses gave testimony, and a number of experts spoke on related topics, for example, applicable laws or broader evidence of the prevalence of SGBV during conflict. The testimonies were given before a panel composed of experts (other than those who testified) who presented a 'finding' towards the end.

The hearings have been presented as an occasion to tell and hear the 'truth' about what had happened. In 2011, the first hearing entitled 'True Voices of Women under the Khmer Rouge' was presented as a non-judicial, transitional justice mechanism for survivors of the Khmer Rouge, providing a forum for truth-telling about SGBV that took place during that time.[32] The hearing originated in a project that 'sought to reveal the truth about the prevalence of gender-based violence during the Khmer Rouge rule and, in doing so, uncovered a hidden part of Cambodian history'.[33]

In addition to truth-telling, the idea that they are being organised in spite of the tide of history working against them runs across the hearings. The first hearing was presented as organised because of 'great difficulties accessing justice and few opportunities to have their [survivors of SGBV perpetrated during the Khmer Rouge regime] stories heard'[34] and as complimenting the ECCC by 'ensur[ing] that sexual violence was included in the historical account of atrocities'.[35] In contrast, the report of the second hearing expresses impatience with the ECCC, with 'the inability or unwillingness of formal judicial mechanisms to deliver justice for survivors of gender-based crime'.[36]

How these notions of spite, truth and history-making work together is made clear in the foreword to the report from the first hearing written by Sok Sam Oeun, Executive Director of CDP. Here, he explains, the aim was 'to provide a forum for the survivors of sexual violence during the Khmer Rouge period to tell their stories and contribute to creating an accurate historical record of the crimes perpetrated under Khmer Rouge rule'.[37] He described the project as necessary to 'break the silence and impunity surrounding sexual violence'.[38] He quoted from

32 Alison Barclay and Beini Ye (eds), 'Women's Hearing: True Voices of Women under the Khmer Rouge, Report on the Proceedings of the 2011 Women's Hearing on Sexual Violence under the Khmer Rouge Regime' (Report, Cambodian Defenders Project, May 2012) 1.
33 Ibid.
34 Ibid 2.
35 Ibid.
36 Theresa de Langis, 'Asia-Pacific Regional Women's Hearing on Gender-Based Violence in Conflict: Report on the Proceedings 2012' (Report, Cambodian Defenders Project, December 2012) 3.
37 Sok Sam Oeun, 'Foreword' in Alison Barclay and Beini Ye (eds), 'Women's Hearing: True Voices of Women under the Khmer Rouge, Report on the Proceedings of the 2011 Women's Hearing on Sexual Violence under the Khmer Rouge Regime' (Report, Cambodian Defenders Project, May 2012) iv.
38 Ibid.

a speech given by Wallström, via video-link at the hearing, in which she stated that 'the history of rape has been a history of denial . . . every speaker who adds their voice to this debate is helping to end centuries of silence that have made rape an effective "secret weapon"'.[39]

Yet, although the hearings were presented as breaking silences, they were nevertheless silencing some experiences. Notably, all three hearings were exclusively about women's experience of SGBV. The one Cambodian man who testified spoke about the rape and murder of his sister.[40] Furthermore, in all the reports of the hearings, SGBV is used interchangeably with rape, as if rape was not only *one* form of SGBV, but *the* form. Somewhat contradicting this forefronting of rape as the primary form of SGBV is the link made to violence against women. The latter two hearings were partly funded by the UN Trust Fund to End Violence against Women, and this link is particularly apparent at the third hearing, which was presented as aiming 'to raise awareness [of young Cambodians] of SGBV and initiate discussion about responses to past crimes and prevention of future violence against women'.[41] By these means, in this alternative forum, SGBV during the Khmer Rouge period becomes sedimented as an issue that affects women and one that has a continuing impact on violence against women into the present.

The focus on women is reinforced by the opening of a new exhibition in March 2016, 'Sorrows and Struggles: Women's Experience of Forced Marriage during the Khmer Rouge Regime', at the Tuol Sleng Genocide Museum ('Tuol Sleng') in Phnom Penh.[42] Together with the Choeung Ek Killing Fields located about 10 kilometres away, Tuol Sleng stands as the primary museum and memorial of the Khmer Rouge regime. As such, it is an important space to which both Cambodians and foreigners come to remember, honour the victims and learn about the period and the regime. A new museum director was recently appointed and much has since happened. In addition to the introduction of an audio tour and the opening of a room specifically designed for reflection, the exhibition on the Khmer Rouge marriages is located in two rooms on the third floor, above the space which, when the place served as Security Centre S-21, was reserved for female prisoners.[43]

39 Ibid.

40 Barclay and Ye (eds), above n 32, 6.

41 'Women's Hearing with the Young Generation' (Panel Statement, Cambodian Defenders Project, 24 September 2013) 1.

42 George Wright, 'Tuol Sleng Exhibition to Tell Stories of Forced Marriage', *The Cambodia Daily* (online) (29 February 2016) <https://www.cambodiadaily.com/news/tuol-sleng-exhibition-to-tell-stories-of-forced-marriage-109152/>.

43 Audrey Wilson, 'Veil Lifting on Cadres' Unwanted Weddings', *Phnom Penh Post* (online) (27 February 2016) <http://www.phnompenhpost.com/post-weekend/veil-lifting-cadres-unwanted-weddings>.

The first room is meant to be interactive, featuring a model of a wedding ceremony as it occurred during the Khmer Rouge.[44] There is a makeshift altar and marks on the floor to indicate where visitors should stand. On one of the walls is a large print of the only known photo of a wedding ceremony from the period, said to depict the wedding between Nun Huy (also known as Huy Sre), head of re-education centre S-24, and Prok Khoeun (also known as Prak Samuth), an official at S-24 and later deputy of an interrogation team at S-21. Huy is believed to have been later killed when a prisoner escaped.[45] Across the room hang two rows of dark grey fabric with anonymous quotes, alternating between English and Khmer, written in white/silver by people who wed in such ceremonies: 'I take medicine daily to help with my mental trauma', one says. 'I did not know at all who my husband was', says another. The walls in the second room hold posters with information about the exhibition and about the particularities of marriage during the regime. Anonymous quotes are printed to form the shape of a silhouette, possibly showing the image of Prok Khoeun: 'Often have violence in the family', 'My baby died of malnutrition', 'I was afraid the children would hate their father', 'We feel no affection for each other' and 'My husband threatened to kill me'. There are seven panels scattered around the room with testimonies by six women and one man. Each testimony on the panels differs somewhat: a woman describes trying to resist being married but eventually being forced, and how she was later violently forced to consummate the marriage. Another woman tells how she was forced to marry a man who was Cham (Muslim)[46] and that she eventually decided to convert to Islam. A third woman describes a marriage characterised by domestic violence. While the pamphlet that introduces the exhibitions states it sought to include a man's perspective and thereby 'acknowledge . . . [men's] suffering as victims of forced marriage',[47] the exhibition is clearly about the suffering of women.

Like the hearings, the exhibition frames the testimonies within a context of violence against women and presents women as the primary victims. According to the local newspaper, the *Phnom Penh Post*, work on the exhibition began after a meeting with the Women's Association of the Ministry of Culture and Fine Arts and, as the museum director put it in an interview for the article, 'We really want to focus on the impact to women'.[48] The exhibition draws heavily on a research project by Theresa de Langis that recorded Cambodian women's oral histories.[49]

The testimonies in the civil society hearings and at the museum are all presented as in spite, in particular in spite of silencing. Perhaps also in spite of the ECCC

44 The following description is from my visits to the place in June 2016.

45 Wilson, above n 43.

46 Cham is a Muslim minority group in Cambodia. *Case 002* hears a charge of genocide against the Cham.

47 Text from presentation to exhibition. Photo on file with author.

48 Wilson, above n 43.

49 Cambodian Women's Oral History Project: Life Stories of Survival under the Khmer Rouge Regime, 'Testimonies' <http://cambodianwomenoralhistory.squarespace.com/>.

and its omission of a charge of rape outside marriage. If the aim is to shed light, or rather, to listen to experiences of SGBV, it is also important to listen to the way in which the testimonies are framed. At both the hearings and at the museum, the subject who has experienced SGBV is framed as a woman.

I now turn to the testimonies by Sou Sotheavy[50] which provide one example of an experience that is impossible to hear because of the framing of the testimonies in these two spaces. Notably, it was at the ECCC that Sotheavy testified, appearing twice, in relation to first the forced population movement and then the regulation of marriage. While the charge of forced population movement was never presented by the ECCC as one of gender-based harm, it did hold these dimensions,[51] something that Sotheavy's testimony clearly brought to the surface.

Sotheavy's courtroom testimony

> On 17 April 1975, I lived at the Olympic Stadium with the transgendered people. Khmer Rouge evacuated us from that Olympic Stadium. A lot of Khmer Rouge soldiers came to our place and we were ordered to leave the city at gunpoint. We were not given enough time to pack our luggage. They, upon reaching my room, opened – fired at us. My four friends died including Saray, Dy, Roatha, and Phalla. I was completely terrified. I bore witness to this execution.[52]

50 My account of her testimonies draws from a variety of sources such as the trial transcripts from her testimony on forced population movement ('Trial transcript 27 May 2013'). However, because the ECCC has at the time of writing (November 2016) not yet published the trial transcript for her testimony on the marriages, I use a video showing parts of her testimony that is available on the ECCC website: *Session 1 – 24 August 2016 – Case 002/02 – EN/FR* (24 August 2016) ECCC <https://www.eccc.gov.kh/en/video/trial-video/session-1-24-august-2016-case-00202-enfr>; *Session 2 – 24 August 2016 – Case 002/02 – EN/FR* (24 August 2016) ECCC <https://www.eccc.gov.kh/en/video/trial-video/session-2-24-august-2016-case-00202-enfr>; *Session 3 – 24 August 2016 – Case 002/02 – EN/FR* (24 August 2016) ECCC <https://www.eccc.gov.kh/en/video/trial-video/session-3-24-august-2016-case-00202-enfr>; *Session 1, 27 May 2013 (English/French)* (27 May 2013) ECCC <https://www.eccc.gov.kh/en/session-1-27-may-2013-englishfrench> together with the reports by two trial monitors: *KRT Monitor Case 002/02 – Issue 64 (22–25 August 2016)* (14 September 2016) Khmer Rouge Trial Monitor <https://krtmonitor.org/2016/09/14/krt-monitor-case-00202-issue-64-22-25-august-2016/>; 'Segment on Forced Marriage Begins', *Cambodia Tribunal Monitor* (23 August 2016) <http://www.cambodiatribunal.org/2016/08/23/segment-on-forced-marriage-begins/>; 'Civil Party Sou Sotheavy Continues Testimony about Forced Marriage', *Cambodia Tribunal Monitor* (24 August 2016) <http://www.cambodiatribunal.org/2016/08/24/civil-party-sou-sotheavy-continues-testimony-about-forced-marriage/>. I also interviewed Sotheavy in Phnom Penh on 4 June 2016, transcripts on file.

51 Diana Sankey, 'Recognition of Gendered Experiences of Harm at the Extraordinary Chambers in the Courts of Cambodia: The Promise and the Pitfalls' (2016) 24 *Feminist Legal Studies* 7.

52 Sou Sotheavy, Trial transcript 27 May 2013, 11.

Thus begins Sotheavy's statement at the ECCC on suffering in relation to the evacuation of Phnom Penh. As Diana Sankey points out, the forced evacuation from Phnom Penh displays gendered dimensions of harm, something that becomes evident when paying attention to social understandings of harm and to pre-existing socio-economic and legal status.[53] Sotheavy's testimony brings these dimensions to light. She begins by testifying to the existence of a community of transgendered people in Phnom Penh and bears witness to the summary execution of her friends. Her journey, if forced movement can be called such, was difficult. As she left the city, she joined others who were being evacuated. At one point, she and a friend were stopped by a small group of Khmer Rouge soldiers. While Sotheavy was told to wait, her friend was raped. She saw how pregnant women pushed carts, and she saw the corpses of Buddhist monks, of soldiers from the previous regime and civilians. She walked without food or rest. Finally, she arrived at her childhood home village. She continued to wear women's clothes and keep her hair long, but was 'severely discriminated . . . [and] had to hide it [her identity]'. So, she cut her hair and concealed her gender identity.[54] Eventually, she joined a mobile work unit and, as a consequence, moved around, staying at many different places. During the coming years, she was raped on multiple occasions, she exchanged sex for food and protection, she was abused for her transgender nature, accused of moral offences and, as a result, was sent to prison.[55]

Among Sotheavy's friends who, like her, were entertainers and/or transgender before the Khmer Rouge period, few survived and those who did suffered because of this. In a ground-breaking empirical study on gender-based violence against sexual minorities during the Khmer Rouge regime, Nakagawa[56] interviewed and collected testimonies from 48 people, most of whom identified as male-to-female transgender persons, but the study also included some gay men, lesbian women and female-to-male transgender persons. Nakagawa finds that violence against transgender people was extremely common and that most of her interviewees were threatened, abused and/or harassed. They all tried to hide their sexuality and/or identity during the regime. Nakagawa documents stories of rape and of exchanging sex for food or protection.[57] Notably, Nakagawa also frames her study in terms of breaking the silence. The testimony that is the epigraph to her introduction sets the frame: 'I have never talked about it to anyone. I never talked because it seemed shameful.'[58]

53 Sankey, above n 51.
54 Sou Sotheavy, Trial transcript 27 May 2013, 11–12, 15, 18.
55 *Cambodia Tribunal Monitor* articles, above n 50; Interview with Sou Sotheavy (Phnom Penh, 4 June 2016).
56 Kasumi Nakagawa, 'Gender-Based Violence against Sexual Minorities during the Khmer Rouge Regime' (Report, 2015).
57 Ibid 61–4.
58 Ibid 16.

Sotheavy speaks openly about her experiences during the regime. In October, or possibly August 1977,[59] she was forced to marry. She had on numerous previous occasions refused, but she had been relocated to Svay Hill where she was breaking rock and she could no longer say no. She spoke with a fellow worker, a woman she did not know, and they decided that if there was going to be a wedding, they should try to find each other. There were 107 couples married that day, and Sotheavy and the woman managed to find each other and be married. When they returned to a house occupied by Sotheavy's relatives, they realised spies were monitoring them, checking whether they would consummate the marriage. For weeks, the spies checked on the couple. When asked, Sotheavy told them they had already consummated the marriage, but they did not believe her, claiming that because she was transgender she could not have done so. Eventually, Sotheavy was called to a meeting and told that she would be 'smashed' – ie killed – unless they consummated the marriage. So they did. Her wife became pregnant, but as they lived at different work locations and Sotheavy was ill, she was not able to visit her daughter.[60]

What are we to make of Sotheavy's testimony? While she tells her story as a woman, during the regime she was forced to live as a man. Part of her experience is this very harm and the harm of having been targeted for her sexuality, as she describes it. These are many experiences of sexual violence, yes, and also of gendered harm. And even as there is sorrow and hurt, her testimony does not originate from a position of shame. Instead, when talking to me she expresses a sense of pride about having testified:

> I informed them [the Court] that I was a LGBT, a man who loved man: I said about the abuse and violence against me and the forced marriage imposed upon me and I asked the Court to consider [it]. Thus, more than one hundred people who attended the hearing returned home and said, 'there was an old woman who was actually a third-gender person, a man who loves man. She dared to speak before the court'. Thus, I am proud as people are aware of my story.[61]

Sotheavy appeared before the Court as a civil party, a victim who successfully applied to participate in the case. She was not a witness, but a victim who participates in the case and who has been chosen to appear to give testimony on behalf of other civil parties and victims. As briefly noted in the introduction, court rooms are not known to be conducive to testimony on traumatic experiences. The legal demands on witness testimony mean that the narrative has to be coherent, logical and contain (correct) factual details, requirements that often stand in direct opposition to the way in which trauma operates. At the ECCC,

59 Sotheavy's testimonies differ as to which month the wedding was held.
60 *Cambodia Tribunal Monitor* articles and ECCC videos, above n 50.
61 Interview with Sou Sotheavy (Phnom Penh, 4 June 2016).

these demands are extended to civil parties who give testimony and statements of suffering. In the first trial at the ECCC, the lawyers for civil parties were lambasted for not having properly prepared their clients.[62] Civil parties were, like witnesses, questioned and cross-examined. Expressions of anger by victims were denounced and any display of too much emotion was criticised by the judges. Now, with the second trial, the civil parties who testify remain mostly within the confines of their assigned roles. Sotheavy's testimonies are exemplar in this regard.[63] Tears flow down her cheeks, and while she expresses emotion, she remains composed as she narrates her story and replies calmly to questions. In her testimony, the loss of her family, the hard labour, the imprisonment and the torture all become parts of her experiences of the regime, alongside, and probably compounded by, the experience of having to hide her gender, the sexual violence and being forced to marry. Remarkably, in spite of the court's rules of evidence and procedure that run counter to the workings of trauma, her testimony on the (trans)gendered harms of evacuation and forced marriage, with its aspects of both sexual violence and gender-based injury, forges a space in which it is heard and recorded.

The gender of sexual and/or gender-based violence in armed conflict

Sotheavy's experiences and testimonies challenge and complicate what is becoming the accepted story about SGBV during the Khmer Rouge period in a number of ways. Her testimony does not fit into the frame of the testimonies at the Women's Hearings or the 'Sorrows and Struggles' exhibition, but at least some of her experiences can be heard at the ECCC.

First, Sotheavy's testimonies operate in a curious way in relation to the said silencing of testimonies on SGBV. By speaking out about the experiences, forging a space for them to be heard, her speech act becomes, as Mona Lilja suggests, an act of resistance.[64] But power is multifaceted and it is rarely as simple as a dominant narrative (of silence) being challenged by a testimony. This is perhaps particularly the case when it comes to testimonies on rape, as rape occupies a paradoxical position. As Nicola Henry suggests, rape occurring during war has long 'been viewed and treated . . . as abhorrent, incomprehensible and unspeakable, yet at the same time as inevitable, excusable or even laudable'.[65] Here, some testimonies

62 See, eg, Transcripts of Proceedings, *Prosecutor v Kaing Guek Eav alias Duch* (ECCC Trial Chamber) ('*Duch Transcripts*') 9 July 2009, 53; and Eric Stover, Mychelle Balthazard and Alexa K Koenig, 'Confronting Duch: Civil Party Participation in *Case 001* at the Extraordinary Chambers in the Courts of Cambodia' (2011) 93(882) *International Review of the Red Cross* 502, 522.

63 See video recordings of her testimonies at *Session 1, 27 May 2013 (English/French)* (27 May 2013) ECCC <https://www.eccc.gov.kh/en/session-1-27-may-2013-englishfrench>.

64 Lilja, above n 6, ch 6.

65 Nicola Henry, 'The Fixation on Wartime Rape: Feminist Critique and International Criminal Law' (2014) 23 *Social & Legal Studies* 93, 95.

on rape are picked up, repeated and given broader public coverage, some even becoming powerful in themselves. These testimonies figure in relation to various narratives, not always conducive to eliminating rape in conflict or challenging the structures that tolerate or even condone SGBV more broadly.[66] As Cynthia Enloe has pointed out, sometimes making rape visible can be 'dangerously easy'.[67] What is notable about Sotheavy's appearance and her testimonies is the way in which she demonstrates this paradoxical position of testimonies on SGBV: she speaks inside the Courtroom, in spite of the place being reputed for silencing victims of SGBV, but she is excluded from speaking at the alternative forums, despite these being presented as offering a place for truth-telling about SGBV during the Khmer Rouge. What will ultimately be registered in the legal judgment is yet to be seen. The acts of inclusion and exclusion seem to be constant.

Second, Sotheavy speaks in spite of a dominant narrative of women being victims of SGBV. The exclusive focus on women's suffering at the hearings and its dominance at the museum means that Sotheavy's experiences do not fit. The focus solely on women as victims of SGBV is not exclusive to the ECCC or Cambodia. Based on an examination of the discursive construction of gender-based violence during conflict in organisations and institutions concerned with the protection of civilians in armed conflict as well as international courts and tribunals dealing with its aftermath, Charli Carpenter argues that gender-based violence is exclusively framed in relation to women and excludes the experiences of civilian men and boys.[68] In her reading, much of the violence that would be categorised as gender based if the victim was a woman, is either characterised as a gender-neutral crime – torture, for example – or not recognised at all if the victim was a man, occluding the gender dimensions of the harm. What Sotheavy's testimonies show is that SGBV does not affect only women. Indeed, some of her remarks, as well as some made in the testimonies in Nakagawa's study, suggest that people were targeted by the Khmer Rouge for their (homo)sexuality or transgender identity.

The focus on women as the victims of SGBV during conflict has meant that examinations of its legacies, if examined at all, tends to focus on post-conflict domestic violence and violence against women. It is now well documented that armed conflict leads to heightened levels of domestic violence in its aftermath. Conflict has an impact on state formation, ideology and political economy, all of which in turn tends to disadvantage women and impact domestic violence.[69]

66 See, eg, Dubravka Žarkov, *The Body of War: Media, Ethnicity, and Gender in the Break-Up of Yugoslavia* (Duke University Press, 2007).

67 Cynthia Enloe, *Maneuvers: The International Politics of Militarizing Women's Lives* (University of California Press, 2000) 109.

68 R Charli Carpenter, 'Recognizing Gender-Based Violence against Civilian Men and Boys in Conflict Situations' (2006) 37 *Security Dialogue* 83.

69 Katherine Brickell, 'Towards Intimate Geographies of Peace? Local Reconciliation of Domestic Violence in Cambodia' (2015) 40 *Transactions of the Institute of British Geographers* 321.

However, this does not mean that the impact of all forms of SGBV during the Khmer Rouge period, or any other conflict, can or should be understood within the framework of domestic violence or violence against women. Consider, for example, the post-conflict situation for LGBT communities in Cambodia, which Sotheavy describes as plagued by state and community violence, arrest and imprisonment.[70] While it is not a criminal offence to engage in same-sex activities in Cambodia, there are no protections available in the form of anti-discrimination laws or other means of sanctioning those who violate the rights of LGBT people.[71] But perhaps LGBT is not the right term to use. As Sotheavy explains:

> The Khmer word for us is third-gender people while in English they may refer to us as gay, transgender, msm [men having sex with men] or lesbian. In Khmer we only have one word to call ourselves. A woman who loves woman is a third-gender person; a man who loves man is also a third-gender person. Even the bisexual people are third-gender people. We call ourselves simply like that with this word that does not contain any discrimination; it is a good word. We have coined this word. In the past people called us Kteuy which sounded very harsh for us in this modernised society and [is] a very dirty term to describe us. For this reason, we gather together to advocate for recognition of our status as third-gender people.[72]

Sotheavy is one of few activists working for the rights of third-gender people, having in 2000 established her own NGO, the Cambodian Network for Men Women Development, which aims to achieve recognition of the rights of third-gender persons. For her, the promise of human rights stands in contrast to the medicalisation of third-gender persons, which she claims is the predominant approach taken by international donors and NGOs: 'They only focus on health issue. They do not care if [people of third-gender] are beaten, mistreated or hospitalised.'[73] What we need to ask is how the lives of third-gender communities in Cambodia today are affected by the structures and attitudes established or impacted by the Khmer Rouge period and the SGBV that then occurred. This is a question foreclosed if the legacy of SGBV perpetrated during conflict is understood as, primarily, domestic violence suffered by women.

The third way in which Sotheavy's testimony challenges what has become the dominant framing of SGBV during the Khmer Rouge regime is the tendency for SGBV to be confined to sexual violence, occluding the recognition of

70 Interview with Sou Sotheavy (Phnom Penh, 4 June 2016).

71 Vicente S Salas, 'Being LGBT in Asia: Cambodia Country Report' (Report, UNDP, USAID, 2014). See also Heidi Hoefinger, Pisey Ly and Srorn Srun, 'Sex Politics and Moral Panics: LGBT Communities, Sex/Entertainment Workers and Sexually Active Youth in Cambodia' in Katherine Brickell and Simon Springer (eds), *The Handbook of Contemporary Cambodia* (Routledge, 2016) 315.

72 Interview with Sou Sotheavy (Phnom Penh, 4 June 2016).

73 Ibid.

gender-based violence. Sotheavy speaks not only about sexual violence, but about a multitude of sexual *and* gender-based harms. She testifies to the gendered harms of forced evacuation and her experience of having to live as a man, which cannot be encompassed by sexual violence alone. The charge of the regulation of marriage at the ECCC opens a new space for consideration of harms that are gendered but not necessarily sexual,[74] but the judgment on this charge is yet to come and it is not currently clear where it is heading. During the trial, many of the questions posed to those testifying focused on the consummation of the marriage – the act of sex/rape. Sotheavy's testimonies, however, demonstrate just how manifold SGBV can be. Yes, she experienced rape and sexual violence, but also the violence of having to live as a man, of having to get married as a man, of having to consummate her marriage as a man and possibly also of being targeted specifically because of her transgender status or her sexuality as a man loving men.

Conclusion

In a study on the representations of sexual violence in Democratic Republic of the Congo (DRC), Charlotte Mertens and Maree Pardy draw attention to a discursive formation they call 'sexurity', a tripartite amalgam of discourses on the securitisation of sexual violence, the sexualisation of security and the language of crisis.[75] They argue that this amalgam of discourses has framed how sexual violence in the DRC is understood and approached, to the extent it has 'opened up certain pathways for highly warranted actions, but it has done so by foreclosing others, for example those that might address the consequences of non-sexual forms of violence, including the violence of poverty, landlessness and lack of education and health services'.[76] Drawing on Didier Fassin's concept of 'political anaesthesia', they explain that '[p]olitical anaesthesia does not indicate a lack of commitment to addressing suffering; rather, it presumes that all necessary knowledge about the conditions of that suffering has now been established'.[77] It seems to me that SGBV during the Khmer Rouge period is presented through certain discursive formations that institute a similar form of political anaesthesia. Here, though, it is not the language of security or rape as weapon of war, but of SGBV that is blinkered as (sexual) violence against women. While this is not necessarily wrong or incorrect, it forecloses other experiences of SGBV, as Sotheavy's testimonies reveal. In spite of the power of the dominant story, her testimonies challenge the stereotype that victims of SGBV are only ever women, and her experience during the regime offers a more complex and inclusive story

74 I discuss this in depth in Elander, above n 7.
75 Charlotte Mertens and Maree Pardy, '"Sexurity" and Its Effects in Eastern Democratic Republic of Congo' (2017) 38 *Third World Quarterly* 956.
76 Ibid 13.
77 Ibid 2.

of multiple forms of SGBV than has to date been told in both the ECCC and alternative civil society hearings.

Sotheavy makes herself heard and if there is a silence to break, she breaks it. Her courage, and that of many others like her, complicates the reductive dominant narrative on SGBV during conflict and its effects, and challenges us all to reject its certainties and exclusions.

Part III

Alliances: Making queer lives matter

7 The (im)possibility of queering international human rights law

*Ratna Kapur**

In August 2015, after footage emerged of members of the Islamic State (IS) throwing a gay man off of a roof in Tal Abyad, Syria, the UN Security Council called its first organised session on gay rights that was open to all member states.[1] In a closed-door meeting, sponsored by the United States and Chile, the Security Council focused on IS and its ongoing persecution of lesbian, gay, bisexual and transgender (LGBT) Syrians and Iraqis.[2] Thirteen of the 15 countries sitting on the Security Council participated in the meetings, with China, Russia, Nigeria and Malaysia present, but silent, and Chad and Angola remaining absent. The event was celebrated as a landmark where the Security Council had taken up the cause of LGBT rights for the first time in its 70-year history.[3]

The question that I seek to examine in this chapter is how have we arrived at a point where the location of LGBT rights within a security discourse marks a moment to be celebrated? Or, to put it slightly differently, what ever happened to

* I am extremely grateful to Gauri Pillai for her invaluable research assistance. My thanks also to Dianne Otto for both her comments and editorial inputs.

1 Such informal meetings are known as Arria-Formula sessions, and were initiated in 1993 by Diego Arria, the Venezuelan Ambassador to the United Nations, to create a venue for the Security Council to be briefed by NGOs on a variety of issues on the Council's agenda.

2 Michael K Lavers, 'Islamic State Focus of U.N. Security Council's First LGBT meeting', *Washington Blade* (online) (24 August 2015) <http://www.washingtonblade.com/2015/08/24/islamic-state-focus-of-u-n-security-councils-first-lgbt-meeting/>.

3 The Security Council has since released a statement on the killing of 49 people and wounding of 53 others at Pulse, a gay nightclub in Orlando on 12 June 2016, by Omar Mateen, a 29-year-old security guard. The act was described in the media as the deadliest terrorist attack in the United States since the 9/11 attacks. The resolution, apparently speaking for all members, 'reaffirmed that terrorism in all its forms and manifestations constitutes one of the most serious threats to international peace and security'. See 'Security Council Press Statement on Terrorist Attack in Orlando, Florida' (Press Release, SC/12399, 13 June 2016) <http://www.un.org/press/en/2016/sc12399.doc.htm>; Kerry Brodie, 'In a Historic First, U.N. Security Council Convenes to Discuss LGBT Rights', *Human Rights Campaign* (24 August 2015) <http://www.hrc.org/blog/in-a-historic-first-u.n.-security-council-convenes-to-discuss-lgbt-rights>; US Department of State, 'UN Security Council Holds Inaugural Meeting on LGBT Issues' (Press Release, 24 August 2015) <https://globalequality.wordpress.com/2015/08/24/un-security-council-holds-inaugural-meeting-on-lgbt-issues/>.

queer radicality? My central claim is that queer engagement with human rights has taken the radicality out of queer rather than resulting in the queering of international human rights. While there are undoubtedly temporal moments when the radicalism of the project emerges, these are quickly quenched by the lure of normativity and glitter of respectability. I argue that the potential for queer radicality remains on the outskirts of human rights, rather than within its embrace, and that these possibilities are abundant outside of the parameters of the liberal imaginary within which human rights remain immersed.

De-radicalising queer in international human rights advocacy

During the course of the past decade, queer advocacy has acquired considerable prominence in international human rights advocacy. It has become the new focus of academics and activists working in the field of sexuality and sexuality studies. While there is a distinction often made between LGBT and queer, the former referring to fixed identities, and the latter as a critical anti-normative project, this distinction becomes blurred in international human rights advocacy, globally and locally, with 'Q' at times being added as part of the LGBT acronym, and LGBT at times doing 'queer' work. While the repeated invocation of queer historically constituted a social bond among homophobic persons, its contemporary appropriation and redeployment by queer persons for radical political purposes has produced its own set of racial and cultural exclusions.[4] Even though queer is understood as providing the critical intellectual impulse that puts into question normativity and drives the political agenda, such drives frequently end up reinforcing the dominant normative order of sexuality and gender rather than producing freedom from this order in the context of human rights.[5] In other words, such interventions in the context of human rights have often moved in the direction of gay governance, where sexuality becomes both normalised and naturalised, and the critical capacities of queer are shorn away through the assimilative and normative gravitational pull of human rights. Queer appears unable to transform or destabilise the normative foundations of human rights that remain firmly embedded in dualistic gender categories and a gender hierarchy,[6] as well as a set of racial and cultural exclusions. In fact, as I argue, queer itself has gone normative.

In the international legal arena, LGBT human rights advocacy at the formal level has invariably been directed at legal inclusion and the bestowal of rights on those subjects who have been disenfranchised, subordinated, stigmatised, criminalised and regarded as less than human. There is no doubt that this remains

4 Judith Butler, *Bodies that Matter: On the Discursive Limits of 'Sex'* (Routledge, 1993) ch 8.

5 Dianne Otto, 'Queering Gender [Identity] in International Law' (2015) 33 *Nordic Journal of Human Rights* 299.

6 Ibid.

a compelling and important aspect of the queer political project, especially given that LGBT persons in large swathes of the world are reduced to truncated, incapable subjects, subjected to exploitation as well as extreme forms of violence, and rendered precarious through lack of legal recognition.[7] While this goal is laudable, in this section I question the claim that such degradations can be alleviated by human rights interventions, especially as they have largely failed to challenge the normative framework within which sexuality is addressed. Moreover, these interventions have at times in fact not only inscribed a set of sexual normativities of their own, but also reproduced racial and cultural binaries between those societies that are seen as 'progressive' and 'civilised', and those societies that remain in a state of transition until the human rights of their LGBT persons are secured.

The prescriptive 'gay' international

The universalising impulse of international human rights advocacy has masked the exclusions on which human rights have been based, where the world's others have featured as subjects to be rescued from their oppressive cultures, histories and civilisational backwardness.[8] At the same time, inclusion is based on alignment with the dominant sexual, gender, cultural and racial norms that structure the human rights project.

Within the arena of human rights, in the specific struggle for LGBT rights we are witnessing a polarised response to the sexual subject. At one end, there is an increased criminalisation of LGBT lives, where not just the sex act but the very identity of homosexuals is criminalised, such as in Nigeria, Uganda, Kenya, Ethiopia, Democratic Republic of the Congo and, to some extent, Russia.[9] In societies where gays and lesbians are denied legal recognition, such denial mobilises resistance as well as a claim for social inclusion. At the opposite end of the spectrum the struggle for rights claims has challenged the pathologising and criminalising of homosexuality, resulting in legal recognition in countries such as Nepal, Cambodia, Chile, South Africa, several European countries and the United States. The judicial or legislative recognition of same-sex marriages is generally regarded as the culmination point of LGBT advocacy and the struggle for legitimacy and

7 UN High Commissioner for Human Rights, Discriminatory Laws and Practices and Acts of Violence against Individuals Based on Their Sexual Orientation and Gender Identity, UN GAOR, 19th sess, Agenda Items 2 and 8, UN Doc A/HRC/19/41 (17 November 2011); UN High Commissioner for Human Rights, Discrimination and Violence against Individuals Based on Their Sexual Orientation and Gender Identity, UN GAOR, 29th sess, Agenda Items 2 and 8, UN Doc A/HRC/29/23 (4 May 2015).

8 Makau Mutua, 'Savages, Victims, and Saviors: The Metaphor of Human Rights' (2001) 42 *Harvard International Law Journal* 201.

9 See list of countries criminalising homosexuality and same-sex conduct at '76 Countries Where Homosexuality is Illegal' on Colin Stewart, *Erasing 76 Crimes* (12 August 2016) <https://76crimes.com/76-countries-where-homosexuality-is-illegal/>.

equality.[10] At the international level, recognition through the adoption of the non-binding but influential Yogyakarta Principles on the Application of International Human Rights Law in Relation to Sexual Orientation and Gender Identity ('Yogyakarta Principles'), as well as the Human Rights Council's recent decision to establish a Special Procedure appointing an independent expert on sexual orientation and gender identity, are two moments that mark the zenith of LGBT advocacy within the human rights apparatus.[11] In the choice between criminality and legitimacy, the latter is clearly preferable to being an ostracised criminal deviant. The struggle for recognition through rights would seem an obvious strategy, given that it affords access to economic and social inclusion, public standing and legibility – all of which are the core objectives of human rights pursuits. Doubtless, it is important that rights continue to be pursued by and for illegible constituencies. In the context of homosexuality, it is indeed better to have legal recognition, including the option to get married as a gay person, as opposed to having an active law that not only persecutes homosexual conduct, but also criminalises the very identity of homosexuals. There seems no reasonable argument against invoking human rights to challenge legal provisions that call for life imprisonment or the death penalty for being gay.

At the same time, we need to inquire into the work that queer is doing in international human rights. As Dianne Otto has argued, the Yogyakarta Principles, while important, are largely based on biological assumptions about sexuality

10 See list of countries that have legalised same-sex marriage at 'Countries Where Gay Marriage is Legal', *Ranker* <http://ranker.com/list/countries-where-gay-marriage-is-legal/web-infoguy>; see also Robert Wintemute, 'From "Sex Rights" to "Love Rights": Partnership Rights as Human Rights' in Nicholas Bamforth (ed), *Sex Rights: The Oxford Amnesty Lectures* (Oxford University Press, 2005) 186.

11 Office of the High Commissioner for Human Rights, 'Council Establishes Mandate against Violence and Discrimination Based on Sexual Orientation and Gender Identity' (Media Release, 28 June 2016) <http://www.ohchr.org/en/NewsEvents/Pages/DisplayNews.aspx?NewsID=20220&LangID=E>; Yogyakarta Principles. There are several significant references to LGBT rights building up the to the Yogyakarta Principles, including, for example, Human Rights Council, 'Joint Statement on Human Rights Violations Based on Sexual Orientation and Gender Identity', 3rd sess, (1 December 2006); Human Rights Council, 'Joint Statement on Human Rights, Sexual Orientation and Gender Identity – Delivered by Argentina on Behalf of 66 States' (18 December 2008) <http://arc-international.net/global-advocacy/sogi-statements/2008-joint-statement/>; Human Rights Council, 'Human Rights, Sexual Orientation and Gender Identity', 27th sess, Agenda Item 8, UN Doc A/HRC/27/32 (2 October 2014); Office of the High Commissioner for Human Rights, 'Combatting Discrimination Based on Sexual Orientation and Gender Identity' <http://www.ohchr.org/EN/Issues/Discrimination/Pages/LGBT.aspx>, as well as the report of the Office of the High Commissioner for Human Rights, 'Born Free and Equal: Sexual Orientation and Gender Identity in International Human Rights Law', UN Doc HR/PUB/12/06 (2012); and its campaign for the equal rights of LGBT persons: Office of the High Commissioner for Human Rights, 'UN Human Rights Office Launches Unprecedented Global Campaign for Lesbian, Gay, Bisexual and Transgender Equality' (Media Release, 26 July 2013) <http://www.prweb.com/releases/2013/7/prweb10967571.htm>.

located in a dualist heteronormative framework that ignores the dynamic understandings of gender and gender identity as socially constructed. Gender remains confined to two categories, male and female, with the 'gay' family constructed as monogamous, nuclear and having an emphasis on procreation. And gender identity continues to be associated with transgender persons rather than as something every person possesses.[12]

Queer radicality that promised to delink gender as well as sexuality from naturalised, normalised, biological categories, finds itself swept into the normative vortex of human rights. In other words, queer advocacy finds itself doing the very governance work in sexual rights that it sought to challenge. It is thus traversing the same route as gender, where governance feminism has increasingly aligned itself with the regulatory apparatus of the state and the normative order of gender, as well as walking the corridors of power within the UN system.[13] The increased visibility of LGBT groups in Human Rights Council meetings and the fact that the Security Council has taken cognisance of this issue are significant, but they do not speak to progress or indicate success in queering human rights. To the contrary, they serve as evidence of the de-radicalisation of queer in human rights.

One of the earliest moments to alert us to this de-radicalisation emerged when a cache of thousands of disturbing photos taken by US army persons in Abu Ghraib prison during the then US-led invasion of Iraq hit the headline news in late 2003. Jasbir Puar analysed the responses to these photos, revealing how they were almost exclusively presented through a sexual lens, where Iraqi prisoners were being intentionally humiliated through sexualised practices that were assumed to be repulsive, emasculating and shameful to Muslims. Occluded in such a reading were the racial, cultural and gendered dimensions of the torture. These erasures reinforced the liberal media's homophobic practice of caricaturing Muslims, here through traumatic images of pure abjection that violently satirise Muslim sexuality/ subjectivity as primitive and grotesque. The brutally racist and sexist dimensions that fell out of this avidly consumed cache of photographs remained largely unquestioned by queer scholars and advocates, thereby leaving in place the Western supposition that repressed sexuality is a defining characteristic of the West's most prominent, adversarial, cultural 'other' – namely, 'the Muslim'. Queer operated to shore up US 'sexual exceptionalism' that is used to indoctrinate the sexual subject into a belief in liberal superiority. Egregious acts such as torture were turned into a 'positive register of the valorisation of (American) life' that continues to mark it as progressive and inclusive.[14]

12 Otto, above n 5, 310–11.

13 Janet Halley, *Split Decisions: How and Why to Take a Break from Feminism* (Princeton University Press, 2006); Janet Halley, P Kotiswaran, C Thomas et al, 'From the International to the Local in Feminist Legal Responses to Rape, Prostitution/Sex Work and Sex Trafficking: Four Studies in Contemporary Governance Feminism' (2006) 29 *Harvard Journal of Law and Gender* 335.

14 Jasbir K Puar, *Terrorist Assemblages: Homonationalism in Queer Times* (Duke University Press, 2007) 3.

What emerged was the collusion of homosexuality and American nationalism generated through the rhetoric of patriotic inclusion as well as homonationalism pursued by gays and queers.[15] In other words, 'queer' came to be deployed in ways that were complicit with dominant formations of sexuality as 'homonormativity'. Sexual exceptionalism continues to operate in ways that include some queer subjects, that is, those who conform or assimilate – the 'good homosexuals' – while it simultaneously casts out non-compliant sexual, gender and racial others. 'Queer' comes to be aligned with a set of (white) secular norms which reinforce the racist representations of Islam and Muslims as homophobic and culturally backward, where practices such as gay marriage serve as a marker for the distinction between a racialised, primitive, Muslim population and upright, proper, homosexual citizens. It thus serves not as a signifier of sexual identity or sexual subversion, but merely as a defused inscription of socio-political difference within a larger modality of hierarchical regulation and governance of gender, sexuality and gender identity.

Similarly, the meeting by the Security Council to discuss LGBT rights in light of the IS attacks on gays in Syria and Iraq did not necessarily advance the rights of those on whose behalf such closed meetings were held. It did, however, provide further justification for the deployment of deadly weaponry in an already confused and lethal militaristic map that has produced untold civilian casualties and traumas in the Middle East. A focus on human security has come to increasingly appropriate progressive agendas, as has been similarly evident in the women's human rights sphere, specifically in the context of sexual violence against women, anti-trafficking and gender, peace and security.[16] To all intents and purposes, the meeting was more about the propaganda war than about advancing the rights of LGBT persons, within Syria or globally. Exhibiting the already endless list of atrocities committed by IS serves as one of the continuing justifications for the bombardment of an already devastated landscape and population, and a non-UN-sanctioned military intervention where no one is held accountable for the lives lost and harms done. Such meetings are not coupled with a change in strategy to defeat IS that may save more LGBT lives; indeed, the military strategy remains unaffected and completely disconnected from these discussions. Further, as discussed in the context of the Abu Ghraib photos, it may be that such a response exacerbates the image of Muslims as misogynist, sexist, homophobic and culturally backward. And it also poses a dilemma for the Middle Eastern/Arab queers who seek to oppose oppression within their communities without serving the militaristic justifications and brutalities inflicted by the sponsors of the US-led military bombardments of Syria and elsewhere.

A further related consideration that puts the radical credentials of queer into question is the often one-dimensional paternalistic reasoning that if legal

15 Ibid 77.

16 Ratna Kapur, 'Gender, Sovereignty, and the Rise of a Sexual Security Regime in International Law and Postcolonial India' (2013) 14 *Melbourne Journal of International Law* 317.

recognition of homosexuality and/or same-sex marriage is permissible in the United States, Canada or France, it is because these societies are just inherently better, more civilised and mature than, say, Uganda or the Caribbean or other 'underdeveloped' parts of the world, including India. Such reasoning deflects attention, for example, from the way in which Christian evangelicals from the United States have been implicated in partly producing an anti-gay agenda not only in Uganda, but also in other African countries such as South Sudan and Democratic Republic of the Congo.[17] It is not Islamic orthodoxy but Christian evangelicalism from the United States that is driving a homophobic agenda, easily received within a context where conservative sexual and gender norms, constituted partly by the legacies of the colonial past, continue to resonate in the postcolonial present. Economic sanctions or the withdrawal of aid by countries whose citizens are implicated in producing or reinforcing homophobia in the very places being punitively targeted by such measures, requires that both the injury and the restorative/rehabilitative interventions be rigorously problematised.

And, finally, a position that continues to associate human rights and freedom with the West, while certain African, Islamic and non-Western societies and their leaders are cast as retrogressive and barbaric, does not implicate the ways in which homophobia continues to flourish in Western liberal democracies. Abhorrence of homosexuality and the homosexual continues to exist as an ideological position *across* these hemispheric divides. For example, while 2015 saw the striking down of discriminatory bans on same-sex marriage in the United States, and more legal protections based on sexual orientation and gender identity have been enacted at the municipal level, the American right wing continues to support anti-gay legislation within the United States as well as in other parts of the world, including in Uganda and Russia. Similarly, shortly before the move to legalise same-sex marriages in France in May 2013, Paris witnessed some of the largest protests seen since the 1960s, vast rallies by those opposed to the move to legalise same-sex marriage; opposition which has been sustained and continuous.[18]

17 Among those US evangelicals who have led the anti-gay campaign in Uganda and elsewhere is Scott Lively, co-author of *The Pink Swastika*, a book in which he argued that homosexuals were the true inventors of Nazism and responsible for the Nazi atrocities. See Scott Lively and Kevin Abrams, *The Pink Swastika: Homosexuality in the Nazi Party* (Veritas Aeterna Press, 4th edn, 2002). See also Antony Loewenstein, 'US Evangelicals in Africa Put Faith into Action, but Some Accused of Intolerance', *The Guardian* (online) (19 March 2015) <https://www.theguardian.com/world/2015/mar/18/us-evangelicals-africa-charity-missionaries-homosexuality>.

18 'France: ION 2013-404 of 17 May 2013 Opening Marriage to Couples of the Same Sex', *Fabregat Perulles Sales* (29 May 2013) <http://www.fabregat-perulles-sales.com/blog/france-loi-n-2013-404-du-17-mai-2013-ouvrant-le-mariage-aux-couples-de-personnes-de-meme-sexe/>; Tom Heneghan, 'French Conservatives March against Government "Family-phobia"', *Reuters* (online) (2 February 2014) <http://www.reuters.com/article/us-france-protests-idUSBREA110AG20140202>; Kim Willsher, 'France's Future at Risk from "Unnatural Families", Say Conservative Protestors', *The Guardian* (online) (3 February 2014) <http://www.theguardian.com/world/2014/feb/02/france-protests-families-paris-lyon>.

Postcolonial queering of human rights?

In human rights, queer has been critiqued precisely for replicating agendas that are based on prevalent models in the United States and Europe, erasing or marginalising articulations of non-Western perspectives on sex and sexuality, while also shoring up the purported civilisational superiority of Western states. At one level, the critique suggests that the gay rights movement is nothing more than a neo-colonial enterprise that annuls the possibility of a valid, postcolonial, Asian narrative of the homoerotic/homosocial.[19] As Joseph Massad argues, the production of a specific sexual subject in LGBT international human rights advocacy is a culturally imperialistic imposition of Western ontology on Arabs.[20] He states that a certain modern Western conception of sexuality and sexual identity is seen as replacing other non-Western/indigenous forms of sexual practices that are not hinged to 'identity'.[21] Momin Rahman similarly argues that there are no monolithic or consistent cultural formations of Muslim or Islamic notions of sexuality and that the 'Western' version of gay sexuality is itself culturally specific.[22] Rahman does, however, question Massad's contention that there has been a consistent trajectory of the 'gay international' in the global arena, pointing to empirical assessments confirming that different NGOs and international organisations have had mixed results in their advocacy.[23]

There have been several efforts at trying to negotiate the terrain between a prescriptive 'gay international' and taking an anti-Western stand that does not slip into an essentialising, authentic Third World position – that is – to retrieve the *critical* value of queer. Elaborating on the dilemma posed when evaluating the impact of Western discourses of LGBT rights on Third World contexts, Rahul Rao questions whether it is possible to find an effective language in which 'to criticize the hierarchies and supremacism that lurk within the cosmopolitan politics of LGBT solidarity without minimizing or ignoring the impressiveness of communitarian homophobia'.[24] The suggestion is that there is a danger of slipping into a hegemonic communitarian approach that arrogates to itself both the right to determine who is/is not 'authentically' queer, and the right to prescribe how sexual identities and practices *ought* to be expressed in a non-Western context. In light of this danger, Rao asks whether the 'gay international' offers anything useful in terms of solidarity with 'traditional' sexual ontologies that are experienced as problematic by the sexually stigmatised subject in the

19 Stewart Chang, 'The Postcolonial Problem for Global Gay Rights' (2014) 32 *Boston University International Law Journal* 329.

20 Joseph Massad, 'Re-orienting Desire: The Gay International and the Arab World' (2002) 14 *Public Culture* 361; Joseph Massad, *Desiring Arabs* (University of Chicago Press, 2007).

21 Massad, 'Re-orienting Desire', above n 21, 361–2.

22 Momin Rahman, *Homosexualities, Muslim Cultures and Modernity* (Palgrave MacMillan, 2014).

23 Ibid 80.

24 Rahul Rao, *Third World Protest: Between Home and the World* (Oxford University Press, 2010) 176.

postcolonial domestic space, and that exact tremendous personal costs.[25] What emerges is the need for contemporary modes of queerness to be in conversation with the 'global gay identity', as well as with the local genealogies, practices and idioms of same-sex desire, whose diverse manifestations cohere within a single nationality or territory.

Similarly, Gayatri Gopinath resists any effort to counter the franchise of the 'gay international', a product of the Euro-American imperium, through the resurrection of a Third World, authentic lesbian subject.[26] She dislodges the fixed, prescriptive understandings of same-sex desire, using a 'queer diaspora' framework and her specific focus on queer female diasporic subjectivity.[27] She seeks a more nuanced approach through an examination of what are recognisable cultural texts such as musical genres, films, novels and videos that are both transnational as well as rooted in the politics of the local.[28] For example, in her discussion of Bollywood cinema, Gopinath focuses on queer female subjectivities in popular culture in order to disrupt the representations of nationalist, jingoistic, anti-foreign narratives that are closely aligned with Indian national identity, as well as the male-male relationship that finds its way into such narratives as a part and parcel of the patriarchal, national story. She offers a postcolonial queer analysis that stands in sharp contrast to the ideological grain of progressive, liberal, feminist and First World signifiers of non-heterosexual sexualities, while resisting the lure to resurrect a Third World, authentic lesbian subject as a counter to the franchise on the 'gay international'. Her position is not to eulogise the formation of a postcolonial queer female subject within Indian popular culture, but to illustrate how such formations are both capable of migrating and pollinating other cultural spaces in ways that do not fit within a homosexual/heterosexual, male/female, us/them, the West and the Rest theoretical binaries.[29] While Gopinath does not specifically present her argument in the context of human rights, her analysis is useful to consider for such a context. Given the tension between universalist prescriptions of human rights and cultural relativism, seeking a queer negotiation beyond this destructive binary remains crucial. Such arguments retain the possibility of queer radicality and its normatively disruptive and subversive possibilities, though the question remains whether this radicality can be sustained once brought within perimeters of human rights.

The arguments of Massad, Rao, Gopinath and others open up the possibility for scrutinising how postcolonial sexual subjectivities are constructed and deployed, and moves us away from a thesis based exclusively on the dialectics of sexual repression/excess and sexual liberation. While both sexual repression as

25 Ibid 178; Rahul Rao, 'Queer Questions' (2014) 16 *International Feminist Journal of Politics* 199.

26 Gayatri Gopinath, *Impossible Desires: Queer Diasporas and South Asian Public Cultures* (Duke University Press, 2005).

27 Ibid 6–7.

28 Ibid 21.

29 Ibid 50.

well as sexual excess and deviancy have been modes of characterising the native subject and have today been incorporated into the justification for ostensibly emancipatory imperial interventions in non-Western territories, the sexual liberation thesis based on a rights agenda does not examine how such moves reinforce the state's regulatory authority and power to paralyse the overt enunciation of sexual subjectivities. Similarly, the liberationist critiques risk slipping into a search for *authentic Asian* practices, identities and sexual subjectivities.

Despite the more nuanced positions by postcolonial scholars, it remains evident that the contemporary discourse of homosexuality at an international level, and specifically within the context of human rights advocacy, continues to be inevitably presupposed and constituted against a cultural 'other'.[30] The hegemonic Euro-American signifiers for same-sex love/non-heterosexual desire are fast becoming the prescribed blueprint across the world. The prescriptive gay subject is based on specific assumptions, including the idea that this subject exists in opposition to heterosexuality and that the fulfilment of same-sex desire and identity can be found through public visibility and inclusion in the heteronormative structures and the patriarchal institutions of the family. This powerful articulation of the end goals of same-sex desire marginalises and de-legitimates other articulations and subjectivities in the non-Euro-American contexts. The ultimate performance of this identity rests in an 'out of the closet' LGBT identity that is prescribed as the antidote for all Third World settings. This strategy assumes something about freedom and what (queer) freedom *should* look like – that is, outness as opposed to the closet. My argument is that such a strategy based on the recovery and inclusion of 'queer voices' or 'same-sex desire' is not up to the task of countering the newly emerging hegemonic, colonising queer in human rights.

The influential framework of 'coming out' narratives also tends to repudiate the varied genealogies and modalities of queer subjectivity, instead locating the issue of sexuality within the narrow dialectic of visibility and invisibility. It neither captures the very real and particular dangers, anxieties, ambivalences, dilemmas and crises of homoerotic experience, nor the plural and diverse ways in which gender, gender identity and sexuality may be experienced, lived and performed in different cultural contexts.[31] Invisibility at times comes at a high emotional cost,

30 Amr Shalakany, 'On a Certain Queer Discomfort with Orientalism' (2007) 101 *American Society of International Law Proceedings* 125 (Shalakany further complicates the relationship between Orientalism or Western prescriptions of sexuality and the human rights of sexual minorities in the context of Egypt).

31 Brinda Bose and Subhabrata Bhattacharyya (eds), *The Phobic and the Erotic: The Politics of Sexualities in Contemporary India* (Seagull Books, 2007); Arvind Narrain and Gautam Bhan (eds), *Because I Have a Voice: Queer Politics in India* (Yoda Press, 2005).

but may be a necessary form of self-protection – which may also mean the protection of others – in many parts of the world, especially but not only where homosexuality is criminalised, and where being an out queer automatically means risking all modes of direct and indirect penalisation. The gaining of queer selfhood through visibility may involve great losses, ranging from familial and social rejection and ostracism, to being deprived of home, livelihood and services, to discrimination and humiliation, to violent assault and sometimes even death at the hands of the bigoted and/or the ignorant.

It is certainly problematic to allege that the out 'gay international' produced by hegemonic 'Western' notions of sexuality/sexual subjectivity is clear evidence of an imposition by 'the West on the Rest', as Massad suggests, yet it is just as problematic to assume a monolithic 'Rest' in this equation, for the West's 'others' form a set constituted by heterogeneous, culturally specific, internally differentiated yet cohesive subsets committed to varied ideologies, groupings, practices and knowledge paradigms. Moreover, given such diversity, it is obvious that queer subsets within the set of any particular queer culture may be wholly or partially invisible to one another, may function hierarchically, and/or may not have a common language or common interactive ground: for instance, metropolitan queers may have no grasp of what it means to be queer in provincial/rural contexts, and vice versa; queer men and queer women might have different priorities and approaches to complex identity or rights issues, and so on. It may be that queerness is not something that requires visibility through rights, which paradoxically can produce invisibility through its normative thrust, but rather, recognition as already existing and thriving within certain contexts and cultures, on the outskirts of human rights, a strategy to which I return in the final segment of this chapter. Such already present queerness renders queer human rights advocacy an intervention rather than a liberation. As an intervention, human rights can also become a form of cultural imperialism, as well as un-freedom for the 'other'. The argument here is not that there should be no engagement with rights. Continuous engagement is essential if only to push back the hegemonic drive of human rights that assumes to itself the power to determine how to be gay in the world or what constitutes oppression and the sources of oppression for LGBT persons in different parts of the world. Continuous engagement reveals what gets occluded or erased in human rights' self-appointed role as saviour and how queer becomes complicit in this project. There remains a need to complicate ideas of human rights as a progressive force that continues with the efforts of the queer project, together with questioning the faith that it has the ability to remedy, repair or restore the lives of stigmatised sexual 'others'.

The limits of queer

While the enjoyment of human rights remains an important political project, such endeavours do not necessarily contain the possibility of producing the radical outcomes and transformations that have inspired queer politics. Rights remain tenuous and ambivalent and do not resolve the hatreds and animosities that continue to circulate, even after recognition has been secured.[32] In fact, the voracious reach and spread of LGBT advocacy has marginalised or erased the multiple forms and arrangements that constitute gender and gender identity in different cultural contexts. Human rights have a proclivity to aggravate the stigmatisation and precariousness of those queers who remain unintelligible either because they fail or refuse to conform to gender and sexual norms. At the same time, they function to incorporate the sexual subject into the regulatory apparatus of the state, where, for example, the recognition of the rights of same-sex couples enabled them to walk with the state to 'tie the knot', eventually hoping to parent or adopt a child, and embrace all of the trappings of heteronormative, reproductive bliss. The end result is not an emancipated sexual subject, but one who is regulated and sequestered in and through the normative scaffolding of (hetero)sexual rights.

My argument is that there is a need to recognise the limited possibilities of queering the terrain of human rights when the sexual subject comes to claim her rights. The radical moment is transient or fleeting, given that rights are a discursive space amenable to a number of competing and powerful agendas. Ultimately, the de-queering of queer in human rights appears inevitable.

In the international arena, LGBT human rights advocacy has incorporated gay sexuality into a linear regulatory framework. It is arguable that an uncomplicated approach to sexual subjectivity based on identity and framed within the heterosexual/homosexual binary is to be welcomed, given the prevailing and malicious pockets of homophobia that continue to circulate. And given the precarity of LGBT rights, such a strategy may be all that stands between LGBT people and the virulent homophobia of orthodox and conservative religious groups at the international and domestic levels. While these interventions may be breaching the borders of heteronormativity, the point is that protection from persecution and intelligibility of some sexual minorities through human rights is neither radical nor transformative, but regulatory. Through moulding illegitimate desire into a mimesis of more approved forms, queering international human rights appears to involve nothing more than the wholesale pursuit of the aspirations

32 For example, in 2013, the Indian Supreme Court reversed a lower court ruling in 2009 that read down section 377 of the Indian Penal Code, 1860, an old colonial law that criminalised sodomy (regardless of sexuality): *Suresh Kumar Koushal v NAZ Foundation* (2013) 1 SCC 1 (2014) (11 December 2013) (Supreme Court of India). Yet, even during the period when homosexuality had been decriminalised, queer lives remained precarious. In a case decided shortly after the 2009 decision, the Allahabad High Court ordered the Aligarh Muslim University to reinstate Professor Ramchandra Siras, who was dismissed from his university post in 2010 on the grounds of gross misconduct. Siras was gay. *Dr Shrinivas Ramchandra Siras v The Aligarh Muslim University*, Civil Misc Writ Petition No 17549 of 2010 (1 April 2010) (High Court of Allahabad). The Court agreed with the petitioner's argument that the actions of the university violated his fundamental rights to privacy as well as equality under the Constitution. Yet, within days of the Court ruling ordering his reinstatement, Siras was found dead in his home, under suspicious circumstances, and his death remains unsolved. Siras was in all likelihood murdered despite his legal victory and the fact that homosexuality had been decriminalised at the time his case was heard.

sanctioned and valorised by the heterosexual regime, in order to prove their own humanity, feel 'normal' and have a sense of stability and social belonging. It emerges as a governance project. In the move towards 'normality', the 'abnormality' of the queer subject is sanitised, and rendered less objectionable to the 'normal' and 'natural' heterosexual majority. While it is important to give greater acknowledgement to the moments of social disruption produced by same-sex marriage, that is, to identify the queer moment, the logic underlying the act and its outcomes mandate deeper scrutiny. After all, it is in the small moments, in the minutiae of daily life within the larger frames of relationships, as in marriage, adoption, conception or consensual sex, that state power is most immediately exercised and felt, and where it regulates, manages and governs.

Beyond anti-normativity/normativity

The anti-normativity impulse of queer theory, which has brought a rich and radical brand of politics to the understanding of sexuality and gender,[33] seems to have lost steam in its engagements with human rights. As it is increasingly brought within the vision of human rights, queer sexuality ends up as normalised, naturalised, procreative and universalised. While the challenges to colonial and persecutory laws have been important, the radicality of queer has been lost in this pursuit. The more queer finds traction within the arena of human rights, the more embedded it has become within dominant racial, religious and cultural norms that continue to operate along an inclusionary and exclusionary divide. This pursuit may be indicative of how queer itself may have gone normative. Even though queer has invariably sought to distinguish itself from normative projects, and from LGBT politics that have been cast as a distinctly more liberal enterprise, it is not apparent that this distinction has been maintained in the field and practice of human rights.

There has been a provocative call from some quarters to distance the queer project from anti-normativity as its default position.[34] This move is based on the insight that queer critique continues to be persistently pursued by the norm that devours nearly everything and anything that seeks a space beyond or outside the norm. This call invites scholars and advocates to think about 'what might queer theory do if its allegiance to antinormativity was rendered less secure?'[35] More specifically, what does it mean to think about queer that is not just a defence against normativity and identitarian politics? The challenge is not intended as a call to disengage with critique, but to explore the alternative spaces that critique

33 David M Halperin, *Saint Foucault: Towards a Gay Hagiography* (Oxford University Press, 1995); Lee Edelman, *Homographesis: Essays in Gay Literary and Cultural Theory* (Routledge, 1994).

34 Robyn Wiegman and Elizabeth A Wilson, 'Introduction: Antinormativity's Queer Conventions' (2015) 26(1) *Differences: A Journal of Feminist Cultural Studies* 1.

35 Ibid 1.

may open up in terms of histories, sexuality, political and social desires, as well as affect.

In line with the concern that underlies this challenge, I have questioned how anti-normativity has been helpful in the field of human rights.[36] The critiques of the human rights project have exposed the discursive operations of rights and how it emerges as a governance project primarily concerned with ordering the lives of non-European peoples, rather than as a liberating force. Central to this critique is how the pre-given liberal rational subject of human rights is contingent and one of the prime effects of power. While the resistive subject of human rights has challenged and disrupted the governing norms that structure the human rights project, these temporal moments have not translated into a lasting and larger transformative project. Instead, as I argue in this chapter, anti-normativity does not appear to have helped in the discovering and uncovering of what has been muted in normativity. Anti-normativity may generate continuity in the field, but once queer has gone normative, what then remains of queer emancipatory possibilities?[37] For example, David L Eng has argued that the emergence of what he describes as 'queer liberalism' affirms the freedom and familial ties of specific types of queer subjects to the exclusion of race, which is consigned to the 'dustbin of history', rather than exposing and engaging with how race and sexuality are mutually constitutive and coeval.[38] Some scholars have argued in favour of rejecting the anti-normative stance of queer politics as a way in which to create the possibility of engagement with the dynamism of the norm, which is more extensive and differentiated than an anti-normative stand allows for.[39] According to this position, normal, norms and normativity are complex, and an oppositional anti-normative stand obscures this complexity and 'immobilises the activity of norms'.[40]

While this turn speaks to the vibrant possibilities that remain unexplored in queer politics, I remain sceptical of the underlying assumption, namely that 'the norm, or normative space, knows no outside', and that there is no place from which to claim to be exterior to the norm, and to 'possess an otherness which would actually make it other'.[41] It may be that within legal terms and the human

36 Kapur, above n 16.

37 See David L Eng, Judith Halberstam and José Esteban Muñoz, 'Introduction: What's Queer about Queer Studies Now?' (2005) 23(3–4) *Social Text* 1. Eng et al have described how this result in queer politics more generally is the equivalent of queer liberalism: '[m]echanisms of normalization [that] have endeavored to organize not only gay and lesbian politics but also the internal workings of the field itself, attempting to constitute its governing logic around certain privileged subjects, standards of sexual conduct, and political and intellectual engagements': at 4.

38 David L Eng, *The Feeling of Kinship: Queer Liberalism and the Racialization of Intimacy* (Duke University Press, 2010) x–xiv, 57.

39 Wiegman and Wilson, above n 35, 11, 14.

40 Ibid 14.

41 François Ewald, 'A Power Without an Exterior' in Timothy J Armstrong (ed), *Michel Foucault Philosopher: Essays Translated from the French and German* (Harvester Wheatsheaf, 1992) 169, 173.

rights arena, norms abound; yet this project is itself bounded and limited by a liberal scaffolding which provides little space for radical alternatives or for the 'failed' queer who refuses normative compliance.[42] I conclude by suggesting that we need to move beyond the anti-normative/normative duality. We need to investigate more thoughtfully and consciously what possibilities for queer radicality lie beyond normativity, as well as anti-normativity, that remain constrained within the liberal imaginary. This requires that we decentre the almost unquestioned alignment of queer with the Euro–American genealogy, US mappings of queer and US political projects.[43]

Recapturing queer radicality

In this vein, I turn to the radical and imaginary possibilities that lie outside the limited circumference of human rights. This involves looking into spaces beyond the liberal imaginary that are not illiberal but non-liberal, and where there exist an abundant supply of queer possibilities and radicality. I show how this can be done with the story of *Lalla* (also known as *Lal Ded* or *Lalleswari*), a young female mystic from the fourteenth century who was born in and around 1320 in modern day Kashmir, a divided state in northern India. While there are few biographical facts available about her life, what is known is that Lalla was married at the age of 12, wherein she was subjected to untold physical abuse and mistreatment. At the age of 26, she chose to leave her marital home, renouncing the material life including her marriage and defying all social conventions by forging her life as a mystic within the tradition of the Kashmiri Shaivite sect of renouncers.[44] Lalla became an ascetic who wandered about naked, creating and writing mystic poetry called a *vatsun* or *Vakh* (speech, or more accurately, utterance) and reciting proverbs as part of her process of sustained introspective contemplation.[45] Her poetry witnesses a breaking away from socially and sexually

42 Sara Ahmed, *The Promise of Happiness* (Duke University Press, 2010).

43 Anjali Arondekar and Geeta Patel, 'Area Impossible: Notes Toward an Introduction' (2016) 22 *GLQ: A Journal of Lesbian and Gay Studies* 151.

44 The basis of this philosophy lies in texts composed between the fourth and eighth centuries (the *Saiva-agamas*) that concern the structure of the cosmos and how to acquire release from the cycle of birth and death. This release is secured by recognising the ineffable and unitary essence of the universe that is known as the Shiva-principle. While there are many variants of the Saivite tradition, in the non-dualist branch of this tradition, there is a recognition that the phenomenal world is real only to the extent that it is perceived as existing through consciousness and that no object can exist independent of perception. This position culminates in the view that there is no world outside of the self. For discussion, see Ranjit Hoskote, *I, Lalla: The Poems of Lal D d* (Ranjit Hoskote trans, Penguin, 2012).

45 In one of her verses, Lalla states: 'My guru gave me only one advice – from outside transfer the attention within. That became Lalla's initiation. That is why I began to wander naked.' Whether Lalla was a nude ascetic makes little difference to her inward journey where all vestiges of materiality including the body are relinquished. Other female mystics have similarly wandered naked, including Akka Mahadevi, who lived in South India in the twelfth century. Defying all social norms and customs, she wandered nude with only her long hair covering

defined norms and experiencing a new way of being free. It is at times highly erotic as her quest for self-realisation is also a quest for unconditional love. This self-realisation and freedom is found in the resolution of her identity as a separate individual being, into that which will give her freedom: a conscious self, from where the world is perceived and wherein the world also resolves.

Lalla deplored religion and religious practice, especially rituals and external worship that for her could never provide the means for what she describes as self-realisation or freedom. Her life and poetry are exemplary of her own position to refuse a life governed by social expectations and their accompanying prohibitions and constraints. While Lalla's inward journey is neither sexually explicit nor based on sexual identity, her journey at the metaphysical and philosophical level represents an experience outside of binary thought rather than reliant on sexual acts and identities, which tend to be the focus of human rights advocacy. To be more specific, it represents a position outside the norm that does not exist in opposition to it, but thrives despite its presence. It is a position that simultaneously produces dissidence and also introduces the possibility for wide-ranging political and epistemological transformation.

Human rights constitute a 'civilised' community and a privileged circle of certain kinds of human beings and human alliances, an inclusion and legitimacy that is denied to failed queer subjects. Lalla's story serves as the metaphor for the crowd of outcasts, like the 'homosexual dissident' that works towards a radical alternative mode of being.[46] It is not a location that is based on sex acts or sexuality, but is a direction that queer politics can take in order to retain or resume its radicality. While it may be argued that this position represents a form of sexual evasiveness, when homosexual sex-acts may demand visibility and an aggressive strategy of 'show and tell' in a homophobic world, such a response obscures that which is queer about this kind of strategy – the productive possibilities that lie in recapturing a radicality based on an alternative epistemology. The queering of human rights ultimately takes us in the direction of more rights, but does not necessarily retain a radical politics or the possibility of queering of human rights. In fact, as discussed, it may take us along the road to respectability and harbour within it a lethal and destructive agenda – of militarisation and violence as resolution, which marked the Security Council meeting on LGBT rights with which this chapter began.

Queer becomes implicated in the production of governmental power through which it also acquires visibility and presence, ultimately collaborating with the very power it sets out to challenge. Its subversive capacities recede, and it becomes a technique for assimilation and co-optation. The story of Lalla proposes another

her body: ibid; Jaishree Kak, 'Introduction' in *Mystical Verses of Lallā: A Journey of Self Realisation* (Jaishree Kak trans, Motilal Banarsidass Publishers, 2007); Jaishree Kak Odin, *To the Other Shore: Lalla's Life and Poetry* (Vitasta, 1999).

46 Leela Gandhi, 'A Case of Radical Kinship: Edward Carpenter and the Politics of Anti-Colonial Sexual Dissidence' in Brinda Bose and Subhabrata Bhattacharyya (eds), *The Phobic and the Erotic: The Politics of Sexualities in Contemporary India* (Seagull Books, 2007) 92.

possible trajectory, that is, perhaps a utopian space that opens up possibilities of developing radical alternative associations that are not based on gender binaries or sexual hierarchies. Linking queer to a tradition and context that has been projected historically as backward and uncivilised not only brings it into close alliance with that which is *productively* different as well as indeterminate, but also repudiates the heteronormative/homonormative and reproductive processes that continue to ensnare queer when it steps onto the terrain of human rights and strip it of its radicality.

8 Homoglobalism

The emergence of global gay governance

*Aeyal Gross**

In September 2016, the UN Human Rights Council appointed an Independent Expert on protection against violence and discrimination based on sexual orientation and gender identity (SOGI).[1] Less than a month later, the World Bank President announced the appointment of an advisor on SOGI, a newly created senior position tasked with promoting lesbian, gay, bisexual, transgender and intersex (LGBTI) inclusion throughout the work of the World Bank.[2] Both developments are part of a wider trend of global institutions beginning to engage with LGBT/LGBTI[3] issues.

In this chapter, I identify and analyse these developments, arguing that we are witnessing an emerging phenomenon I call 'global gay governance' (GGG). By 'gay governance', following the work of scholars on governance feminism,[4] I mean the forms in which LGBT advocacy and ideas get incorporated into

* Previous versions of this chapter were presented at the Symposium to Celebrate the Work of Dianne Otto held at SOAS, the University of London, September 2016, and at the Faculty Seminar, Tel-Aviv University Faculty of Law, November 2016. I am grateful to the participants in these forums for their helpful comments. Thanks to Roy Mattar and Idan Seger for their research assistance. Thanks to Mimi Oorloff for her assistance in preparing the chapter for publication in this volume. Special thanks to Di Otto for inviting for me to be part of this book and for her many suggestions. Special thanks to Catriona Drew for her excellent editorial and substantive suggestions.

1 See below nn 79–89 and accompanying text.

2 'World Bank Announces New Advisor on Sexual Orientation and Gender Identity Issues' (Press Release, 27 October 2016) <http://www.worldbank.org/en/news/press-release/2016/10/27/world-bank-announces-new-advisor-on-sexual-orientation-and-gender-identity-issues>.

3 I use the terms LGBT or LGBTI depending on the original use to which I cite.

4 See Janet Halley, Prabha Kotiswaran, Hila Shamir and Chantal Thomas, 'From the International to the Local in Feminist Legal Responses to Rape, Prostitution/Sex Work and Sex Trafficking: Four Studies in Contemporary Governance Feminism' (2006) 29 *Harvard Journal of Law and Gender* 335.

state, state-like and state-affiliated power. In previous work,[5] I showed that gay governance occurs at the municipal, national and global levels. This chapter extends this work by focusing on GGG at the level of global institutions.

Even before the recent appointments, the growing engagement of global institutions with LGBT issues had attracted academic attention. Rahul Rao for example, has described the International Financial Institutions' (IFI) campaign against homophobia as 'global homocapitalism'.[6] Others have addressed the United Nations' engagement with LGBT issues.[7] These institutional developments are, I suggest, part of an emerging 'homoglobalism'. The rise of homoglobalism cannot be detached from recent developments at the national level – the dramatic shifts from the depiction of the homosexual as a threat to the nation,[8] to the notion of the homosexual as embedded in the nation, or of LGBT rights as *de rigeur* in the branding of states as liberal and democratic.[9] Some of this process has been captured in the discussion of 'homonationalism', described by Jasbir Puar as 'nationalist homonormativity', whereby 'domesticated' gay entities provide ammunition for strengthening the nationalist project,[10] and by growing interest in the use of LGBT rights by states (especially but not only Israel) for public diplomacy and propaganda purposes, often referred to as 'pinkwashing'.[11]

5 Aeyal Gross, 'Gay Governance: A Queer Critique' in Janet Halley, Prabha Kotiswaran, Rachel Rebouche and Hila Shamir (eds), *Governance Feminism: A Reader* (University of Minnesota Press, forthcoming 2017).

6 Rahul Rao, 'Global Homocapitalism' (2015) 194 *Radical Philosophy* <https://www.radicalphilosophy.com/article/global-homocapitalism>.

7 See, eg, Elizabeth Baisley, 'Reaching the Tipping Point?: Emerging International Human Rights Norms Pertaining to Sexual Orientation and Gender Identity' (2016) 38 *Human Rights Quarterly* 134; Anthony S Winer, 'Levels of Generality and the Protection of LGBT Rights before the United Nations General Assembly' (2015) 41 *William Mitchell Law Review* 80; Eduard Jordaan, 'The Challenge of Adopting Sexual Orientation Resolutions at the UN Human Rights Council' (2016) 8 *Journal of Human Rights Practice* 298; Françoise Girard, 'Negotiating Sexual Rights and Sexual Orientation at the UN' in Richard Parker, Rosalind Petchesky and Robert Sember (eds), *Sex Politics: Reports from the Front Lines* (Report, Sexual Policy Watch, 2007) 311 <http://www.sxpolitics.org/frontlines/book/pdf/capitulo9_united_nations.pdf>; Tina Beattie, 'Whose Rights, Which Rights? – The United Nations, the Vatican, Gender and Sexual and Reproductive Rights' (2014) 55 *Heythrop Journal* 1080.

8 See Aeyal M Gross, 'Between the Homosocial and the Homoerotic: Gays/Military in Comparative and International Law' in A-Ch Kiss and Johann G Lammers (eds), *Hague Yearbook of International Law* (Martinus Nijhoff, 2001) vol 13, 86.

9 See, eg, Katherine Franke, 'Dating the State: The Moral Hazards of Winning Gay Rights' (2012) 44 *Columbia Human Rights Law Review* 1; David Paternotte, Manon Tremblay and Carol Johnson (eds), *The Lesbian and Gay Movement and the State: Comparative Insights into a Transformed Relationship* (Ashgate, 2011).

10 Jasbir K Puar, *Terrorist Assemblages: Homonationalism in Queer Times* (Duke University Press, 2007) 36–40. See also Jasbir Puar, 'Rethinking Homonationalism' (2013) 45 *International Journal of Middle East Studies* 336, 337.

11 Aeyal Gross, 'The Politics of LGBT Rights in Israel and beyond: Nationality, Normativity, and Queer Politics' (2015) 46 *Columbia Human Rights Law Review* 81; Sarah Schulman, *Israel/Palestine and the Queer International* (Duke University Press, 2012).

The changing relationship between LGBT rights and the state has given rise to complex questions about the appropriation of LGBT rights both internationally and domestically.[12] However, the appropriations at the national and global levels can differ. While GGG is only in its infancy, it is already receiving concerted opposition. Many states oppose treating violence and discrimination on LGBT grounds as a human rights issue. Of course, there is also opposition at the national level. But at the global level, the opposition is interstate, rather than intrastate, and the political context is different. Moreover, as I will show, the emergence of homoglobalism is fragile and dependent upon factors that are politically, temporally and also, to some degree, personally contingent.

Puar describes homonationalism as an analytic category deployed to understand and historicise how and why a nation's status as 'gay-friendly' has become desirable in the first place,[13] and posits that homonationalism 'goes global' as it undergirds US imperial structures through, in her words, 'an embrace of a sexually progressive multiculturalism justifying foreign intervention'.[14] I argue in this chapter that the shifts by global institutions, as well as the associated activism by LGBT advocates, are not limited in their impact to the politicised use of LGBT rights by states. I argue further that what I call GGG is not limited to, and quite different from, the global aspects of homonationalism described by Puar. The shifts discussed also change attitudes towards LGBT issues at the global level, a change that is advocated not only by global North states, but by some states from the global South, as well as by civil society activists. These shifts go beyond the politicised use of a state's status or image as gay friendly, and its wish to vilify other states as homophobic or to justify intervention, even if these elements also exist. The gay governance framework I offer, and specifically the GGG framework, considers not only the changing attitude of the state to homosexuality, but also the growing participation of LGBT advocacy and ideas – and sometimes people – in governance itself.

The discussion proceeds as follows. In the first part, I address the emergence of GGG in the attempts of the United Kingdom and the United States on the one hand, and IFIs on the other, to export LGBT rights through aid conditionality and other financial measures. In the second part, I explore recent developments at the United Nations primarily – but not only – in its human rights institutions. In conclusion, I highlight some common challenges presented to LGBTI human rights advocates by both tracks of homoglobalism: the financial and the human rights dimensions. I argue that in assessing the trend towards GGG there is a need to carry out a cost-benefit analysis that assesses the promise of advancing LGBT rights at the global level against the risk of co-option by global institutions for their own purposes.

12 See Gross, 'The Politics of LGBT Rights', above n 11; Franke, above n 9.

13 Puar, 'Rethinking Homonationalism', above n 10, 336.

14 Ibid.

The emergence of global gay governance: Exporting rights and imposing conditionality[15]

The United Kingdom, the World Bank and gay conditionality

In 2011, then British Prime Minister David Cameron announced that a state's domestic policy towards LGBT rights would henceforth be a factor in determining UK aid policy. States that criminalised homosexuality could lose financial aid unless they reformed.[16] Britain is 'one of the premier aid givers in the world', said Cameron. It wants countries that receive its aid to adhere to 'proper human rights', including in how they treat gay men and lesbians.[17] Rao has called this 'gay conditionality'.[18] It provides a telling example of GGG because of the way in which LGBT rights are used within a power structure. Later, in 2013, after same-sex marriage was legalised in the United Kingdom, Cameron said he wanted to 'export' gay marriage to the entire world as part of the 'global race . . . to export more and sell more'.[19]

Cameron's conditionality announcement provoked angry (and arguably homophobic) reactions from many political and religious leaders in Africa. A Ugandan presidential advisor accused Cameron of having an 'ex-colonial mentality' and of treating Ugandans 'like children'.[20] A broad coalition of African social justice activists expressed concern over Cameron's statements and similar decisions by several other donor countries in relation to Uganda and Malawi. 'While the intention may well be to protect the rights of LGBTI people on the continent', they said, 'the decision to cut aid disregards the role of the LGBTI and broader social justice movement on the continent and creates the real risk of a serious backlash against LGBTI people'.[21] Instead, the activists urged the British government to expand its aid to community-based LGBTI programmes aimed at fostering dialogue and tolerance, and support national and regional human

15 Some of the discussion in this section draws on parts of Gross, 'Gay Governance', above n 5.

16 'Countries that Ban Homosexuality Risk Losing Aid, Warns David Cameron', *The Guardian* (online) (30 October 2011) <http://www.theguardian.com/politics/2011/oct/30/ban-homosexuality-lose-aid-cameron>.

17 BBC News, 'Transcript Philip Hammond Interview', *The Andrew Marr Show*, 30 October 2011 (David Cameron) <http://news.bbc.co.uk/1/hi/programmes/andrew_marr_show/9627898.stm>.

18 Rahul Rao, 'On "Gay Conditionality", Imperial Power and Queer Liberation', *Kafila* (1 January 2012) <https://kafila.online/2012/01/01/on-gay-conditionality-imperial-power-and-queer-liberation-rahul-rao/#more-11088>.

19 Christopher Hope, 'David Cameron: "I Want to Export Gay Marriage around the World"', *The Telegraph* (online) (24 July 2013) <http://www.telegraph.co.uk/news/politics/10200636/I-want-to-export-gay-marriage-around-the-world-says-David-Cameron.html>.

20 'Uganda Fury at David Cameron Aid Threat over Gay Rights', *BBC News* (online) (31 October 2011) <http://www.bbc.com/news/world-africa-15524013>.

21 'Statement on British "Aid Cut": Threats to African Countries that Violate LGBTI Rights', *Pambazuka News* (online) (27 October 2011) <http://www.pambazuka.net/en/category.php/advocacy/77470>.

rights mechanisms to ensure the inclusion of LGBTI issues in their protective and promotional mandates. They further urged the United Kingdom to support the 'entrenchment' of LGBTI issues into broader social justice issues through the financing of locally led and nationally owned projects.[22]

The perceived attempt to 'export' gay marriage has been blamed for an escalation of homophobic violence in some parts of Africa,[23] and a backlash against 'gay conditionality' has been reported in several countries.[24] For example, shortly after Cameron's statement, the President of Ghana declared he would never legalise homosexuality, and religious groups used Cameron's speech as an opportunity to foster homophobia,[25] while Nigeria introduced a bill criminalising same-sex marriage.[26]

In Uganda, gay conditionality turned from threat to reality. Some of Uganda's budget support was suspended over concerns about its attitude to gay rights.[27] In February 2014, the World Bank announced it would indefinitely delay a US $90 million health-care loan to Uganda because of its anti-gay law.[28] The money in question had been earmarked to address maternal mortality, which is extremely high in Uganda.[29] Aid conditionality with regard to health-care systems has a problematic history, in the past requiring 'economic restructuring', including the cutting of social expenditure under the so-called Washington Consensus.[30]

22 Ibid.

23 See also Rahul Rao, chapter 1, this volume, 'A tale of two atonements'.

24 For a discussion of the backlash showing that homosexuality is portrayed in several African countries by a hostile media, and by the political elite as an imported cultural abomination, see Stephen Wood, 'Sexuality, Development and Continued Colonialism?', *An Institute of Development Studies Blog* (3 November 2011) <https://participationpower.wordpress.com/2011/11/03/sexuality-development-and-continued-colonialism/>.

25 Luis Abolafia Anguita, 'Aid Conditionality and Respect for LGBT People Rights' in *The Global Context: Sexuality and Geopolitics, Selected Texts* (SPW Working Paper No 7, Sexual Policy Watch, April 2012) 9 <http://www.sxpolitics.org/wp-content/uploads/2012/04/spw-wp7-the-global-context-sexuality-and-politics.pdf>. On Ghana, see also Scott Long, 'Backlash in Ghana: New Anti-Gay Legislation Discussed' on Scott Long, *A Paper Bird* (3 November 2011) <http://paper-bird.net/2011/11/03/backlash-in-ghana-new-anti-gay-legislation-discussed/>.

26 Anguita, above n 25.

27 See 'Uganda Fury at David Cameron', above n 20.

28 J Lester Feder, 'World Bank Delays $90 Million Loan to Uganda as Bank President Blasts Anti-Gay Laws', *BuzzFeed News* (online) (28 February 2014) <http://www.buzzfeed.com/lesterfeder/world-bank-delays-90-million-loan-to-uganda-as-bank-presiden#.kr32Bve0G>.

29 Scott Long, 'Uganda, the World Bank and LGBT Rights: Winners and Losers' on Scott Long, *A Paper Bird* (10 March 2014) <http://paper-bird.net/2014/03/10/uganda-the-world-bank-and-lgbt-rights-winners-and-losers/>.

30 Sue McGregor, 'Neoliberalism and Health Care' (2001) 25 *International Journal of Consumer Studies* 82; Alicia Ely Yamin, 'Power, Suffering and Courts: Reflections on Promoting Health Rights through Judicialization' in Alicia Ely Yamin and Siri Gloppen (eds), *Litigating Health Rights: Can Courts Bring More Justice to Health?* (Harvard University Press, 2011) 340.

The possibility of health care again becoming a victim of conditionality resonated alarmingly.[31]

Since the enactment of anti-homosexuality legislation in Uganda, other donors too have slashed or suspended aid.[32] Project and budget support worth about US $140 million has been suspended or redirected by the World Bank, the United States and several European countries. While some human rights groups have advocated continuing these sanctions,[33] health officials, activists and NGOs have warned of the impact on health-care services, particularly for HIV/AIDS patients.[34]

Some Ugandan activists have been critical of aid cuts, protesting that they do not want the people of Uganda to suffer because of the government's political choices. They support only strategic cuts to specific sectors that fail to demonstrate respect for human rights and which support the anti-gay bill.[35] Advocates note that there are many 'horrible laws' in Uganda. Singling out the anti-gay bill is patronising and increases the vulnerability of LGBT people to homophobia.[36] The different positions taken by advocacy groups, even within Uganda itself, attest to the real dilemmas raised by the issue of conditionality.

In 2015, after the Ugandan Constitutional Court struck down the new anti-gay legislation for procedural reasons,[37] the Ugandan President said the law was no longer necessary and he would no longer pursue it.[38] Although the country's previous law criminalising 'carnal knowledge . . . against the order of nature' (which carried the threat of life imprisonment) remained in force, international pressure may have affected the President's decision to desist from further pursuing the new legislation that targeted homosexuality more specifically, dramatically increasing sentences compared to existing legislation and criminalising LGBT rights advocacy in Uganda.[39] Can we assume, then, that international pressure was useful here? Obviously making this judgment is difficult, but it is an important

31 See Peter Dunne, 'LGBTI Rights and the Wrong Way to Give Aid' (2012) 12 *Harvard Kennedy School Review* 66.

32 'Briefing: Punitive Aid Cuts Disrupt Healthcare in Uganda', *IRIN* (online) (2 April 2014) <http://www.irinnews.org/printreport.aspx?reportid=99878>.

33 Aaron Dorfman, Kevin Robert Frost, Chad Dobson et al, *Joint CSO Letter to World Bank on Discrimination in Uganda's Health Sector*, The Council for Global Equality <http://globalequality.org/newsroom/latest-news/1-in-the-news/203-worldbankcsoletter>.

34 'Briefing: Punitive Aid Cuts', above n 32.

35 Scott Long, 'From Uganda: Guidelines for Action against the Anti-Homosexuality Bill' on Scott Long, *A Paper Bird* (5 March 2014) <http://paper-bird.net/2014/03/05/from-uganda-guidelines-for-action-against-the-anti-homosexuality-bill/>.

36 'Briefing: Punitive Aid Cuts', above n 32.

37 *Oloka-Onyango v Attorney General*, Petition No 8, 1 August 2014 reported in [2014] UGCC 14 (Constitutional Court of Uganda).

38 Joe Williams, 'Uganda's President Says New Anti-Gay Laws "Not Necessary"', *Pink News* (online) (16 September 2015) <http://www.pinknews.co.uk/2015/09/16/ugandas-president-says-new-anti-gay-laws-not-necessary/>.

39 For a discussion of the differences between the existing and the proposed laws, see 'Uganda Action Alert: Dismiss the Anti-Homosexuality Bill' (16 October 2009) Outright Action

factor if we are to calculate the costs and benefits of GGG. In such a calculation, we would also need to consider whether this case risked the lives of women (and babies) to save the lives of gay people – as it should not be acceptable to advocate for LGBT rights at the expense of the rights of other groups. For a more exact assessment, we would need to know on the one hand whether the loan suspension indeed damaged maternal health and on the other whether it played a role in preventing the reintroduction of the anti-gay legislation. We would also need to account for the effects of the backlash on LGBT lives. All in all, the story of gay conditionality points to the risks inherent in GGG. Once LGBT rights are incorporated into global governance, they can be appropriated to reinforce or strengthen the political and/or economic power of Northern states over states in the global South, and potentially harm vulnerable populations.

The United States and global gay governance

In 2011, then US Secretary of State Hillary Clinton addressed the need for global consensus on the recognition of the human rights of LGBT individuals everywhere: 'The Obama Administration defends the human rights of LGBT people as part of our comprehensive human rights policy and as a priority of our foreign policy.'[40] In US embassies, Clinton said, diplomats are raising concerns about specific cases and laws, and working with a range of partners to strengthen human rights protections for all. In Washington, the State Department created a task force to support and coordinate this work.[41] A memorandum issued by President Obama directed US foreign aid agencies to engage regularly with governments, citizens, civil society and the private sector to foster awareness of LGBT human rights.[42] Ugandan officials responsible for anti-LGBT human rights abuses were banned from entering the United States.[43]

Further signs of the expanding scope and power of US-led global LGBT advocacy were evident in 2015, when the State Department announced the

International <https://www.outrightinternational.org/content/uganda-action-alert-dismiss-anti-homosexuality-bill>.

40 Hillary Rodham Clinton, 'Remarks in Recognition of International Human Rights Day' (6 December 2011) US Department of State <http://online.hillsdale.edu/file/presidency/lecture-6/Clinton--Remarks-in-Recognition-of-International-Human-Rights-Day.pdf>.

41 Ibid.

42 See *Presidential Memorandum – International Initiatives to Advance the Human Rights of Lesbian, Gay, Bisexual and Transgender Persons* (6 December 2011) The White House <https://www.whitehouse.gov/the-press-office/2011/12/06/presidential-memorandum-international-initiatives-advance-human-rights-l>; Chris Johnson, 'Obama, Clinton Push Int'l LGBT Rights', *Washington Blade* (online) (6 December 2011) <http://www.washingtonblade.com/2011/12/06/obama-administration-takes-action-on-intl-lgbt-rights/>.

43 Michael K Lavers, 'U.S. to Ban Uganda Officials for LGBT Rights Abuses', *Washington Blade* (online) (19 June 2014) <http://www.washingtonblade.com/2014/06/19/u-s-ban-uganda-officials-lgbt-rights-abuses/>.

appointment of a special envoy to advocate for the rights of LGBT people.[44] The executive director of the International Gay and Lesbian Human Rights Commission called this a 'welcome development and historic moment in the US government's progress in promoting the dignity and equality of LGBT people around the world'.[45] At the same time, argued Adebisi Alimi, many outside the United States were concerned that the appointment might be more symbolic than substantive, and that the symbolism might be 'negative' – why focus on LGBT violence and discrimination, rather than gender violence, poverty, child labour and so on? Moreover, there is a risk that the envoy might look like 'a white person trying to save brown and black LGBT people from their brown and black oppressors', reinforcing the notion that 'homosexuality is something white people in Western countries do that is then imported into African countries'.[46] This is an idea that LGBT activists in Africa have worked hard to debunk. These questions resonated when US officials – including Secretary of State John Kerry in Nigeria and President Obama in Kenya – raised the issue of gay rights during visits to Africa.[47]

At the same time, the importance of the US-led campaign to LGBT activists around the world, who often work in extremely difficult conditions, should not be underestimated and, indeed, this support is often gratefully acknowledged.[48] However, it is also necessary to consider whether the US position, as formulated by Clinton and Obama, entails risks in its implementation. Some differences are evident between the UK position, as expressed by Cameron, and the Clinton-Obama messages, which not only omit explicit advocacy of gay conditionality, but also endorse a less proselytising style, with Clinton herself acknowledging the United States' own problematic record on LGBT rights.[49] Nevertheless, it remained 'unclear whether those countries that target and discriminate against

44 Sylvan Lane, 'Kerry Establishes LGBT Envoy to Advocate for Rights Overseas', *The Boston Globe* (online) (5 February 2015) <http://www.bostonglobe.com/news/nation/2015/02/05/secretary-state-john-kerry-establishes-new-post-lgbt-envoy-advocate-for-rights-overseas/zW9x9QfPFsBGsnQbAdoOKL/story.html?event=event25>.

45 Michael K Lavers, 'State Department Envoy to Promote Global LGBT Rights', *Washington Blade* (online) (5 February 2015) <http://www.washingtonblade.com/2015/02/05/state-department-envoy-promote-global-lgbt-rights/>.

46 Adebisi Alimi, 'Why I Oppose the United States' Special Envoy for LGBT Human Rights', *The Daily Beast* (online) (3 October 2015) <http://www.thedailybeast.com/articles/2015/03/10/why-i-oppose-the-united-states-special-envoy-for-lgbt-human-rights.html>.

47 Michael K Lavers, 'Kerry Raises LGBT Rights with Nigerian President', *Washington Blade* (online) (22 July 2015) <http://www.washingtonblade.com/2015/07/22/kerry-raises-lgbt-rights-with-nigerian-president/>.

48 Ugandan activist Frank Mugisha, for example, said that, thanks to Clinton and others, 'we are no longer alone'. Frank Mugisha, 'Gay and Vilified in Uganda', *The New York Times* (23 December 2011).

49 Scott Long, 'More on Hillary and Barack' on Scott Long, *A Paper Bird* (9 December 2011) <http://paper-bird.net/2011/12/09/more-on-hillary-and-barack/>. See also the distinction Rao draws between Cameron's and Clinton's statements. Rao, 'On "Gay Conditionality"', above n 18.

gay and lesbians would have their funding cut',[50] even though neither Clinton nor Obama had mentioned conditionality.[51] Eventually, the United States was one of the countries that suspended health-related aid to Uganda because of its violation of LGBT rights, although it promised that the cuts would not affect essential health services, agricultural programming or initiatives in democracy and governance.[52]

The question of weighing the costs and benefits of US LGBT global advocacy – and thus more broadly of the processes I describe as homoglobalism – resonated in the mainstream media when the *New York Times* ran a story in December 2015 entitled 'US Support of Gay Rights in Africa May Have Done More Harm than Good'.[53] Gay Nigerians were reported as blaming not only Nigerian society and authorities for the harassment and violence that was triggered by the new anti-gay law, but also the United States, whose support, some argued, had made things considerably worse. The new law was widely regarded, according to the article, as a response to US pressure. A great deal of US money and diplomacy had been deployed in Africa which had opened conversations on a previously taboo subject, but which also made gay men and lesbians more visible and so more vulnerable to harassment and violence.[54]

Unsurprisingly, the *New York Times* story drew criticism. Some argued that the article's focus on Nigeria failed to take sufficient account of the way in which the risk of losing US money may have persuaded the Ugandan government not to revive the Anti-Homosexuality Act 2014, or how public criticism by the US ambassador and others may have led to the release in Malawi of men arrested on homosexuality charges.[55] The US State Department criticised the article as fundamentally misrepresenting the situation of LGBTI people in Africa,

50 Karen McVeigh, 'Gay Rights Must Be Criterion for US Aid Allocations, Instructs Obama', *The Guardian* (online) (7 December 2011) <https://www.theguardian.com/world/2011/dec/07/gay-rights-us-aid-criteria?INTCMP=SRCH>; cf Steven Lee Myers and Helene Cooper, 'US to Aid Gay Rights Abroad, Obama and Clinton Say', *The New York Times* (7 December 2011).

51 Long, 'More on Hillary and Barack', above n 49. For a comparative critical discussion of Cameron's and Clinton's statements, see also Adam J Kretz, 'Aid Conditionality as (Partial) Answer to Antigay Legislation: An Analysis of British and American Foreign Aid Policies Designed to Protect Sexual Minorities' (2013) 7 *Vienna Online Journal on International Constitutional Law* 476.

52 'Briefing: Punitive Aid Cuts', above n 32; Philippa Croome, 'U.S. Suspends Some Aid to Uganda over Anti-Gay Law', *Reuters* (online) (13 March 2014) <http://www.reuters.com/article/2014/03/13/us-uganda-usa-idUSBREA2C1Y120140313#f6T8is6jwDt6pMPF.97>; Peter Baker, 'Uganda: Anti-Gay Law Draws Sanctions', *The New York Times* (20 June 2014).

53 Norimitsu Onishi, 'US Support of Gay Rights in Africa May Have Done More Harm than Good', *The New York Times* (21 December 2015).

54 Ibid.

55 Colin Stewart, 'N.Y. Times: Pro-Gay U.S. Makes Life Worse for Gay Africans' on Colin Stewart, *Erasing 76 Crimes* (20 December 2015) <https://76crimes.com/2015/12/20/n-y-times-pro-gay-u-s-makes-life-worse-for-gay-africans/>.

emphasising that the State Department always works in close consultation with local groups in civil society and affected communities, based on the principle to 'do no harm'.[56] Similar sentiments were expressed by Frank Mugisha, the Executive Director of Sexual Minorities Uganda, who stated that the United States follows the lead of local activists before taking action on their behalf, and that LGBTI people in Uganda sounded the global alarm because the proposed legislation placed lives at risk.[57] Mugisha argued that Ugandan activists advised the US government on how to minimise harm, 'and they listened'. In his account, it is African politicians who employ the narrative of a 'neo-colonial' phenomenon in order to maintain their power at the expense of LGBTI people. Mugisha does not deny the backlash, but argues that, if there is greater violence now that LGBTI people are more visible, the blame lies with homophobia, not funding.[58]

These statements are important because if we want to evaluate the way in which GGG involves an exercise of power along the global North/South divide, we should not only look at the power axis between states. States also exercise power over individuals within their jurisdiction, and if actions by the global North reinforce the power of LGBT individuals and groups who are vulnerable in relation to their home states, then this must also be considered. Describing GGG as an exercise of North/South imperial power is only part of a complex grid of costs and benefits. A cost-benefit analysis must also consider what GGG means for other power relationships, including the empowerment (or weakening) of LGBTI individuals and communities, and their civil society advocacy organisations.

The international financial institutions

In 2014, the World Bank implemented 'gay conditionality' in its decision regarding Uganda. This decision, along with other initiatives such as the World Bank and International Monetary Fund's contributions to the 'It Gets Better' pro-LGBT campaign, and World Bank attempts to build an economic case against homophobia, is part of what Rao calls 'global homocapitalism'.[59] Analysing these developments – to which should be added the recent appointment of a SOGI advisor at the World Bank mentioned earlier – Rao argues, drawing on critical analysis of IFI's engagement with gender issues, that the World Bank may be (again) exemplifying the tendency of imperial governmentality to legitimate its

56 Michael K Lavers, 'State Department Defends LGBT Rights Efforts in Africa', *Washington Blade* (online) (22 December 2015) <http://www.washingtonblade.com/2015/12/22/state-department-defends-lgbt-rights-efforts-in-africa/>. See also the Letter to the Editor by Tom Malinowski, Assistant Secretary of State for Democracy, Human Rights and Labor, 'Support for Gay Rights in Africa', *The New York Times* (29 December 2015).

57 Frank Mugisha, Executive Director, Sexual Minorities Uganda, Letter to the Editor, 'Support for Gay Rights in Africa', *The New York Times* (29 December 2015).

58 Ibid.

59 Rao, 'Global Homocapitalism', above n 6, 38–42.

will to power by humanitarian justifications.[60] Rao argues that the approach of IFIs obscures their own culpability in producing the conditions of homophobia, which allows them to position themselves as external to the problems they seek to alleviate, as a progressive force, at a time when the devastating effects of capitalist crisis and austerity threaten to bring them into disrepute.[61]

But the question to be considered here is not only how anti-homophobia measures may 'pinkwash' the IFIs, but also what the additional costs (however hidden) of this form of GGG are. The controversy about the effect of GGG on the situation of LGBT people in Africa highlights the complexity of carrying out a cost-benefit analysis of gay governance. How can we assess the costs of pinkwashed IFIs? How do we calculate the costs of backlash (more homophobia) and harm to other groups (less maternal healthcare in Uganda)? In making these assessments, we should consider which costs are merely symbolic – their imperial or colonial resonance – and which are material – the risk of increased levels of homophobia, and greater harm to other groups.

The aspects of emerging GGG suggest then a package deal, one that makes LGBT rights advocacy complicit in pinkwashing IFIs and risks harming LGBT rights and other causes, at the same time potentially strengthening local advocacy, changing government policies and making some lives safer. Therefore, the emergence of GGG creates a familiar double bind: the draw of harnessing powerful global institutions to the LGBT cause on the one hand, thereby doing a lot of good, and the risk of co-option on the other, which can result in considerable harm.

The emergence of global gay governance: LGBT human rights discourse in the United Nations

Advocacy and governance in UN human rights bodies

The development of LGBT rights discourse at the United Nations has emerged in stages: first, through the work of UN expert-based human rights treaty bodies and human rights special procedures; second, through civil society advocacy; and, third, the stage we are at today, through a combination of state involvement and strong UN leadership, especially by former UN Secretary-General Ban Ki-moon and former High Commissioner for Human Rights, Navi Pillay. It is only at this third stage that we see the recognition of LGBT rights in UN bodies that are composed of states.[62] Furthermore, in 2011, the UN Office of the High Commissioner for Human Rights (OHCHR) launched a campaign called 'Free and Equal',[63] which promotes LGBT rights from within the UN Secretariat. As part of this campaign, the OHCHR released various videos advocating LGBT

60 Ibid 39.
61 Ibid 38.
62 Baisley, above n 7.
63 UN Free and Equal <https://www.unfe.org/>.

rights, some of which featured messages from high-profile individuals including Ki-moon and Pillay, as well as others from within the LGBT community, advocating the issue in diverse ways.[64]

Despite facing hostility from many states, LGBT rights advocacy has seen some success at the United Nations. In 1994, the Human Rights Committee, which monitors implementation of the International Covenant on Civil and Political Rights (ICCPR)[65] and comprises experts acting in an independent capacity, found that a statute in Tasmania criminalising sex between men violated the right to privacy.[66] Since then, the Committee has also held that the ICCPR requires equal treatment of same-sex couples by the law,[67] but found that the ICCPR does not require states parties to recognise same-sex marriage.[68] In another significant decision, it found that convicting a person for displaying pro-gay posters breached the right to freedom of expression.[69]

Other UN human rights treaty bodies, as well as the Human Rights Committee, have addressed LGBT rights in concluding observations, given after reviewing states' periodic reports, and in general comments interpreting their treaty provisions.[70] However, it was the Human Rights Committee's decisions in individual complaints, launched under the ICCPR's Optional Protocol, that drew much attention and signalled the emerging interpretation of universal human rights norms as offering protection – even if limited – in this area.

Recognition of LGBT rights in the UN-Charter-based human rights bodies, comprised of states, has been much more contested.[71] Developments have therefore come much later and only after some notable failures, such as the decisions not to proceed with a resolution on 'Human Rights and Sexual Orientation' at the Commission on Human Rights in 2003 and 2004, and at the Human Rights

64 See, eg, 'Ban Ki-Moon's Call To World Leaders at the UN', UN Free and Equal <https://www.unfe.org/en/actions/world-leaders>; 'Navi Pillay Knows We Need to Start Changing the World', UN Free and Equal <https://www.unfe.org/en/actions/navi-pillay-psa>.

65 International Covenant on Civil and Political Rights, opened for signature 16 December 1966, 999 UNTS 171 (entered into force 23 March 1976).

66 Human Rights Committee, *Communication No 488/1992*, 50th sess, UN Doc CCPR/C/50/D/488/1992 (31 March 1994) ('*Toonen v Australia*').

67 Human Rights Committee, *Communication No 941/2000*, 78th sess, UN Doc CCPR/C/78/D/941/2000 (18 September 2003) ('*Young v Australia*'); Human Rights Committee, *Communication No 1361/2005*, 89th sess, UN Doc CCPR/C/89/D/1361/2005 (30 March 2007) ('*X v Colombia*').

68 Human Rights Committee, *Communication No 902/1999*, 75th sess, UN Doc CCPR/C/75/D/902/1999 (17 July 2002) ('*Joslin v New Zealand*').

69 Human Rights Committee, *Communication No 1932/2010*, 106th sess, UN Doc CCPR/C/106/D/1932/2010 (31 October 2012) ('*Fedotova v Russian Federation*').

70 Paula Gerber and Joel Gory, 'The UN Human Rights Committee and LGBT Rights: What Is It Doing? What Could It Be Doing?' (2014) 14 *Human Rights Law Review* 403.

71 Dianne Otto, 'Transnational Homo-Assemblages: Reading "Gender" in Counter-Terrorism Discourses' (2013) 4(2) *Jindal Global Law Review* 79; Eduard Jordaan, 'The Challenge of Adopting Sexual Orientation Resolutions at the UN Human Rights Council' (2016) 8 *Journal of Human Rights Practice* 298.

Council (which replaced the Commission) in 2005, because of fierce opposition from the Organisation of the Islamic Conference and the Holy See.[72] In 2010, the UN General Assembly adopted its first resolution on LGBT issues, which called for an end to extrajudicial killings of persons based on their sexual orientation.[73] The following year, the Human Rights Council, by a narrow margin, adopted a resolution, presented by South Africa, Brazil and others, which expressed grave concern over acts of violence committed against individuals because of their sexual orientation and gender identity and called on the High Commissioner for Human Rights to report on the extent of the problem.[74] The resulting report – 'Discriminatory Law and Practices and Acts of Violence against Individuals Based on Their Sexual Orientation and Gender Identity' – was published in December 2011[75] with a follow up in 2015.[76] In 2016, the Human Rights Council decided to appoint an Independent Expert to deal with protection against violence and discrimination based on sexual orientation and gender identity.[77]

These gains have been hard won.[78] Discussions at the Human Rights Council over the resolution calling for the appointment of the Independent Expert, for example, were a battleground.[79] The resolution proposing the appointment was

72 Matthew Waites, 'Critique of "Sexual Orientation" and "Gender Identity" in Human Rights Discourse: Global Queer Politics Beyond the *Yogakarta Principles*' (2009) 15 *Contemporary Politics* 137, 141; Baisley, above n 7, 149–50.

73 Resolution on Extrajudicial, Summary or Arbitrary Executions, GA Res 65/208, UN GAOR, 65th sess, Agenda Item 68(b), UN Doc A/RES/65/208 (30 March 2011).

74 Human Rights Council, Human Rights, Sexual Orientation and Gender Identity, GA Res 17/19, UN GAOR, 17th sess, Agenda Item 8, UN Doc A/HRC/RES/17/19 (14 July 2011).

75 Human Rights Council, Discriminatory Laws and Practices and Acts of Violence against Individuals Based on Their Sexual Orientation and Gender Identity, UN GAOR, 19th sess, Agenda Items 2 and 8, UN Doc A/HRC/19/41 (17 November 2011).

76 Human Rights Council, Discrimination and Violence against Individuals Based on Their Sexual Orientation and Gender Identity, UN GAOR, 29th sess, Agenda Items 2 and 8, UN Doc A/HRC/29/23 (4 May 2015).

77 Human Rights Council, Protection against Violence and Discrimination Based on Sexual Orientation and Gender Identity, GA Res 32/2, UN GAOR, 32nd sess, Agenda Item 3, UN Doc A/HRC/RES/32/2 (12 July 2016).

78 Waites, above n 72, 141 and sources cited therein.

79 For a compilation of the debate, see 'Compilation of the Adoption of the 2016 SOGI Resolution' (Compilation Report, ILGA, 30 June 2016) <http://ilga.org/downloads/SOGI_Resolution_Vote_compilation.pdf>. See also 'Appointing an Independent Expert on Sexual Orientation and Gender Identity: An Analysis of Process, Results and Implications: 32nd Session of the Human Rights Council, June 13 – 1st July, 2016' (Report, Arc International, 2016) <http://arc-international.net/wp-content/uploads/2016/08/HRC32-final-report-EN.pdf>. For the full amendments, see Pakistan: Amendment to Draft Resolution A/HRC/32/L.2/Rev.1, UN GAOR, 32nd sess, Agenda Item 3, UN Doc A/HRC/32/L.71–A/HRC/32/L.81 (29 June 2016).

brought to the Human Rights Council by several Latin American states.[80] The Organisation of Islamic Cooperation (except Albania) objected to the appointment and proposed 11 different amendments to the resolution.[81] While those that would have undermined the mandate altogether, by deleting all references to sexual orientation and gender identity, were rejected, seven were accepted and incorporated into the text of the resolution.[82]

Most of the seven amendments read as a litany of familiar objections to the encroachment of human rights on domestic or cultural space – the 'protection of sovereignty',[83] the importance of 'respecting regional, cultural and religious value systems', the need for 'joint ownership of human rights', the need to pay attention to the 'relevant domestic debates at the national level on matters associated with historical, cultural, social and religious sensitivities'[84] and to consider human rights in an 'objective and non-confrontational manner'.[85] But less familiar was an amendment to the Preamble 'deploring the use of external pressures and coercive measures against states, particularly developing countries, including through the use and threat of use of economic sanctions and/or application of conditionality on official development assistance, with the aim of influencing the relevant domestic debates and decision-making processes at the national level'.[86]

Read out of context, this paragraph could be mistaken for a critical discussion of homonationalism or pinkwashing. Yet here the critique is by states *opposing* UN recognition of LGBT rights by proposing to delete any reference to sexual orientation or gender identity. In what could be termed homophobic-nationalism, states are here participating in *white*washing – dressing up their homophobia as global South opposition to conditionality, denial of cultural difference and trampling of sovereignty.[87] Once we focus on the global, it is crucial that we look not only at the *pro*-LGBT states and their political use of LGBT rights,[88] but also at the *anti*-LGBT states and *their* political use of the topic. When we discuss GGG, we should also discuss the governance (global or otherwise) that is part of its backlash.

80 'Compilation of the Adoption', above n 79, 3, 7–9. The states were Argentina, Brazil, Colombia, Costa Rica, Mexico and Uruguay.

81 Ibid.

82 Ibid 3.

83 Ibid 54, Ninth Amendment.

84 Ibid 43, Fifth Amendment.

85 Ibid 34, Third Amendment.

86 Ibid 46, Seventh Amendment.

87 For a discussion of the ways in which sexual minorities became 'pawns' in an international 'sensitivity game', see Eric Heinze, 'Sexual Orientation and International Law: A Study in the Manufacture of Cross-Cultural "Sensitivity"' (2001) 22 *Michigan Journal of International Law* 283.

88 For a discussion of the growing support by states of LGBT advocacy at the UN level and the dilemmas this creates, see Long, 'More on Hillary and Barack', above n 49.

Following the adoption of the Independent Expert resolution, in September 2016, the Human Rights Council appointed a Thai national, Vitit Muntarbhorn, to the newly created position,[89] a choice that continues efforts to shift the face of UN LGBT rights activism, and GGG, to the global South. In the same month, the Secretary-General addressed a meeting of government leaders at a high-level side-event of the United Nations' LGBT Core Group.[90] Notably, Muntarbhorn joins Ki-moon and Pillay, all non-white voices outside the West, as leaders of SOGI rights within the United Nations – not an insignificant development, especially when the leading role of global South states in challenging these developments is recalled. This is in contrast to the economic strategies aimed at promoting LGBTI rights, where the United Kingdom and the United States take a leading role.

The developments promoted by human rights bodies are important and promising to many, but also raise the concern that they may create more backlash than emancipatory change on the ground. South African human rights activist, Gabriel Hoosain Khan, has argued that the appointment of an Independent Expert on SOGI seems remote from the realities of culture, geography and poverty of black LGBTI youth in South African townships. '[W]hat does an independent expert mean to a black gender non-conforming woman tortured by police in Zimbabwe?', he asks, concerned that human rights 'has little to do with the messy colonial, racial, gendered, sexualized, classed realities of humans'.[91]

This question also arose with the unlikely arrival of LGBT rights issues at the UN Security Council in the form of an informal closed meeting on the persecution of LGBT Syrians and Iraqis by the so-called Islamic State (ISIS).[92] For Scott Long, the meeting was at best 'useless' and at worst likely to 'cause more killings', giving ISIS 'an easy chance to affirm its law and write its defiance of the Security Council in blood'.[93] Indeed, there have been reports of a rise in the number of ISIS executions for homosexual acts after the meeting.[94] Long argues that putting

89 See 'Vitit Muntarbhorn', UN Human Rights Office of the High Commissioner <http://www.ohchr.org/EN/Issues/SexualOrientationGender/Pages/VititMuntarbhorn.aspx/>

90 'Ban Calls for Continued Efforts to Secure Equal Rights for LGBT community', *UN News* (online) (21 September 2016) <http://www.un.org/apps/news/story.asp?NewsID=55014#.WC7RFuZ97b0>.

91 Gabriel Hoosain Khan, 'The UN, Seen from Khayelitsha: Guest Post' on Scott Long, *A Paper Bird* (6 July 2016) <https://paper-bird.net/2016/07/06/the-un-seen-from-khayelitsha/>.

92 Michael K Lavers, 'Islamic State Focus of U.N. Security Council's First LGBT Meeting', *Washington Blade* (online) (24 August 2015) <http://www.washingtonblade.com/2015/08/24/islamic-state-focus-of-u-n-security-councils-first-lgbt-meeting/>.

93 Scott Long, 'The UN Security Council Debates Gays and ISIS: Why This Is a Bad Idea' on Scott Long, *A Paper Bird* (23 August 2015) <http://paper-bird.net/2015/08/23/the-un-security-council-terrible-idea/>.

94 Scott Long, 'New ISIS Execution for "Sodomy": Attention, UN Security Council' on Scott Long, *A Paper Bird* (17 September 2015) <http://paper-bird.net/2015/09/17/new-isis-execution-attention-un-security-council/>.

LGBT victims of ISIS under the symbolic protection of the United States and the Security Council would make sense only if there was something the United States and the United Nations could and would do to help them.[95] If all they can do is talk, argues Long, the *only* result is the cost to gay lives. Many LGBT groups, however, support and encourage these processes. The Council for Global Equality – an organisation that describes its mission as 'advancing an American foreign policy inclusive of sexual orientation and gender identity'[96] – in granting an award to Samantha Power, US Ambassador to the United Nations, for her support of LGBT rights abroad, praised the Security Council meeting as the 'centrepiece' of her work.[97] The Security Council engaged with the topic again in 2016, following the mass killings in a US gay night club in Orlando, and for the first time adopted a statement expressly mentioning sexual orientation.[98]

In response to the governance feminism critique in the context of international law, Dianne Otto has argued that, while gender-focused resolutions of the Security Council may amount to co-option, they can nonetheless create opportunities for further feminist engagement both locally and globally.[99] She argues that the subsequent development of monitoring mechanisms, for example, provide an opportunity for feminist activism.[100] Gender-based Security Council resolutions are, then, a double-edged sword: they provide 'footholds' for feminist activism, on the one hand, and a means for the Security Council to enhance its legitimacy and power, on the other.[101] The resolutions divert attention away from the underlying structural causes of armed conflict (in particular, the inequitable distribution of global power and wealth) while, at the same time, providing a powerful organising tool for local, national, regional and international feminists networks and

95 Ibid.

96 The Council for Global Equality <http://globalequality.org/>.

97 Michael K Lavers, 'Council for Global Equality Honors Samantha Power in D.C.', *Washington Blade* (online) (14 October 2015) <http://www.washingtonblade.com/2015/10/14/council-for-global-equality-honors-samantha-power-in-d-c/>. In 2016, Power spoke on LGBT issues at a Human Rights Campaign event in New York, where she highlighted the Security Council meeting. See Michael K Lavers, 'Samantha Power: LGBT Equality Not "Special Category of Rights"', *Washington Blade* (online) (12 March 2016) <http://www.washingtonblade.com/2016/03/12/samantha-power-lgbt-equality-not-special-category-of-rights/>.

98 UN, 'Security Council Press Statement on Terrorist Attack in Orlando, Florida' (Press Release, SC/12399, 13 June 2016). For a discussion of the significance of this statement, see Somini Sengupta, 'After Orlando, Gay Rights Moves off Diplomatic Back Burner', *The New York Times* (15 June 2016).

99 Dianne Otto, 'Power and Danger: Feminist Engagement with International Law through the UN Security Council' (2010) 32 *Australian Feminist Law Journal* 97, 112–13.

100 Ibid 115.

101 Dianne Otto, 'Beyond Stories of Victory and Danger: Resisting Feminism's Amenability to Serving Security Council Politics' in Gina Heathcote and Dianne Otto (eds), *Rethinking Peacekeeping, Gender Equality and Collective Security* (Palgrave Macmillan, 2014) 157, 158.

movements.[102] The shifts described by Otto in her own position over time point to how future assessment of the SOGI rights developments occurring at the United Nations – in both the human rights system and the Security Council – will require examining the effects they generate, in a way similar to that offered by Otto in relation to gender issues.

In any case, the changes described here – particularly the fact that states, as well as UN officials, are taking a leading role in advocacy for LGBT rights – point further to the nature of emerging GGG, whereby advocacy is led by national governments through their membership of key UN institutions. Elizabeth Baisley considers the states and high-ranking UN officials involved to be the most effective norm entrepreneurs in this area – achieving more success than individual experts within the UN system and civil society organisations, which nevertheless continue to play an important advocacy role.[103] However, success needs to be weighed against the costs involved. One cost is that the issue of LGBT rights is now a feature of transnational political contestations, with some states, as well as some global institutions, using their support for LGBT rights to bolster their superiority, and others using their opposition to LGBT rights to fuel accusations of neo-imperial interference with their domestic affairs, thereby whitewashing their own reputations. Moreover, the content of the discourse generated at this stage of development shies away from the language of 'sexual rights' utilised earlier by NGOs at UN forums, to a terrain that deploys accepted terms drawn from the existing human rights system. The focus is particularly on violations of civil and political rights of people based on their sexual orientation and gender identity.[104] While this language shift may account for some of the success of those supportive of LGBT rights because they are not advocating for 'new rights' or 'special rights',[105] the inclusion (or some would argue appropriation) of LGBT rights into the existing human rights framework may also have a restricting effect as discussed in the next section. Assessing the costs and benefits of the GGG that is emerging in UN institutions is therefore complicated, not only because of the risk of states pinkwashing themselves by advocating for LGBT rights, while ignoring other human rights issues and vilifying oppositional states, but also because of the risk that global LGBT rights governance spreads a certain restricted version of sexuality, focused more on identities than on sexual rights and freedoms – a risk to which I now turn.

102 Dianne Otto, 'Contesting Feminism's Institutional Doubles: Troubling the Security Council's Women Peace and Security Agenda' in Halley et al, above n 5.

103 Baisley, above n 7, 161–5.

104 Ibid 162.

105 See Navi Pillay's insistence on this point in her video statement from 2012: UN Human Rights, 'Pillay on Homophobia: Punish Violence and Hatred, Not Love!' (7 May 2012) <https://youtu.be/5-_kzl-_mrg>. On this topic, see also Jena McGill, 'SOGI . . . So What?: Sexual Orientation, Gender Identity and Human Rights Discourse at the United Nations' (2014) 3 *Canadian Journal of Human Rights* 1.

The SOGI framework revisited

An important moment in the genealogy of the current SOGI human rights framework was the adoption of the Yogyakarta Principles on the Application of International Human Rights in Relation to Sexual Orientation and Gender Identity ('Yogyakarta Principles') in 2007.[106] The Principles were prepared by a group of human rights experts, and launched at the Human Rights Council.[107] Since then, the SOGI language and framework have defined the mandate of both the UN Independent Expert and the World Bank advisor. Principle 3 of the non-binding Yogyakarta Principles, entitled 'The Right to Recognition before the Law', declares that '[p]ersons of diverse sexual orientations and gender identities shall enjoy legal capacity in all aspects of life', and that '[e]ach person's self-defined sexual orientation and gender identity is integral to their personality and is one of the most basic aspects of self-determination, dignity and freedom'. Thus, the Principles interpret states' existing human rights obligations to include ensuring that all persons are accorded legal capacity without discrimination on the basis of sexual orientation or gender identity.

The concept of sexual orientation – assigning people an identity based on the gender of their object-choice being identical or opposite to their own gender – as reflected in the Yogyakarta Principles definition,[108] has its historical and cultural origins in modern Western states, but not of all humanity subscribes to it.[109] Nor do all societies subscribe to an understanding of sexuality that divides people into two categories – hetero- and homosexuals. In societies where men have sex with men regardless of any specific sexual identity, for example, to attach a sexual orientation label would be to impose a Western model that categorises men having sex with men as an identity, as a distinct and autonomous feature of the self.

While the SOGI framework avoids other Western categories such as 'gay' and 'lesbian', in an attempt to be more open to sexual and gender diversities, its categories of sexual orientation and gender identity[110] still universalise a Western cultural framework, giving charges that the West is seeking to 'export' its own values a great deal of legitimacy. Neville Hoad, for example, asks whether the universalisation of 'the homosexual' as a trans-historical trans-spatial subject in human rights law closes down spaces for other participants in same-sex acts

106 Alice M Miller and Mindy J Roseman, 'Sexual and Reproductive Rights at the United Nations: Frustration or Fulfilment?' (2011) 19(38) *Reproductive Health Matters* 102, 108; Waites, above n 72, 137.

107 Waites, above n 72, 141.

108 *Yogyakarta Principles* (Introduction, fn 1).

109 See David M Halperin, *One Hundred Years of Homosexuality: And Other Essays on Greek Love* (Routledge, 1990).

110 For a critique of the category of gender identity in the Yogyakarta Principles, see Dianne Otto, 'Queering Gender [Identity] in International Law' (2015) 33 *Nordic Journal of Human Rights* 299.

in various places.[111] Attempting to 'transform participants in certain corporeal intimacies into homosexual persons' may, he argues, do a disservice to the majority of participants in same-sex acts outside the West.[112] Similarly, Sonya Katyal argues that focusing on identity-based protections in order to achieve equality for sexual minorities fails to take into account individuals who fall out of the neatly circumscribed categories of sexual identity.[113]

For Joseph Massad, it is the discourse of the LGBT advocacy groups, which he collectively calls the 'Gay International', which both produces gays and lesbians where they do not exist and represses same-sex desires and practices that refuse to be assimilated into its sexual epistemology. In relation to the trials of men accused of 'debauchery' at the 'Queen Boat' club in Cairo, Massad argues that a crackdown on gay men followed increased visibility of Westernised, Cairo-based, upper- and middle-class Egyptian men who identified as gay. The Gay International, argues Massad, misses an important distinction: that what is being repressed by the Egyptian authorities is not same-sex sexual practices, but, rather, the sociopolitical identification of these practices with the Western identity of gayness. In his harsh critique of the international gay rights project, Massad argues that by exporting gay identity, this movement imposes the hetero/homo binary on societies where it may not exist, and incites a discourse on homosexuality that will paradoxically make same-sex sex less feasible.[114] Against Massad's argument, it is important to consider whether international gay identity is indeed a product of 'universalisation' through human rights, or whether it is actually exported through the globalised world of information, tourism, money and media. In my view, while Massad misses identifying the main agents of 'export', and also offers an account of identities being 'implanted', which is too simplistic,[115] the point remains that addressing the ways in which identities are exported and globalised remains critical in application of the SOGI framework.

Queer theory has taught us that the binary hierarchical categories of gender and sexuality (men/women, heterosexual/homosexual) are themselves part of the problem, as this structure mandates that every person must have a gender and sexual orientation that is legible in terms of these binaries. Yet the Yogyakarta Principles, and the subsequent adoption of the SOGI framework as central to

111 Neville Hoad, 'Arrested Development or the Queerness of Savages: Resisting Evolutionary Narratives of Difference' (2000) 3 *Postcolonial Studies* 133.

112 Ibid 152.

113 Sonya Katyal, 'Exporting Identity' (2002) 14 *Yale Journal of Law and Feminism* 97, 100.

114 Joseph Massad, 'Re-Orienting Desire: The Gay International and the Arab World' (2002) 14 *Public Culture* 361. See also Joseph Massad, *Desiring Arabs* (University of Chicago Press, 2007).

115 See also Aeyal Gross, 'Queer Theory and International Human Rights Law: Does Each Person Have a Sexual Orientation?' (2007) 101 *American Society of International Law Proceedings* 129; Amr Shalakany, 'On a Certain Queer Discomfort with Orientalism' (2007) 101 *American Society of International Law Proceedings* 125; Rahul Rao, *Third World Protest: Between Home and the World* (Oxford University Press, 2010) 176–9.

GGG, have not challenged these binaries, but instead have helped to further naturalise them. It is true, as Vanja Hamzić argues, that the Yogyakarta Principles framework does not explicitly crystallise a binary concept of homo/hetero-sexuality and it avoids the explicit language of immutability.[116] But as I have shown, its understanding of sexual orientation does not escape the identitarian locus of Western sexuality. An alternative route was offered by the Sexual Rights Initiative, in the discussion that preceded the Human Rights Council's decision to appoint a SOGI Independent Expert. The Initiative suggested a broad framing of *sexual rights* which would not be limited to addressing violations of the rights of LGBTI people but extended to include sex workers, others who suffer discrimination due to their sexual or gender expression, women seeking access to abortion and other reproductive rights, and the issue of sex education in schools for everyone.[117] However, this option was rejected in favour of the SOGI approach.[118] It is thus concern with discrimination on the grounds of SOGI, rather than sexual rights, that is central to the human rights dimension of GGG.

When assessing this new form of governance, it is also necessary to address critiques that point to the heteronormative assumptions that underpin international human rights law more generally.[119] Other critiques point to the LGBT embrace of liberal rights discourse as devoid of a focus on the development agenda,[120] and as being drawn into a neoliberal narrative of private individual rights, in which gay rights serve as a marker of a civilisational divide between states.[121]

These concerns highlight some of the costs of GGG, but the picture at the UN level, as discussed, is more complex. For example, individuals from the global South have assumed a leading promotional (as well as oppositional) role and states

116 Vanja Hamzić, 'The Case of "Queer Muslims": Sexual Orientation and Gender Identity in International Human Rights Law and Muslim Legal and Social Ethos' (2011) 11 *Human Rights Law Review* 237, 240.

117 'SRI Calls for Political and Legal Framing that Recognizes Full Range of Sexual Rights' (7 June 2016), Sexual Rights Initiative <http://sexualrightsinitiative.com/2016/topics/abortion/sri-calls-for-political-and-legal-framing-that-recognizes-full-range-of-sexual-rights/>.

118 See on this process Scott Long, 'Selling Out: The Gays and Governmentality' on Scott Long, *A Paper Bird* (2 November 2016) <https://paper-bird.net/2016/11/02/selling-out-the-gays-and-governmentality/>.

119 Wayne Morgan, 'Queering International Human Rights Law' in Carl Stychin and Didi Herman (eds), *Law and Sexuality: The Global Arena* (University of Minnesota Press, 2001) 208; Kristen L Walker, 'Capitalism, Gay Identity, and International Human Rights Law' (2000) 9 *Australasian Gay and Lesbian Law Journal* 58; Brenda Cossman, 'Gender Performance, Sexual Subjects and International Law' (2002) 15 *Canadian Journal of Law and Jurisprudence* 281; Aeyal Gross, 'Post/Colonial Queer Globalisation and International Human Rights: Images of LGBT Rights' (2013) 4(2) *Jindal Global Law Review* 98.

120 Andrew Park, 'A Development Agenda for Sexual and Gender Minorities' (Report, Williams Institute, June 2016) <http://williamsinstitute.law.ucla.edu/wp-content/uploads/Development-Agenda-for-Sexual-and-Gender-Minorities.pdf>.

121 Carl F Stychin, 'Same-Sex Sexualities and the Globalization of Human Rights Discourse' (2004) 49 *McGill Law Journal* 951, 953–61.

opposing LGBT rights have appropriated counter-hegemonic arguments as apologia for homophobia. The GGG, which has emerged in the context of UN human rights advocacy, has adopted the SOGI framework rather than the potentially more radical sexual rights framework, but in so doing has gained access to and successes in UN bodies as unlikely as the Security Council. The human rights dimension of GGG shares some features with the financial dimension discussed earlier, but is also different in many regards, particularly with regard to who the key players are.

Conclusion

In this chapter, I have pointed to the emergence in recent years of GGG. In conclusion, it is important to recognise just how fragile this emerging phenomenon is. Unlike, for example, the growing recognition of women's rights, which is occurring against a background where international law explicitly recognises women's equality in various human rights treaties, with a treaty dedicated specifically to the issue, GGG is building from a much weaker starting point. This is not only because of the absence of explicit recognition within international law when it comes to LGBT equality, which allows oppositional states to make the argument that the SOGI concept is not one recognised at all in international law,[122] but also because LGBT people are a relatively small minority, often not represented or visible. The fragility of GGG is also apparent in the continuing objections to the recognition of LGBT rights, most recently seen in the failed attempt, in the UN General Assembly,[123] to suspend the establishment of the mandate of the SOGI Independent Expert, questioning its 'legal basis'.[124] The fragility of the recognition of LGBT rights, and consequently of GGG, is also apparent in the shifts in US positions. The United States only started to take a leading role during the Obama Administration, which undoubtedly influenced developments at the United Nations. With the election of Donald Trump and the subsequent change of Administration, the future US role in GGG is unpredictable, and may affect future developments.[125] Moreover, with both Pillay and Ki-moon being replaced, it is not clear whether the strong UN leadership on this issue will continue.

122 For a discussion of these arguments, see Baisley, above n 7, 150–4; Ignacio Saiz, 'Bracketing Sexuality: Human Rights and Sexual Orientation: A Decade of Development and Denial at the UN' (2004) 7 *Health and Human Rights* 48.

123 Outright Action International, 'United Nations SOGI Mandate Safeguarded in Face of Hostility' (Press Release, 21 November 2016) <https://www.outrightinternational.org/content/united-nations-sogi-mandate-safeguarded-face-hostility>.

124 For the draft resolution proposed by Sierra Leone, see Sierra Leone: Draft Resolution, Report of the Human Rights Council, UN GAOR, 3rd Comm, 70th sess, Agenda Item 67, UN Doc A/C.3/70/L.66 (16 November 2015).

125 See Michael K Lavers, 'Future of U.S. LGBT Envoy Remains Unclear', *Washington Blade* (24 January 2017) <http://www.washingtonblade.com/2017/01/24/future-u-s-lgbt-envoy-remains-unclear/>.

I also want to say a few words about how homoglobalism, as discussed in this chapter, compares to Puar's discussion of homonationalism. Her focus is on the recent protections provided for some homosexual bodies – mainly white people living in Western pro-gay states. The changes described here show how, when gay governance goes global, it not only enters geopolitics by pitting gay-friendly states against states which are hostile to LGBT rights, but also promotes the global protection of LGBT people, including those in anti-gay states, and engages a variety of actors in advocacy, including a diverse range of states, civil society and global institutions. As I have argued, at the global level, the questions of the role of pinkwashing and homonationalism take a different turn, especially when LGBT advocacy is instigated by NGOs and by states and UN leaders from the global South. It is therefore not possible to explain the way in which states vote on LGBT rights at the United Nations only through the prism of homonationalism, which considers 'the circumstances through which nation-states are now vested with the status of "gay-friendly" versus "homophobic"'.[126] Whereas the global dimensions of the homonationalism discussion point to the way in which states leverage their support (real or perceived) of LGBT rights to mark themselves as civilised or progressive and to brand others as uncivilised, the GGG developments taking place at the global level require that we also engage critically with the actions (and agency) of opposing states.

I have focused on gay governance questions arising at the level of global institutions, where states leverage both advocacy for and opposition to LGBT rights as both part of, and as a response to, GGG. I have examined GGG as it is emerging along two different tracks – through the global financial and human rights systems. While both tracks use the SOGI framework, the first is led by powerful states (the United States and the United Kingdom) from the global North, and by IFIs. In the second track emerging at the United Nations, particularly in its human rights system, states and UN officials from the global South are taking a leading role. A meeting point between the two tracks took place when it was agreed to adopt an amendment to the UN Human Rights Council resolution appointing the SOGI Independent Expert, which condemned gay conditionality. This indicates that we are now witnessing a few developments occurring at the same time: the emergence of states from the South taking the lead on LGBT rights together with civil society and UN leadership; the appropriation by some global North states of LGBT rights for political purposes; and both critical opposition to this appropriation by various actors, and cynical opposition to it by homophobic-national (or rather heteronational) states.

Both tracks of GGG risk co-option, backlash, exporting Western concepts of identity, pinkwashing, whitewashing and legitimating violation of the human rights of others in the name of LGBT rights. Both tracks have also seen some successes, including heightened awareness and emphatic condemnation of the serious threats to life and well-being faced by LGBT people in many parts of

126 Puar, above n 10, 337.

the world. It is not possible to carry out a full cost-benefit analysis at this early stage, but some current aspects of GGG – such as suspending aid directed at maternal healthcare, or using LGBT rights to pinkwash states and institutions – are clearly objectionable. Other aspects raise more complex questions of rhetoric versus reality and of the risks of backlash as well as of exporting identities in a way that may create harm – all risks that those involved in global LGBT rights advocacy must take into account.

9 Governing (trans)parenthood

The tenacious hold of biological connection and heterosexuality

Anniken Sørlie *

> I have only thought that I am a man without sperm, and there are many men who are and who can be fathers . . . [To be legally registered as a father] is important for me. It is so important, in fact, that I haven't been able to think of anything else.[1]

> [P]regnant men engender a critical re(conceive)ing of the idea that sex is biologically determined, that pregnancy is necessarily sexed as female, and that one's sex, gender identity and identification as mother/father neatly align.[2]

In states like Argentina, Portugal, Sweden, Denmark, Malta, Ireland and Norway, laws have recently been amended or new laws enacted to facilitate change of legal gender. Most importantly, the requirements of sterilisation or infertility have been abolished.[3] At the core of these reforms, especially since 2012[4] onwards, are the fundamental human rights principles of individual autonomy, integrity, non-discrimination and dignity. If not yet a global trend, the recent legal reforms represent a paradigm shift in law's conception of gender.

Concepts of legal gender are being constructed in response to legal claims brought by transgender[5] litigants.[6] In the case of the United Kingdom, A Sharpe

* My thanks to Dianne Otto, Anne Hellum and May-Len Skilbrei for their valuable comments and feedback on earlier drafts of this chapter.

1 Informant interviewed in 2015 in conjunction with my doctoral project. The informant was registered in Norway as female at birth and has a female personal identification number. He identifies as a man. Note, all interview translations are by the author.

2 Lara Karaian, 'Pregnant Men: Repronormativity, Critical Trans Theory and the Re(conceive)ing of Sex and Pregnancy in Law' (2013) 22 *Social & Legal Studies* 211, 212–13.

3 I use *legal* or *registered gender* to refer to gender specific national identity numbers or insurance numbers, gender according to birth certificates and passports.

4 In 2012, Argentina adopted Ley de Identidad de Género [Act on Gender Identity] (Argentina) 9 May 2012, No 26.743.

5 Transgender, trans or trans* have emerged as umbrella terms for trans identities. For the purpose of this chapter, I use transgender to refer to people whose birth-assigned gender mismatches their gender identity, and wish to, or have, changed their legal gender.

6 A Sharpe, *Foucault's Monsters and the Challenge of Law* (Routledge, 2010) 88–9.

is concerned that 'the body has been privileged in legal (re)constructions of sex, or, more particularly, the (binary) categories male and female'.[7] This describes the situation under earlier Norwegian administrative practice on change of legal gender, but also, as will be demonstrated, under recently reformed Norwegian law. Before 2016, transgender people in Norway, who sought correction of their legal gender and wanted biological children, had to conceive or beget children before completing the legal gender recognition process. In many states, surgical removal of reproductive organs served as a precondition for correction of legal gender, considered necessary in order to rule out legal men giving birth and legal women begetting children.[8] However, in an increasing number of states, including Norway, this has changed: both legal men and legal women can give birth to children as a result of new gender recognition laws that base correction of legal gender on self-declaration, repealing earlier requirements of surgical interventions.[9] By way of this change, assumed reproductive capacity, or its absence, is no longer a decisive element in legal gender categories. It breaks – at least to some extent – the strong medico-legal link that previously characterised gender recognition practices. In the aftermath of these new rules, new questions emerge for human rights bodies, activists and NGOs. How, for example, should law deal with the diversity of legal genders it now recognises? Is a legal woman always a 'woman' for legal purposes?

This leads to the question of how current Norwegian law governs and should govern parenthood in relation to transgender parents. Informed by Michel Foucault's concept of 'governmentality',[10] I see law as one of many 'tactics' used to govern and order the population.[11] Rather than being the most significant tactic, law interweaves with others, such as the media and politics, which, seen as a whole, govern the population and construct what is understood as legitimate and illegitimate parenthood. Particularly important to my argument is how, according to Foucault, the 'legal complex', understood as inter alia statutes, legal codes, legal institutions, texts and norms, is permeated by non-legal forms of knowledge and expertise, such as the medical.[12] This is a point of departure for

7 Ibid 108.

8 'Report of the Interdepartmental Working Group on Transsexual People' (Report, Home Office, April 2000) 21 <http://docs.scie-socialcareonline.org.uk/fulltext/wgtrans.pdf>; Prop. 1972:6 Kungl. Maj:ts proposition nr 6 år 1972 [Proposition to Riksdagen (bill)] (Sweden) 23.

9 For an overview of legal reforms, see Jens M Scherpe (ed), *The Legal Status of Transsexual and Transgender Persons* (Intersentia, 2015).

10 Michel Foucault introduced the notion of 'governmentality' in his lecture at the Collège de France in February 1978. Michel Foucault, 'Governmentality' (Pasquale Pasquino trans) in Graham Burchell, Colin Gordon and Peter Miller (eds), *The Foucault Effect: Studies in Governmentality with Two Lectures by and an Interview with Michel Foucault* (University of Chicago Press, 1991) 87.

11 Ibid 87–104.

12 Nikolas Rose and Mariana Valverde, 'Governed by Law?' (1998) 7 *Social and Legal Studies* 541, 542–3.

my thinking of how law works in constructing gender and 'normality'. Legal parenthood has been based on the biological two-sex model, reconstituting conventional norms of binary gender and (hetero)sexuality. I examine how gender emerges as a 'problem' for law when transgender litigants claim legal recognition of their gender identity, especially in the context of parenthood.[13] When the 'problem' of gender emerges before and under law, gender as biology and medical 'truth', referred to as 'biologic' by Sharpe,[14] is questioned.

By focusing on the legal recognition of transgender people and laws that regulate the field of reproduction and parenthood in Norway, I examine how law works as a tactic in governing parenthood and gender by promoting certain forms of living arrangements, gender identities and kinship relations while dismissing others as invalid or irrelevant. This provides a window into what law is doing and why law matters. This leads to the question of whether it is necessary for law to apply gendered parental categories (mother, father and co-mother) at all, or whether terms referring to functions, like being pregnant or giving birth, should replace the current parental categories and thereby remove legal concepts that do not match the identity or functions of all the people they are supposed to apply to.

The chapter unfolds in three sections. The first presents the legal backdrop against which the rights of transgender people have emerged, and subsequently how international and European human rights law, as well as Norwegian law, are constructing gender. In the second section, I look at the establishment of parenthood under the Act Relating to Children and Parents 1981 ('Children Act')[15] and how the rules apply to transgender parents. The continuing operation of biologic is clearly apparent, working as a constant reminder of the 'otherness' of parents whose gender identity differs from their birth-assigned gender. The third section provides a more thorough discussion of how law works to govern parenthood and why law matters. I argue that, even though law does not preclude transgender parents, parenthood is regulated in such a way that transgender people appear as other to the norm. I conclude by suggesting that it would be beneficial to gender-neutralise parenthood under the law as a way of covering all gender identities, including those that the law currently marginalises or does not recognise at all.

13 Michel Foucault, *Seksualitetens Historie I: Viljen til Viten* (Espen Schaaning trans, Pax, first published 1976, 1999 edn) [trans of: *Histoire de la sexualité 1: La volonté de savoir*].

14 A Sharpe, *Transgender Jurisprudence: Dysphoric Bodies of Law* (Cavendish, 2002) 9–10.

15 Lov om barn og foreldre [Act Relating to Children and Parents] April 1981, No 7 [Ministry of Children, Equality and Social Inclusion trans, 2014 <https://www.regjeringen.no/en/dokumenter/the-children-act/id448389/>] ('Children Act'). All laws and preparatory work refer to Norway, except where otherwise indicated.

The road to legal men giving birth and its legal framework: The ambiguous scope of gender

Against the backdrop of universal human rights, the rights of transgender people have only recently started to be recognised. Legal developments have focused on rights related to legal recognition of preferred gender identity, and on expanding coverage of anti-discrimination provisions to include the grounds of gender identity/expression. In this section, I provide a brief overview of these developments, starting with the jurisprudence of the European Court of Human Rights (ECtHR), turning then to the work of international human rights mechanisms and finally to describing the recent developments in Norwegian law.

The European Court of Human Rights – acknowledging gender as social yet holding on to biology

Because transgender people have brought claims to the ECtHR, its jurisprudence has played a crucial role in developing and clarifying the obligations of states parties under the European Convention of Human Rights (ECHR),[16] to protect and respect transgender people's human rights. In these cases, gender explicitly emerges as a problem for law by way of appearing as a question. Most complaints have been tried as a matter of the right to respect for one's private life under article 8. Nevertheless, it is now uncontested that gender identity falls within the proscribed grounds of discrimination under article 14, which prohibits discrimination in the enjoyment of all ECHR rights and freedoms.[17] Article 8, by contrast, only protects individuals against arbitrary interference with their privacy or family life by public authorities, although it does place positive obligations on states to ensure that everyone's right to private life is respected.[18] According to the ECtHR, respect for human dignity and human freedom constitute the very essence of the ECHR, and the notion of personal autonomy is an important principle in the interpretation of article 8.[19] The right to respect for private life covers the personal integrity of a person and encompasses issues such as personal

16 Convention for the Protection of Human Rights and Fundamental Freedoms, opened for signature 4 November 1950, 213 UNTS 221 (entered into force 3 September 1953) ('ECHR') is incorporated into Norwegian law by Lov om styrking av menneskerettighetenes stilling i norsk rett (menneskerettsloven) [Human Rights Act] 21 May 1999, No 30 ('Human Rights Act'). The incorporation gives precedence to the Convention if it comes into conflict with other Norwegian law. Human Rights Act § 3.

17 See, eg, *Identoba v Georgia* (European Court of Human Rights, Chamber, Application No 73235/12, 12 May 2015) [96]. Protocol No 12 to the Convention for the Protection of Human Rights and Fundamental Freedoms, opened for signature 4 November 2000, ETS No 177 (entered into force 1 April 2005) sets forth a general prohibition of discrimination: see article 1. To date, Norway has signed, but not ratified, the optional protocol.

18 *Van Kück v Germany* (2003) VII Eur Court HR 1, [70].

19 *Goodwin v the United Kingdom* (2002) VI Eur Court HR 1, [90].

identity and personal development.[20] States parties have a positive obligation to take measures to ensure that transgender people can live in accordance with their gender identity by amending identity documents that refer to gender.[21] However, states' obligations beyond the question of mere correction of gender understood as binary have not been explicitly clarified.

In 1997, when the first and so far only case on transgender parenthood brought to the ECtHR was heard, the ECtHR had not yet identified any obligation on states parties to legally recognise transgender people's gender identity. In *X, Y and Z v UK*,[22] the United Kingdom refused to register X (post-operative female-male 'transsexual')[23] as the father of Z (conceived by donor insemination and born to his partner Y). The ECtHR found the United Kingdom not to be in contravention of the applicants' right to respect for family life under article 8 because of the state's interest in maintaining a coherent system of law, arguing that it would lead to inconsistency if somebody who was not legally a man was registered as a father and that such a change to the law could have negative implications for children. The question now is whether the ECtHR will, in future cases, find that states are obliged to register transgender parents in alignment with their legal gender when gender recognition laws are based on self-determination.

It was not until 2002, in *Christine Goodwin v UK*, that the ECtHR ruled decisively in favour of transgender people seeking legal gender recognition.[24] Goodwin, a post-operative male-female transgender person, argued inter alia that the ECHR required the United Kingdom to modify her birth certificate to recognise her preferred gender. The ECtHR agreed, finding no decisive reason for chromosomes to be determinative when establishing a 'transsexual's' legal gender.[25] Thereby, gender was acknowledged as a social construct and it was accepted that legal gender is not always synonymous with biological gender. Yet, Goodwin's case, and others that have since been considered by the ECtHR, have all involved people who have undergone or intend to undergo gender-confirmation surgery. Furthermore, in the rulings, 'transsexualism' has been treated as a medical condition for which gender-confirmation[26] treatment has been understood as providing relief. The ECtHR's analysis has been carried out along this medical pathway. Thus, in these cases, the ECtHR has not raised

20 Torkel Opsahl, *Internasjonale Menneskerettigheter: En Innføring* (Institutt for Menneskerettigheter, 2nd edn, 1996) 44–6; *Pajić v Croatia* (European Court of Human Rights, Chamber, Application No 68453/13, 23 February 2016) [61].

21 *Goodwin v the United Kingdom* (2002) VI Eur Court HR 1.

22 *X, Y and Z v The United Kingdom* (1997) II Eur Court HR 143.

23 In its case law the ECtHR uses the term 'transsexual' to refer to most of the transgender applicants. Many consider this term to be offensive and pathologising trans identities. See above n 5.

24 *Goodwin v the United Kingdom* (2002) VI Eur Court HR 1.

25 Ibid [82].

26 Gender reassignment surgery is another term often used. However, I use *confirmation*, as this term reflects that the purpose of the surgery is to confirm and not *reassign* a person's gender.

concern about the legitimacy of requiring gender-confirmation surgery.[27] So, even though the ECtHR has claimed to recognise gender as a social category, in practice it has not distinguished it from biology or medical science. Therefore, the biological two-sex model continues to provide the basis for legal gender.

In 2015, in *YY v Turkey*,[28] the ECtHR found that a refusal by Turkish courts to authorise access to gender-confirmation surgery for a transgender person, on the ground that he was not permanently infertile (a condition of court authorisation), encroached on his right to respect for his private and family life under article 8.[29] The core question for the majority was whether the non-procreation requirement was necessary in order to protect the health of transgender people. Since Turkish authorities failed to justify the requirement in light of article 8, the ECtHR ruled that Turkish authorities violated the applicant's privacy rights, finding that freedom to establish gender is an essential part of the ECHR.[30] Although not dealing with the question of medical intervention as a precondition for correction of legal gender directly, but entry to gender-confirmation surgery which leads to correction of registered gender, the consequence of the ruling is a move in the direction of separating reproductive capacity from the biological basis of gender categories.[31] Yet the ECtHR seems reticent to take a clear stand about whether gender is biologically or socially determined.[32]

The Council of Europe Commissioner for Human Rights, the Committee of Ministers and the Parliamentary Assembly have all recommended that states abolish sterilisation and other harmful procedures as criteria for legal gender recognition, based on the view that requiring gender-confirmation surgery as a precondition to altering legal gender violates the human rights of transgender people, including the right to bodily integrity and self-determination.[33] If followed, the recommendations will foster a construction of gender that will have significant implications in many different areas of life. Yet, even though the recommendations

27 See, eg, *Goodwin v the United Kingdom* (2002) VI Eur Court HR 1.

28 *YY v Turkey* (European Court of Human Rights, Chamber, Application No 14793/08, 10 March 2015).

29 Peter Dunne, 'Commentary: *YY v Turkey*: Infertility as a Pre-condition for Gender Confirmation Surgery' (2015) 23 *Medical Law Review* 646, 647–8.

30 Ibid 646, 648–50.

31 See ibid 646.

32 Pending cases before the Court on gender-confirmation surgery and transsexualism as preconditions for correction of registered gender: *AP v France* (Application No 79885/12, 5 December 2012), *Garçon v France* (Application No 52471/13, 13 August 2013) and *Nicot v France* (Application No 52596/13, 13 August 2013).

33 See, eg, Commissioner for Human Rights, 'Human Rights and Gender Identity' (Issue Paper, Council of Europe, 29 July 2009) [3.2.1]; Committee of Ministers, 'Recommendation CM/Rec(2010)5 of the Committee of Ministers to Member States on Measures to Combat Discrimination on Grounds of Sexual Orientation or Gender Identity' (Recommendation No CM/Rec(2010)5, Council of Europe, 31 March 2010) cl 35; Parliamentary Assembly, 'Discrimination on the Basis of Sexual Orientation and Gender Identity' (Resolution No 1728 (2010), Council of Europe, 29 April 2010) [16.11.2].

are clear, they fail to address how states are to implement the changes. For example, do they now have an obligation to protect pregnant or breast-feeding legal men from sex/gender discrimination and an obligation to recognise transgender people's gender identity in relation to registration of parenthood?

International law – combating sterilisation – yet blind to its consequences

In international human rights law, sex/gender has also been traditionally understood in binary male/female categories.[34] While there has been some progress in the context of women's rights towards understanding gender as a social category, it remains moored on a biological base, understood as 'sex'.[35] More recently, human rights treaty bodies and many of the Special Procedures of the UN Human Rights Council (and its predecessor the Commission on Human Rights) have explicitly recognised that discrimination on the basis of gender identity is prohibited by the non-exhaustive anti-discrimination clauses in international human rights instruments.[36] Yet little attention has been paid to specific human rights obligations with regard to gender identity, let alone transparenthood.

Several human rights treaty bodies have now expressed concern about requiring medical intervention as a precondition for correction of registered gender, recommending that states abolish such requirements. In its 'Concluding Observations' to Belgium (2014), Finland (2014) and Slovakia (2015), the Committee on the Elimination of Discrimination against Women recommended that sterilisation, as a requirement for legal gender recognition, be abolished.[37] Also in 2015, the Committee against Torture recommended that China (Hong Kong) remove preconditions, such as sterilisation, for legal gender recognition.[38]

34 See generally Dianne Otto, 'International Human Rights Law: Towards Rethinking Sex/ Gender Dualism and Asymmetry' in Margaret Davies and Vanessa Munro (eds), *A Research Companion to Feminist Legal Theory* (Ashgate Companion Series, 2013) 197.

35 Dianne Otto, 'Queering Gender [Identity] in International Law' in Anne Hellum (ed), *Human Rights, Sexual Orientation, and Gender Identity* (Routledge, 2017) 299.

36 Anne Hellum, 'Vern mot Diskriminering på grunnlag av seksuell legning, kjønnsidentitet og kjønnsuttrykk – religiøse kjønnsdogmer i møte med internasjonal og norsk rett' in Reidun Førde, Morten Kjelland and Ulf Stridbeck (eds), *Festskrift til Aslak Syse 70 år* (Gyldendal, 2016) 191.

37 UN Committee on the Elimination of Discrimination against Women (CEDAW), Concluding Observations on the Seventh Periodic Report of Belgium, 59th sess, UN Doc CEDAW/C/ BEL/CO/7 (14 November 2014) [45]; UN CEDAW, Concluding Observations on the Seventh Periodic Report of Finland, 57th sess, UN Doc CEDAW/C/FIN/CO/7 (10 March 2014) [29]; UN CEDAW, Concluding Observations on the Combined Fifth and Sixth Periodic Reports of Slovakia, 62nd sess, UN Doc CEDAW/C/SVK/CO/5-6 (25 November 2015) [37].

38 UN Committee against Torture, Concluding Observations on the Fifth Periodic Report of China with respect to Hong Kong, China, 56th sess, UN Doc CAT/C/CHN-HKG/CO/5 (3 February 2016) [29].

However, trans-specific issues have yet to be adequately addressed by international human rights treaty bodies.[39]

As early as 2001, two of the Human Rights Council's Special Procedures made reference to human rights abuses suffered by transgendered people, in the context of the question of torture and extrajudicial, arbitrary and summary executions.[40] Since then, other Special Procedures have raised the issue within mandates covering human rights defenders, health and minority issues.[41] In 2013, and again in 2016, the Special Rapporteur on Torture recommended that states abolish and outlaw sterilisation as a requirement for legal gender recognition because it constituted torture and/or other cruel, inhuman and degrading treatment.[42] If states follow these recommendations and bring domestic law into compliance with international human rights law by adopting gender recognition acts based on self-determination, legal gender will be detached from reproductive capacity. Legal men will, for example, like in Norway, be able to give birth. However, none of these bodies has made recommendations about how they should be implemented in practice or what effect legal gender should have on parenthood.

The Yogyakarta Principles on the Application of International Human Rights Law in Relation to Sexual Orientation and Gender Identity ('Yogyakarta Principles') also do not address these matters directly. Adopted in 2007 by a group of LGBT human rights experts and advocates to provide guidance in interpreting existing human rights law, the Principles are not legally binding, but as more formal bodies rely on them, their potential to guide legal developments increases.[43] The Yogyakarta Principles clearly state that the universal right to

39 Rikki Holtmaat and Paul Post, 'Enhancing LGBTI Rights by Changing the Interpretation of the Convention on the Elimination of All Forms of Discrimination Against Women?' in Hellum, above n 35, 319.

40 Report of the Special Rapporteur on the Question of Torture and Other Cruel, Inhuman or Degrading Treatment or Punishment, UN GAOR, 56th sess, Agenda Item 132(a), UN Doc A/56/156 (3 July 2001) [17]; Asma Jahangir, Report of the Special Rapporteur on Extrajudicial, Arbitrary and Summary Executions, UN ESCOR, 57th sess, Agenda Item 11(b), UN Doc E/CN.4/2001/9 (11 January 2001) [50].

41 Hina Jilani, Report of the Special Representative of the Secretary General on Human Rights Defenders, UN ESCOR, 62nd sess, UN Doc E/CN.4/2006/95/Add.1 (22 March 2006) [290]; Paul Hunt, Report of the Special Rapporteur on the Right of Everyone to the Enjoyment of the Highest Attainable Standard of Physical and Mental Health, UN ESCOR, 60th sess, Agenda Item 10, UN Doc E/CN.4/2004/49 (16 February 2004) [33], [38]–[39]; Gay McDougall, Report of the Independent Expert on Minority Issues, UN ESCOR, 62nd sess, Agenda Item 14(b), UN Doc E/CN.4/2006/74 (6 January 2006) [28], [42].

42 Juan E Méndez, Report of the Special Rapporteur on Torture and Other Cruel, Inhuman or Degrading Treatment or Punishment, UN GAOR, 31st sess, Agenda Item 3, UN Doc A/HRC/31/57 (5 January 2016) [72(e)]; Juan E Méndez, Report of the Special Rapporteur on Torture and Other Cruel, Inhuman or Degrading Treatment or Punishment, UN GAOR, 22nd sess, Agenda Item 3, UN Doc A/HRC/22/53 (1 February 2013) [88].

43 Michael O'Flaherty, 'The Yogyakarta Principles at Ten' in Hellum, above n 35, 280.

recognition before the law includes the right to have your self-defined gender legally recognised without the requirement of medical interventions.[44] Yet, while recognising that transgender people have the right to found a family, and that no family should face discrimination because of the gender identity of any of its members, they are, as the soft law mentioned above, silent about parental categories for LGBT people as a matter of legal recognition.[45] Therefore, even though the Principles are clear on self-declared gender and the right to non-disclosure of gender identity,[46] they do not directly address the problem of heteronormative and cisnormative[47] domestic parenting laws.

Norwegian law – self-declared binary gender

Returning to Norway, the binary gender-specific national identity number is based on physical sex characteristics at birth. Before 2016, a person's national identity number could be changed on the condition of completed gender-confirmation treatment, including hormonal therapy, real-life-experience living as the preferred gender for a minimum of 12 months and removal of testes or ovaries.[48] Since this administrative practice was established in the 1970s, Norway was one of the first states to provide for correction of legal gender.[49] By implication, at this point the law recognised gender as social. Yet clear-cut boundaries between male and female bodies were maintained, as no other genders were recognised and a correction was reliant on alignment of the body with biological sex. Gender assignment at birth continued to be based on physical sex characteristics and the gender binary.

As a result of amendments to Norway's anti-discrimination legislation in 2013, the prohibition of discrimination was extended to include gender identity and gender expression.[50] In 2014, the Equality and Anti-Discrimination Ombud concluded that the Ministry of Health and Care Services violated this legislation

44 Yogyakarta Principles, principle 3.

45 Yogyakarta Principles, principle 24.

46 Yogyakarta Principles, principles 3, 6.

47 Cis is a term used to refer to people who self-identify with their birth-assigned gender.

48 Directorate of Health, 'Rett til rett kjønn – Helse til alle kjønn: Utredning av vilkår for endring av juridisk kjønn og organisering av helsetjenester for personer som opplever kjønnsinkongruens og kjønnsdysfori' (Report, Ministry of Health, April 2015) 36, 43–7; See generally Anniken Sørlie, 'Legal Gender Meets Reality: A Socio-Legal Children's Perspective' in Hellum, above n 35, 353.

49 Lag (1972:119) om fastställande av könstillhörighet i vissa fall [Gender Recognition Act] (Sweden) 21 April 1972; Gesetz über die Änderung der Vornamen und die Feststellung der Geschlechtszugehörigkeit in besonderen Fällen [Act on Change of Names and Gender] (Germany) 10 September 1980, BGBl I, 1980, 1654; Norme in materia di rettificazione di attribuzione di sesso [Gender Recognition Act] (Italy) 14 April 1982, No 164.

50 Lov om forbud mot diskriminering på grunn av seksuell orientering, kjønnsidentitet og kjønnsuttrykk [Sexual Orientation Anti-Discrimination Act] 21 June 2013, No 58. The Act applies in all sectors of society except from within family life and other purely personal relationships. Sexual Orientation Anti-Discrimination Act § 2.

when requiring a diagnosis of transsexualism, hormonal therapy and gender-confirmation surgery for correction of legal gender.[51] This determination increased the pressure to abolish medical requirements for change of legal gender.[52] The Norwegian Parliament then adopted the Act on Change of Legal Gender 2016 ('Gender Recognition Act'), which entered into force on 1 July 2016.[53] The Act provides for change of legal gender from the age of 16 based on self-declaration. For children between the ages of 6 and 16, parental consent is required. If only one parent gives their consent, children at this age may change their legal gender if the County Governor, by way of an individual decision, finds correction of legal gender to be in the best interests of the child.[54]

Legal gender therefore develops from biological determination at birth to self-declaration for people who have reached the age limits prescribed by the Act. Hence, gender recognition breaks the biological link between legal gender and parenthood, which had earlier seemed logical, as reproductive capacity is no longer tied to legal gender. However, the Act relies on the gender binary by way of providing only two gender options. The Act also does not challenge the role of physical sex characteristics for gender assignment at birth. This means that biology continues to serve as the basis of legal gender orthodoxy, but that law accepts gender as social for people over the age of 6. By constructing gender, the Act shapes contemporary norms about gender, which play a powerful role in governing expressions and practices of gender. The Act grants 'authenticity' to certain forms of gender identity and the distinction between 'normal' and 'abnormal' emerges – a distinction which medical science previously constructed, before gender appeared as a problem for law. As pointed out above, it can be questioned whether law fully recognises gender as social, or if biology still plays a decisive role also in other relations – for example, in relation to parenthood.

Parenthood under Norwegian law: The heterosexual, dualistic and biological norm

Law also governs ways of becoming a family with children, through provisions on assisted conception, egg donation and adoption. In Norway, assisted conception is available to same-sex and different-sex couples as a part of the public health

51 Statement, Norwegian Equality and Anti-Discrimination Ombud, Case No 14/840, 9 September 2014 <http://www.ldo.no/nyheiter-og-fag/klagesaker/2014/18840-diskriminering-pa-grunn-av-kjonnsidentitet/>.

52 For work of great significance in advocating for change, see, eg, 'The State Decides Who I Am: Lack of Legal Gender Recognition for Transgender People in Europe' (Report, Amnesty International, 2014).

53 See generally Anniken Sørlie, 'Rettighetssubjekter i Endring: Den Fødende Mannen' in Ingunn Ikdahl and Vibeke Blaker Strand (eds), *Rettigheter i Velferdsstaten: Begreper, Trender, Teorier* (Gyldendal, 2016) 227.

54 Lov om endring av juridisk kjønn [Act on Change of Legal Gender] 17 June 2016, No 46, §§ 2, 4, 5 ('Gender Recognition Act').

service. It preconditions dual parenthood by way of requiring either marriage or a stable relationship resembling marriage.[55] Conversely, adoption is available to single persons, as well as couples.[56] Norwegian law does not permit surrogacy or egg donation.[57] In this section, I explore how parenthood is established under the Children Act and how the rules apply to transgender parents. The focal point is to examine whether the rules follow a presumed biological link between parenthood and gender, or whether the rules recognise gender as social.

The term 'legal parents' means 'those persons who have established parenthood in a manner recognised by legislation'.[58] Parenthood means the child's mother, father or co-mother pursuant to the Children Act or the Adoption Act 1986.[59] Mere registration of parenthood in the Population Register has no legal effect if it does not comply with the rules in these Acts.[60] Legal parenthood entails rights and obligations for the legal parents and, in parallel, it provides rights for the children vis-à-vis their parents. The Children Act is based on the premise that a child is to have two legal parents.[61] In the Population Register and on birth certificates, parents are not categorised as mother, father or co-mother, but simply registered as an individual who has children. Children are registered with information about their parents that lists their names.[62] In this chapter, focus is given to legal parenthood following from the three categories recognised in the Children Act.

Motherhood

Until 1997, motherhood was not regulated by law, but based on the biological principle of *mater semper certa est* (the mother is always certain).[63] However, technological advances in medicine that enabled egg donation generated a need for regulation of motherhood, even though the Act Relating to the Application

55 Lov om humanmedisinsk bruk av bioteknologi m.m. [Biotechnology Act] 5 December 2003, No 100, § 2-2 ('Biotechnology Act').
56 In 2001, registered partners were given the right to adopt the child of their partner. Lov om endringer i lov 28. februar 1986 nr. 8 om adopsjon og i lov 30. april 1993 nr. 40 om registrert partnerskap [Act Amending the Adoption Act and the Act on Civil Partnership] 15 June 2001, No 36. In 2008, the Adoption Act was amended so as to give same-sex couples the right to adopt in general. Lov om endringer i ekteskapsloven, barnelova, adopsjonsloven, bioteknologiloven mv. [Act Amending the Marriage Act, the Children Act, the Adoption Act and the Biotechnology Act] 27 June 2008, No 53.
57 Biotechnology Act § 2-15, § 2-18.
58 Commission on Paternity, 'NOU 2009:5 Farskap og annen morskap' ['Norwegian Official Report'] (2009) [3.1].
59 Adoption Act.
60 Ibid [14.7.4].
61 Children Act § 5; Prop. 105 L (2012–2013) [Proposition to the Storting (bill)] 52–3.
62 Prop. 74 L (2015–2016) Lov om endring av juridisk kjønn [Proposition to the Storting (bill)] [8.5.3].
63 Lov om endringer i lov av 8. april 1981 nr. 7 om barn og foreldre (barnelova) m.v. [Act Amending the Children Act] 13 June 1997, No 39.

of Biotechnology in Medicine 1994 did not allow for this.[64] It was still possible that donated eggs could be acquired in a foreign state.[65] As explained in the preparatory work, the Children Act takes the view that a child's biological kinship with the person bearing the child to delivery should be attributed greater weight than any genetic kinship with another woman or egg donor.[66] Therefore, the biological principle, which says that the 'woman' who gives birth to the child is the child's legal mother, was codified into the Children Act in 1997.[67] This regulates giving birth as an exclusively female function. The determination of legal motherhood moves from egg to uterus, and can be changed only by adoption.

According to the Gender Recognition Act, as a main rule, legal gender shall apply when applying other statutes and regulations. Yet an exception is made when it comes to parenthood. If it is 'necessary' to establish parenthood and parental responsibility pursuant to the Children Act, birth-assigned gender shall be applied.[68] Therefore, a legal man who gives birth will be assigned parenthood pursuant to the rules on motherhood. The rationale for this is that the conditions for fatherhood or co-motherhood are not fulfilled. The purpose is to ensure that parenthood can be established and to avoid uncertainty about how parenthood is established.[69] The rules on motherhood break with the main rule on self-declared and social legal gender. As a consequence, law treats gender identities, which differ from birth-assigned gender, as justifying differential treatment under the Children Act. In this way, law does not recognise gender or pregnancy as social. Law continues to govern giving birth as a female function, rendering legal men giving birth invisible and not 'really' men (or fathers). Motherhood is 'always' biology.

Fatherhood

The rules governing paternity are closely linked with regulation of who the child's mother is. When a child is born in wedlock, the *pater est* rule applies[70] and the legislator assumes the biological likelihood that the husband is the father of the child. That is, the man who is married to the mother at the time of birth is the father of the child, irrespective of whether or not the latter is the biological

64 Lov om Medisinsk Bruk av Bioteknologi [Act Relating to the Application of Biotechnology in Medicine] 5 August 1994, No 56 (repealed).

65 Ot.prp. nr.33 (2007–8) [Proposition to the Odelsting (bill)] [9.2.1]; Inge Lorange Backer, *Barneloven: Kommentarutgave* (Universitetsforlaget, 2nd edn, 2008) 46–7.

66 Ot.prp. nr. 56 (1996–7) Om lov om endringer i lov 8. April 1981 nr 7 om barn og foreldre (barnelova) [Proposition to the Odelsting (bill)] ch 3.

67 Children Act § 2.

68 Gender Recognition Act § 6.

69 Prop. 74 L (2015–2016) [Proposition to the Storting (bill)] 37.

70 Shortening of *pater est quem nuptiae demonstrant* (the true father is established through marriage). The *pater est* rule has been stated by statutory law since 1892. Children Act Commission, 'NOU 1977: 35 Lov om barn og foreldre' [Norwegian Official Report] (1977) 12.

father.[71] At the outset, the rule is based on the biological principle, but it applies as well to assisted conception. The basis for the rules governing paternity and determination of fatherhood is thus of a social nature.[72] The rule is meant to ensure the integrity of the family as a social unit and that the child will be cared for by both parents.[73] This means that for paternity, social kinship and the best interests of the child, rather than biological kinship as for motherhood, is seen as more favourable. With the *pater est* rule, the biological principle yields to governmental support for the nuclear family and its privileged position in society.[74]

For heterosexual cohabitants or parents not living together, the law requires active deeds on the part of the father. The father must declare paternity either during pregnancy or after the child is born and the mother has to agree with the paternity.[75] Social kinship is given less weight because of the couple's form of living arrangement. This marks marriage as the preferred living arrangement. The distinction between the rules of paternity in marriage and in cohabitation is founded on the rationale that cohabitants are a diverse and shifting group. The presumption that the mother's cohabitant is the child's father is therefore weaker than for marriage.[76]

Furthermore, legal paternity can be allocated or altered by a court ruling on the basis of a DNA test or, if the analysis provides no conclusive answer (or has not been conducted), based on the probability that the person is the father because of the mother having had sexual intercourse with the man in question.[77] In the case of assisted conception, paternity can be attributed if the husband or cohabitant consented to the conception and it is probable that the child was born as a result of assisted conception.[78] Legal paternity can never be allocated to a donor by way of a court ruling.[79]

Paternity established on the basis of marriage or declaration can be changed if another man declares paternity, provided the mother and the person who initially was assigned paternity consent in writing and a DNA analysis confirms paternity.[80] With the consent of the parties, biological evidence gives grounds for paternity, whereas social paternity provides no opportunity to change a biologically established paternity. The only way to do this is through adoption.

71 Children Act § 3. See generally Backer, above n 65, 73–80.
72 Ot.prp. no.33 (2007–8) [Proposition to the Odelsting (bill)] [9.2.2].
73 Prop. 105 L (2012–13) Endringer i barnelova (farskap og morskap) [Proposition to the Storting (bill)], [4.1.1]–[4.1.4].
74 Sigrun Saur Stiklestad, 'Det biologiske prinsipps skiftende anvendelse' (2007) 24 *Nytt Norsk Tidsskrift* 138, 143.
75 Children Act § 4; Prop. 105 L (2012–2013) Endringer i barnelova (farskap og morskap) [Proposition to the Storting (bill)] [4.3].
76 Prop. 105 L (2012–13) Endringer i barnelova (farskap og morskap) [Proposition to the Storting (bill)] [4.2.4].
77 Children Act §§ 6, 9. See generally Backer, above n 65, 56–8, 100–18.
78 Children Act § 9.
79 Ibid § 9.
80 Ibid § 7.

According to the Gender Recognition Act, for a legal woman who begets a child with her own semen, legal parenthood is established based on the rules on paternity, as described above.[81] The legal woman cannot, in this case, be the legal mother. Nor are the requirements for co-motherhood fulfilled, as discussed in the next section. In a similar way, the rules on fatherhood cannot be applied to establish parenthood for a legal man who gives birth since the person who gives birth is the child's mother. When birth-assigned gender and gender identity conflict, birth-assigned gender wins out in determining parenthood. The rules (re)constitute the biological link between semen and man/father. In regulating families, the wording of the law does not recognise a legal woman who begets a child as a woman.

Co-motherhood

The woman to whom the mother is married at the time of birth, when the child is born after assisted conception, is considered to be the co-mother.[82] The prerequisites are that she has consented to conception and that the couple has used a known donor in an approved health institution.[83] The *pater est* rule is thus applied to regulate co-motherhood despite the absence of biological or genetic kinship. As explained in the preparatory work, this approach was based on considerations of the best interests of the child and of gender equality.[84] For women cohabitants, co-motherhood can be acquired by declaration, in the same manner as for fatherhood,[85] or allocated by a court ruling if the co-parent consented to conception.[86] The rules for assigning and declaring co-motherhood are thus founded on social parenthood and the consent of both lesbian cohabitants or married partners. Here, the Act differs from the otherwise increased emphasis on biology with regard to fatherhood.[87]

The rules on co-motherhood also apply if the partner of a legal woman (who has changed her legal gender) avails herself of assisted conception by the use of donor semen. Since the requirements for co-motherhood are fulfilled, it is not necessary to apply the birth-assigned gender in order to establish parenthood.[88] Thereby, in the case of co-mother, the rules recognise gender as social.

81 Prop. 74 L (2015–2016) [Proposition to the Storting (bill)] 37.
82 The term *co-father* is not a legal term and is not applied in any regulation on parenthood.
83 Children Act § 3.
84 Ot.prp. nr.33 (2007–2008) [Proposition to the Odelsting (bill)] [9.6.1.2].
85 Children Act § 4.
86 The rules in §§ 6–9 apply likewise for a co-mother to the extent that they are fitting. The legal effects of co-motherhood are the same as for fatherhood. Children Act §§ 4a, 9.
87 Backer, above n 65, 50.
88 Prop. 74 L (2015–2016) [Proposition to the Storting (bill)] 37.

Disrupting the biological link

As illustrated above, the basis of the parental rules under the Children Act remains that of a man and a woman whose legal genders match their birth-assigned genders. A father is presumed to be a cisman and a mother a ciswoman. As recognition of the rights of lesbian couples to assisted conception challenged the male/female parenting dyad, the new legal term 'co-mother' was introduced. The Act also establishes that a child cannot have both a father and a co-mother, as this would be too much of a violation of the biological principle, since there will always be a 'father' when donor insemination is not used, as explained in the preparatory work.[89] Nor can a child have two legal mothers or co-mothers. Although the Act opens social parenthood as a basis for legal parenthood, such as for co-motherhood, it remains anchored in the biological principle.

As we have seen, the Gender Recognition Act challenges the biological parenting dyad by making it possible for legal men to give birth and legal women to produce semen. Yet whereas the basis for legal genders is in motion from biologic to social recognition, the birth-assigned gender, which is based on biological characteristics at birth, continues to be the basis for the establishment of legal parenthood. In relation to parenthood, law governs gender as biological.

However, rules that govern parenthood by treating gender as biological are not unique to Norway. For example, in Denmark, Sweden and the Netherlands, the person who gives birth is the child's mother, irrespective of legal gender.[90] The one exception may be the Gender Recognition Act 2004 (UK), which states that '[t]he fact that a person's gender has become the acquired gender under this Act does not affect the status of the person as the father or mother of a child'.[91] The provision is ambiguous, but in the view of Stephen Gilmore, it is likely that it refers to parenthood prior to legal gender recognition, meaning that parenthood before transitioning remains the same after legal gender recognition. Gilmore suggests that, after recognition of preferred gender, legal parenthood can be acquired in keeping with legal gender, which would mean that a transgender man could be legal father, as wished for by my informant quoted at the start of this chapter.[92]

89 Children Act § 4a; Ot.prp. nr.33 (2007–8) [Proposition to the Odelsting (bill)] [9.6.1.2].

90 Natalie Videbæk Munkholm, 'Legal Status of Transsexual and Transgender Persons in Denmark' in Jens M Scherpe (ed), *The Legal Status of Transsexual and Transgender Persons* (Intersentia, 2015) 147, 171; Prop. 2012/13: 107 [Proposition to Riksdagen (bill)] (Sweden) 18–22; Marjolein van den Brink and Jet Tigchelaar, 'The Equality of the (Non) Trans-Parent: Women Who Father Children' in Marjolein van den Brink, Susanne Burri and Jenny Goldschmidt (eds), *Equality and Human Rights: Nothing but Trouble?* (SIM special, 2015) 247, 249–50.

91 Gender Recognition Act (UK) c 7.

92 Stephen Gilmore, 'The Legal Status of Transsexual and Transgender Persons in England and Wales' in Jens M Scherpe (ed), *The Legal Status of Transsexual and Transgender Persons* (Intersentia, 2015) 183, 200, 203.

So why has the legislature held onto the traditionally presumed link between gender and parenthood categories? Why not change the wording of the Act so as to comply with the purpose of the Gender Recognition Act, which is self-determined gender, or even better gender-neutralise the rules regarding parenthood in the Children Act? The law cannot prevent forms of genetic kinship that do not conform with the paradigm of 'normality' produced and governed by law. For example, since transgender people undergoing gender-confirmation treatment are unable to arrange for the preservation of their eggs in Norway, because surrogacy is not permitted, one of my young transgender informants told me that he is travelling abroad to preserve his eggs to ensure that his partner can carry and give birth to his child.[93] He will be genetically related to his child, whereas his partner will be biologically related by way of carrying their child. Since his partner will give birth, she will be the child's mother. It would be in line with the objectives of the rules on parenthood, such as ensuring the integrity of the family and ensuring the best interests of the child by ensuring that the child has two legal parents, if he is assigned fatherhood to the child born by his partner.[94] If he gave birth, he would automatically be assigned motherhood. By overcoming the limitations imposed by law, these parents will challenge the 'normal' biological link between gender and reproduction. This means that the rules on parenthood under the Children Act are no guarantee for presumed biological parent/child relations, and as we have seen above, they are inconsistent in whether or not transgender peoples' gender identity is recognised.

Governing (trans)parenthood

So, how are the Gender Recognition Act and the Children Act governing parenthood? In particular, what are their effects in the lives of transgender Norwegians? As Foucault argues, in modern societies power operates through normative discourses, which lead to the normalisation of certain conduct and behaviour. Law works as an important medium that produces power,[95] which works to discipline populations by defining what are normal ways to live and what are not.

93 Informant interviewed 2015. Since surrogacy is not permitted in Norway preservation of eggs has not been provided for transgender people who are starting hormone therapy and undergoing gender-confirmation surgery. Biotechnology Act § 2-15; Directorate of Health, 'Evaluering av bioteknologiloven 2015: Oppdatering om status og utvikling på fagområdene som reguleres av loven' (Report, Directorate of Health, 2015) [2.2.9.3]. To date, the Biotechnology Act is under revision and biotechnology options for transgender people are considered.

94 It is uncertain how this would work out in practice. Yet, if they are married, as a main rule the *pater rest* rule shall apply.

95 See, eg, Jane Scoular, 'What's Law Got to Do with It? How and Why Law Matters in the Regulation of Sex Work' (2010) 37 *Journal of Law and Society* 12, 26–8.

Exceptions to the rule of self-declared legal gender are regulated by section 6 of the Gender Recognition Act. The provision establishes which rules to apply when the rules on establishment of parenthood under the Children Act do not fit the situation of transgender people conceiving children, clarifying what conception of gender operates in relation to parenthood. For example, giving birth is not a function only legal women or people identifying as women have. Yet the rules do not reflect this situation. When the rules on parenthood do not fit the 'reality', the provision requires that birth-assigned gender shall be applied at the expense of (legal) gender. The operation of power of this provision is not by way of precluding transgender people from establishing families with children, like the requirements of sterilisation or infertility did previously. Rather, it draws on normative expectations embedded in this provision. The operation of power works by way of governing what the population sees as 'normal' and their wish to be 'normal', and not by way of coercion. It is a shift from how the requirement of surgery governed the population and how the less visible form of power of today's legislation works. Yet this less visible form of power affects the personal experiences of transgender people and shapes the wider expectations of society by constituting subjects based on conventional norms. In relation to transgender people, the provision works by way of implying that they are not 'real' men or women even though their legal gender indicates that they are. It imposes certain limits on the expulsion of the biologic of gender from the law. The line is drawn at parenthood and reproduction.

The enactment of the Gender Recognition Act did not lead to a subsequent change of the wording of the Children Act to bring it into compliance with the new situation. This probably enabled a more rapid introduction of the Act, which was beneficial to transgender people because it abolished medical requirements for change of legal gender. At the same time, this works to limit the effects of the change and protect cisgendered conventions relating to both gender and sexuality. The power of the Children Act works through its gender-specific wording, in other words from the texts as such, which constructs heterosexual, married, cisgender families as the norm. In 'denying' the realities of transgendered people's lives, the Act constructs normative expectations about gender and parenthood, which reconstitute and reconfirm their 'otherness'. Rather than challenging conventional norms, the Act thereby pursues and supports these norms and their power in normalising the population.

Yet most people never look at the specific wording of legislation and, as was argued in the preparatory work to the Gender Recognition Act, parents are not listed as mother, father or co-mother in the National Population Register or on birth certificates, unlike in Sweden.[96] In 2014 and 2015, Swedish courts found that a mismatch between a person's gender identity/legal gender and gendered parental status in the Swedish Population Register was in breach of article 8 (privacy) and article 14 (non-discrimination) of the ECHR in relation to both the

96 Prop. 74 L (2015–16) [Proposition to the Storting (bill)] [8.5.3].

parent and the child. It is, as argued by the Administrative Court in Gothenburg, in compliance with the best interests of the child to register parents in such a way that parents' 'change of gender' is not involuntarily disclosed. The courts concluded that a legal man who gives birth, and a person who changes legal gender after giving birth, can be registered as a father.[97] Such registration was considered to be in keeping with the object of population registration, which is to secure correct and relevant information about individuals. In the view of the Swedish courts, to register a legal man as a mother implies that he is registered as a woman, and as a consequence his gender identity is not fully legally recognised.[98]

Even though the Norwegian Population Register registers parents differently from the Swedish register, other Norwegian laws and regulations also apply cisgendered categories of parenthood. If we look at the National Insurance Act 1997 provisions on pregnancy, birth and adoption benefits, the terms 'man', 'woman', 'mother' and 'father' appear throughout.[99] These rules actively impact on the lives of trans-parents. Indeed, the new legislation specifies that these rules also apply to those who have changed their legal gender, yet, the terms are used in application forms for parental benefits and for assisted conception,[100] which means that applicants are forced to disclose their gender history. These rules are therefore a constant reminder of 'otherness' – of not being recognised as a parent on an equal footing with cisparents. Here, law continues to disqualify transgendered parenthood as fully normal, signalling transgender people's questionable fitness for parenthood. This might affect not only the well-being of transgender parents,

97 *A and B v Skatteverket* [Swedish Tax Agency], Förvaltningsrätten i Göteborg [Administrative Court in Gothenburg], 11435-13, 30 October 2014. The appeal made by the Swedish Tax Agency was rejected by Kammarrätten i Göteborg [Administrative Court in Gothenburg], 6186-14, 5 October 2015. *Warren Kunce v Skatteverket* [Swedish Tax Agency], Förvaltningsrätten i Stockholm [Administrative Court in Stockholm], 24685, 14 April 2015. The appeal made by the Swedish Tax Agency was rejected by Kammarrätten i Stockholm [Administrative Court of Appeal in Stockholm], 3201-14, 19 July 2015. Cf Kammergericht in Berlin [Higher Regional Court], 1. Zivilsenat 1 W 48/14, 30 October 2014. In 2011, the German Constitutional Court ruled that the requirement of sterilisation under the Act on Change of Names and Gender was in breach of the German Constitution and the ECHR, and annulled the requirement. Bundesverfassungsgericht [German Constitutional Court], 1 BvR 3295/07, 11 January 2011.

98 Förvaltningsrätten i Göteborg [Administrative Court in Gothenburg], 11435-13, 30 October 2014.

99 Lov om folketrygd [National Insurance Act] 28 February 1997, No 19.

100 See, eg, Søknad om foreldrepenger, mødrekvote eller fedrekvote ved fødsel [Application on Parental Benefits, Mother's Quota or Father's Quota at Birth] (Form No NAV 14 to 05.09, NAV) <https://www.nav.no/internett/no/Person/Skjemaer-for-privatpersoner/skjemaveileder/vedlegg?key=267385&veiledertype=privatperson>; Varsel om avvikling av foreldrepermisjon [Notice of Parental Leave] (Form No 703147e, Meløy Kommune); Tilrettelegging/omplassering pga graviditet [Adaptation/Reposition Due to Pregnancy] (Form, Norwegian Labour Inspection Authority); Samtykke til assistert befruktning fra ektefelle/registrert partner/samboer [Consent to Assisted Conception from Spouse/Registered Partner/Cohabitant] (Form No Q-0314B, Folkeregistermyndigheten).

but also indirectly their children. As argued by the Swedish courts mentioned above, there is no reason to not see birth-giving legal men as fathers.

The 2016 legislative change operates quietly to shape normality by maintaining the fictive link between legal men and semen and legal women and eggs, thereby privileging a cisgendered reality. Law's power does not work by way of prohibiting particular forms of parenthood, such as it does for egg donation, surrogacy and assisted conception. On the contrary, in relation to transgender parenthood, the wording of the law operates behind the appearance of trans inclusion, interweaving with other tactics in governing gender identities, rewarding preferable forms of (cis)parenthood and casting doubt on the legitimacy of others.

One of my informants, a woman in her 20s, says: 'I would of course see myself as a mother, but I'm not sure how that would work out on paper. It would have felt quite weird to be defined as a father, creepy actually . . . I am a woman.'[101] She, like all the other transgender people I have interviewed, would identify as the parent matching their gender identity if they have children. However, the wording of the Act reflected in many application forms will signal that they are not 'really' women or men. The same informant says: 'Being trans is a part of my identity, but not a significant part of my identity. Being trans has evolved from figuring prominently, to wind up in the background [to being a woman].' To introduce the Gender Recognition Act and not amend related laws works against the purpose of the Act, which is to recognise gender identity based on self-determination. Instead of diminishing the relevance of being transgender, it is continually foregrounded by law's representation of the 'otherness' of trans-parents. Norwegian rules on parenthood create a hierarchy of preferred parents where matters of gender identity, sexual orientation, whether you are in a relationship and whether you use a 'proper' form of conception all matter.

Norwegian law is based on the male/female gender dualism. No other genders are recognised, and biology serves as the predominant basis of determining gender in the context of recognising legal parenthood. Would it not be preferable to introduce gender-neutral terms into the laws regulating and establishing parenthood? The use of gendered terms could be replaced with language that relates to the function or substance that the law is governing: such as pregnancy, cash benefits for the birth-giving parent or caring parent, protection against discrimination on the grounds of pregnancy or becoming or being a parent, access to abortion and parental leave.[102] This would include all parents no matter what their gender identity or sexual orientation, and contribute to ending reliance on gender and sexuality hierarchies based on biologic. It could be a way to disrupt the tenacity of rigid normative and socially constructed dualistic gender roles that

101 Informant interviewed 2015.

102 Other scholars have also suggested this as a possible option. See, eg, Sheelagh McGuinness and Amel Alghrani, 'Gender and Parenthood: The Case for Realignment' (2008) 16 *Medical Law Review* 261, 282; van den Brink and Tigchelaar, above n 90, 247, 259; Karaian, above n 2, 211–30.

continue to rely on biologic, even as they purport to recognise trans-parenthood. It would be in compliance with the best interests of the child that shall be a primary consideration in all actions concerning children, as it would ensure that the child has legal parents.[103] Furthermore, it would diminish the role of law in creating authenticity and normalising subjects which could positively influence the well-being of transgender parents and thereby also their children.

I have argued that recent developments in the legal and social regulation of gender identity and parenthood hold fast to the importance of biological foundations, heterosexual family forms and cisnormativity. In Norway, the Children Act, in combination with the Gender Recognition Act, while not explicitly excluding transgender parenthood, establishes a governing hierarchy of parenthood, gender identities and sexualities that normalises heterosexuality and reinstates the biological link between birth/legal woman and semen/legal man. Law's recognition of gender as social and fluid is extremely limited. A great deal depends on the subject matter. In the case of parenthood, law refuses the full inclusion of transgender people, and returns to the biologic of the two-sex model. I suggest that it may be time to adopt gender-neutral parental categories under the law, arguing that gender-neutral terms would better include and reflect the reality of parents living in contemporary Norway, and many other parts of the world. Gender-neutral parenthood would also help to realise the human rights principles of self-identification, personal integrity and autonomy that underlie new laws relating to change of legal gender. The goal should be to recognise transgender people's gender identity in all aspects of their lives.

103 Convention on the Rights of the Child, opened for signature 20 November 1989, 1577 UNTS 3 (entered into force 2 September 1990) art 3. Incorporated into the Human Rights Act.

Part IV

Risks: Troubling statehood, sovereignty and its borders

10 Queer border crossers

Pragmatic complicities, indiscretions and subversions

*Bina Fernandez**

> Borders are set up to define the places that are safe and unsafe, to distinguish us from them. A border is a dividing line, a narrow strip along a steep edge. A borderland is a vague and undetermined place created by the emotional residue of an unnatural boundary. It is in a constant state of transition. The prohibited and forbidden are its inhabitants. Los atravesados live here: the squint-eyed, the perverse, the queer, the troublesome, the mongrel, the mulato, the half-breed, the half dead; in short, those who cross over, pass over, or go through the confines of the 'normal'.[1]

Gloria Anzaldúa's words provide an apt preface to the concerns of this chapter with borders, and the people who cross them, those whom she calls *los atravesados*. In a Spanish–English dictionary, the source verb '*atravesar*' means 'to cross, to pierce, to lay across, to go through (a situation or crisis)' and also 'to obstruct and to interfere'.[2] With Anzaldúa, I view queer border crossers as transgressors of boundaries whose disruptions of normative categories may be contradictory, provocative and alien, but have critical and transformative possibilities.

By invoking at the outset the work of Chicana lesbian feminist activist Gloria Anzaldúa, I engage the anti-identitarian and anti-normative traditions in queer critique that Anzaldúa pioneered a few years before the 'canonical' texts of queer theory by Judith Butler and Eve Sedgwick were published. It is nearly 30 years since Anzaldúa's pioneering work, and the robust scholarship on queer migrations that has since emerged acknowledges that 'queer' is a contested term, and goes beyond the identitarian categories of lesbian, gay, bisexual, transgender and intersex (and the diverse gender and sexual identities and practices

* I am grateful to Debolina Dutta and Dianne Otto for their comments on this chapter. Their thoughtful feedback enriched my thinking and helped me clarify arguments in the chapter. I also thank Isabella Ofner for her meticulous assistance with the references.

1 Gloria Anzaldúa, *Borderlands/La Frontera: The New Mestiza* (Aunt Lute Books, 1987) 25.

2 See, eg, Britannica, 'Atravesar', Nglish: Translation and English Learning <http://www.nglish.com/spanish/en/atravesar?rr=L1>; Henry Neuman and Giuseppe Marco Antonio Baretti, *Neuman and Baretti's Dictionary of the Spanish and English Languages* (William Kerr & Co, 1842) vol 1, 85 (definition of 'atravesar').

not captured by these terms). 'Queer' is used as a tool of critique that offers 'resistance to regimes of the normal' and is simultaneously 'calibrated to account for the social antagonisms of nation, race, gender, and class as well as sexuality'.[3]

'Borders' are also contested: they are not merely the physical markers of territory, lines on the map, barbed wire fences or check posts that demarcate divisions between states. Borders are ideological constructs that generate particular identities, denote power relationships and the ontological boundaries of political space. Anzaldúa described the border as '*una herida abierta* [an open wound] where the Third World grates against the First and bleeds'.[4] She challenged the imperial imposition of the (US) border that violently divided her people, yet inevitably failed to contain them. Borders are 'polysemic', carrying meanings that are contingent on context and perspective.[5] They may denote national cultural belonging, may be constitutive of the production of gender, sexualities, families and households, confer membership privileges of entitlements and protections due to national citizens, filter out 'desirable' from 'undesirable' workers and construct labour relations, and under globalisation, may also be irrelevant to the circulation of certain types of commodities, services and finances.

In focusing on queer border crossers, this chapter seeks to explore what happens when these two inherently unstable signifiers 'queer' and 'border' intersect. In doing so, I aim to move beyond the limited narrative of such individuals crossing international borders to 'escape repression in the global South and gain freedom in the global North', and ask instead, what are the modes of inclusion, dissidence, subversion or normalisation that are produced when queers cross the border? How do the boundaries of the nation-state and citizenship get redrawn? While queer border crossers may be categorised by states as migrants, asylum seekers, refugees, economic migrants, family or partner migrants, business travellers and tourists; in this chapter I restrict my discussion to the first three categories, with the caveat that all these categories have fuzzy often overlapping boundaries, and that they must be recognised as contingent on the prior existence of nations and borders.

The chapter is structured as follows: the second section outlines some of the significant victories of LGBTI struggles for the recognition of gender and sexuality as grounds for migration and asylum seeking. I show that while there has been progress, particularly in immigration law in the past few decades, recognition of LGBTI asylum seeker claims has been troubled. In the third section I examine the practices of the law and activist responses in two domains: the practices around 'credibility' of LGBTI applicants for migration and asylum; and, second, the paradoxes of sexual (in)visibility related to LGBTI claims. Here, I argue that although such practices may be viewed as 'pragmatic complicities' supporting

3 Eithne Luibhéid and Lionel Cantú Jr (eds), *Queer Migrations: Sexuality, US Citizenship, and Border Crossings* (University of Minnesota Press, 2005) x–xi.

4 Anzaldúa, above n 1, 25.

5 Étienne Balibar, *Politics and the Other Scene* (Verso, 2002) 81.

individual claimants, they legitimate the reification of identity politics and a homonationalist consolidation of power. In the concluding fourth section, the chapter introduces the 'no borders' position, differentiating it from an 'open borders' position, and develops my argument for why the former offers emancipatory possibilities for a politics of *los atravesados* or queer border crossers that seeks to transform, rather than accommodate to, existing social structures.

Reforms in LGBTI immigration and asylum law

In the nineteenth century, nation-states' prerogatives and capacity to control the entry of *los atravesados* to their territories became the mode of signalling state authority, indeed their very 'stateness'. National identities were deeply entwined with ideologies of race, ethnicity, class and sexuality, particularly in settler colonial countries like the United States, Australia and Canada. Citizenship became naturalised as delimited by the nation, and immigration legislation enacted in this period[6] explicitly denied entry to a long list of people considered undesirable: lunatics, criminals, sex workers, polygamists, paupers, people unable to take care of themselves without becoming a public charge, people suffering from contagious disease, anyone convicted of a crime of 'moral turpitude', people deemed to have 'psychopathic personalities', 'deviants', homosexuals and 'non-white' populations (Asians, Africans, Eastern Europeans).

The ban on people with mental illness was interpreted in practice to exclude lesbians, gays and gender non-conformist people in the United States, Australia and Canada. These restrictions were tightened in the mid twentieth century in the United States (and to a lesser degree in the other two countries), largely in response to the Cold War wave of anti-Communist paranoia.[7] As Margot Canaday observes, 'homosexuals were, like communists, not only unnatural but dangerously subversive' unworthy of entry and citizenship.[8] In 1952, the Diagnostic and Statistical Manual of Mental Disorders, published by the American Psychiatric Association, officially classified homosexuality as a 'sociopathic personality disturbance'; in the same year, the McCarran–Walter Act's ban on psychopathic personalities was used for the first time by the Immigration and Naturalization Service in the United States to explicitly refuse immigration of lesbians and gays. It was only in the 1990s that these explicitly discriminatory provisions of the law were removed in the United States and several other countries, allowing individual lesbian and gay applicants to make immigration applications. Notwithstanding these changes, lesbians and gays continued to face significant barriers to

6 For instance, see An Act Supplementary to the Acts in Relation to Immigration, USC (1875); Immigration Restriction Act 1901 (Cth); Immigration Act, C 1906.

7 Randolph W Baxter, '"Homo-Hunting" in the Early Cold War: Senator Kenneth Wherry and the Homophobic Side of McCarthyism' (2003) 84 *Nebraska History* 118. Margot Canaday, '"Who Is a Homosexual?": The Consolidation of Sexual Identities in Mid-Twentieth-Century American Immigration Law' (2003) 28 *Law and Social Inquiry* 351.

8 Canaday, above n 7, 355.

immigration over the next two decades, due to the inability of lesbian and gay couples to marry, and the legal non-recognition of their families.

Australia and Canada were the first countries to allow immigration of the same-sex partners of nationals in the late 1980s, through compassionate and humanitarian visas that were issued by ministerial discretion. Today, around 20 countries[9] recognise immigration rights for bi-national same-sex couples, *if one of them is a citizen*. These countries have followed two distinct routes to such recognition. The first route is the creation of an immigration sponsorship category broad enough to include same-sex relationships. This was the path adopted by Australia in 1991, through the introduction of the Emotional Interdependency visa category to allow non-familial migration (amended in 2000 to the family stream same-sex interdependency visa); the majority of countries subsequently followed this pathway. Initially, many of these countries continued to make discriminatory distinctions between heterosexual and homosexual relationships – for instance, in the proviso for the number of years prior to and post-entry that the couple was required to provide evidence of a continued relationship. Since 2000, these differences have been gradually eliminated, and same-sex couples enjoy the same rights as opposite-sex couples to sponsor their non-citizen partners, or to include their partner in visa applications. The second route to recognition of same-sex immigration rights is through civil unions legislation, which confers some of the rights of heterosexual marriage, including partner sponsorship. This route was adopted by Norway, Iceland, Denmark and Switzerland.

Until very recently, the United States was the major outlier from this group of countries that recognise same-sex partner immigration rights. According to a study using US census data conducted by the Williams Institute in 2010, there were an estimated 28,500 bi-national same-sex couples and nearly 11,500 same-sex couples in which neither partner was a US citizen.[10] However, estimates of actual numbers exceeded these 40,000 couples, as many would be unlikely to declare their status to authorities. Thus, over 40,000 lesbian and gay bi-national couples were prevented from sponsoring their non-citizen partners to live in the United States.

In a comparative analysis of the United States, Israel and Australia, S Iimay Ho and Megan Rolfe argue that the structure of political opportunity constrained the efforts of gay rights advocates in the United States.[11] In contrast, in Israel and Australia, access to elite allies, ministerial autonomy and parliamentary politics

9 These include Canada, Australia, New Zealand, Norway, Sweden, Denmark, Finland, Iceland, the Netherlands, Germany, France, Spain, Portugal, Belgium, Switzerland, Ireland, the United Kingdom, South Africa, Brazil, Israel and, most recently, the United States.

10 Craig J Konnoth and Gary J Gates, 'Same-Sex Couples and Immigration in the United States' (Report, The Williams Institute, November 2011) <http://williamsinstitute.law.ucla.edu/wp-content/uploads/Gates-Konnoth-Binational-Report-Nov-2011.pdf>.

11 S Iimay Ho and Megan E Rolfe, 'Same-Sex Partner Immigration and the Civil Rights Frame: A Comparative Study of Australia, Israel, and the USA' (2011) 52 *International Journal of Comparative Sociology* 390.

allowed activists to successfully use a civil rights frame to legitimise their cause and reduce opposition. Conservatives in the United States succeeded in mounting significant opposition at state and federal levels, which culminated in the regressive 1996 Defense of Marriage Act (DOMA) that restricted marriage to the union of one man and one woman, and allowed states to refuse recognition of same-sex marriages granted under the laws of other states.[12] This restrictive definition of 'marriage' to heterosexual couples thus aggressively reinforced the bar against same-sex couples receiving federal marriage benefits, including the right to sponsor a non-citizen partner.[13] These restrictions were recently lifted with two Supreme Court decisions: the 2013 ruling in *Windsor v United States* that section 3 of DOMA was unconstitutional, and the 2015 ruling in *Obergefell v Hodges* that state-level bans on same-sex marriage were unconstitutional. The US Department of Homeland Security now reviews immigration visa petitions filed on behalf of a same-sex spouse in the same manner as those filed on behalf of an opposite-sex spouse.[14]

In contrast to same-sex immigration reforms, legislative reforms that recognise the eligibility of lesbians and gays to be considered refugees and asylum seekers have been slower to be implemented and are still deeply contested, even in the core countries that accept immigration of same-sex partners. Drawing on the extensive scholarship documenting these struggles across national contexts, I identify below some of the key reform moments in this history.[15]

12 John Medeiros, 'Immigration after DOMA: How Equal Is Marriage Equality?' (2014) 35 *Hamline Journal of Public Law & Policy* 196.

13 Logan Bushell, '"Give Me Your Tired, Your Poor, Your Huddled Masses" – Just as Long as They Fit in the Heteronormative Ideal: US Immigration Law's Exclusionary and Inequitable Treatment of Lesbian, Gay, Bisexual, Transgendered, and Queer Migrants' (2012) 48 *Gonzaga Law Review* 673; Daniela G Domínguez, Bernadette H Solórzano and Ezequiel Peña, 'Nonheterosexual Binational Families: Resilient Victims of Sexual Prejudice and Discriminatory Immigration Policies' (2012) 8 *Journal of GLBT Family Studies* 496.

14 See Department of Homeland Security, 'Implementation of the Supreme Court Ruling on the Defense of Marriage Act' (21 July 2015) <http://www.dhs.gov/topic/implementation-supreme-court-ruling-defense-marriage-act>.

15 See Arwen Swink, 'Queer Refuge: A Review of the Role of Country Condition Analysis in Asylum Adjudications for Members of Sexual Minorities' (2006) 29 *Hastings International and Comparative Law Review* 251; Sabine Jansen, 'Fleeing Homophobia, Asylum Claims Related to Sexual Orientation and Gender Identity in Europe' in Thomas Spijkerboer (ed), *Fleeing Homophobia: Sexual Orientation, Gender Identity and Asylum* (Taylor and Francis, 2013) 1; Jenni Millbank, 'Sexual Orientation and Refugee Status Determination over the Past 20 Years: Unsteady Progress through Standard Sequences?' in Thomas Spijkerboer (ed), *Fleeing Homophobia: Sexual Orientation, Gender Identity and Asylum* (Taylor and Francis, 2013) 32; Heather Scavone, 'Queer Evidence: The Peculiar Evidentiary Burden Faced by Asylum Applicants with Cases Based on Sexual Orientation and Identity' (2013) 5 *Elon Law Review* 389; Nan Seuffert, 'Haunting National Boundaries LBGTI Asylum Seekers' (2013) 22 *Griffith Law Review* 752; Rachel A Lewis, '"Gay? Prove it": The Politics of Queer Anti-Deportation Activism' (2014) 17 *Sexualities* 958; Amy Shuman and Carol Bohmer, 'Gender and Cultural Silences in the Political Asylum Process' (2014) 17 *Sexualities* 939;

The 1951 UN Convention Relating to the Status of Refugees ('Refugee Convention') defines a refugee as a person who is outside their country of citizenship because they have well-founded grounds for fear of persecution because of their race, religion, nationality, membership of a particular social group or political opinion, and is unable to obtain sanctuary from their home country or, owing to such fear, is unwilling to avail themselves of the protection of that country.[16]

As the Refugee Convention did not explicitly include lesbians and gays as a group requiring protection, in the first three decades, lesbian and gay applications for refugee status were routinely denied until the Netherlands became the first Northern nation to recognise sexual orientation as grounds for protection from persecution,[17] followed by the United States in 1990 in the *Matter of Toboso-Alfonso*,[18] Canada in a 1991 ruling by the Supreme Court in *(AG) v Ward* and other countries such as Australia and the United Kingdom.[19] In the 1990s, international human rights organisations like Amnesty International and Human Rights Watch argued that protection from homosexual and gender-based persecution fell within the purview of refugee rights. The LGBTI rights activism by these organisations documented persecution on the basis of gender and sexual orientation around the world. This documentation was partially responsible for the UN High Commissioner for Refugee's (UNHCR) Guidelines on International Protection: Gender-Related Persecution in 2002, which recognised that 'membership of a particular social group' entailed sharing a common characteristic which is '*innate, unchangeable, or which is otherwise fundamental to identity, conscience or the exercise of one's human rights*'.[20] The Guidelines explicitly stated that sexual orientation should be considered as 'membership of a particular social group' and thus a relevant ground in claims for protection against persecution under the Refugee Convention.

Two additional important steps forward taken in these Guidelines were the recognition first, that the criminalisation of homosexuality could amount to persecution; and, further, that even when there is no explicit criminalisation, a claimant can establish a valid claim if the state condones the persecution or fails to protect the claimant from persecution. Second, the Guidelines recognised that non-state actors may also be responsible for persecution. Subsequently, the UNHCR has issued additional guidance, resource documentation and guidelines

Amy Shuman and Wendy S Hesford, 'Getting Out: Political Asylum, Sexual Minorities, and Privileged Visibility' (2014) 17 *Sexualities* 1016.

16 Convention Relating to the Status of Refugees, opened for signature 28 July 1951, 189 UNTS 137 (entered into force 22 April 1954).

17 Jansen, above n 15, 1.

18 Scavone, above n 15, 393.

19 Millbank, above n 15.

20 UN High Commissioner for Refugees, Guidelines on International Protection: Gender-Related Persecution within the Context of Article 1A(2) of the 1951 Convention and/or its 1967 Protocol Relating to the Status of Refugees, UN Doc HCR/GIP/02/01 (7 May 2002) (emphasis in original).

on sexual orientation and gender identity claims (in 2008 and 2011) which explicitly included LGBTI persons as among those migrants who 'may be at particular risk at international borders'.[21] Similar legislative action followed within the European Union: in 2004, EU member states adopted a Council directive that specified sexual orientation as 'membership in a particular social group', which by 2015 was recognised in 24 EU countries either through case law or national legislation.[22]

In an authoritative, longitudinal, comparative review of LGBTI refugee case law in the United Kingdom, Australia, New Zealand and Canada, Jenni Millbank outlines the development of legislative reforms through a sequence of steps that have been (and continue to be) undertaken by countries, which include:[23]

- acceptance of sexual orientation as constituting 'membership of a particular social group' in refugee claims;
- recognition that criminalisation of homosexuality is persecutory;
- acknowledgement that non-state actors are often primary agents of persecution;
- development of information related to LGBT issues in the country of origin;
- rejection of the role of 'discretion reasoning' (which allowed countries to deny LGBT claimants asylum on the grounds that they would be safe if they were discreet about expressing their sexual orientation); and
- recognition of multiple, intersecting harms as persecution and not 'mere' discrimination.

Notwithstanding these gains, Millbank argues that the recognition of sexual orientation within refugee status determination processes progressed unsteadily, with large 'symbolic' legislative gains not quite matched by equivalent advances in legal practice, especially at lower judicial levels.[24]

To conclude this section, two observations about same-sex immigration and asylum law reforms are worth noting. First, the reforms discussed are relevant to a very small handful of countries. Queer border crossers who negotiate the borders of the majority of countries where such reforms do not apply must do so through various means of subterfuge, and are constantly at risk of exposure

21 Office of the High Commissioner for Human Rights, Recommended Principles and Guidelines on Human Rights at International Borders, 69th sess, Agenda Item 69, UN Doc A/69/CRP. 1 (23 July 2014).

22 Alejandro Rada, 'Persecution on the Grounds of Sexual Orientation and Gender Identity – Asylum Rights, Procedures and Decisions in the European Union' (Report, Observatory for Sociopolitical Developments in Europe, March 2016) <http://www.sociopolitical-observatory.eu/uploads/tx_aebgppublications/2016-03_ENG_Expertise_Asylum_rights_for_LGBTI.pdf>.

23 Millbank, above n 15, 36.

24 Ibid.

to laws that discriminate against and criminalise homosexuality and 'deviance', however defined.

Second, the parameters of 'successful' legislative reform in these countries are crucially contingent on structural and normative markers of difference such as race, citizenship and class, that mediate which queer migrants actually cross borders, and how. Queer border crossers without a partner who is a citizen or permanent resident have only two possible, individualised, routes of legal entry: to apply as a refugee or asylum seeker, or to apply under an economic immigration category (such as the highly skilled migrant programmes). In the latter case, usually only one spouse/partner needs to meet the selection criteria in order for both to enter the country. The income, education and skills requirements of these visa categories preclude the vast majority of potential migrants (gay or otherwise) from considering applications. Border laws thus work to produce a select group of lesbian and gay border crossers as 'acceptable' citizens.

Practices of LGBTI immigration and asylum law

By 'practices of the law', I refer not only to the activities of functionaries of the state who make, interpret and implement laws, but also to the interstitial engagements of LGBTI claimants and activists who are affected by the law – who conform to, ignore, resist, challenge or subvert it, and in so doing, reconstitute (though not always 'queer') the law. I focus here on two aspects of immigration and asylum law to which scholars have drawn attention: first, the need for LGBTI claimants to establish the credibility of their cases; and, second, the paradoxes of sexual (in)visibility and (in)discretion produced through the practice of asylum law. I conclude the section with reflections on the contradictions and tensions wrought by the pragmatic complicities with LGBTI immigration and asylum law.

Telling tales: The credibility of LGBTI individuals' claims

Close scrutiny of evidence to establish the *credibility* of LGBTI applicants is undertaken in the practice of both immigration and asylum law. The demand for evidence in immigration applications requires proving the credibility of the bi-national couple's relationship; the demand for evidence in asylum cases has a higher credibility requirement of, first, proving their sexual and/or gender identity, and, second, proving that they are persecuted because of it. While the specific demand for evidence may vary, the demand itself must be marked as a mechanism that legitimates the state's authority and assures citizens of its control of the border and the nation.

In countries that accept same-sex partner immigration, applicants must marshal credible evidence of a relationship. Depending on the country, this may be done through proof of marriage or domestic partnership; or it may be through personal testimony, testimonies of others as witness to the relationship, proof of joint residence, joint banking accounts, travel and so on. In many countries, proof of the stability and longevity of the relationship also needs to be established, and these requirements have in the past been more stringent than those for heterosexual couples.

Within the limited parameters of countries that accept same-sex partner migration, it is worth reflecting on the exclusions and inclusions effected through the credibility practices of immigration law. First, establishing the credibility of the relationship does not necessarily guarantee entry for *all* bi-national couples. As I pointed out previously, non-citizen bi-national couples are excluded. Further, bi-national couples in which the non-national partner has a chronic illness (such as HIV), a disability or is 'too old' can be excluded on grounds that they would be a potential burden on the state because they would be unable to support themselves. Thus, the recognition of a bi-national same-sex relationship can be precarious and contingent on the inherently productivist assumptions underlying contemporary border control practices. There is also an implicit exclusion of people based on their class and education, as only those with the requisite financial capacity (to pay the required fees) and language capacity and internet literacy (to navigate complex application systems that are often now online) are in a position to apply for same-sex partner migration.

Second, immigration inclusion for bi-national couples is achieved in practice through homonormative appropriations of the construct of a 'good citizen'. Lisa Duggan defined homonormativity as 'a politics that does not contest dominant heteronormative assumptions and institutions, but upholds and sustains them, while promising the possibility of a demobilized gay constituency and a privatized, depoliticized gay culture anchored in domesticity and consumption'.[25] Lesbian and gay couples make their immigration claims by establishing their status as happy families and productive workers. Audrey Yue offers an insightful analysis of how homonormativity plays out in the immigration of younger Asian men as the same-sex partners of older Anglo-Australian men. She describes this pairing of the 'rice and potato queen' as constituted through the sedimented histories of colonialism and the 'unequal neocolonial and neoliberal geopolitics of how marginalised groups within and outside the nation, are forced to conform to the norm so as to make claims to the resources of mobility'.[26]

Establishing credibility is more difficult for LGBTI asylum seekers, in part because sexual and gender orientation are relatively new grounds, accepted only since 2002 under the Refugee Convention as constituting 'membership of a particular social group'. Although the broader principle of sexual orientation and gender-related persecution was accepted, individual LGBTI claimants still have to present credible evidence of, first, the persecution they have suffered, and, second, their sexual and/or gender identity. Evidence of persecution entails four aspects: evidence about the source of persecution, the location of persecution, that the

25 Lisa Duggan, *The Twilight of Equality? Neoliberalism, Cultural Politics, and the Attack on Democracy* (Beacon Press, 2003) 50.

26 Audrey Yue, 'Same-Sex Migration in Australia: From Interdependency to Intimacy' (2008) 14 *Journal of Lesbian and Gay Studies* 239, 255–6.

persecution is sufficiently severe and that it warrants a 'well-founded fear'. Initially, many LGBTI asylum applicants struggled to establish credible claims against the state as a 'source' as the existence of anti-sodomy statutes in the country of origin was considered the only evidence of persecution – that is, that the applicants were in violation of the laws of their country.[27] Non-state actors (family, community, employers and so on) as perpetrators of persecution were also not traditionally within the purview of political asylum cases, where the state was typically considered the source of persecution. Similarly, persecution within the private domain of the home was excluded from consideration. These exclusions particularly invalidated the dangers experienced by lesbian asylum seekers who typically faced violence within families.[28] Establishing that the persecution is severe, and not 'merely' everyday discrimination and oppression is the next requirement, which is linked to the need to establish 'well-founded fear'. Refugee law establishes a legal requirement to negotiate the intensely subjective emotion of fear in a rights claim, necessitating a complex subject positioning situated at the spatial and temporal intersections of bodily integrity, pain and trauma, sexual shame, erotic agency and desires, as well as other positions such as race, nationality, religion, gender and class.[29]

Further, LGBTI applicants must prove their sexual and/or gender identity, and in order to credibly do so, they must fit their experiences into stereotypical asylum seeker narratives acceptable to immigration authorities in the global North. Some of the assumptions underlying decision-making in asylum cases are that all lesbians and gays engage in cross-gender identification, are active in queer social spaces, are knowledgeable about queer culture, are sexually active but always only with persons of the same gender, don't have children, and if they have not 'come out', they will (or should) when they arrive in the country of immigration. These assumptions about identities and behaviours, even the terms LGBTI, are based on gendered, racialised and classed assumptions of a Western white gay male norm, and in effect erase experiences along the spectrum of sexual and gender diversity, and may lead to judgments such as the one below in the case of a Lebanese asylum seeker in Australia:

> [T]he applicant's oral evidence to the Tribunal was that he had had no relationship with anyone who shared his sexual orientation since he left school – a period of over 20 years, spanning his entire adult life to date – either in Lebanon or in Australia. He does not claim ever to have spoken to a homosexual since then. He asks the Tribunal to accept that this was because

27 Scavone, above n 15, 411.

28 See Susan A Berger, 'Production and Reproduction of Gender and Sexuality in Legal Discourses of Asylum in the United States' (2009) 34 *Signs* 659; Bushell, above n 13; Rachel Lewis, 'Lesbians under Surveillance: Same-Sex Immigration Reform, Gay Rights, and the Problem of Queer Liberalism' (2010) 37(1) *Social Justice* 90.

29 Senthorun Raj, 'Affective Displacements: Understanding Emotions and Sexualities in Refugee Law' (2011) 36 *Alternative Law Journal* 177.

he was, as he has said, a 'closet gay'. In my view this is implausible, and is far more consistent with his being heterosexual.[30]

The evidentiary demands of the asylum process and Eurocentric models of identity as 'outness' necessitate the presentation of an 'authentic' or genuine LGBTI person such that those with previous histories of passing or concealment (as in the case of the Lebanese applicant above) create a 'credibility gap' in their narratives. Furthermore, cases primarily based on testimonial evidence can be considered personal and subjective, vulnerable to 'adverse credibility'.[31]

Paradoxes of sexual (in)visibility and (in)discretion

The credibility requirement in the practice of the LGBTI asylum law has produced paradoxes of sexual (in)visibility. At different times and places, queer border crossers have been expected to, or compelled to disavow their sexualities, be 'discreet' or invisible, in order to avoid state surveillance or persecution (whether perpetrated by the state or non-state actors). Thus, in countries that do not allow same-sex partner immigration (which included the United States until very recently), such couples were often forced into invisibility as an adaptive strategy to deflect attention from the foreign partner's absence of legal status. This invisibility led to an underestimation of the number of such couples in the United States.[32] Forced invisibility is accompanied by fear of separation and deportation, and often necessitates staying under the radar of the government, which in turn has resulted in restricted access to essential services such as health care, education and housing.[33]

Asylum seekers too were forced into invisibility, as initially 'discretion reasoning' was used as a common ground for the rejection of LGBTI applicants. This was the claim that if applicants lived 'discreetly' (basically, became invisible) in their country of origin, they could avoid persecution. Widely applied until the late 1990s (until sexual orientation was recognised as constituting 'membership in a particular social group'), the discretion argument worked against lesbian asylum applicants in particular, as women are already less visible in the private sphere, and 'less likely to engage in targeted public activities'.[34]

Since the early 2000s, landmark judgments in Australia (2003), New Zealand (2004), the Netherlands (2007) and the United Kingdom (2010) have rejected 'discretion reasoning' as grounds for denying LGBTI applications.[35] These

30 Ibid 178.
31 Scavone, above n 15, 395–6.
32 Domínguez et al, above n 13.
33 Karma R Chávez, 'Identifying the Needs of LGBTQ Immigrants and Refugees in Southern Arizona' (2011) 58 *Journal of Homosexuality* 189.
34 Shuman and Bohmer, above n 15, 241.
35 Jansen, above n 15.

judgments led to intense debates on whether or not they were 'bad law'.[36] While it is beyond the scope of this chapter to enter into these debates, what can be noted here is that the rejection of 'discretion reasoning' has only been partial, and resistance to LGBTI asylum claims persists now through the heightened scrutiny of credibility.

The paradoxes of visibility produced were made most apparent in the highly publicised case of Brenda Namigadde, a lesbian asylum seeker from Uganda who was initially denied asylum in the United Kingdom on the grounds that the UK government could not 'see' that she was lesbian in Uganda. The publicity around her case 'ironically produced the very visibility [the British state] claimed it could not "see"', as Brenda became visible to the Ugandan government and public, facing life imprisonment charges and death threats.[37] Thus, 'in order to survive Brenda is expected to still prove in the UK that she is a lesbian and at the same time to prove that she is not a lesbian in Uganda'.[38]

New practices of ***indiscretion*** have been generated by LGBTI responses to the demands of credibility and (in)visibility framed through 'discretion reasoning', which compel applicants to 'prove' their gender and sexual identities through 'hyper-visible' public performances of sexuality that are sometimes explicitly sexual, as a means of resisting deportation.[39] Illustrative of this is the experience of Kiana, an Iranian film-maker and gay rights activist documented by Rachel Lewis.[40] Kiana was initially told by UK officials that her asylum claim was rejected on the grounds that she could return to Iran and live 'discreetly'. The release of her short documentary *Cul de Sac* which depicted her in an explicit lesbian sex scene, and its dissemination through multiple social media networks, resulted in a reversal of the decision, on the grounds that it was no longer possible for her to return and be discreet about her sexual orientation. Paradoxically, performing her identity as an out lesbian film-maker activist makes her un-deportable, but problematically also reproduces gendered, racial and classed stereotypes (of lesbians as butch, out and outspoken women who like to hang out in bars).[41] Similar projects of queer migrant activism resisting deportation of undocumented LGBTI individuals, such as the Toronto-based campaign 'Let Alvaro Stay' and

36 James C Hathaway and Jason Pobjoy, 'Queer Cases Make Bad Law' (2012) 44 *New York University Journal of International Law and Politics* 315; Jenni Millbank, 'The Right of Lesbians and Gay Men to Live Freely, Openly, and on Equal Terms Is Not Bad Law: A Reply to Hathaway and Pobjoy' (2012) 44 *New York University Journal of International Law and Politics* 497. See also other articles in the same issue of *New York University Journal of International Law and Politics*.

37 Rachel Lewis, 'Deportable Subjects: Lesbians and Political Asylum' (2013) 25(2) *Feminist Formations* 174, 180.

38 Melanie Nathan, 'UK Judge & "Blogger" Precedent – "The Brenda Namigadde Effect": Another Ugandan's Deportation Stayed' on *LezGetReal: A Gay Girl's View on the World* (8 March 2011), quoted in Lewis, above n 37.

39 Shuman and Bohmer, above n 15; Shuman and Hesford, above n 15.

40 Lewis, above n 37.

41 Ibid.

Julio Salgado's collaborative visual arts project 'I am Undocuqueer', draw on personal testimony and political protest imagery, but as Melissa White points out, rely on methodological nationalisms and visibility politics to make their claims hearable to the state.[42]

Pragmatic complicities?

Taken together, the practices of breaking, re-making, and sometimes reinforcing immigration and asylum law have generated 'successes' for (some) LGBTI border crossers. Yet our appraisal of these successes must consider the instability of such gains, as even when the credibility of both identity and persecution is reasonably established, immigration officials are often inconsistent in their interpretations of case law and can be surprisingly inventive in their contorted counter-explanations justifying the denial of eligibility for asylum.[43]

More critically, and without diminishing the gains achieved through LGBTI activist practices, we must pay attention to the ways in which queer border crossers become legible to the state through the establishment of credible evidence and responding to the contradictory demands of (in)visibility. This legibility works through prior acceptance of the official categories of trans-border movement (migrant, refugee, asylum seeker) sanctioned by states and supranational bodies. Legal legibility is also rendered through racialising colonialist LGBTI identity categories understood in very specific ways. For example, by privileging 'coming out', public (hyper) visibility, particular kinds of white desirable citizens (productive, skilled, healthy) and homonormative happy families.

Queer struggles in this modality not only ossify an identitarian politics, they set up yet another missionary rescue project, reinforcing queer border crossers as 'victim subjects' incapable of exercising agency. Citizenship in a country of the global North and its attendant entitlements (rights, welfare) are privileges that are contingent on conformity with these normative identity categories and subject positions. While such strategies may be pragmatic complicities with official regimes of knowledge about non-citizen queer lives, they produce a homonationalist[44] consolidation of power consonant with capitalist accumulation, the biopolitics of control over population movements and liberal rights discourses. They simultaneously leave unproblematised the methodological nationalism of normative constructs of state borders and territorially based citizenship.[45]

42 Melissa Autumn White, 'Documenting the Undocumented: Toward a Queer Politics of No Borders' (2014) 17 *Sexualities* 976.

43 Millbank, above n 15, 14.

44 Jasbir Puar, 'Rethinking Homonationalism' (2013) 45 *International Journal of Middle East Studies* 336; Jasbir K Puar, *Terrorist Assemblages: Homonationalism in Queer Times* (Duke University Press, 2007).

45 Liisa H Malkki, 'Refugees and Exile: From "Refugee Studies" to the National Order of Things' (1995) 24 *Annual Review of Anthropology* 495; Andreas Wimmer and Nina Glick

If, however, we remind ourselves of José Esteban Muñoz's articulation of '*[q]ueerness [as] essentially about the rejection of a here and now and an insistence on potentiality or concrete possibility for another world*',[46] we can envision alternative imaginaries that allow critical refusal of queer pragmatics, to think and act beyond 'pragmatic complicities' of the here and now outlined above. One such imaginary would be to consider how a politics of 'no borders' resonates with the anti-normative thrust of a queer politics. Before I sketch the outline of these possibilities, I first clear the conceptual ground by distinguishing the 'no borders' from the 'open borders' perspective.

Border controls, 'open borders' and 'no borders'

The control of human mobility across state borders is one of the most politically urgent, yet divisive, issues of the twenty-first century, entangled as it is in concerns about employment, the economy, threats to national identity, terrorism and national security. Demographic pressures, colonial and neo-colonial legacies of structural inequality, poverty and conflict and the expansion of global transport and communication options have propelled increasing numbers of people to cross international borders. Yet border control policies to contain this migration have intensified, particularly in countries of the global North. Such policies are not only exercised at the border: they are activated in the surveillance of internal mobility, access to employment, social services and governance structures. They are exercised in the migrant origin countries in the global South, through aid and education programmes designed to encourage people to 'stay put', particularly on the African continent. They are also increasingly exercised in 'buffer zones': territories 'excised' from the nation (such as Christmas Island for Australia) or outside national or regional borders in transit countries such as Libya or Indonesia (for Europe and Australia respectively) or in detention 'holding' countries (such as Nauru for Australia).

Scholarship and activism in the past three decades has drawn attention to the ways in which border control policies have established an oppressive 'global apartheid'[47] that is gendered, heteronormative, racialised and classed. State border control policies are deeply implicated in the production and maintenance of relations of power and dependency through two circuits of global mobility. In the privileged circuit, highly skilled professional elites from both the global North and the global South experience free mobility, usually through regular channels of migration, while in the underprivileged circuit, unskilled migrants experience

Schiller, 'Methodological Nationalism and Beyond: Nation-State Building, Migration and the Social Sciences' (2002) 2 *Global Networks* 301.

46 José Esteban Muñoz, *Cruising Utopia: The Then and There of Queer Futurity* (New York University Press, 2009) 1 (emphasis added).

47 Nandita Sharma, 'Anti-Trafficking Rhetoric and the Making of a Global Apartheid' (2005) 17(3) *NSWA Journal* 88; Michael Clemens, 'A Labor Mobility Agenda for Development' (Working Paper No 201, Centre for Global Development, January 2010).

immobility, or constrained mobility, through irregular 'undocumented' channels of migration.[48]

Calls for liberalising border controls vary in the *degree* of liberalisation: they may offer an easing of quantitative restrictions, allowing larger numbers of migrants and/or asylum seekers. The 2015 pledge to welcome an increased intake of 800,000 Syrian refugees by Germany and 14,000 by Australia is in this mode. This modality does not disturb existing political arrangements in any significant way, as there is still a selective process of determining eligibility – who is 'fit' to enter the nation. The 'open borders' or 'no borders' perspectives are more radical in that they envision the free movement of *all* people. They point to the absurdity of the Universal Declaration of Human Rights' recognition of the right to emigrate, without corresponding recognition of the right to immigrate and the 'fundamental . . . contradiction between the notion that emigration is widely regarded as a matter of human rights while immigration is regarded as a matter of national sovereignty'.[49]

Although the terms 'open borders' and 'no borders' are often used interchangeably, there are important distinctions worth signalling.[50] The framework of mobility in the 'open borders' perspective assumes the continued existence of nation-states and territorial borders, but articulates new modalities of citizenship and entitlements. Most liberal political arguments are situated in this framework, which defends open borders on egalitarian principles with the argument that freedom of movement within and across borders is an undeniable liberal right, and on the utilitarian principle that free mobility maximises collective utility.[51] Yet the right to free movement confronts an intractable deadlock in liberal political theory with the right to national self-determination. The latter is premised on border controls as central to the construction of shared identity and political membership. This presents a paradox that liberal political theorists have reconciled by either prioritising one or the other right: John Rawls argues that rich countries have the right to bar migrants from poor countries on grounds of the right to protect national interest;[52] Michael Dummett makes the opposite case for freedom of mobility on the grounds of freedom of thought and action.[53] Other theorists have developed compromise positions that propose relatively open

48 Saskia Sassen, 'Two Stops in Today's New Global Geographies: Shaping Novel Labor Supplies and Employment Regimes' (2008) 52 *American Behavioral Scientist* 457.
49 Myron Weiner, 'Ethics, National Sovereignty and the Control of Immigration' (1996) 30 *International Migration Review* 171, 171.
50 Harald Bauder, 'Perspectives of Open Borders and No Border' (2015) 9 *Geography Compass* 395.
51 Joseph H Carens, 'Aliens and Citizens: The Case for Open Borders' (1987) 49 *Review of Politics* 251.
52 John Rawls, *The Law of Peoples: With, the Idea of Public Reason Revisited* (Harvard University Press, 2001).
53 Michael Dummett, *On Immigration and Refugees* (Taylor and Francis, 2001).

borders[54] and modalities of citizenship to accommodate new notions of the national and entitlements that are not merely contingent citizenship of '*jus soli*' (meaning 'right of the soil', or birthright citizenship granted to anyone born in the territory of a state) or '*jus sanguinis*' (meaning 'right of blood', or citizenship granted through descent, where one or both parents are citizens of the state). Thus, Veit Bader[55] proposes 'open borders' conjoined with the concept of 'domiciliary citizenship' as a form of citizenship based on residence. Similarly, Ayelet Shachar develops the concept of '*jus nexi*' that is premised on the principle of a 'real and effective link' and 'genuine connection of existence, interests and sentiments' to determine entitlements of irregular migrants or non-status persons as having a claim to citizenship entitlements.[56] Aligned with the liberal political perspective, the neoliberal economic perspective supports open borders because they are assumed to optimise efficiency and productivity globally; border controls conversely are assumed to distort labour markets. Yet the liberal perspective that promotes free labour mobility serves the interests of cross-border global capital accumulation that is achieved through the exploitation of the cheapest (migrant) labour.[57]

In contrast, 'no borders' advocates propose a more radical framework that 'calls into question the legitimacy of the global system of national states itself and the related global system of capitalism'.[58] It envisions a political and social reorganisation of societies that includes the elimination of borders and controls on mobility.[59] Bridget Anderson et al argue that:

> A radical No Borders politics acknowledges that it is part of revolutionary change. If successful, it will have a very profound effect on all of our lives for it is part of a global reshaping of economies and societies in a way that is not compatible with capitalism, nationalism, or the mode of state-controlled belonging that is citizenship. It is ambitious and requires exciting and imaginative explorations, but it is not utopian. It is in fact eminently practical and is being carried out daily.[60]

54 Veit Bader, 'Fairly Open Borders' in Veit Bader (ed), *Citizenship and Exclusion* (St Martin's Press, 1997) 28; Jonathan Seglow, 'The Ethics of Immigration' (2005) 3 *Political Studies Review* 317.

55 Veit Bader, 'The Ethics of Immigration' (2013) 12(3) *Constellations* 331.

56 Ayelet Shachar, *The Birthright Lottery: Citizenship and Global Inequality* (Harvard University Press, 2009).

57 Nick Gill, 'Whose "No Borders"? Achieving Border Liberalization for the Right Reasons' (2009) 26(2) *Refuge* 107.

58 Bridget Anderson, Nandita Sharma and Cynthia Wright, 'Editorial: Why No Borders?' (2009) 26(2) *Refuge* 5, 11.

59 Pam Alldred, 'No Borders, No Nations, No Deportations' (2003) 73 *Feminist Review* 152; Nandita Sharma, 'No Borders Movement and the Rejection of Left Nationalism' (2003) 37(3) *Canadian Dimension* 37.

60 Anderson et al, above n 58, 12.

The examples they provide of this ongoing practical political project include a wide variety of groups, those that are explicitly political movements such as the *Sans Papiers* in France, *Sin Papeles* in Spain and the 'No one is Illegal' and 'Don't Ask Don't Tell' campaigns in the United States, but also groups such as Doctors of the World, who operate without consideration of nationality or residence status. Central to their political vision is the concept of rights to 'the commons' as a political, social and economic alternative vision of the future.[61]

Although Anderson et al distance themselves from the notion of 'utopia' as some abstract, unrealisable project, the counter-border activism to which they refer (above) as pre-figurations of the state of 'no borders' can potentially also signal the possibilities of what Muñoz describes as a *concrete* utopia. In contrast to an 'abstract utopia' that is untethered to historical consciousness, Muñoz deploys the concept of a concrete utopia to describe the critical politics of hope that is positioned in relation to historically situated struggles:

> In our everyday lives abstract utopias are akin to banal optimism . . . Concrete utopias can also be daydream-like, but they are the hopes of a collective, an emergent group, or even the solitary oddball who is the one who dreams for many. Concrete utopias are the realm of educated hope.[62]

The potential of concrete utopia is thus realised through collective action; it is a 'backward glance that enacts a future vision'.[63] It is this critical politics of hope that I wish to activate in the discussion below.

Queer alignments with 'no borders' politics

In this concluding section, I draw out some of the emancipatory possibilities inherent in an alignment of queer politics with the vision of 'no borders'. I outline below a few interrelated challenges offered by the 'no borders' perspective, and discuss how these challenges resonate with the experiences and activism of queer border crossers and activists.

First, the 'no borders' perspective offers a challenge to the sedentarist bias and temporal amnesia in our understandings of human migration. We must remember that migration is an essential human activity and human beings have always been on the move for varied reasons, even as these movements have often been forced, or restricted. Colonisation generated massive forced migration through the slave trade and indentured labour. It also shaped settler colonial nations like the United States, Canada and Australia, and countries in South America,

61 Bridget Anderson, Nandita Sharma and Cynthia Wright, '"We Are All Foreigners" No Borders as a Practical Political Project' in Peter Nyers and Kim Rygiel (eds), *Citizenship, Migrant Activism and the Politics of Movement* (Taylor and Francis, 2012) 73.

62 Muñoz, above n 46, 3.

63 Ibid 3–4.

through (ongoing) violence and subjugation of indigenous populations and mass migrations of 'free' labour to the colonies. Industrialisation also resulted in controls on mobility related to the creation and maintenance of 'free labour' for nascent capitalism. In these different histories, borders as we understand them today either did not exist or were ignored, or the control of mobility was exercised along different criteria – for instance, class-based seigneurial control over serfs' mobility, poor laws and vagrancy laws, and gender-based male control over women's mobility. The introduction of border controls over migrants, as a 'problem' that needed to be 'managed', emerged in the late nineteenth century as a feature of the nation-state-based organisation of citizenship, in contrast to the loose controls exercised by earlier city-based, or even empire-based, models of citizenship.[64]

From the 'no borders' perspective, then, the apparatus of contemporary border controls by nation-states is far from a logically inevitable, immutable outcome of the progressive development of nation-states. Rather, from this perspective, we could critique the inherent assumption of linear notions of development as sequential progress that holds the 'developed' global North as the normative standard, and pay attention instead to the diverse historically and culturally specific practices and structural arrangements around mobility, including queer mobilities. This critical attention to histories is particularly important for a queer politics of the border, as it allows us to interrogate the ways in which colonial and imperial states were, and continue to be, implicated in the production of homophobic laws that have generated global flows of queer refugees.

Following from above, a 'no borders' perspective challenges the nation-state centrism inherent in the presumption of the state's power to control cross-border mobility. As scholars have argued, the state enforces but also *produces* the border. The structural violence inherent in border controls (wherever they are exercised) is that they situate border crossers within relationships of power, vulnerability and dependency. They also make untenable differentiations through the categories such as 'migrant', 'asylum seeker' and 'refugee'. From this perspective, appeals to the state in LGBTI immigrant and asylum cases reinforces and reproduces this structural imbalance of power and dependency. As I have discussed above, such appeals necessitate pragmatic complicities in the marshalling of evidence to demonstrate 'credibility' and 'visibility' to functionaries of the state. Yet, in doing so, as White cautions, activists need to heighten their awareness of the ways in which demands for better, 'improved' laws and regulations may reinforce the nation-building project.[65] Such an awareness would be foundational to any emancipatory project that is *not* nation-state centric.

64 John Torpey, *The Invention of the Passport: Surveillance, Citizenship and the State* (Cambridge University Press, 2000); Marlou Schrover, Joanne van der Leun, Leo Lucassen et al (eds), *Illegal Migration and Gender in a Global and Historical Perspective* (Amsterdam University Press, 2008).

65 White, above n 42.

Third, and related, is the challenge to the normative liberal construction of citizens as free and equal (implicitly homogenous) individuals with rights, entitlements and obligations, who 'belong' to a nation either through descent (*jus sanguinis*) or through birth (*jus soli*). The parameters of belonging and the inclusion of some as citizens are, however, invariably predicated on the exclusion of others as 'non-citizens'. As we have seen, LGBTI applicants for immigration and asylum have to prove themselves 'deserving' recipients of state benevolence and, if they fail, they fall into irregular or 'non-status', and become vulnerable to deportation. The unfortunate effect is the reinforcement of a 'deserving'–'undeserving' dichotomy in which some queer subjects are deemed worthy of citizenship. The hierarchy of oppression and sympathy produced through this 'queer migrant exceptionalism' is sutured on to the differentiated hierarchies of social, political and economic inequalities that exist even among citizens. Dissatisfaction with existing models of citizenship has generated a rich scholarship on citizenship,[66] including on queer citizens,[67] which is beyond the purview of this chapter. All I wish to do here is signal, first, that from a 'no borders' perspective, citizenship would have to be detached from its current mooring in the nation-state. Second, it would be worthwhile for explorations in this area to offer queer perspectives on existing practices of 'irregular citizenship',[68] practices of cultural citizenship,[69] and the multiple ways in which citizenship is no longer a territorially bound, nation-state centric institution or statute, but a 'collective practice'[70] that is transforming the boundaries of belonging.

The fourth challenge of 'no borders' is to global capitalism. It recognises that borders function to produce differentiated labour regimes that can be exploited and dispossessed by capitalist forces.[71] A 'no borders' position resists the capitalist social relations dependent on productivist assumptions that encourage the entry of 'skilled workers' and on social reproductivist assumptions allowing entry of heteronormative families as well as unskilled workers essential to the care economy. This challenge forces queer politics to take class hierarchies and the

66 See, for example, Aihwa Ong, *Flexible Citizenship: The Cultural Logics of Transnationality* (Duke University Press, 1999); Seyla Benhabib, *The Rights of Others: Aliens, Residents, and Citizens* (Cambridge University Press, 2004); Shachar, above n 56.

67 Arnaldo Cruz-Malave and Martin F Manalansan (eds), *Queer Globalizations: Citizenship and the Afterlife of Colonialism* (New York University Press, 2002); Luibhéid and Cantú, above n 3.

68 Peter Nyers, 'Forms of Irregular Citizenship' in Vicki Squires (ed), *The Contested Politics of Mobility: Borderzones and Irregularity* (Routledge, 2011) 184.

69 See, for example, Fatima El-Tayeb, *European Others: Queering Ethnicity in Postnational Europe* (University of Minnesota Press, 2011); Renato Rosaldo, 'Cultural Citizenship, Inequality, and Multiculturalism' in Rodolfo D Torres, Louis F Mirón and Jonathan Xavier Inda (eds), *Race, Identity, and Citizenship: A Reader* (Blackwell Publishers, 1999) 253.

70 Etienne Balibar, 'The Nation Form: History and Ideology' in Etienne Balibar and Immanuel Wallerstein (eds), *Race, Nation, Class: Ambiguous Identities* (Verso, 1991) 86.

71 Teresa Hayter, *Open Borders: The Case against Immigration Controls* (Pluto Press, 2000).

global precariat[72] more seriously than it has hitherto, and move beyond token acknowledgement of class as a dimension of intersectionality.

Finally, moving beyond the obsession with the state, a 'no borders' perspective challenges our predispositions to xenophobia (and I hope I am not being too optimistic here). As Leo Tolstoy famously (though possibly apocryphally) said: 'there are two primary stories: a person goes on a journey or a stranger comes to town'. Within these two archetypal plots, xenophobic reactions to the migrant stranger are not just a phenomenon of our contemporary age of anxieties. Erasing the salience of borders has the potential to diminish our fear of the foreigner, which is often premised on racialised, gendered, heterosexed, classed and national understandings of an 'us', positioned against a threatening 'stranger/other'. It offers the opportunity to explore the histories of queer travellers and the affective possibilities that are generated.[73] Perhaps also, the potential to open up new notions of 'belonging' that are not premised on exclusions, expanding our horizons of what is politically possible and morally desirable.

72 Guy Standing, *The Precariat: The New Dangerous Class* (Bloomsbury Academic, 2011).

73 Leela Gandhi, *Affective Communities: Anticolonial Thought, Fin-de-Siècle Radicalism, and the Politics of Friendship* (Duke University Press, 2006).

11 Queering international law's stories of origin

Hospitality and homophobia

Nan Seuffert

The project of 'queering' international law suggests excavating concepts of sexuality and sexual conduct in its formative moments. This chapter argues that two of the works of the sixteenth-century Spanish theologian Francisco de Vitoria provide rich grounds for excavation. These works are often included in the genealogy of international law and sometimes in the formative moments of the modern Law of Nations. Vitoria's influential work challenged prevailing justifications for the imperialist Spanish project of the invasion of Mesoamerica, replacing them with universal natural law duties of friendship and hospitality owed by the people of the 'New World' to the Spanish, facilitating the Spanish imperial project.

Little scholarly attention has been directed at unpacking the allegory of Sodom and Gomorrah, 'sodomy' and hospitality in Vitoria's work, or on the implications of these theological concepts for the development of international law. Focusing on hospitality and sodomy, this chapter analyses Vitoria's work, positioned at the cusp of European imperialism and the inception of modern international law, in the historical and theological contexts in which it was written. It first briefly traces the importance of hospitality in early interpretations of the allegory of Sodom. It then considers the emergence of the contested and amorphous category of 'sodomy' in the eleventh century. In this context, it analyses the pivotal importance of sodomy in Vitoria's work on the Law of Nations. It argues that Vitoria's work engages with biblical, theological and scholarly debates and discourses on both hospitality and sodomy, elucidating the significance of the Sodom allegory to Vitoria's justification of Spanish invasion. 'Queering' international law requires attention to the sedimentation of these discourses of sexuality in its inception and their continuing resonances and reiterations in international law, especially in relation to the treatment of non-normative sexual and gender minorities in human rights and refugee law, and in relation to indigenous peoples' self-determination claims.

Vitoria and international law

Vitoria has been referred to as 'one of the most influential political theorists in sixteenth-century Catholic Europe'.[1] Although he was primarily a Dominican theologian, powerfully influenced by St Thomas Aquinas, he regarded theology as the 'mother of sciences' and claimed as his topic all of divine and natural law, which he saw as the realm of jurisprudence. He was the master of a number of Spanish theologians and jurists known as the 'School of Salamanca', famous internationally principally for their achievements in jurisprudence and moral philosophy. It is Vitoria's two influential lectures, 'On the Indians Lately Discovered'[2] and 'On the Law of War Made by the Spaniards on the Barbarians',[3] which engaged with Spanish discourses on the invasion of Mesoamerica,[4] that contributed to the development of international law[5] and the justifications for European imperialism and colonisation,[6] as well as the law applied to first nation peoples in what later became the United States.[7] While Hugo Grotius is sometimes cast as the 'father' of modern international law,[8] Vitoria's work is seen by some legal scholars as providing its 'primitive' origins,[9] as influencing Grotius, and as providing an early focus on the relationships between nations.[10] As Robert A Williams has argued, Vitoria

> inaugurated the first critical steps towards a totalizing jurisprudence of international order – a Law of Nations intended to regulate all aspects of the

1 Anthony Pagden and Jeremy Lawrance (eds), *Vitoria: Political Writings* (Cambridge University Press, 1991) xiii.
2 Francisco de Vitoria, 'On the American Indians' in Pagden and Lawrance (eds), above n 1, 231.
3 Francisco de Vitoria, 'On the Law of War' in Pagden and Lawrance (eds), above n 1, 293.
4 Anthony Pagden, *The Fall of Natural Man: The American Indian and the Origins of Comparative Ethnology* (Cambridge University Press, 1982) 66.
5 Franciscus de Victoria, 'De Indis et de ivre belli relectiones' in James Brown Scott and Ernest Nys (eds), *The Classics of International Law* (John Pawley Bate trans, Carnegie Institution, 1917). See also Arthur Nussbaum, *A Concise History of the Law of Nations* (Macmillan, 1947) 63; Jane McAdam, 'An Intellectual History of Freedom of Movement in International Law: The Right to Leave as Personal Liberty' (2011) 12 *Melbourne Journal of International Law* 1, 7.
6 Antony Anghie, 'Francisco de Vitoria and the Colonial Origins of International Law' (1996) 5 *Social & Legal Studies* 321.
7 Felix S Cohen, 'The Spanish Origin of Indian Rights in the Law of the United States' (1942) 31 *Georgetown Law Journal* 1, 17.
8 Chantal Thomas, 'What Does the Emerging International Law of Migration Mean for Sovereignty?' (2013) 14 *Melbourne Journal of International Law* 1, fn 136.
9 David Kennedy, 'Primitive Legal Scholarship' (1986) 27 *Harvard International Law Journal* 1, 1.
10 See Illena M Porras, 'Constructing International Law in the East Indian Seas: Property, Sovereignty, Commerce and War in Hugo Grotius' *De Iure Praedae* – The Law of Prize and Booty, or "On How to Distinguish Merchants from Pirates"' (2006) 31 *Brooklyn Journal of International Law* 741, 745 fn 8, 756, 770–1.

> relationships between independent states . . . initiat[ing] the process by which the European state system's legal discourse was ultimately liberated from its stultifying, expressly theocentric, medievalized moorings and was adapted to the rationalizing demands of Renaissance Europe's *secularized* will to empire.[11]

This argument positions Vitoria's work as progressing beyond explicitly theocentric, stultifying and Medieval foundations, towards rational secularism. Williams, like some others, sees Vitoria as making a break with the past, moving towards a secular order in which Christendom is relegated to the parochial, a place alongside, rather than integrated into, the state.[12]

More generally, the argument for the significance of Vitoria's work to the development of a secularised international law assumes a movement from foundations in theocentric universal jurisdiction based on the authority of the Pope, or the Holy Roman Emperor, to a set of universal principles for a Law of Nations based on natural law.[13] While Williams figures Vitoria as taking just 'first steps', his work, and that of other legal scholars, pays scant heed to how deeply embedded religious, and particularly Thomist, ideas remain in Vitoria's work. The shift that his work embodies is described as a *displacement* of divine law and Papal authority by natural law, as though natural law is not also closely based on divine law.[14]

Yvonne Sherwood argues that Vitoria rewrote, rather than left behind, the theological underpinnings of the justifications for Spain's imperial move into Mesoamerica, emphasising the extent to which his work is steeped in Christian theology and arguing that Western modernity more generally is allied to a Christian framework which tends to be taken for granted.[15] Indeed, Vitoria responded to both the theological and the legal problems raised by the Spanish invasion. Vitoria's reliance on Aquinas, the theologian whose work is formative for another discipline, Western (Christian) philosophy,[16] in his discussion of 'just war' and his development of ideas of sovereignty and 'right reason', reveals the extent to which Christian ideas are embedded in the roots of international law.

11 Robert A Williams, *The American Indian in Western Legal Thought: The Discourses of Conquest* (Oxford University Press, 1990) 96–7, citing Cohen, above n 7, 9–21 (emphasis added).
12 Williams, above n 11, 106; Yvonne Sherwood, 'Francisco de Vitoria's More Excellent Way: How the Bible of Empire Discovered the Tricks of [the Argument from] Trade' (2013) 21 *Biblical Interpretation* 215, 216–17.
13 Kennedy, above n 9, 11–12.
14 Sherwood, above n 12, 259, fn 100, citing Anghie, above n 6, 31, and Pagden, above n 4, 63.
15 Sherwood, above n 12, 219; Martti Koskiennemi, 'International Law and Raison D'état: Rethinking the Prehistory of International Law' in Benedict Kingsbury and Benjamin Straumann (eds), *The Roman Foundations of the Law of Nations: Alberico Gentili and the Justice of Empire* (Oxford University Press, 2010) 297, 298.
16 Margaret Denike, 'The Sex of Right Reason: Aquinas and the Misogynist Foundations of Natural Law' in Maria Drakopoulou (ed), *Feminist Encounters with Legal Philosophy* (Routledge, 2013) 20.

Aquinas's particular emphasis on natural reason leading to recognition of reproduction as the ultimate purpose of man, coupled with his linking of the allegory of Sodom to misuse of the natural power of reproduction, informed the Spanish law of 1497 prohibiting crimes 'against God's natural order', discussed below, contributing to the debates on Spain's conquest of the new world, and also infusing Vitoria's work. The next part of this chapter considers hospitality in the allegory of Sodom, and the emergence of the category of sodomy.

Sodom and Gomorrah, hospitality and sodomy

The biblical allegory of Sodom is often assumed in popular contemporary political debates to be a story of God's punishment of a city for 'sodomy', defined as the particular sexual act of anal penetration of one man by another. Ideas about 'sodomy' as unnatural and against God's divine laws have unevenly infiltrated the development of rights discourses and international human rights conventions and provided grist for contemporary conservative arguments against legislation decriminalising sodomy, prohibiting discrimination on the basis of sexual orientation and recognising same-sex marriage. Partly in response to these contemporary arguments, recent scholarship has challenged the assumption that the allegory of Sodom can be reduced to punishment for sodomy, arguing that the Sodomites were punished for breaches of hospitality, and that any punishment for sexual transgressions was not focused on sodomy so narrowly defined.[17] Indeed, the term 'sodomy' was not coined until the eleventh century, and is inherently amorphous and ill-defined.[18] This section considers three aspects of recent scholarship on the allegory that are relevant to the shape and interpretation of Vitoria's work. First, it discusses the importance of hospitality in the allegory of Sodom. Second, it analyses the historical framing of the allegory, which oscillates between an emphasis on hospitality and an emphasis on sexual transgression, and which is pertinent to Vitoria's emphasis on hospitality in his justification of Spanish presence in Mesoamerica. Third, it considers the ambiguity and instability in the term 'sodomy', particularly in the work of Aquinas, which was important to Vitoria's work.

Recent scholarship questions the strength of the link between the Sodom allegory, found in the Old Testament of the Bible in Genesis 19, and what became known as 'sodomy' and 'Sodomites'. Instead, it is argued that Sodom can be seen as a founding allegory about the importance of hospitality, and of God's 'total

17 John Boswell, *Christianity, Social Tolerance, and Homosexuality: Gay People in Western Europe from the Beginning of the Christian Era to the Fourteenth Century* (University of Chicago Press, 1981); Jonathan Goldberg, 'Introduction' in Jonathan Goldberg (ed), *Reclaiming Sodom* (Routledge, 1994) 1; Robert Alter, 'Sodom as Nexus: The Web of Design in Biblical Narrative' in Jonathan Goldberg (ed), *Reclaiming Sodom* (Routledge, 1994) 28; Mark D Jordan, *The Invention of Sodomy in Christian Theology* (University of Chicago Press, 1997); Louis Crompton, *Homosexuality and Civilization* (Belknap Press, 2003) 36.

18 Jordan, above n 17.

divine judgment'[19] for breaches of hospitality. In the version of the Bible used by Vitoria, from a translation in the sixteenth century, Lot was a foreigner, or visitor, staying in Sodom.[20] In the evening two angels came to the city of Sodom in the form of men and Lot invited them into his house as their servant, to stay the night. After initially declining, they went to Lot's house and 'he made them a feast'. The next part of the story is crucial to its interpretation:

> [T]he men of the city beset the house both young and old, all the people together. And they called Lot, and said to him: Where are the men that came in to thee at night? Bring them out hither that we may know them. Lot went out to them, and shut the door after him, and said: no not so, I beseech you, my brethren, do not commit this evil.
>
> I have two daughters who as yet have not known man: I will bring them out to you, and abuse you them as it shall please you, so that you do no evil to these men, because they are come in under the shadow of my roof. But they said: Get thee back thither. And again: Thou camest in, said they, as a, stranger, was it to be a judge? Therefore we will afflict thee more than them. And they pressed very violently upon Lot: and they were even at the point of breaking open the doors.
>
> And behold the men [angels] put out their hand, and drew in Lot unto them, and shut the door. And them, that were without, they struck with blindness from the least to the greatest, so that they could not find the door.

The angels then told Lot to gather his family together and bring them 'out of this city: [f]or we will destroy this place, because their cry is grown loud before the Lord, who hath sent us to destroy them'. The Lord then 'rained upon Sodom and Gomorrah brimstone and fire'.

Interpreting this allegory as one of punishment for same-sex copulation relies on interpreting 'to know' as knowledge in a sexual sense. However, it has been argued that the Hebrew verb 'to know' is very rarely used in the Bible to refer to sexual intercourse (contrary to popular opinion). Derick Sherwin Bailey suggests that 'in only 10 of its 943 occurrences in the Old Testament does it refer to carnal knowledge'.[21] Lot's offer of his daughters is sometimes taken to signify the sexual nature of the use of 'to know'.[22] However, others point out that in the parallel story in Judges 19, in which the men of Gibeah gather at the door of a host asking for the guest to be brought out so that they may 'know' him, and the host's daughter is offered as a bribe to satisfy them, the demand to 'know' is interpreted

19 Ibid 31.

20 Vitoria used the Latin Vulgate Bible. The Douay-Rheims translation of Genesis 19 from the Vulgate Bible is available online at 'Genesis – Chapter 19', *Vulgate.org* <http://vulgate.org/ot/genesis_19.htm>.

21 Boswell, above n 17, 94, citing Derick Sherwin Bailey, *Homosexuality and the Western Christian Tradition* (Longmans, 1955) 2–3.

22 See Goldberg, 'Introduction', above n 17, 6.

as a breach of hospitality without sexual connotations.[23] Recognition of the importance of hospitality in the Old Testament (and more broadly, as discussed below), reflecting times when inns were unavailable outside of urban centres and travellers were dependent upon hosts for survival, is central to these arguments.

Mark D Jordan argues that many contemporary scholars agree that the Sodom allegory of sudden divine judgment and utter destruction is better read as a story of punishment for breach of hospitality than as a story about same-sex copulation.[24] Early interpretations of the allegory, found in the writings of Ezekiel, Jesus and the Talmudists, support this argument, viewing the transgressions in Sodom as sins of inhospitality, arrogance born of an overabundance of wealth and leisure, and Sodom's mistreatment of aliens and the poor.[25] Contemporary queer scholarship also suggests that the allegory should be read in the context of the broader saga of Abraham, of which it forms a part.[26] In Genesis 18, just prior to the Sodom allegory, Abraham pleads with God to spare the city if it has just 10 righteous men. This suggests that God had decided to punish Sodom prior to the arrival of the angels hosted by Lot. The only reference to the reason for God's prior wrath is that 'the men of Sodom were wicked and sinners before God exceedingly',[27] which is consistent with the other references to Sodom as gluttonous, inhospitable, arrogant and uncharitable.

In the contemporary consensus, in early interpretations the sexual overtones of the allegory were minor, if they figured at all. One interpretation is that Lot, a sojourner himself, was entertaining visitors at night without the permission of the city elders, which resulted in the citizens of the city showing up at his house.[28] The demand by the men of Sodom was simply to bring them out so that they might 'know' who they were.[29] Their inhospitable behaviour at Lot's door confirms God's decision, already made, to punish, and sudden divine judgment is visited on Sodom as the result of this breach of hospitality.

However, over time, interpretations of Sodom as an allegory including sexual transgressions emerged. Philo, a Helenistic Jewish philosopher born in 25 BCE, in his text *On Abraham* recounts numerous sins of the Sodomites arising 'from gluttony and lewdness' resulting from wealth fed by a prolific harvest, and offers an early inclusion of sexual and gender transgressions:

> they threw off from their necks the law of nature and applied themselves to deep drinking of strong liquor and dainty feeding and forbidden forms of intercourse. Not only in their mad lust for women did they violate the marriages of their neighbors, but also men mounted men without regard for

23 Boswell, above n 17, 95–6.
24 Jordan, above n 17, 30, citing Bailey, above n 21, and Boswell, above n 17, 93–7.
25 Crompton, above n 17, 136; Jordan, above n 17, 31.
26 Jordan, above n 17, 36.
27 Ibid 37, quoting Genesis 13.
28 Boswell, above n 17, 93–4.
29 Ibid 94.

> the sex nature which the active partner shares with the passive . . . [and] became like women . . . corrupting in this way the whole race of man.[30]

The emphasis here is still on overindulgence, which *leads to* forbidden forms of intercourse, 'men mounting men' and the gender transgression of active and passive sex roles, corrupting 'the whole race of man'.[31]

By the fifth century, Augustine, widely acknowledged as playing a crucial role in determining Western Christian attitudes to sexuality, and influential in Vitoria's work, referred to Sodom as a place where sexual intercourse between males had become commonplace, and was widely accepted.[32] The basis of the invention of the category of sodomy, as the sin of the men of Sodom, has been traced to an eleventh-century theologian, Peter Damian.[33] As Jordan has argued, reducing the sin of Sodom to sodomy is part of a process of 'thinning' the allegory of its other meanings, and ignoring the centrality of the sins of excess, gluttony and greed to punishment by God's divine judgment.[34] Reducing the allegory to a link between 'unnatural' sexual intercourse and the inhabitants of a particular city also involved a high level of abstraction; all other traits are erased and the meaning of 'Sodomites' is condensed to sodomy. The term that emerges is amorphous, encompassing at times all non-procreative sexual acts between same-sex and opposite sex partners, at times including bestiality, at times focused on anal intercourse between opposite sex and same-sex partners, and sometimes including married couples. Integral to the chameleon term are 'fundamental confusions and contradictions', which make it particularly useful for 'oppressive legislation and demagoguery'.[35]

Aquinas's (1225–74) *Summa Theologica*[36] played a crucial role in condensing the category of sodomy, positioning it contradictorily as both a sin of middling importance, and one of the gravest of all sins.[37] Aquinas discussed six types of 'luxuria', the vice of excess of venereal pleasure, which is one of seven capital sins, which are all subsidiary to the first sin of pride.[38] The sixth type of venereal excess, dealt with in a relatively short passage, is the 'vice against nature', which includes masturbation, bestiality, sleeping with someone not of the proper sex and the use of improper instruments or 'monstrous and bestial manners'.[39] The worst of the

30 Crompton, above n 17, 136–7, citing Philo of Alexandria, *The Works of Philo* (C D Yonge trans, H G Bohn, 1854) 133–5, [XXVI].
31 Crompton, above n 17, 136–7.
32 Ibid 137; Jordan, above n 17, 34–5.
33 Jordan, above n 17, 29.
34 Ibid.
35 Ibid 7, 9.
36 Thomas Aquinas, *The Summa Theologiae* (Fathers of the English Dominican Province trans, Benziger Brothers, 1974) pt 2-2, q 154, art 12.
37 Jordan, above n 17.
38 Aquinas, above n 36, pt 2-2, q 154, art 12; Jordan, above n 17, 144–51.
39 Aquinas, above n 36, pt 2-2, q 154, art 11.

vices against nature is bestiality.[40] Focusing on the *structure* of Aquinas's work suggests that, positioned in the middle of the vice against nature, itself of a subsidiary class of sins, same-sex sexual conduct is a 'middling species of a subsidiary class of sins'.[41] On the other hand, one passage in Aquinas suggests that it is one of the gravest sins, as it disrupts God's order for nature:

> Just as the order of right reason is from man, so the order of nature is from God himself. And so in *sins against nature* [the vice against nature], in which the very order of nature is violated, an injury is done to God himself, the orderer of nature.[42]

Jordan argues that this statement is linked to three readings of earlier texts by Aquinas, which, first, shift interpretation of the Sodom allegory from a focus on the ferocity of God's divine judgment to a response to a certain type of sin, a collection of acts that pervert natural reproductive powers; second, link it to cannibalism and bestiality, positioning it as an atrocity beyond reason and therefore beyond the human; and, third, dictate that it not be named, prescribing silence.[43] These readings contradict the reading of the vice against nature as less serious than other sins, such as adultery, deflowering and abduction, because it does not harm one's neighbour. The vice against nature therefore oscillates in Aquinas's work between a middling sin and one of the gravest.

Aquinas's linking of sodomy, cannibalism and bestiality resonates with a long tradition of links between sexual excess, cannibalism, festivals, feasts and human sacrifice in the Bacchanalia. As described by the Roman historian Titus Livius, orgies of wine and sex 'extinguished all sense of modesty' and escalated out of control until '[w]hoever would not submit to defilement, or shrank from violating others, was sacrificed as a victim' and frenetically consumed.[44] These rituals or festivals were linked with the pleasures of city life, and the ample supply of luxuries, princely wealth and the 'effeminacy' of the enemy.[45] They provide a moral cautionary tale, plotting Rome's decline at a time when its power was increasing; a moral decline attributable to foreigners, women and plebians.[46]

40 Jordan, above n 17, 144–6; Michael J Horswell, *Decolonizing the Sodomite: Queer Tropes of Sexuality in Colonial Andean Culture* (University of Texas, 2005) 33.

41 Jordan, above n 17, 143–7.

42 Aquinas, above n 36, pt 2-2, q 154, art 12 (emphasis added).

43 Jordan, above n 17, 148–56; Horswell, above n 40, 33.

44 Anthony Pagden, *The Uncertainties of Empire: Essays in Iberian and Ibero-American Intellectual History* (Ashgate, 1994) ch 7, 19. For an accessible translation of Titus Livius, *The History of Rome* (Canon Roberts trans, Dent, 1905), see 'Livy's History of Rome: Book 39', *Everyman's Library* <http://mcadams.posc.mu.edu/txt/ah/Livy/Livy39.html>.

45 Livius, above n 44, vol 6, ch 39.

46 P G Walsh, 'Making a Drama Out of a Crisis: Livy on the Bacchanalia' (1996) 43 *Greece & Rome* 188, 188–9.

The injunction against speaking about same-sex sexual acts, combined with an imperative to regulate and prohibit,[47] resulted in a third type of instability in the category of sodomy. Aquinas obliquely refers to the prohibited sexual act[s], which he says are 'unnamable' and 'against nature', and which he then sets aside.[48] This injunction is produced by an anxiety that mentioning sodomy will performatively encourage it – it is simultaneously one of the gravest sins against God's order and nature, *and* easily spreads like an epidemic. Silence also intensifies the transgression and simultaneously heightens the eroticisation of the forbidden, another of its contradictions.[49] These characteristics of the vice against nature – as one of the gravest violations of God's order, as a slippery category and as an unspeakable sin – become important to shaping justifications for Spain's invasion of Mesoamerica.

Spanish imperialism and sodomy

Understanding the debate with which Vitoria's work engages, and the framing of the allegory of Sodom used in the Spanish conquest of the New World, requires consideration of the political and religious context, including the deployment of sodomy in the Spanish Inquisition, the law on sodomy and the centrality of ideas about sodomy to Spain's invasion of the New World.

The theological-juridical-political context

In his lectures, Vitoria responded to two sets of issues arising from the Spanish presence in the New World over the previous 40 years. The claim of the Spanish Catholic monarchs to Mesoamerica was based on the Papal Bulls of Donation made by Pope Alexander VI in 1493, which, 'by the authority of Almighty God', granted possession and 'full free and integral power, authority and jurisdiction'[50] in lands and islands inhabited by non-Christians discovered west of a north-south line located to the west of the Azores Islands (territory to the east of the line was granted to Portugal).[51] The Bulls reflected Spain's agreement to convert the indigenous peoples to the Catholic faith in return for a trade monopoly which was intended to finance the deal.[52]

The first issue to which Vitoria responded was a theological one. Initially, the Spanish viewed the Mesoamericans as animals, fit only for slavery.[53] In 1511,

47 See Leslie J Moran, *The Homosexual(ity) of Law* (Routledge, 1996) 33.
48 Jordan, above n 17, 150.
49 Ibid 156.
50 Williams, above n 11, 81, citing Sydney Z Ehler and John B Morrall (eds trans), *Church and State through the Centuries* (Biblo and Tannen, 1967) 156.
51 Stephen C Neff, *Justice among Nations: A History of International Law* (Harvard University Press, 2014) 110.
52 Ibid.
53 Lewis Hanke, *Aristotle and the American Indians: A Study in Race Prejudice in the Modern World* (Indiana University Press, 1975) 14–15.

the Dominican Antonio de Montesinos preached a radical sermon in the Caribbean warning that the Spanish invaders' souls were in danger as a result of their treatment of the peoples of Mesoamerica. Implicit in his exhortation, 'Are they not men?' was reference to Spanish procreation with them – if they were animals, then the Spaniards had been committing bestiality.[54] In response, the 'Leyes de Burgos' were enacted, regulating the establishment of *Ecomiendas*, granting individual Spaniards monopolies on the indentured labour of groups of Mesoamericans and regulating their treatment. While these laws nominally recognised the Mesoamericans as human, they still reflected contempt, and the indigenous peoples were still exploited, with significant declines in population.[55]

The second issue to which Vitoria responded was a theological-juridical-political question, raised in discussions on the 'Leyes de Burgos' of a just basis for the Spanish presence in the New World. In response, King Ferdinand asked loyal lawyer-scholars and theologians to draft regulations for future royal conquest.[56] The infamous 1513 *Requerimiento*, as a charter of conquest, unequivocally relied on the authority conferred by the Pope, who was said to have temporal jurisdiction above the princes and over the whole world, in the Bulls of 1493:

> [A]s best we can, we ask and require you that . . . you acknowledge the Church as the ruler and superior of the whole world . . . But if you do not do this, and maliciously make delay in it . . . we shall powerfully enter into your country, and shall make war against you in all ways and manners that we can, and shall subject you to . . . the Church and [to] their highnesses; we shall take you, and your wives, and your children, and shall make slaves of them, and as such shall sell and dispose of them as their highnesses may command; and we shall take away your goods, and shall do you all the mischief and damage that we can . . . [and] the deaths and losses that shall accrue from this are your fault, and not that of their highnesses, or ours, nor of these cavaliers who come with us.[57]

Read in a language that they could not understand, and blaming the indigenous peoples for violence and death resulting from the Spanish invasion, the *Requerimiento* performativity claimed land for the Spanish, based on assumed authority of the Pope.[58] However, Spanish conquistadores, such as Hernán Cortés, failed to abide by even these biased rules, by, for example, attacking the Aztecs without just cause, raising questions about the legitimacy of Spain's presence in Mesoamerica.[59]

54 Ibid.

55 Ibid.

56 Williams, above n 11, 89–91.

57 Sherwood, above n 12, citing Patricia Seed, *Ceremonies of Possession in Europe's Conquest of the New World, 1492–1640* (Cambridge University Press, 1995) ch 3, 69; see also ibid 88–93.

58 Ibid 230–8.

59 Hernán Cortés, 'Tercera Carta-Relación de Hernán Cortés al Emperador Carlos V, Coyacán, 15 de Mayo de 1522' in *Cartas de Relación* (Porrúa, first published 1522,

By the time Vitoria wrote in the 1530s, Spain was attempting to achieve both secular and ecclesiastical autonomy from Papal Rome.[60] Vitoria's reliance on the natural law principles of the Thomists provided a good fit for Spain's political project of gaining autonomy from Rome's pontifical authority for civil and ecclesiastical orders.[61] Vitoria's project therefore had a theological-juridical-political orientation, which involved drawing jurisdictional boundaries between the domains of the Pope and the monarchs.[62]

The vice against nature and 'sodomy'

At the time of Spain's early imperialistic forays, the Catholic monarchs issued an edict in 1497 reflecting Aquinas's categorisation of the 'vice against nature' as one of the gravest sins disrupting God's natural order:

> Among the other sins and crimes that offend our Lord God and defame our lands, the worst is the crime committed against the natural order; . . . laws should be used to punish this nefarious crime, unworthy of naming, destroyer of the natural order, punished by divine justice; through which nobility is lost and the heart becomes cowardly. And it begets little firmness in faith; and it is abhorrence in the eyes of God, who is so angered as to deliver unto humankind pestilence and other torments on earth; and from this sin is born shame and insult toward people and lands that consent to it; . . . any person of any status . . . who commits the nefarious crime against nature . . . [shall] be burned in the flames of fire on the spot.[63]

This characterisation reflects the thinning and condensing of the allegory of Sodom. Implicit in the reference to God delivering 'pestilence and other torments on earth' is that Sodom was destroyed exclusively because of the threat of sodomy, without reference to gluttony, overindulgence and breaches of hospitality. Gender transgression is also targeted in the references to defaming of lands and undermining the masculinity of the nation, its nobility and courage. The edict reflects the European obsession linking women and female sexuality with evil during the 'Golden Age of Man', resulting, for example in England, in a 'church- and state-backed campaign of unmitigated violence against women' facilitated through the witch hunts of the Malleus Maleficarum of 1486.[64]

2015 edn) 129, 132–3. Thanks to Dr Luis Gómez Romero for assisting with this analysis and for translation.

60 Williams, above n 11, 96; Pagden and Lawrance (eds), above n 1, xviii–xxiv, 85.
61 Williams, above n 11, 96.
62 See Sherwood, above n 12, 245–6.
63 Horswell, above n 40, 60, citing Rafael Carrasco, *Inquisición y represión sexual en Valencia: historia de los sodomitas (1565–1785)* (Laertes, 1985).
64 Margaret Denike, 'The Devil's Insatiable Sex: A Genealogy of Evil Incarnate' (2003) 18 *Hypatia* 10, 12–14.

This edict was used to mobilise the category of sodomy against 'outsiders' in and out of Spain through the Inquisition. The Spanish were more likely to see sodomites in their long-time enemies the Moors, as well as in other 'foreigners', such as Jews, Germans, French and English, against whom the Inquisition was often directed.[65] In Aragon and Valencia, the Moors were accused of sodomy, a pestilence capable of spreading, 'if these debased kinds of men are not isolated they can drag down the faithful into this corruption'.[66] Fuelled by racial and religious anxieties, sodomy was 'excoriated, feared, and all but hidden from public view', while simultaneously contributing to producing a 'properly' masculine nation in opposition.[67]

This culture of nation-building through attribution of the 'nefarious sin' to internal and external enemies was incorporated into Spain's tactics in the New World, clashing with cultures where same-sex sexual acts sometimes appeared to be tolerated, openly avowed and even institutionalised. A report on the Caribes in 1525, emphasising sodomitic proclivities, resulted in a ruling by the Holy Roman Emperor Charles V declaring that the Indians were slaves as they were irrational, and hence inhuman.[68] In 1526, Gonzalo Fernández de Oviedo's widely influential account of 'native customs' in the New World stated:

> Very common among the Indians in many parts is the nefarious sin against nature; even in public the Indians who are headmen . . . have youths with whom they use this accursed sin, and those consenting youths as soon as they fall into this guilt wear *naguas* [skirts] like women . . . and the other things used by women as adornment; and they do not exercise in the use of weapons, nor do anything proper to men, but they occupy themselves in the usual chores of the house . . . and other things customary to women.[69]

Spanish rule and the expropriation of Indian wealth and land[70] were represented as 'the logical result of God's punishment of the pagan Amerindians for their alleged effeminacy and propensity for homosexual intercourse'.[71]

Michael J Horswell argues that constructions of indigenous sexuality were centrally, not marginally, related to Spain's project of conquest.[72] Portraying

65 Goldberg, above n 17, 6; Crompton, above n 17, 291–2.
66 Crompton, above n 17, 295, citing Carrasco, above n 63, 58.
67 Crompton, above n 17, 314.
68 Ibid 316.
69 Crompton, above n 17, 315, citing Francisco Guerra, *The Pre-Columbian Mind: A Study into the Aberrant Nature of Sexual Drives, Drugs Affecting Behaviour and the Attitude towards Life and Death, with a Survey of Psychotherapy in Pre-Columbian America* (Seminar Press, 1971) 55, citing Gonzalo Fernández de Oviedo, *De La Natural Historia de las Indias* (Ramón de Petras, 1526) folio 44 verso, ch LXXXI.
70 Crompton, above n 17, 315.
71 François Soyer, *Ambiguous Gender in Early Modern Spain and Portugal: Inquisitors, Doctors and the Transgression of Gender Norms* (Brill, 2012) 29.
72 Horswell, above n 40, 75.

indigenous peoples as sodomites, deviant, monstrous and lacking in humanity and rationality meant that they were inferior to the Spanish, could not participate in a natural law based on reason, and could be conquered, consigned to slavery and/or killed.[73] Cannibalism, human sacrifice and sodomy formed a triumvirate trope mobilised to denote barbarity and inhumanity.[74] For example, the coastal peoples of the Tawantinsuyu, with both a woman ruler and sodomites, were described as deviant, monstrous and transgressing natural law.[75] Using the allegory of Sodom, with Spain in the divine role, the conquest of whole societies was justified on the basis of practices of sodomy, or of engagement in human sacrifice and cannibalism and 'in addition' sodomy,[76] or on the more general basis that the Mesoamericans lacked rationality and were therefore incapable of engaging with natural law.[77]

Vitoria, the Law of Nations and Spanish imperialism in the Mesoamerica

Vitoria's two lectures were delivered in the 1530s into this context where these discourses of sodomy infused key laws, policies and practices of the Spanish conquest of Mesoamerica. In this part, the first of three sections considers Vitoria's analysis of reason and ownership of the peoples of Mesoamerica, which is central to his rejection of the universal jurisdiction of the Pope and the Holy Roman Emperor, and lays the foundation for the remainder of his work. The second section analyses his treatment of sodomy in responding to Spanish claims to title in Mesoamerica, and the third analyses his treatment of sodomy and the allegory of Sodom in his arguments justifying Spanish title and rule. Vitoria's arguments reflect the historical trajectory of the allegory; the shifting relationships of hospitality, sexuality and gender in the allegory become an integral part of his work, and therefore of the foundations of international law.

Vitoria on reason and ownership in Mesoamerica

By the late 1530s, theologians, who had been baptising the 'Indians' for some years, baulked at the idea that they lacked rationality. In 1537, Pope Paul III issued two Papal Bulls declaring the Indians to be rational beings.[78] Arguments for the conquest of Mesoamerica, and the early experiment in the extension

73 See Pagden, above n 4, 67–70.

74 Horswell, above n 40, 73–7; Sherwood labels the grouping of cannibalism, human sacrifice, bestiality and sodomy together as the 'Supersins': at above n 12, 242.

75 Horswell, above n 40, 75.

76 Jonathan Goldberg, *Sodometries: Renaissance Texts, Modern Sexualities* (Stanford University Press, 1992) 194–8.

77 Horswell, above n 40, 73–7.

78 Crompton, above n 17, 316.

of European empire to the west, were widely perceived to have failed in the face of mounting evidence of genocide and 'demographic apocalypse'.[79]

In Vitoria's scheme, participation in natural law and ownership was reserved to rational beings. Rejecting the authority of the Papal Bulls, Vitoria posed the question of whether the Mesoamericans were 'true owners' of their territory in public and private law, before the arrival of the Spanish. He recognises the Mesoamericans, whom he refers to as 'Indians',[80] as possessing the power of reason, and as not 'mad':

> [t]hey are not in point of fact madmen, but have judgment like other men [but have in their own way, the use of reason[81]]. This is self-evident, because they have some order [a certain rational order[82]] in their affairs: they have properly organised cities, proper marriages, magistrates, and overlords (*domini*), laws, industries and commerce, all of which require the use of reason. They likewise have a form (*species*) of religion, and they correctly apprehend things which are evident to other men, which requires the use of reason. Furthermore, 'God and nature never fail in the things necessary' for the majority of the species, and the chief attribute of man is reason;
>
> Thus if they seem to us insensate and slow-witted, I put it down mainly to their evil and barbarous education. Even amongst ourselves we see many peasants (*rustici*) who are little different from brute animals.[83]

Here, reason is associated with institutions recognisable to Europeans, and civilisation, such as cities, marriages and magistrates, and allocated to indigenous peoples on that basis, positioning European culture as the universal measure of reason.[84] These peoples, whose cities Hernán Cortés compared to Seville and Cordoba,[85] are characterised as rational and human, but only to the extent that they reflect European institutions back to Europeans. At the same time, they are precariously placed at the margins, on the brink of rationality and humanity, positioned where they might, with education and guidance, be uplifted, but also might, at any moment, slide 'backwards' towards insensate or animal status, lacking in rationality.

Vitoria's finding that the Indians have the capacity to reason, and his conclusion that they are true owners of their land, in both the public and private law senses, is therefore qualified by his positioning them at the margins of rationality.

79 Sherwood, above n 12, 227.
80 Translations of Vitoria often use the term 'Indian' to refer to the peoples of Mesoamerica. Pagden and Lawrance (eds), above n 1, 233.
81 Text in brackets provide alternative translations. See the footnotes in Pagden and Lawrance (eds), above n 1.
82 See Pagden, above n 4, 68.
83 See Victoria, above n 5, 250 (citations omitted).
84 Pagden, above n 4, 67–79; Anghie, above n 6.
85 Pagden, above n 4, 70–2.

Since they have at least the potential for the capacity to reason, the indigenous people are subject to Vitoria's universal natural law, which aligns with the Law of Nations. The Pope's universal jurisdiction and divine law are replaced with a universal natural law.

Vitoria on unjust titles to Mesoamerica: Sodomy as a middling sin of a subsidiary class

Once Vitoria established that the Mesoamericans were rational owners of their land, he rejects seven possible rationales for Spanish rule, including that the Holy Roman Emperor is the master of the whole world, that the Pope is the monarch of the whole world, and that title may be claimed on the basis of discovery, or on the basis of the refusal of the peoples to accept the Christian faith.[86] As a Thomist, Vitoria draws on and responds to the use of Aquinas's work at the time, initially rejecting the argument that sins against nature justify invasion. However, in a move that parallels his equivocation on the rationality of the Mesoamericans, he is more ambivalent on his position in a later passage, which I discuss in the following section. Further, he does not reject the idea that these sins should be punished by monarchs among their own peoples within their jurisdiction.

Vitoria sets out the fifth rationale used by others to justify Spain's conquest on the basis of the Indians' sins against nature as follows:

> Some sins, they [St Antonino and Innocent IV, justifying invasion] say, are not against natural law, but only against positive divine law; and for these the barbarians cannot be invaded. But others, such as cannibalism, incest with mothers and sisters, or sodomy, are against nature; and for these sins they may be invaded . . . in the case of sins against the law of nature the barbarians can be shown that they are committing an offense against God, . . . This is the opinion of St Antonino of Florence . . . and the same opinion is held by . . . Innocent IV . . . He adduces to this purpose the fact that the Sodomites were punished by God (Gen. 19); 'since God's judgments are examples to us, I do not see why the pope, who is the vicar of Christ, should not be empowered to do the same'. . . . and by this argument, they might also, on the pope's authority, be punished by Christian princes.[87]

In this view, the sins that justify invasion are those in Aquinas's oscillating category of the gravest of sins, including sodomy which violates God's natural order and was criminalised in the Spanish edict of 1497. Vitoria reiterates his rejection of the Pope's authority as a basis for this justification: 'Christian princes, even on the authority of the pope', cannot punish sins against the law of nature outside of their

86 Pagden and Lawrance (eds), above n 1, 252–72.
87 Ibid 273.

jurisdiction.[88] Second, he rejects the reliance on Aquinas's singling out of the vice against nature as somehow particularly against God's order more so than other sins, arguing that these sins are not worse than the sins of homicide and blasphemy, which do not justify invasion, and therefore these cannot either.[89] Vitoria here rejects Aquinas's contradictory categorisation of sins against nature as *both* of middling importance *and* as the gravest sins, settling on these sins as of only 'middling' importance.

This interpretation is buttressed by Vitoria's lecture *On Dietary Laws*, delivered in 1537, where he rejects the proposition that Christian princes can wage war on unbelievers due to their 'crimes against nature', any more than for other crimes, explicitly mentioning sodomy. He aligns sodomy with fornication and theft, terming it a 'merely unnatural sin', and noting that murder is a more serious crime.[90] Cannibalism and human sacrifice, which involve the killing of innocent people, justify invasion 'since it is a fact that these barbarians kill innocent men, at least for sacrifice, princes can wage war on them to force them to give up these rituals'.[91] By focusing on the right of individual self-defence of the victims of these sins, and using that to justify defence by a third party, Vitoria avoids any recourse to papal or church authority. This analysis disaggregates sodomy from the other two sins of the triumvirate trope, cannibalism and human sacrifice. Sodomy does not involve the death of innocent people and therefore invasion to punish it is not justified.

Vitoria is clearly concerned with authority for invasion rather than protection of sodomites. Clearing the way for punishment of sodomy once Spain has taken over, he states that Christian princes can compel their non-Christian subjects to give up not only those of their sins and rituals which are against natural law, but also those which are against divine law.[92] Non-Christian princes who have been converted can force their own subjects to give up all of these sins,[93] by abolishing idolatry and other unnatural rituals.[94] His statement that 'Christian princes have no more powers with the authority of the pope, than without it'[95] clarifies that his concern is with the authority of the Pope.

Just titles of the Spanish to the New World: Sodomy as a sin against God's order

Once Vitoria refutes the seven 'unjust' reasons for the assertion of Spanish authority in Mesoamerica, he moves on to the justifications that he considers

88 Ibid.
89 Ibid.
90 Ibid 224.
91 Ibid 225.
92 Ibid 219–29.
93 Ibid 219.
94 Ibid 221.
95 Ibid 223.

legitimate. In considering the fifth of these, Vitoria is, perhaps, more ambivalent than with the previous four.[96] He reiterates his rejection of the Pope's authority as a basis for invasion, but he equivocates on sodomy:

> The next [legitimate] title could be either on account of the personal tyranny of the barbarians' masters towards their subjects, or because of their tyrannical and oppressive laws against the innocent, such as [that which allows[97]] human sacrifice practiced on innocent men or the killing of condemned criminals for cannibalism. I assert that *in lawful defence of the innocent from unjust death, even without the pope's authority, the Spaniards may prohibit the barbarians from practising any nefarious custom or rite*. . . . The barbarians are all our neighbours, and therefore anyone, and especially princes, may defend them from such tyranny and oppression. . . . This applies not only to the actual moment when they are being dragged to death; they may also force the barbarians to give up such rites altogether. If they refuse to do so, war may be declared upon them . . . and if there is no other means of putting an end to these sacrilegious rites, their masters may be changed and new princes set up. In this case, there is truth in the opinion held by Innocent IV and Antonino of Florence, that *sinners against nature* may be punished. It makes no difference that all the barbarians consent to these kinds of rites and sacrifices, or that they refuse to accept the Spaniards as their liberators in the matter.[98]

The use of the phrases '*any* nefarious custom or rite' and 'sinners against nature', which commonly denote the triumvirate of cannibalism, human sacrifice and sodomy, open up the possibility that this passage includes sodomy. The phrase 'sinners against nature' is used with reference to Innocent IV and Antonino, both of whom are cited by Vitoria earlier for the proposition that the Spanish may justify conquest on the basis of breaches of sins against nature, including sodomy.[99] He embraces their opinion, at least with regard to 'putting an end to sacrilegious rites'. This broader interpretation is supported by Anthony Pagden, who points out that while some translations qualify 'sins against nature' with 'when their sins are to the detriment of the innocent', this qualification is not contained in the earliest, most authoritative manuscripts of Vitoria's work.[100]

Vitoria's use of the phrase 'personal tyranny of the barbarians' masters towards their subjects', combined with the broad phrases just discussed, also suggests that

96 Ibid 287, fn 82, Vitoria's choice of words is less certain than in the previous justifications.

97 This phrase suggests that the examples following are of oppressive laws against the innocent, leaving the interpretation of 'personal tyranny of the barbarians' open. Victoria, above n 5, xliv.

98 Pagden and Lawrance (eds), above n 1, 287–8 (first emphasis in original, second emphasis added).

99 Ibid 273. See also above n 90 and accompanying text.

100 Ibid 288, fn 83, xxxiii–xxxvi.

he is invoking the triumvirate trope. A story from Vasco Núñez de Balboa's arrival in Panama in 1513, widely reported by Peter Martyr in 1516,[101] provides some context for linking Vitoria's references to personal tyranny with this trope. Balboa and his men killed the leader of the people of Quarequa and 600 of his warriors. The event is described with terms usually used for the slaughter of animals, stating that they were 'hewed . . . in pieces as the butchers do flesshe from one an arm, from another a leg, here a buttock, there a shoulder', in a scene of carnage.[102] Martyr reported that, after killing the Quarequa people, Balboa found the leader's brother attended by 'smooth and effeminately decked' men who engaged in 'most abominable and unnaturall lechery' whom he 'abused with preposterous venus'. Balboa had 40 of these men 'gyven for a pray to his dogges'.[103] Although the term 'sodomy' is not used here, consistent with the trope of silence surrounding it, the other terms make the reference clear: 'preposterous' here refers to a 'confusion of before and behind' and 'venus' to sexual acts; and the references to abominable and unnatural lechery also invoke sodomy.[104]

Uncannily, Martyr's report operates similarly to the allegory of Sodom, read as a punishment for excesses of wealth and sex, with Balboa positioned as the divine. Combining questions of transgendering, 'effeminately decked' men and sodomy by the elite, it provides a moral purpose for Balboa's slaughter, a righting of transgressions of gender and sexual excess, that evokes (misogynist) disgust in the Spanish, positioning the Spanish as 'properly' masculine in contrast.[105] Presented as a story of degenerate wealth and sexual excess among the elite, it positions Balboa as the friend and saviour of the commoners.[106] This creates a link between the 'right thinking men' of Balboa and the commoners, liberating the commoners from oppressive rulers who are immoral and unfit to lead, and justifying Balboa's brutal conquest.[107]

The event and its portrayal occur in the context of the first meeting of theologians, canon and civil lawyers to discuss the legitimacy of the Spanish conquests in Mesoamerica.[108] Martyr's influential report was published in numerous editions throughout Europe.[109] Vitoria's references to 'any nefarious custom or rite', and the 'personal tyranny' and 'abuse' of rulers, and his insistence that this principle applies not just when people are actually being dragged to death, but justifies stopping these rituals altogether, reasserts sodomy as a

101 Pietro Martire d'Anghiera was an Italian serving in Spain as a councillor of the Indies. The *Decades* (*De Orbo Novo*) was a series of letters and reports of the early invasions of the Spanish. See Goldberg, above n 76, 180.
102 Goldberg, above n 76, 180–3.
103 Ibid 181.
104 Ibid.
105 Ibid.
106 Ibid.
107 Horswell, above n 40, 71–2.
108 Pagden and Lawrance (eds), above n 1, xxix.
109 Goldberg, above n 76, 180.

justification for invasion along with the closely aligned human sacrifice and cannibalism. In this context at least, sodomy is connected with, and collapsed into, inhumane rites and customs, 'those sins against nature which constituted an injury to humanity itself',[110] positioning the Mesoamericans as not human, and justifying Spanish conquest. The justification follows the logic of the Sodom allegory, reflecting the historical trajectory at the moment where whole societies may be punished (by the Spaniards in the position of God) for sins against nature, including the triumvirate of sodomy, cannibalism and human sacrifice.

Vitoria on hospitality

I have argued that Vitoria's intervention in debates about the legitimacy of Spain's titles to Mesoamerica engage with, and pivot around, the debates of his time concerning sodomy, Sodomites and the attendant oscillations and ambivalence in these categories. In this part, I argue that his eight possible just titles for Spain in the New World are shaped by biblical and philosophical traditions of hospitality to which the Sodom allegory is central. I argue that the allegory is 'the shape described by an absence'; while it is not explicitly mentioned, its outline, in which God or his emissaries appear and the Mesoamericans, as hosts, must offer hospitality, informs his duties of hospitality owed by the indigenous Mesoamericans to the Spanish, and his Law of Nations more generally.[111] In effecting a shift to natural law justifications, Vitoria pivots around his equivocal position disaggregating sodomy from cannibalism and human sacrifice, and focuses on duties of love, friendship and hospitality. Vitoria's duties of hospitality, though perhaps more palatable (to Europe), were no less expansionary, and still a trap for the peoples of Mesoamerica.[112]

Vitoria's duties of hospitality

Vitoria begins his discussion of the possible lawful titles 'by which the barbarians could have come under the control of the Spaniards',[113] with a general principal of hospitality, 'natural partnership and communication'.[114] His first rule is justified on the basis that it is part of the Law of Nations, because 'natural reason has established among all [Christian, European] nations' the principle that it is inhuman to treat travellers badly without cause.[115]

110 Pagden and Lawrance (eds), above n 1, xxvii.
111 Avery F Gordon, *Ghostly Matters: Haunting and the Sociological Imagination* (University of Minnesota Press, 1997) 24–5.
112 Sherwood, above n 12, 255.
113 Pagden and Lawrance (eds), above n 1, 277.
114 Ibid 278.
115 Ibid.

> *[T]he Spaniards have the right to travel and dwell in those countries* [of the Mesoamericas], *so long as they do no harm to the barbarians, and cannot be prevented by them from doing so.*[116]

Vitoria initially recognises Mesomericans as having reason, and therefore rights to property and lordship, as discussed above. This brings them under his universal natural law and the Law of Nations, which imposes upon them wide-reaching duties of hospitality, friendship and love in welcoming the Spanish to their lands. Many of these duties are based on the Bible and religious texts, for example, the duty to 'love their neighbours as themselves'.[117] He also notes that it is relevant that hospitality is commended in Scripture, and it follows that 'to refuse to welcome strangers and foreigners is inherently evil'.[118]

The Christian European genealogy of hospitality invoked by Vitoria can be traced back to the Sodom allegory, which participates in founding the duty to behave hospitably to strangers. The limits of the extent of this duty are unclear; Lot offered his daughters to be abused by the men of Sodom as it pleased them in an attempt to divert attention from, and protect, his guests.[119] For this, he is rewarded by the angels, suggesting that sacrificing harm to women family members is the appropriate extent of the duty of hospitality. Jacques Derrida highlights the analogously misogynistic bargaining in the Bible's allegory in Judges 19, with a plot that parallels Sodom, where the townsmen who demand to 'know' the guest are given the guest's concubine to abuse, after which the guest cuts her limb by limb into pieces[120] and, interestingly, God's divine wrath does not rain down on the city of Gibeah and nor does the name of the city come to represent 'unnatural', or anal, or male-to-male sex.[121]

In the biblical hospitality trope that informs Vitoria's duties:

> God or his emissaries appear to human beings in the guise of unknown strangers, challenging the host to prove his worthiness by offering the wanderer food and shelter.[122]

In Vitoria's scheme, where the Spanish have the right to travel and present themselves to the peoples of Mesoamerica, and those people must treat the Spanish hospitably, the Spanish take the place of God's emissaries, if not God himself. The peoples of the New World are challenged to prove their worthiness

116 Ibid (emphasis in original).
117 Ibid 279.
118 Ibid 281.
119 See Jacques Derrida and Anne Dufourmantelle, *Of Hospitality* (Rachel Bowlby trans, Stanford University Press, 2000) 49–150.
120 Ibid 153–5.
121 Jordan, above n 17, 30.
122 Tracy McNulty, *Hostess: Hospitality, Femininity, and the Expropriation of Identity* (University of Minnesota Press, 2006) xiv.

to the Spanish by offering hospitality. While Sodom and sodomy are absent from this discussion, it nevertheless takes the shape of the Sodom allegory.

Vitoria's punishment for breaches of duties of hospitality

In the Sodom allegory, the punishment for breaches of hospitality is the raining down of God's wrath. In Vitoria's scheme, the duties of hospitality are broad and deep, and breaching them justifies the Spanish punishing the Mesoamericans with war. Resisting the Spanish, not allowing them in, or expelling them after they arrive, are not only violations of the right to travel, but are acts of war and, in particular, acts of an unjust war:

> [I]t is an act of war to bar those considered as enemies from entering a city or country, or to expel them if they are already in it. But since the barbarians have no just war against the Spaniards, assuming they are doing no harm, it is not lawful for them to bar them from their homeland.[123]

The Spanish, when doing no harm, must be welcomed. The fundamental offence of the peoples of Mesoamerica becomes any refusal to engage in a loving relationship with the Spaniards.[124] Every encounter between people long resident in a place and the Spanish strangers becomes a potential justification for war.

The biblical bases for Vitoria's duties, such as the commandment to love one's neighbour, and the hospitality trope, are generally duties owed between individuals. Vitoria extends these to require welcoming large groups of Spanish people, who may present themselves in full military regalia, 'armed men, who surround a fearful and defenceless crowd',[125] as they did when reading the *Requerimiento* in Latin:

> [T]hese barbarians are by nature cowardly, foolish and ignorant besides. However much the Spanish may wish to reassure them and convince them of their peaceful intentions, therefore, the barbarians may still be understandably fearful of men whose customs seem so strange, and who they can see are armed and much stronger than themselves. If this fear moves them to mount an attack to drive the Spaniards away or kill them, it would indeed be lawful for the Spaniards to defend themselves, within the bounds of blameless self-defence.[126]

The use of 'understandably' here suggests empathy at the same time as it patronises by assuming inferiority. The scenario challenges the peoples of the New World to

123 Pagden and Lawrance (eds), above n 1, 278.
124 Porras, above n 10, 773.
125 Pagden and Lawrance (eds), above n 1, 276.
126 Ibid 282.

calmly accept an invasion of armed men, and judges their conduct in response by a set of rules to which they have no access, but which are nevertheless claimed to be universal and recognisable by all. Antony Anghie concludes that Vitoria's discussion of breaches of these duties results in justifying 'inevitable and endless' war by the Spanish in response.[127]

Breach of the duties of hospitality also threatens to send the Mesoamericans, who Vitoria has left precariously perched on the brink of rationality and humanity, plunging into the abyss of the inhuman. Vitoria states that as 'nature has decreed a certain kinship among all men', it is against natural law for one man to turn against another without due cause because 'man is not a wolf to his fellow man . . . but a fellow'.[128] This is further equivocation on the status of the Mesoamericans, paralleling the equivocation on sodomy and shoring up the demands for hospitality.

The allegory of Sodom, and biblical hospitality tropes more generally, shape Vitoria's work explicitly in his recognition of the possibility that the punishment for failure to offer hospitality may take the shape of God's sudden divine wrath. In a passage in Vitoria's second lecture, *On The Law of War*,[129] the allegory of Sodom is invoked, suggesting the possibility of punishing a whole society without regard to the individual 'guilt' of each person. The question is whether the killing of guiltless people is lawful when they may be expected to cause danger in the future.[130] Justifying killing everyone even though some are not guilty relies on the allegory of Sodom, where everyone was killed in a demonstration of God's sudden, divine wrath. Vitoria argues that this licence does not extend beyond God.[131] The references to Sodom nevertheless reveal how the allegory continued to shape contemporary thought and his work.

Conclusion

This chapter has argued that Vitoria's lectures on the Law of Nations, positioned at the inception of international law, participate in, and shape, biblical, theological and scholarly debates and discourses interweaving hospitality, homophobia and misogyny. Questions central to international law today, of who may travel, invade and conquer, and who must welcome into their lands, and provide hospitality to, travellers, invaders and outsiders, arise from the shapes provided by the deployment of these ancient discourses at the particular moment of Spain's invasion of Mesoamerica. Sedimented in these shapes and bounds of hospitality and international law are questions of homophobia and misogyny in the recognition

127 Anghie, above n 6, 328; cf Christopher Tomlins, *Freedom Bound: Law, Labor, and Civic Identity in Colonizing English America, 1580–1865* (Cambridge University Press, 2010) 122–31, on Anghie's analysis of Vitoria on Indian sovereignty.
128 Pagden and Lawrance (eds), above n 1, 280, fn 76.
129 Ibid 316.
130 Ibid.
131 Ibid.

of humanity and rationality, and of worthiness in the provision, and punishment for breaches, of hospitality. Like Derrida, I want to promote further inquiry into the extent to which we are heirs to the homophobia and misogyny in these traditions, facing the challenge of embracing the law of hospitality, opening our homes to the other, while rejecting its miring in injustice.[132] This project is crucial to rethinking current responses to urgent issues, such as the treatment of asylum seekers around the world, particularly sexual and gender minorities, and the assertion of self-determination of colonised indigenous peoples.

132 Derrida and Dufourmantelle, above n 119.

12 Resisting the heteronormative imaginary of the nation-state

Rethinking kinship and border protection

*Dianne Otto**

Make love not war.[1]

'This way if you are gay.' Thus read the invitation to Russian sailors, transmitted in Morse code from a waterproof box, lowered into the sea near Stockholm. The box also contained a flashing neon sign of a gyrating singing sailor, clad only in his suggestively bulging underwear, and an invitation in pink Russian script saying 'Welcome to Sweden – Gay since 1944' (the year Sweden decriminalised homosexuality).[2] The mock invitation was directed at Russian submarines, which had reportedly been patrolling Swedish waters (reports that were dismissed by some Swedish commentators as a scare campaign orchestrated by those who stood to profit from increased military spending in Sweden).[3] In the press release that accompanied the launch of the box and its message on 27 April 2015, the Swedish peace group responsible explained that it was launching a new border protection strategy, which it hoped would persuade the Swedish government 'to think in new ways [about responding to threats from Russia] instead of falling back on territorial defence, conscription and rearmament'.[4] And, I would add, the anxious proliferation of walled borders.

The idea of Russian submarines retreating, rather than risking defection by gay sailors, has its own pleasures. But the action by the venerable Swedish Peace and Arbitration Society (SPAS), established in 1883 by Nobel Peace Prize laureate

* Thanks to Kara Connolly for early research assistance, Joan Nestle for inspiration, patience and care, and Mimi Oorloff for consummate editorial skills and enthusiastic support.

1 Anti-war slogan popularised, particularly in the United States, by anti-Vietnam War protests in the 1960s.

2 The Singing Sailor Underwater Defense System <http://www.svenskafreds.se/singingsailor/>.

3 Sven Hultberg Carlsson, 'Russia's "Threat" to Sweden – An Exaggeration?', *Radio Sweden* (online) (7 March 2013) <http://sverigesradio.se/sida/artikel.aspx?programid=2054&artikel=5466480>.

4 Nick Miller, 'The Swedes Introduce the "Singing Sailor", Gay Propaganda to Repel Unwanted Russian Submarines', *The Sydney Morning Herald* (Sydney) (13 May 2015).

Figure 12.1 The singing sailor, Swedish Peace and Arbitration Society, 2015

Klas Pontus Arnoldson,[5] can be read in a number of ways that illustrate some of the risks, as well as possibilities, facing queer thinkers and activists in the present global conjuncture. On the one hand, the spectacle provides a graphic illustration of the 'homonationalism' that marks some of the international advocacy for gay and lesbian rights, whereby sexual liberality joins the long line of indicators of Western superiority[6] and non-Western development.[7] In this reading, SPAS's protest risks buffering present-day geo-political hierarchies of civilisation and backwardness which, in turn, help to justify carceral states. On the other hand, the idea that non-state-based forms of global relationality could offer alternative non-military means of border protection points to the imaginative possibilities of queer ways of thinking. The invitation challenges heteronormative kinship systems that prioritise national loyalties, support militarism and normalise quotidian inequalities. As explained in its press release, SPAS hopes to promote a radical rethinking of state security, which would shift military resources into (transformative) development. The neon protest links together many queer, feminist, critical race and postcolonial efforts to think in new ways about the current paradigm of international law and politics.

On almost every measure, the state-based international legal order is failing. It is proving impossible for states to reach agreement on robust measures to reduce global warming; there is no end in sight for dozens of armed conflicts and militarised stalemates, many of which have been exacerbated by international efforts at intervention; the international trade in arms, both legal and illegal, continues to grow, even in the reputedly less militaristic countries of Scandinavia; the gap between rich and poor keeps widening, exposing the hollowness of the inclusionary promises of prevailing neoliberal economics; the human rights project has been seriously undermined in the name of defending nation-states against terror; and free-trade agreements and dynamics have carved the heart out of democracy everywhere. Yet international law and global politics remain firmly anchored in national imaginaries, as dramatically illustrated by the call to fear-based white patriotism that saw the election of Donald Trump as the next US President. As seen in Trump's election campaign, the technologies of walling states ('I will build a great wall')[8] and sexual panics (Mexican immigrants are 'rapists')[9] both feature prominently in attempts to shore up and continue to privilege and naturalise the nation-state as the primary locus of identity, community, security and well-being.

5 The Swedish Peace and Arbitration Society <http://www.svenskafreds.se/english/>.

6 Jasbir K Puar, *Terrorist Assemblages: Homonationalism in Queer Times* (Duke University Press, 2007) 38–9.

7 Jon Binnie, *The Globalization of Sexuality* (Sage, 2004) 75–7.

8 'Full Text: Donald Trump Announces a Presidential Bid', *The Washington Post* (online) (16 June 2015) <https://www.washingtonpost.com/news/post-politics/wp/2015/06/16/full-text-donald-trump-announces-a-presidential-bid/?utm_term=.cfaa90757acd>.

9 Ibid.

The iron grip that imagined communities of nationhood have on our sense of identity and belonging[10] presents a major obstacle to thinking in radically inclusive and plural ways about law, politics, markets, militaries, individuals and communities. The SPAS is not alone in calling for a radical reconsideration of the way in which things are normally done. In the context of the post-2015 UN development agenda, a coalition of 167 NGOs committed themselves to creating a 'transformative' development model that 'works for everyone';[11] on 10 March 2015, the Women's International League for Peace and Freedom (WILPF) withdrew from its long-standing engagement with the Conference on Disarmament, which it accused of '[m]aintaining the structures that reinforce deadlock';[12] and queer activists are joining other movements demanding human rights, social justice and open borders across the globe, including anti-occupation Jewish queers joining with Palestinians to support the academic and cultural boycott of Israel.[13] These are among mounting efforts to actively rethink the way in which things have been done. What they have in common is the hope that the alternative practices of solidarity and alliance they foster will lay the foundation for an international community based on forms of kinship and human interconnection other than militaristic nationalism.

In this chapter, I join the calls for change. I argue that queer relational practices offer emancipatory non-state-centred imaginaries of human connection and interdependence. I start by examining recent efforts to strengthen the heteronormative underpinnings of the nation-state by measures including the recognition (or rejection) of same-sex marriage as a human rights issue. I then link these internal efforts, to strengthen the identity of the nation-state, with the increasing militarisation of state borders and the use of elaborate border fortifications to project power in the face of alleged external threats and provide reassurance to fearful (heteronormative) national loyalties. I conclude with some thoughts on how queer kinship systems might reshape border protection strategies and promote a shift of military resources into development, as hoped for by the Swedish activists. I am not arguing for a post-state world, although this may be a logical conclusion to draw. Rather, my argument is that the primacy of national loyalty needs to give way to the myriad other assemblages of human kinship that refuse to confine loyalty and connection to the narrow and racially imbued band of 'natural' reproductive ties.

10 Benedict Anderson, *Imagined Communities: Reflections on the Origin and Spread of Nationalism* (Verso, revised edn, 1991).

11 'Feminist Sustainable Development: A Transformative Alternative for Gender Equality, Development and Peace' (Vision Statement, Post-2015 Women's Coalition, 11 March 2015) <http://www.post2015women.com/post-2015-womens-coalition-vision-statement/>.

12 WILPF, 'Statement to the Conference on Disarmament on International Women's Day 2015' (Statement delivered at Conference on Disarmament, 10 March 2015) <http://www.reachingcriticalwill.org/news/latest-news/9559-wilpf-statement-to-the-conference-on-disarmament-on-international-women-s-day-2015>.

13 Sarah Schulman, *Israel/Palestine and the Queer International* (Duke University Press, 2010).

The heteronormative analytics of the normal nation-state

If the precarious lives of sexual and gender minorities are taken seriously as lives that matter,[14] it becomes apparent that the nation-state is so deeply enmeshed in the regulation of sexuality that its very existence depends on it. Heterosexual analytics saturate our everyday lives without most of us even noticing. It is widely recognised that 'responsible' heterosexuality (state-sanctioned, monogamous, adult and reproductive) was a key component of Europe's 'civilising mission'.[15] In Europe, too, the same disciplinary heteronormative sexual configuration has been a core technique of state governmentality.[16] Going further, my argument is that the nation-state is itself made possible by putatively natural heterosexual kinship arrangements. Therefore, to question these arrangements, and give primacy to other forms of relational attachment, will help us to imagine other conceptions of state security, as the SPAS action suggests. Alternative kinship ties will also open new possibilities for challenging the hegemony of loyalties, based on nationhood, that currently structure the international community.

The debate about whether the Vatican properly qualifies as a state for the purposes of admission to full UN membership provides a revelatory starting point. The classic indicia of 'normal' statehood, as conceived, regulated and privileged by international law, include defined territory, permanent population, governmental authority and international independence in the form of the capacity to enter into legal relations with other states.[17] While the Vatican satisfies many of these requirements, more or less, the main stumbling block is its lack of reproductive continuity. Pundits have argued that the Vatican's population of celibate priests and nuns lacks 'permanency' because it is not self-sustaining.[18] This argument recalls the Law of Nations, as explicated by Emmerich de Vattel in 1758, which included the 'right of carrying off women' because '[a] nation cannot preserve and perpetuate itself except by propagation'.[19] This 'right of nations' makes it crystal clear that the nation is, naturally, 'a nation of [heterosexual] men',

14 Judith Butler, 'Indefinite Detention' in *Precarious Life: The Powers of Mourning and Violence* (Verso, 2004) 50.

15 See also Nan Seuffert at chapter 11, 'Queering international law's stories of origin: Hospitality and homophobia'.

16 See generally Michel Foucault, 'Governmentality' (Pasquale Pasquino trans) in Graham Burchell, Colin Gordon and Peter Miller (eds), *The Foucault Effect: Studies in Governmentality with Two Lectures by and an Interview with Michel Foucault* (University of Chicago Press, 1991) 87.

17 Montevideo Convention on the Rights and Duties of States, signed 26 December 1933, 165 LNTS 19 (entered into force 26 December 1934) art 1.

18 M H Mendelson, 'Diminutive States in the United Nations' (1972) 21 *International and Comparative Law Quarterly* 609, 611.

19 Emmerich de Vattel, *The Law of Nations; or Principles of Natural Law, Applied to the Conduct and Affairs of Nations and Sovereigns* (first published 1758, 1844 edn) bk II, ch IX, s 122, 179 <http://www.loc.gov/rr/frd/Military_Law/Lieber_Collection/pdf/DeVattel_LawOfNations.pdf>. Thanks to Rosemary Grey, who drew my attention to this early right of nations.

and that force is justified if used 'to procure women, who are absolutely necessary to its preservation [reproductive continuity]'.[20]

Strangely, this means the non-reproductive Vatican provides one starting point for imagining a queer state – assuming such an entity would even be recognisable as a state. That the nation-state depends so fundamentally on heteronormative reproductive relations for the transfer and reproduction of national loyalty and culture has been entirely overlooked by theorists of nationalism, including Benedict Anderson.[21] Further, as Judith Butler observes, in reproducing the nation and its culture, the state's kinship configurations carry 'implicit norms of racial purity and domination'.[22] This helps to explain the current anxiety of many European states over their falling birth rates and why increasing (racially diverse) immigration is not necessarily seen as the answer.[23] It also explains why same-sex marriage (presumed reproductive) has become so widely embraced in the West, because it promises to (re)produce citizens loyal to the nation-state, rather than outlaws likely to question the idea of state loyalty.

'Taking a break'[24] from normal ways of thinking about other key attributes of statehood – defined territory, governmental authority and international independence – makes it clear that they are all are anchored and stabilised by heteronormative imaginaries, which have helped legitimate claims of sovereignty over territory, shaped modes of governance and made states recognisable as independent international actors. As Michel Foucault argued, the ideal of the 'Malthusian couple' – monogamous, heterosexual, reproductively and socially responsible – is one of the anchors of Western sexual normativity.[25] Understood as the elemental, natural form of human association, conjugal heterosexuality not only produces and disciplines 'normal' interpersonal and familial relationships, but is constitutive of the nation-state, international law's primary subject. Today, almost every aspect of national life is organised along the grid-lines of (patriarchal) heterosexual kinship relationships – census forms, surnames, marriage regulation, birth registration, child custody, tax arrangements, inheritance, wages, education, social security, medical decision-making, funeral arrangements, immigration, insurance, parenting rights, housing and health care assistance and much more.[26]

20 Ibid.

21 Anderson, above n 10.

22 Judith Butler, 'Is Kinship Always Already Heterosexual?' in *Undoing Gender* (Routledge, 2004) 102, 110.

23 Ashifa Kassam, Rosie Scammell, Kate Connolly et al, 'Europe Needs Many More Babies to Avert a Population Disaster', *The Guardian* (online) (23 August 2015) <https://www.theguardian.com/world/2015/aug/23/baby-crisis-europe-brink-depopulation-disaster>.

24 Thanks to Janet Halley for the provocative idea of 'taking a break' in Janet Halley, *Split Decisions: How and Why to Take a Break from Feminism* (Princeton University Press, 2006).

25 Michel Foucault, *The History of Sexuality: An Introduction* (Robert Hurley trans, Vintage, first published 1976, 1990 edn) vol 1, 104–5.

26 See, eg, 'Same Sex: Same Entitlements: National Inquiry into Discrimination against People in Same-Sex Relationships: Financial and Work-Related Entitlements and Benefits' (Report, Australian Human Rights and Equal Opportunity Commission , May 2007), which

Extensive rights and privileges are conferred by the state on married couples, granting them full humanity in the frame of the law. Other sexual relationships, encounters, exchanges and practices are less privileged and, depending on how far they depart from the Malthusian couple standard, may be marked as perverse, anomalous, abnormal, criminal and even unthinkable. It is heteronormativity that makes the imagined community of the nation-state possible, giving such power to national feelings of belonging and attachment that, as Anderson observes, people are willing to die for it.[27]

Colonial administrations clearly understood that the regulation and control of sexuality was essential to their imperial state-building projects. Conjugal reproductive heterosexuality, closely associated with whiteness, was projected as the most civilised expression of sexuality, affirming in the family sphere the modern liberal values of 'civility, self-control, self-discipline and self-determination'.[28] The developing technologies of colonial governance treated sexuality, as described later by Foucault, as an 'especially dense transfer point' of power, endowed with the 'greatest instrumentality'.[29] The criminalisation of 'unnatural' sexual practices was standard procedure. New systems of birth, sex and marriage registration enforced gender binary, monogamy and heterosexuality, and prohibited arranged and child marriages. These colonial technologies of governance rendered perverse many local practices and beliefs about kinship and community responsibility. In a similar vein, there was 'heavy imperial investment' in representing the sexual behaviours of indigenous peoples as deviant.[30] Evolutionary theories were drawn into imperial service, classifying homosexual practices and male effeminacy as signs of the 'arrested development' of savages.[31] As Neville Hoad notes, nineteenth-century evolutionary anthropologists posited sexual promiscuity as the primitive stage of human social organisation. The 'family' emerged through several developmental stages, including incestuous and polygamous relations, until it reached the final stage of the 'civilised family' of state-sanctioned monogamous conjugal reproductive heterosexuality.[32]

identified 58 federal laws that discriminate against same-sex couples, and sometimes their children as well, and a further 21 that potentially discriminate against same-sex couples and families. (Marriage law was not included in the terms of the inquiry.)

27 Anderson, above n 10, 7.

28 Ann Laura Stoler, *Race and the Education of Desire: Foucault's History of Sexuality and the Colonial Order of Things* (Duke University Press, 1995) 8.

29 Foucault, above n 25, 103.

30 Maddee Clarke, 'Are We Queer? Reflections on "Peopling the Empty Mirror" Twenty Years On' in Dino Hodge (ed), *Colouring the Rainbow: Blak Queer and Trans Perspectives – Life Stories and Essays by First Nations People of Australia* (Wakefield Press, 2015) 238, 241; Mark Rifkin, *When Did Indians Become Straight? Kinship, the History of Sexuality, and Native Sovereignty* (Oxford University Press, 2011).

31 Neville Hoad, 'Arrested Development or the Queerness of Savages: Resisting Evolutionary Narratives of Difference' (2000) 3 *Postcolonial Studies* 133.

32 Ibid 140.

Colonial discourses of sexuality were not just concerned with controlling and normalising populations. The tropes of sexuality also served an analytical function by marking the superiority of the Western nation-state. As Teemu Ruskola's study of the anthropomorphic metaphors of colonial international law reveals, the rhetoric of sexual violation was often used to describe (and legitimate) Western expansionism.[33] European states were attributed a normatively masculine position, while non-European states and peoples were understood as expressing deviant forms of masculinity. Africa, for example, was monolithically represented as '*hypermasculine*'[34] and, ironically, Oriental civilisations were considered 'too civilized' and therefore not masculine enough.[35] Thus, as Ruskola argues, imperial homo-erotic 'penetrations' were necessary to produce the 'full sovereign manhood' necessary for acceptance into the international community of modern states.[36] Yet, despite Europe's best penetrative efforts, the standard is one of impossibility for postcolonial states. They continue to be racially and sexually marked as underdeveloped, illiberal, degenerate and threatening to (Western) civilisation. The post-colony is also the site of many counter-heteronormative movements, the diversity of which cannot possibly be captured by language of LGBTI, as Ratna Kapur cautions.[37] Instead, she uses the term 'sexual subalterns' to resist the assimilationism of the neoliberal project and reflect the 'extraordinary range' of these movements in postcolonial states.[38]

In the West, fears about homosexuality threatening the survival of the nation-state became explicit in many of the recent same-sex marriage debates. One of the strident opponents of marriage equality in the United States, law professor Maura Strassburg, asserted that monogamous heterosexual marriage was 'uniquely capable of producing free-thinking and independent individuals who are also capable of choosing to be loyal and trusting citizens'.[39] This view was echoed in the US Congressional debates that preceded the passing of the Defense of Marriage Act 1996 ('DOMA'),[40] when Senator Jesse Helms warned that 'at the heart of this debate is the moral and spiritual survival of this Nation'.[41]

33 Teemu Ruskola, 'Raping like a State' (2010) 57 *UCLA Law Review* 1477.

34 Ibid 1498 (emphasis in original).

35 Ibid.

36 Ibid 1497.

37 Ratna Kapur, 'De-Radicalising the Rights Claims of Sexual Subalterns through "Tolerance"' in Robert Leckey and Kim Brooks (eds), *Queer Theory: Law, Culture, Empire* (Routledge, 2010) 37, 39.

38 Ibid.

39 Maura I Strassberg, 'Distinctions of Form or Substance: Monogamy, Polygamy and Same-Sex Marriage' (1997) 75 *North Carolina Law Review* 1501, 1577.

40 Defense of Marriage Act, Pub L No 104–199, 110 Stat 2419 (1996) 1 USC § 7, 28 USC § 1738C 28, later struck down by the Supreme Court in *US v Windsor* (133 S Ct, 26 June 2013) slip op 2675, 2682–4.

41 Jesse Helms, 142 *Congressional Record* S10068 (daily ed, 9 September 1996), quoted in David L Chambers, 'Polygamy and Same-Sex Marriage' (1997) 26 *Hofstra Law Review* 53, 56.

The DOMA stipulated that marriage was the union of one man and one woman. Adopted by an overwhelming majority of both houses of Congress, it took the unprecedented step of overriding many aspects of American states' powers to regulate marriage – a step that was justified in defence of the nation.[42]

In France, the explosion of opposition to the 1998 bill seeking to recognise same-sex civil partnerships[43] focused on the threat to national culture that would be presented by legally recognised gay couples having children.[44] The bill was eventually adopted, but only after heterosexual (and patriarchal) kinship relations had been protected by banning same-sex couples from adopting children and accessing reproductive technologies.[45] In the subsequent same-sex marriage debates in France, gay men were again depicted as a 'menace to the nation' because they procure foreign surrogates (bypassing French law) and so contaminate the French polity with racially diverse babies.[46] Despite this fear-mongering, same-sex marriage legislation was adopted in 2013,[47] which also allowed same-sex married couples to jointly adopt children, although it pointedly did not extend state aid to help same-sex couples procreate.[48]

Well before same-sex marriage became a battleground, queer sexualities were considered antithetical to the nation. In the West, state efforts to dehumanise and even eradicate sexual dissidents are legion. The common law of England defined the crime of sodomy broadly as the abominable and detestable 'crime against nature', which was, like treason, punished by death.[49] In Europe, homophobic zeal reached its zenith during the Third Reich, when homosexuals were among the 'degenerates' slated for extermination. Heinrich Himmler argued that ties between homosexuals (like Jews) were stronger than their loyalty to the state.[50] On the discovery by his secret police that homosexuals were present in every government and party office, he feared that gay men would hire other gay men when positions

42 Chambers, above n 41, 53, 76.

43 Loi n°99-944 du 15 novembre 1999 relative au pacte civil de solidarité (France) JO, 16 November 1999. The 'pacts of civil solidarity' (PACS) legislation provided civil partnership recognition for any two individuals who organise their lives jointly, regardless of sexual orientation.

44 Butler, above n 22, 110.

45 Ibid.

46 Michael J Bosia, 'Strange Fruit: Homophobia, the State, and the Politics of LGBT Rights and Capabilities' (2014) 13 *Journal of Human Rights* 256, 257.

47 Loi n° 2013-404 du 17 mai 2013 ouvrant le mariage aux couples de personnes de même sexe (France) JO, 18 May 2013.

48 Steven Erlanger, 'Hollande Signs French Gay Marriage Law', *The New York Times* (19 May 2013).

49 William Blackstone, *Commentaries on the Laws of England* (Robert Bell, 1st edn, 1772) bk 4, ch 15, s 4.

50 Geoffrey J Giles, 'The Institutionalization of Homosexual Panic in the Third Reich' in Robert Gellately and Nathan Stoltzfus (eds), *Social Outsiders in Nazi Germany* (Princeton University Press, 2001) 233, 239.

became vacant, and thus that gay cliques would eventually run whole areas of government, destabilising the state.[51]

In an unnervingly similar vein, since the strengthening of Russian laws in 2013 banning 'gay propaganda',[52] the state news media has 'worked hard to portray gay activists as traitors doing the work of foreign powers [meaning particularly the US – perhaps also Sweden?] to undermine the Russian state'.[53] A trial judge sentenced members of the feminist punk rock band Pussy Riot, under earlier legislation, to long terms of imprisonment for questioning Russian democracy, homophobia and gender conformity. He described their protest as 'shatter[ing] the constitutional foundations of the state'.[54] This kind of alarm about gender and sexual non-conformity helped justify the strengthening of Russia's anti-propaganda laws. Even women's crisis centres have now been caught in the legislation's broad net of menacing sexual and gender deviancy, threatening their access to 'foreign' funding.[55]

The heated UN debates over the last decade, about recognising the marginalisation and violence experienced by sexual and gender minorities as human rights violations, have also relied heavily on heterosexualised tropes of the normal nation-state. A solid block of states from the global South, consisting of most African and Caribbean countries and members of the Organisation of Islamic Conference (OIC) (joined often by the Vatican, apparently oblivious to its own queerness), has presented formidable opposition to the idea that such minorities might exist outside the West.[56] They have reflected back the colonial paradigm of sexual degeneracy as a 'white man's disease'[57] and accused the West of imposing their 'perceived cultural superiority'.[58] On the other hand, Western and Latin American states have been eager to display their liberal sexual credentials by advocating for the recognition of GLBTI rights, emphasising the universality of human

51 Ibid.
52 Miriam Elder, 'Russia Passes Law Banning Gay "Propaganda"', *The Guardian* (online) (12 June 2013) <https://www.theguardian.com/world/2013/jun/11/russia-law-banning-gay-propaganda>.
53 Ivan Nechepurenko, 'Russian Newspaper's Scoop? Based on Fake Letters, US Says', *The New York Times* (21 November 2015).
54 Janet Elise Johnson and Aino Saarinen, 'Twenty-First-Century Feminisms under Repression: Gender Regime Change and the Women's Crisis Center Movement in Russia' (2013) 38 *Signs: Journal of Women in Culture and Society* 543, 562.
55 Ibid. The new law requires NGOs receiving foreign funding to register as 'foreign agents'.
56 Dianne Otto, 'Transnational Homo-Assemblages: Reading "Gender" in Counter-Terrorism Discourses' (2013) 4(2) *Jindal Global Law Review* 79.
57 Oliver Phillips, 'Zimbabwean Law and the Production of a White Man's Disease' (1997) 6 *Social & Legal Studies* 471.
58 See, eg, Egypt introducing amendments to draft SOGI resolution UN Doc A/HRC/27/L.27/Rev.1: Human Rights Council, Report of the Human Rights Council on its Twenty-Seventh Session, 27th sess, Agenda Item 1, UN Doc A/HRC/27/2 (22 December 2014).

rights norms and obligations.[59] As Michael Bosia points out, the speeches in these debates can all be read as states articulating a purposeful and often innovative homophobia to serve their own interests, rather than responding to GLBTI rights claims.[60] He argues that many states use queer identities as 'ready-made bogeymen', creating sexual panics which divert attention from the pressures of globalisation and demands from their own populations for increased opportunities and freedoms,[61] a theme to which I return in the next section.

I agree that states that present themselves as gay-friendly also have a homophobic agenda.[62] Their goal is to domesticate (civilise) queer expressions and communities of desire by granting them normalising rights. Domestication buttresses GLBTI loyalties to the nation-state and encourages responsible reproductive practices, minimising the potential for alternative arrangements, outside state control, which may disrupt their national projects.[63] Lisa Duggan has described this as the 'sexual politics of neoliberalism' or the 'new homonormativity'.[64] As she argues, this frustrates the democratic potential of sexual dissidence by extending familial rights and privileges to those who model their relationships on the heterosexual, monogamous, reproductive norm. Jasbir Puar has aptly described this process as 'biopolitical reorientation',[65] whereby the quid pro quo for admission into the heterosexual institutions of the nation is to abandon queer and feminist critiques of the monogamous heteronormative family.[66] The granting of rights can de-radicalise a movement, and patriotism can demand abandonment of queer curiosity.[67]

It is not, as commonly believed, that marriage in the West (and elsewhere) has shifted from its pre-modern incarnation of serving to consolidate alliances between men or lines of descent and protect male property interests, to becoming a matter of individual freedom and choice. Rather, disguised as individual choice, the privileging of dyadic heteronormative marriage, and its gradual extension to same-sex couples, provides a powerful means of instituting primary loyalty to the modern nation-state,[68] helping to make territorial sovereignty and state

59 See, eg, Human Rights Council, 'Joint Statement on Human Rights, Sexual Orientation and Gender Identity – Delivered by Argentina on Behalf of 66 States' (18 December 2008) <http://arc-international.net/global-advocacy/sogi-statements/2008-joint-statement/>.

60 Bosia, above n 46.

61 Ibid 266.

62 Otto, above n 56.

63 Butler, above n 22, 104.

64 Lisa Duggan, 'The New Homonormativity: The Sexual Politics of Neoliberalism' in Russ Castronovo and Dana D Nelson (eds), *Materialising Democracy: Towards a Revitalised Cultural Politics* (Duke University Press, 2002) 175, 190.

65 Puar, above n 6, 211.

66 Margaret Denike, 'What's Queer about Polygamy?' in Robert Leckey and Kim Brooks (eds), *Queer Theory: Law, Culture, Empire* (Routledge, 2010) 137, 145.

67 See also Dianne Otto at 'Introduction: Embracing queer curiosity', this volume.

68 Butler, above n 22, 103; Hoad, above n 31, 139.

governance possible in chaotic times. Heterosexual (presumed biological) kinship arrangements are thus constitutive of the modern nation-state and, it follows, of the 'normal' system of state-centred international law. It underpins a system of human (dis)connectedness that is endangering us all.

The border protection strategies of the normal nation-state

The broader context in which these contestations and (re)alignments over sexuality are taking place is the increasing precarity of the nation-state itself, due largely to global developments, in which it may nevertheless be implicated. More familiar threats, like the fear of Russian expansionism that prompted the Singing Sailor invitation and civil conflicts spilling into neighbouring states, have been eclipsed by the devastating effects of neoliberal economic globalisation which has created a vast underclass of people living precarious lives. The borders of nation-states have become increasingly porous, in the face of increased demands for cheap labour mobility and ever-larger flows of desperate (and hopeful) people seeking economic opportunities while also often fleeing intractable conflicts and environmental disasters. At the same time, fears about international terrorism have skyrocketed, fanned by perversely sexualised and racialised bigotry, as has anxiety about transnational criminal networks trafficking people as well as weapons, drugs, diamonds, ivory and all manner of contraband. While the movement of people and goods across borders has always been highly regulated, involving immigration and customs officials, border police, military back-up and extensive technological systems of international cooperation, border security has now, in national imaginaries, reached crisis point.

Control of borders, and thus of defined territory, is another of the key attributes of statehood. Borders are an important marker of the limits of domestic jurisdiction and governmental power, although the jurisdiction of states extends extra-territorially where they exercise 'effective control'.[69] In recent years, we have seen states take unprecedented measures to secure their borders, primarily by employing the kind of aggressive shows of force that SPAS, WILPF and other peace groups oppose. Many of these measures are in violation of international legal obligations. This includes breaching the sovereignty of neighbouring states, using force arbitrarily, denying due process to many of those attempting to cross, *refoulment* of refugees and asylum seekers, extrajudicial executions, indefinite detention, and the use of torture and other forms of cruel, inhuman and degrading treatment. Borders have, in many instances, become zones of state lawlessness. The 'frenzied' wall-building that has accompanied these developments[70] spectacularly symbolises the sense of crisis for the nation. At the same time, the spectacle provides some

69 See, eg, Human Rights Committee, General Comment No 31: The Nature of the General Legal Obligation Imposed on States Parties to the Covenant, 80th sess, UN Doc CCPR/C/21/Rev.1/Add. 13 (26 May 2004).

70 Wendy Brown, *Walled States, Waning Sovereignty* (Zone Books, 2010) 8.

measure of reassurance that the imagined community of the nation-state can be protected from menacing outsiders.

While not a new technique of border security, never before have walls proliferated in such numbers.[71] There are currently almost 70 border walls.[72] They project the image of fortress nation-states determined to impose order in a world of uncertainty and chaos produced by terrorism, criminal networks and amorphous globalisation. The displays of impregnability also serve to deny our global interdependence. The main enthusiasts for projecting sovereign power in this way include the United States, Israel, India, Saudi Arabia, Morocco, Turkey, Uzbekistan, Turkmenistan, Kenya, Botswana, Egypt, China and North Korea.[73] Walls are also increasingly commonplace in Europe, at its perimeters as well as within its Schengen free-travel zone.[74] Yet there is little proof that militarisation and walling are effective as a means of border security. Instead of acting as a deterrent, there is a great deal of evidence that they simply make crossing borders more perilous. Clearly undeterred, millions of people continue to cross borders as 'irregular' migrants. According to the International Organisation on Migration, in the first half of 2016 alone, over 3,700 people had gone missing or died in the process.[75]

So how has the increasingly lawless securitisation of borders been justified in a post-Cold War world that celebrated the fall of the Berlin Wall less than three decades ago? Here, again, the analytics of sexuality have played an important role in stoking the fear and panic that has manufactured public support. Recall that those directly responsible for the 9/11 atrocities were cast as sexually dubious by reports in the West of their apparent preference for masculine company while on earth, and their hopes for reward in the form of eternal access to virgins in the afterlife.[76] Ever since, the intonation of sexual perversity has assisted the Western project of denigrating Islam and demonising its adherents, casting a pall of suspicion and fear of contagion. These sexualised tropes have helped fuel the panic that has made walls, and the lawlessness and death that they foster, seem both necessary and desirable. As Puar contends, the 'invocation of the terrorist as a queer, nonnational, racially perverse other [became] part of the normative script

71 Barbara Tasch, 'The Number of Border Walls around the World More than Quadrupled in 25 Years – Here's Why', *Business Insider Australia* (online) (15 November 2016) <http://www.businessinsider.com.au/more-border-walls-around-world-2016-11>.

72 Ibid.

73 Brown, above n 70, 8–19.

74 Matthew Holehouse and Isabelle Fraser, 'Migrant Crisis: European Council President Tusk Warns Schengen on Brink of Collapse', *The Telegraph* (online) (23 November 2016) <http://www.telegraph.co.uk/news/worldnews/europe/eu/11991098/Migrant-crisis-Donald-Tusk-warns-that-Schengen-is-on-brink-of-collapse-latest-news.html>.

75 IOM's Global Migration Data Analysis Centre, 'Dangerous Journeys – International Migration Increasingly Unsafe in 2016' (2016) (4) *Data Briefing Series* 1 <https://missingmigrants.iom.int/sites/default/files/gmdac_data_briefing_series_issue4.pdf>.

76 Anna M Agathangelou, 'Power, Borders, Security, Wealth: Lessons of Violence and Desire from September 11' (2004) 48 *International Studies Quarterly* 517, 530.

of the US war on terror'.[77] This undertone of erotic depravity also helped then US President Bush to declare the advent of a 'different kind of conflict against a different kind of enemy' in 2001,[78] a manoeuvre that simultaneously released him from the need to comply with existing law and signalled the necessity of different law(lessness) to deal with the new emergency of endless war. The idea of perpetual conflict has since been buttressed by the proliferation of border walls and their sense of permanency.

Also compounding the nervousness about security and undocumented (perverse, racialised and potentially terrorist) migration, and helping to justify extreme border protection measures in defence of the nation, is the spike in anti-trafficking crusades, driven largely by the United States.[79] These crusades rely heavily on traditional narratives of innocent and helpless Third World women, unable to exercise free will, needing to be rescued from the sexual depravity and exploitation of (foreign) traffickers, and even sometimes their own (backward) families.[80] The anxiety induced by these images has enabled states to adopt draconian laws that impose harsh criminal penalties on supposed traffickers as well as, in many cases, on their purported victims;[81] laws which are then applied more generally. These laws have, in turn, justified states devoting substantially increased financial and administrative resources to border surveillance, security police and detention facilities, all cloaked in a 'mantle of righteousness'[82] that claims to be protecting defenceless women and children. In fact, these efforts have made matters worse for many women, who see themselves as economic migrants, but are treated as victims of trafficking.

Outside the reassuring boundaries of state-based affiliation, any man can be a sexually deviant terrorist or trafficker, any woman – especially if she wears a veil – can be a supporter and/or reproducer of terrorists, and any person who defies the heteronormative order in other ways, such as sex workers and queers, can potentially contaminate national loyalties and heteronormative purity. These sexually charged figurations of threatening outsiders utilise sexuality productively, in the Foucauldian sense of instrumentalising it as a transfer point of power. As Gayle Rubin describes this process, sexual acts are burdened 'with an excess of significance' making them available to 'function as signifiers for personal and social

77 Puar, above n 6, 37.

78 'Radio Address of the President to the Nation' (15 September 2001) The White House: President George W Bush <https://georgewbush-whitehouse.archives.gov/news/releases/2001/09/20010915.html>.

79 Janie Chuang, 'The United States as Global Sheriff: Using Unilateral Sanctions to Combat Human Trafficking' (2005–6) 27 *Michigan Journal of International Law* 437.

80 Jayashri Srikantiah, 'Perfect Victims and Real Survivors: The Iconic Victim in Domestic Human Trafficking Laws' (2007) 87 *Buffalo University Law Review* 157, 191–5.

81 Janie A Chuang, 'Exploitation Creep and the Unmaking of Human Trafficking Law' (2014) 108 *American Journal of International Law* 609.

82 Karen E Bravo, 'Exploring the Analogy: Modern Trafficking in Humans and the Trans-Atlantic Slave Trade' (2007) 25 *Boston University International Law Journal* 207.

apprehensions to which they have no intrinsic connection'.[83] The mystification of sexuality, at least in Western societies, she says, makes sex a productive site for the generation of 'rage, anxiety, and sheer terror' which, in turn, enables the state to enact new laws and regulations that extend its control even more deeply into our intimate lives.[84] With regard to border protection, the image of the sexually perverse migrant, in its many avatars,[85] has helped to fuel the panic and fear that has justified otherwise unthinkable restrictions on individual rights and freedoms, the otherwise indefensible militarisation of borders, and an otherwise inconceivable wall-building frenzy. In the process, attention is diverted from the 'real' crises of the systemic injustices of neoliberal economics, the burgeoning global trade in arms and military equipment, escalating environmental destruction and the resurgence of xenophobia, racism, misogyny and homophobia as national values.

It is therefore not coincidental that we have seen the intensification of militarised empire at the same time as gay 'victories' – like the legalisation of same-sex marriage – are being celebrated, at least in some parts of the world. They are both measures designed to fortify the power and autonomy of the nation-state. From within, this fortification is advanced by either redrawing or reinforcing their heteronormative 'internal frontiers'[86] with displays of either sexual liberality or conservatism. On the border, efforts to restore confidence in the idea of national unity, purity and transmissibility take the form of heightened securitisation which (ostensibly) will protect the nation from deviant intrusions. The technologies of same-sex marriage (or opposition to it) and walling states are both strategies aimed at rejuvenating the nation, in the face of the uncertainties and disruptions of the neoliberal present. Both technologies engage what Cynthia Weber describes as the 'sexualised orders of international relations',[87] produced through particular encodings of genders and sexualities that shore up, privilege and naturalise the nation-state as the primary locus of identity, community, security and well-being. As a consequence, the failures of the state-based international economic, legal and political order are occluded, critique is branded as disloyalty, even treasonous, and alternative imaginings of kinship and belonging become unthinkable. International law and global politics remain firmly anchored in militaristic, heteronormative, national imaginaries, in which other hierarchies of inequity are also securely sedimented.

83 Gayle Rubin, 'Thinking Sex: Notes for a Radical Theory of the Politics of Sexuality' in Carole S Vance (ed), *Pleasure and Danger: Exploring Female Sexuality* (Routledge, 1984) 267, 297.

84 Ibid 279.

85 See also Ratna Kapur, *Makeshift Migrants and Law: Gender, Belonging and Postcolonial Anxieties* (Routledge, 2010).

86 Stoler, above n 28, 7.

87 Cynthia Weber, *Queer International Relations: Sovereignty, Sexuality and the Will to Knowledge* (Oxford University Press, 2016) 22.

Non-state queer relational imaginaries: Thinking in new ways about border protection

State-authorised heteronormative kinship ties hardly exhaust the field of life-affirming and life-sustaining relational connections. If we release kinship from the fixed, presumptively biological parameters enforced by the nation-state, and embrace Butler's understanding of kinship 'as a set of practices that institutes relationships of various kinds which negotiate the reproduction of life and the demands of death',[88] we start to see how it can be 'self-consciously assembled from a multiplicity of possible bits and pieces'.[89] Indeed, many forms of heterosexual parenthood already rely on social rather than biological connection. In the context of 'queer *non*-biokinship',[90] the technologies of adoption, surrogacy, donor insemination, other forms of reproductive assistance and various parenting arrangements between gay men, lesbians, non-sex-specific and transgender people have produced many more filial relations that are not based on biological connections or confined to only two parents. Many others have committed themselves to bringing their children up queerly, often against great odds.[91] Despite this, the emerging legal language of queer parenting remains mired in a heteronormative script.[92]

However, even these alternative family arrangements do not exhaust the possibilities. Around the world, queer communities, whether or not they are publicly visible, are founded on alternative kinship ties that, as Butler observes:

> constitute a 'break-down' of traditional kinship that not only displaces the central place of biological and sexual relations from its definition but gives sexuality a separate domain from that of kinship, which allows for the durable tie to be thought outside the conjugal frame and thus opens kinship to a set of community ties that are irreducible to family.[93]

Kinship possibilities are multiplicitous, and not necessarily dependent on the state for recognition and rights in order to engender a sense of belonging and self-worth.

Many queer people have self-consciously set about building alternative communities, based on non-reproductive kinship ties, thereby seeking to diffuse the

88 Butler, above n 22, 102–3.

89 Ibid 126, quoting Sarah Franklin and Susan McKinnon, 'New Directions in Kinship Study: A Core Concept Revisited' (2000) 41 *Current Anthropology* 275.

90 Stu Marvel, 'Polymorphous Reproductivity and the Critique of Futurity: Toward a Queer Legal Analytic for Fertility Law' (2013) 2(4) *Jindal Global Law Review* 298, 305.

91 Eve Kosofsky Sedgwick, 'How to Bring Your Kids Up Gay: The War on Effeminate Boys' in Steven Bruhm and Natasha Hurley (eds), *Curioser: On the Queerness of Children* (University of Minnesota Press, 2004) 139.

92 See Anniken Sørlie at chapter 9, 'Governing (trans)parenthood: The tenacious hold of biological connection and heterosexuality', this volume.

93 Butler, above n 22, 127.

nation or at least reduce its hold on their loyalties and lives. They have sought to establish relations of care, intimacy, pleasure, shared values, self-esteem, economic interdependence, community obligation and public visibility, recognising diverse sexual and intimate relations, and non-binary expressions of gender, as worthy of respect, affirmation, protection and celebration. Many of these communities have also explicitly sought to challenge other exclusionary practices that anchor nation-states, like hierarchies of class, race, religion and ethnicity. They are characteristically urban communities, readily visible in cosmopolitan cities like Buenos Aires, Cape Town, London, Manila, New York, Rio de Janeiro, Shanghai, Sydney, Taipei, Tel Aviv and Tokyo. These communities have 'cultivated unprecedented kinds of commonality, intimacy, and public life'.[94] They also include long-established, although stigmatised, *hijra* communities spread across South Asia,[95] *kathoey* (third gender) communities in Thailand,[96] and relatively recent formations like the sister-girl and brother-boy networks of support in Australian indigenous communities.[97] Many of these queer kinship communities are transnational, like the 'underground railway' between queer communities in Kampala and Paris that provides safe passage for Ugandan activists,[98] the members of the NGO Proud Lebanon that have welcomed queer refugees from Syria into the relative safety of their community,[99] and the bonds of solidarity and support between Palestinians and anti-occupation Jewish queers to which I alluded earlier.[100]

In the past, active resistance to state regulation of sexuality was the hallmark of many queer communities in the West. Michael Warner describes the resistance that was at the heart of gay and lesbian politics in the United States until the 1990s (when same-sex marriage started to dominate the gay political agenda)

94 Michael Warner, 'Beyond Gay Marriage' in Wendy Brown and Janet Halley (eds), *Left Legalism/Left Critique* (Duke University Press, 2002) 259, 264.

95 Dredge Byung'chu Käng-Nguyễn, 'The Search for Intelligible Life in the Genderqueer Imaginary: Conceptualizing Transgenderism Independent of Homosexuality' in *The 1st Annual International Graduate Research Conference on Social Sciences and Humanities, Theme 'Harmony in Diversity', 2–3 April 2009, Bangkok, Thailand* (Proceedings of the Conference, Faculty of Social Sciences and Humanities, Mahidol University, 2009) 248, 258 <http://citeseerx.ist.psu.edu/viewdoc/download?doi=10.1.1.454.7359&rep=rep1&type=pdf#page=58>.

96 Ladda Waiyawan and Penchan Sherer, 'Sexuality and Sexual Discourses of *Katheoy*: Living with HIV/ AIDS in I-Saan' in *The 1st Annual International Graduate Research Conference on Social Sciences and Humanities, Theme 'Harmony in Diversity', 2–3 April 2009, Bangkok, Thailand* (Proceedings of the Conference, Faculty of Social Sciences and Humanities, Mahidol University, 2009) 57, 59.

97 Crystal Johnson, 'Napanangka: The True Power of Being Proud' in Hodge (ed), above n 30, 21; Brie Ngala Curtis, 'Kungakunga: Staying Close to Family and Country' in Hodge (ed), above n 30, 35.

98 Bosia, above n 46, 262.

99 James Longman, 'Gay Community Hit Hard by Middle East Turmoil', *BBC News* (online) (29 October 2014) <http://www.bbc.com/news/world-middle-east-29628281>.

100 Schulman, above n 13.

as emanating from an 'ethical vision of queer politics'.[101] Among the principles that this ethical vision rested upon was alertness to the 'invidiousness' of the institution of marriage and other state-regulated institutions, which are 'designed both to reward those inside it and discipline those outside it'.[102] In his list of those rendered 'queer' by marriage law, Warner includes 'adulterers, prostitutes, divorcees, the promiscuous, single people, unwed parents, [and] those below the age of consent'.[103] Warner's catalogue is reminiscent of Rubin's earlier mapping of sexual hierarchy in the United States, maintained by a broader set of laws, which she describes as establishing a 'charmed circle' of 'good' heteronormative, reproductive, vanilla sexuality, and locating 'bad' sexuality at the 'outer limits'.[104] These American catalogues resonate with Kapur's identification of sexual subalterns in the contemporary Indian context, which includes '*kush*, queer, *hijra*, *kothis*, *panthis*'[105] and others who are tarred with threatening Indian culture and nationhood, like sex workers, homosexuals and lesbians.[106] Being inclusive of demonised sexual communities, who are excluded from the charmed circle, was fundamental to earlier queer politics in the West, which refused to accord legitimacy to only some forms of consensual sex. In 1972, for example, the US National Coalition of Gay Organizations called for the 'extension of the legal benefits of marriage [not marriage itself] to all persons who cohabit regardless of sex or numbers'.[107]

Much changed with the end of the Cold War and the dramatic rise of neoliberal economic globalisation. The emerging homonormative agenda of Western and Latin American states, which extended the circumference of the charmed circle to include same-sex de facto and marital unions, has splintered many queer communities. The effect has been to weaken relational ties that rested on radical sexual politics, alternative relational economies and communities unbound from the nation-state. Some of the earlier inclusivity of queer communities has been blunted by the lure of respectability that comes with legal recognition and human rights. Inadvertently – sometimes purposefully – many GLBTI activists have given credence to nationalist evolutionary discourses by portraying same-sex marriage as the high water-mark of 'civilisation'.[108] Western-domesticated sexual identities have been projected by some advocates as universal, thereby stigmatising, disqualifying and silencing resistive Western and non-Western practices and

101 Warner, above n 94, 264.
102 Ibid 264–5.
103 Ibid 265.
104 Rubin, above n 83, 281.
105 Kapur, above n 37, 39.
106 Ibid 69–87.
107 Warner, above n 94, 265.
108 See, eg, William N Eskridge, *The Case for Same-Sex Marriage: From Sexual Liberty to Civilized Commitment* (Free Press, 1996); and Robert Wintemute, 'From "Sex Rights" to "Love Rights": Partnership Rights as Human Rights' in Nicholas Bamforth (ed), *Sex Rights: The Oxford Amnesty Lectures 2002* (Oxford University Press, 2005).

expressions of community and desire.[109] While the recognition of same-sex marriage means that some former deviants have been welcomed into the nation-state's charmed circle of good sexuality, the demonisation of those who remain on the outer limits has intensified.

Yet there are also those in queer communities who remain committed to radical sexual politics and to forging relational ties with all those living precariously on the outer limits, not just sexual and gender outsiders. Some bonds of queer relationality have been strengthened and extended in reaction to the exclusionary effects of the new respectabilities.[110] There is so much more to be done. As Lisa Duggan argues, the neoliberal 'recoding' of some of the key aspirations of queer movements – equality, freedom and the right to privacy – needs to be actively resisted.[111] The struggle to invest rights with emancipatory grammars that help to articulate a world in which justice is possible must continue.[112] And, as SPAS urges through the device of the Singing Sailor, we need to utilise our transnational relational ties to think beyond imagined communities of nationality that rely on militarism and walls to deliver security. The neon message of gay solidarity points to the possibility that alternative kinship practices suggest non-violent methods of border protection, or may end the need for border 'protection' altogether.

Hannah Arendt's powerful critique of the devastation wreaked by nationalist states asks whether there are other modes of belonging that can be 'rigorously non-nationalistic'.[113] Like Butler, I think we should understand Arendt's question as 'an inducement, an incitement, a solicitation', as 'part of the discursive process of beginning something new'.[114] Queer communities suggest some contours of non-nationalistic modes of belonging, starting with the incitement that it is non-reproductive kinship ties that give communities the desire to be diverse, resistive and inclusive. Further, at the heart of practices of queer belonging is the inclusion of sexual and gender 'outcasts' – a variable grouping of those excluded from the charmed circle of normative sex and relationships. Queer kinship engages dynamic ties based on what Duggan describes as the 'democratic potential of

109 Joseph Massad, 'Re-Orienting Desire: The Gay International and the Arab World' (2002) 14 *Public Culture* 361.

110 Karma R Chávez, Ryan Conrad and Yasmir Nair for Against Equality, 'Against Equality, Against Inclusion' in Sandeep Bakshi, Suhraiya Jivraj and Silvia Posocco (eds), *Decolonizing Sexualities: Transnational Perspectives, Critical Interventions* (Counterpress, 2016) 215. See also 'Against Equality: Queer Challenges to the Politics of Inclusion' (online archive) <http://www.againstequality.org/>.

111 Duggan, above n 64, 190.

112 Wendy Brown, 'Suffering Rights as Paradoxes' (2000) 7 *Constellations* 230, 240.

113 Judith Butler and Gayatri Chakravorty Spivak, *Who Sings the Nation-State? Language, Politics, Belonging* (Seagull Books, 2010) 49, discussing Hannah Arendt, 'The Decline of the Nation State and the End of the Rights of Man' in *The Origins of Totalitarianism* (Harcourt, 1994) 267.

114 Ibid 55.

sexual [and gender] dissidence',[115] Warner as an 'ethical vision of queer politics'[116] and Gayatri Spivak as 'persistent critique'.[117] They are ties that refuse to be walled in by national loyalties, and refuse to accept the civilisational hierarchies, inequitable distributional arrangements and militaristic geopolitics that structure the international community of states.

So what do queer kinship practices offer to border protection strategies? This leads me first to a prior question, posed by Spivak, which is to ask what part of the state remains useful?[118] Her answer, which I read as queer, is that we need the state to be an 'instrument of redistribution'.[119] Indeed, one of the aspirations of the SPAS action was to promote the redistribution of military resources to development. We also need the state to hold onto and strengthen, but not control or homogenise, the public spheres of politics – local, national, transnational, regional and global – without which we are reduced to 'bare life'.[120] Both the redistributive and democratic aspects of the state have been severely eroded, if not destroyed, by the global spread of neoliberal economics which demand a minimal state in the sense of political engagement and distributional justice, and a strengthened state with regard to militarised security. As Butler proposes, we need to find ways to open up an analytics of power that would include sovereignty as one of its features, but would also be able to talk about the kinds of mobilisations and containments of populations that are not conceptualisable as the acts of a sovereign, and which proceed through different operations of state power.[121] That is, we need to reimagine the state in a way that is not built on national loyalties. Instead, we should expect it to be an entity that emerges from modes of belonging which resist and escape state regulatory power and refuse all hierarchies of human worth. It is everyone's responsibility to foster everyday practices of inclusion, freedom and equality in our communities, however they are defined and wherever they are located.

Having reimagined the state as in some respects an ally, rather than an adversary in all respects, the question of reimagining border security becomes more thinkable. We can start to reconceive the border as a site that is 'regulated' for queer purposes – to 'smash' the charmed circle and recognise durable kinship ties based on diverse relational practices and community ties that do not conform to the conjugal family; to further the redistributive efforts of the state by welcoming crossings by those most disadvantaged by global analytics of power; and to refuse 'falling back on territorial defence, conscription and rearmament' and walled fortifications. Instead, border 'security' should rely on enriched critical thinking

115 Duggan, above n 64, 63.
116 Warner, above n 94, 264.
117 Butler and Spivak, above n 113, 108.
118 Ibid 80.
119 Ibid 98.
120 Giorgio Agamben, *Homo Sacer: Sovereign Power and Bare Life* (Daniel Heller-Roazen trans, Stanford University Press, 1998).
121 Butler and Spivak, above n 113, 102.

and engaged political discussion which enable its negotiation peacefully and cooperatively. This is not cosmopolitanism in an abstract sense, but as affective, embodied and material human connectedness.

The paradoxes facing queer efforts to change meanings, unsettle taxonomies and invert conventions in international law and politics present many challenges. As Butler observes, we need the 'thinkability' of human lives for politics, yet nation-states set the terms of that thinkability.[122] This makes engagement with politics an endeavour that risks reaffirming state regulatory power. Further, as queer relationalities extend across national boundaries, challenging the state's control of kinship arrangements and displacing the primacy of national loyalty, they become entangled in imperial histories of racial hierarchy and exploitation. And as queer communities become more visible and more adept at providing safety and affirmation, they risk commodification and commercialisation as a central feature of neoliberal urban governance. Despite these difficulties, we need to value queer curiosity, and the critical thinking that it enables, and continue the struggle to build queer kinship networks in and beyond the nation-state. Queer communities give voice and substance to emancipatory imaginaries of community and life that will one day release us from the militaristic, inequitable and anti-democratic grip of national loyalty and carceral modes of defence and security.

Conclusion

The nation-state is made possible by the powerful personal and cultural feeling of national belonging which, as I have argued, is founded on heteronormative kinship ties, now extended by some states to include same-sex filial relations. These state-regulated family arrangements instil and naturalise primary loyalty to the nation-state. Relational ties that invoke human solidarities that are inconsistent with the national story of belonging are demonised, criminalised or pathologised. Sexuality and gender non-conformity are particularly amenable to this type of instrumentalisation. The danger of these arrangements lies in the enormous power of the state to serve elite and inequitable neoliberal interests in the name of the nation, and foreclose or devalue other imaginaries of human kinship and connection. Newly domesticated queer bodies help to reinforce nationalist projects and reduce the space for living and imagining alternatives.

In the current global conjuncture, the continued primacy of state interests and loyalties is endangering us all. Global warming continues, a new arms race is underway, right-wing bigotry and hatred is spreading, states of emergency have become commonplace, the flows of people fleeing conflicts, environmental degradation, poverty, persecution and terror are endless, and market demands are threatening what remains of democratic governance. Border protection has become more brutal and lawless, as states take unprecedented measures, including

122 Butler, above n 22, 106.

the construction of more and more walls, to assert their sovereignty and ensure that it is understood that we are divided and separated along national lines.

We urgently need to reshape border protection strategies and shift military resources into transformative development 'that works for everyone'. Communities based on queer kinship ties offer us hope that human solidarities and loyalties can break free of the bonds of the nation-state and extend to include others, particularly those most disadvantaged by the brutal heteronormative ordering that states impose. We need to foster and value transnational queer assemblages of human belonging that are much harder to colonise and domesticate than their nationalist counterparts.

Bibliography

Agamben, Giorgio, *Homo Sacer: Sovereign Power and Bare Life* (Daniel Heller-Roazen trans, Stanford University Press, 1998)

Agathangelou, Anna M, 'Power, Borders, Security, Wealth: Lessons of Violence and Desire from September 11' (2004) 48 *International Studies Quarterly* 517

Ahmed, Sara, *The Promise of Happiness* (Duke University Press, 2010)

Alldred, Pam, 'No Borders, No Nations, No Deportations' (2003) 73 *Feminist Review* 152

Alter, Robert, 'Sodom as Nexus: The Web of Design in Biblical Narrative' in Jonathan Goldberg (ed), *Reclaiming Sodom* (Routledge, 1994) 28

Amutabi, Maurice and Mary Lutta-Mukhebi, 'Gender and Mining in Kenya: The Case of Mukibira Mines in Vihiga District' (2001) 1(2) *Jenda: A Journal of Culture and Women Studies* 1

Anderson, Benedict, *Imagined Communities: Reflections on the Origin and Spread of Nationalism* (Verso, revised edn, 1991)

Anderson, Bridget, Nandita Sharma and Cynthia Wright, 'Editorial: Why No Borders?' (2009) 26(2) *Refuge* 5

———, '"We Are All Foreigners" No Borders as a Practical Political Project' in Peter Nyers and Kim Rygiel (eds), *Citizenship, Migrant Activism and the Politics of Movement* (Taylor & Francis, 2012) 73

Anghie, Antony, 'Francisco de Vitoria and the Colonial Origins of International Law' (1996) 5 *Social & Legal Studies* 321

Anzaldúa, Gloria, *Borderlands/La Frontera: The New Mestiza* (Aunt Lute Books, 1987)

Aquinas, Thomas, *The Summa Theologiae* (Fathers of the English Dominican Province trans, Benziger Brothers, 1974)

Arendt, Hannah, *On Violence* (Harcourt, 1970)

Arondekar, Anjali and Geeta Patel, 'Area Impossible: Notes Toward an Introduction' (2016) 22 *GLQ: A Journal of Lesbian and Gay Studies* 151

Atwan, Abdel Bari, *Islamic State: The Digital Caliphate* (Saqi, 2015)

Bader, Veit, 'Fairly Open Borders' in Veit Bader (ed), *Citizenship and Exclusion* (St Martin's Press, 1997) 28

Bailey, Derick Sherwin, *Homosexuality and the Western Christian Tradition* (Longmans, 1955)

Baisley, Elizabeth, 'Reaching the Tipping Point?: Emerging International Human Rights Norms Pertaining to Sexual Orientation and Gender Identity' (2016) 38 *Human Rights Quarterly* 134

Balibar, Etienne, 'The Nation Form: History and Ideology' in Etienne Balibar and Immanuel Wallerstein (eds), *Race, Nation, Class: Ambiguous Identities* (Verso, 1991) 86

———, *Politics and the Other Scene* (Verso, 2002)

Barale, Aina and David M Halperin (eds), *The Lesbian and Gay Studies Reader* (Routledge, 1993) 3

Barnes, Teresa A, *'We Women Worked So Hard': Gender, Urbanization, and Social Reproduction in Colonial Harare, Zimbabwe, 1930–1956* (Heinemann, 1999)

Bauder, Harald, 'The Possibilities of Open and No Borders' (2013) 39(4) *Social Justice* 76

———, 'Perspectives of Open Borders and No Border' (2015) 9 *Geography Compass* 395

Bauman, Zygmunt, Didier Bigo, Paulo Esteves, Elspeth Guild, Vivienne Jabri, David Lyon and R B J Walker, 'After Snowden: Rethinking the Impact of Surveillance' (2014) 8 *International Political Sociology* 121

Baxter, Randolph W, '"Homo-Hunting" in the Early Cold War: Senator Kenneth Wherry and the Homophobic Side of McCarthyism' (2003) 84 *Nebraska History* 118

Beattie, Tina, 'Whose Rights, Which Rights? – The United Nations, the Vatican, Gender and Sexual and Reproductive Rights' (2014) 55 *Heythrop Journal* 1080

Beckles, Hilary McD, *Britain's Black Debt: Reparations for Caribbean Slavery and Native Genocide* (University of West Indies Press, 2013) 195

Benedict, Barbara M, *Curiosity: A Cultural History of Early Modern Inquiry* (University of Chicago Press, 2001) 2

Benhabib, Seyla, *The Rights of Others: Aliens, Residents, and Citizens* (Cambridge University Press, 2004)

Benjamin, Walter, 'Zur Kritik der Gewalt' (1921) 47 *Archiv für Sozialwissenschaft und Sozialpolitik* 809

Berger, Susan A, 'Production and Reproduction of Gender and Sexuality in Legal Discourses of Asylum in the United States' (2009) 34 *Signs* 659

Besada, Hany and Philip Martin, 'Mining Codes in Africa: Emergence of a "Fourth" Generation?' (2015) 28 *Cambridge Review of International Affairs* 263

Bhabha, Homi K, *The Location of Culture* (Routledge, 1994)

Binnie, Jon, *The Globalization of Sexuality* (Sage, 2004)

Blackstone, William, *Commentaries on the Laws of England* (Robert Bell, 1st edn, 1772)

Bob, Clifford (ed), *The International Struggle for New Human Rights* (University of Pennsylvania Press, 2009)

Bose, Brinda and Subhabrata Bhattacharyya (eds), *The Phobic and the Erotic: The Politics of Sexualities in Contemporary India* (Seagull Books, 2007)

Bosia, Michael J, 'Strange Fruit: Homophobia, the State, and the Politics of LGBT Rights and Capabilities' (2014) 13 *Journal of Human Rights* 256

Boswell, John, *Christianity, Social Tolerance, and Homosexuality: Gay People in Western Europe from the Beginning of the Christian Era to the Fourteenth Century* (University of Chicago Press, 1981)

Bravo, Karen E, 'Exploring the Analogy: Modern Trafficking in Humans and the Trans-Atlantic Slave Trade' (2007) 25 *Boston University International Law Journal* 207

Brickell, Katherine, 'Towards Intimate Geographies of Peace? Local Reconciliation of Domestic Violence in Cambodia' (2015) 40 *Transactions of the Institute of British Geographers* 321

van den Brink, Marjolein and Jet Tigchelaar, 'The Equality of the (Non) Trans-Parent: Women Who Father Children' in Marjolein van den Brink, Susanne Burri and Jenny Goldschmidt (eds), *Equality and Human Rights: Nothing but Trouble?* (SIM special, 2015) 247

Brown, Wendy, 'Suffering Rights as Paradoxes' (2000) 7 *Constellations* 230

———, *Walled States, Waning Sovereignty* (Zone Books, 2010)

Bushell, Logan, '"Give Me Your Tired, Your Poor, Your Huddled Masses" – Just as Long as They Fit in the Heteronormative Ideal: US Immigration Law's Exclusionary and Inequitable Treatment of Lesbian, Gay, Bisexual, Transgendered, and Queer Migrants' (2012) 48 *Gonzaga Law Review* 673

Butler, Judith, *Bodies that Matter: On the Discursive Limits of 'Sex'* (Routledge, 1993)

———, 'Against Proper Objects: Introduction' (1994) 6(2–3) *Differences: A Journal of Feminist Cultural Studies* 1

———, 'Is Kinship Always Already Heterosexual?' in *Undoing Gender* (Routledge, 2004) 102

———, 'Indefinite Detention' in *Precarious Life: The Powers of Mourning and Violence* (Verso, 2004) 50

———, *Precarious Life: The Powers of Mourning and Violence* (Verso, 2006)

———, *Frames of War: When is Life Grievable?* (Verso, 2010)

———, 'Violence, Nonviolence: Sartre on Fanon' in *Senses of the Subject* (Fordham University Press, 2015) 171

Butler, Judith and Gayatri Chakravorty Spivak, *Who Sings the Nation-State? Language, Politics, Belonging* (Seagull Books, 2010)

Canaday, Margot, '"Who Is a Homosexual?": The Consolidation of Sexual Identities in Mid-Twentieth-Century American Immigration Law' (2003) 28 *Law and Social Inquiry* 351

Carens, Joseph H, 'Aliens and Citizens: The Case for Open Borders' (1987) 49 *Review of Politics* 251

Carpenter, R Charli, 'Recognizing Gender-Based Violence against Civilian Men and Boys in Conflict Situations' (2006) 37 *Security Dialogue* 83

de las Casas, Bartolomé, *A Brief Account of the Destruction of the Indies* (Project Gutenberg, first published 1542, 2007 edn) <http://www.gutenberg.org/cache/epub/20321/pg20321-images.html>

Castan, Nicole, 'The Arbitration of Disputes under the *Ancien Régime*' in John Bossy (ed), *Disputes and Settlements: Law and Human Relations in the West* (Cambridge University Press, first published 1983, 2003 edn) 219

Castells, Manuel, *The Rise of the Network Society: The Information Age: Economy, Society, and Culture* (Wiley, 2nd edn, 2009) vol 1

Chambers, David L, 'Polygamy and Same-Sex Marriage' (1997) 26 *Hofstra Law Review* 53

Chang, Stewart, 'The Postcolonial Problem for Global Gay Rights' (2014) 32 *Boston University International Law Journal* 329

Chávez, Karma R, 'Identifying the Needs of LGBTQ Immigrants and Refugees in Southern Arizona' (2011) 58 *Journal of Homosexuality* 189

Chávez, Karma R, Ryan Conrad and Yasmir Nair for Against Equality, 'Against Equality, Against Inclusion' in Sandeep Bakshi, Suhraiya Jivraj and Silvia Posocco (eds), *Decolonizing Sexualities: Transnational Perspectives, Critical Interventions* (Counterpress, 2016) 215

Chuang, Janie, 'The United States as Global Sheriff: Using Unilateral Sanctions to Combat Human Trafficking' (2005–6) 27 *Michigan Journal of International Law* 437

———, 'Exploitation Creep and the Unmaking of Human Trafficking Law' (2014) 108 *American Journal of International Law* 609

Ciorciari, John D and Anne Heindel, 'Trauma in the Courtroom' in Beth Van Schaack, Daryn Reicherter and Youk Chhang (eds), *Cambodia's Hidden Scars: Trauma Psychology in the Wake of the Khmer Rouge* (Documentation Center of Cambodia, 2011) 121

Clarke, Maddee, 'Are We Queer? Reflections on "Peopling the Empty Mirror" Twenty Years On' in Dino Hodge (ed), *Colouring the Rainbow: Blak Queer and Trans Perspectives – Life Stories and Essays by First Nations People of Australia* (Wakefield Press, 2015) 238

Cockburn, Patrick, *The Rise of Islamic State: ISIS and the New Sunni Revolution* (Verso, 2015)

Cohen, Felix S, 'The Spanish Origin of Indian Rights in the Law of the United States' (1942) 31 *Georgetown Law Journal* 1

Cohen, Roseann, 'Extractive Desires: The Moral Control of Female Sexuality at Colombia's Gold Mining Frontier' (2014) 19 *Journal of Latin American and Caribbean Anthropology* 260

Comaroff, John L and Jean Comaroff, 'Law and Disorder in the Postcolony: An Introduction' in Jean Comaroff and John L Comaroff (eds), *Law and Disorder in the Postcolony* (University of Chicago Press, 2000) 1

Cooper, Davina, *Challenging Diversity: Rethinking Equality and the Value of Difference* (Cambridge University Press, 2004)

Corrêa, Sonia, Horacio Sívori and Bruno Zilli, 'Internet Regulation and Sexual Politics in Brazil' (2012) 55 *Development* 213

Cortés, Hernán, 'Tercera Carta-Relación de Hernán Cortés al Emperador Carlos V, Coyacán, 15 de Mayo de 1522' in *Cartas de Relación* (Porrúa, first published 1522, 2015 edn) 129

Cossman, Brenda, 'Gender Performance, Sexual Subjects and International Law' (2002) 15 *Canadian Journal of Law and Jurisprudence* 281

Crompton, Louis, *Homosexuality and Civilization* (Belknap Press, 2003)

Cruz-Malave, Arnaldo and Martin F Manalansan (eds), *Queer Globalizations: Citizenship and the Afterlife of Colonialism* (New York University Press, 2002)

Curtis, Brie Ngala, 'Kungakunga: Staying Close to Family and Country' in Dino Hodge (ed), *Colouring the Rainbow: Blak Queer and Trans Perspectives – Life Stories and Essays by First Nations People of Australia* (Wakefield Press, 2015) 35

Cuvelier, Jeroen, 'Money, Migration and Masculinity among Artisanal Miners in Katanga (DR Congo)' (2016) *Review of African Political Economy* 7

Daly, Angela, 'The Law and Ethics of "Self Quantified" Health Information: An Australian Perspective' (2015) 5 *International Data Privacy Law* 144

Davies, Margaret, 'Taking the Inside Out: Sex and Gender in the Legal Subject' in Ngaire Naffine and Rosemary J Owens (eds), *Sexing the Subject of Law* (Sweet & Maxwell, 1997) 25

Davis, Angela, *The Prison Industrial Complex* (AK Press, 1999)

Dean, Jodi, *Publicity's Secret: How Technoculture Capitalizes on Democracy* (Cornell University Press, 2002)

Dembour, Marie-Bénédicte and Emily Haslam, 'Silencing Hearings? Victim-Witnesses at War Crimes Trials' (2004) 15 *European Journal of International Law* 151

DeNardis, Laura, 'Hidden Levers of Internet Control: An Infrastructure-Based Theory of Internet Governance' (2012) 15 *Information, Communication & Society* 720

———, *The Global War for Internet Governance* (Yale University Press, 2014)

DeNardis, Laura and Andrea M Hackl, 'Internet Control Points as LGBT Rights Mediation' (2016) 19 *Information, Communication & Society* 753

Denike, Margaret, 'The Devil's Insatiable Sex: A Genealogy of Evil Incarnate' (2003) 18 *Hypatia* 10

———, 'What's Queer about Polygamy?' in Robert Leckey and Kim Brooks (eds), *Queer Theory: Law, Culture, Empire* (Routledge, 2010) 137

———, 'The Sex of Right Reason: Aquinas and the Misogynist Foundations of Natural Law' in Maria Drakopoulou (ed), *Feminist Encounters with Legal Philosophy* (Routledge, 2013) 20

Derrida, Jacques, 'Force of Law: The "Mystical Foundation of Authority"' (1990) 11 *Cardozo Law Review* 919

Derrida, Jacques and Anne Dufourmantelle, *Of Hospitality* (Rachel Bowlby trans, Stanford University Press, 2000)

Domínguez, Daniela G, Bernadette H Solórzano and Ezequiel Peña, 'Nonheterosexual Binational Families: Resilient Victims of Sexual Prejudice and Discriminatory Immigration Policies' (2012) 8 *Journal of GLBT Family Studies* 496

Duggan, Lisa, 'The New Homonormativity: The Sexual Politics of Neoliberalism' in Russ Castronovo and Dana D Nelson (eds), *Materialising Democracy: Towards a Revitalised Cultural Politics* (Duke University Press, 2002) 175

———, *The Twilight of Equality? Neoliberalism, Cultural Politics, and the Attack on Democracy* (Beacon Press, 2003)

Dummett, Michael, *On Immigration and Refugees* (Taylor & Francis, 2001)

Dunne, Peter, 'LGBTI Rights and the Wrong Way to Give Aid' (2012) 12 *Harvard Kennedy School Review* 66

———, 'Commentary: *YY v Turkey*: Infertility as a Pre-condition for Gender Confirmation Surgery' (2015) 23 *Medical Law Review* 646

Durham, Helen and Katie O'Byrne, 'The Dialogue of Difference: Gender Perspectives on International Humanitarian Law' (2010) 92(877) *International Review of the Red Cross* 31

Edelman, Lee, *Homographesis: Essays in Gay Literary and Cultural Theory* (Routledge, 1994)

Elander, Maria, 'Prosecuting the Khmer Rouge Marriages' (2016) 42 *Australian Feminist Law Journal* 163

El-Tayeb, Fatima, *European Others: Queering Ethnicity in Postnational Europe* (University of Minnesota Press, 2011)

Eng, David L, *The Feeling of Kinship: Queer Liberalism and the Racialization of Intimacy* (Duke University Press, 2010)

Eng, David L, Judith Halberstam and José Esteban Muñoz, 'Introduction: What's Queer about Queer Studies Now?' (2005) 23(3–4) *Social Text* 1

Engle, Karen, 'The Grip of Sexual Violence: Reading UN Security Council Resolutions on Human Security' in Gina Heathcote and Dianne Otto (eds), *Rethinking Peacekeeping, Gender Equality and Collective Security* (Palgrave Macmillan, 2014) 23

Enloe, Cynthia, *Maneuvers: The International Politics of Militarizing Women's Lives* (University of California Press, 2000)

———, 'The Surprised Feminist' (2000) 25 *Signs: Journal of Women in Culture and Society* 1023

———, *The Curious Feminist: Searching for Women in a New Age of Empire* (University of California Press, 2004)

———, 'A Conversation with Cynthia Enloe on Curiosity, Confidence, and Feminist Questions' (2014) 38(2) *Fletcher Forum of World Affairs* 13

Equiano, Olaudah, *The Interesting Narrative of the Life of Olaudah Equiano, or Gustavus Vassa, the African Written by Himself* (Project Gutenberg, first published 1789, 2005 edn) <http://www.gutenberg.org/files/15399/15399-h/15399-h.htm>

Eshun, P A, 'Sustainable Small-Scale Gold Mining in Ghana: Setting and Strategies for Sustainability' in B R Marker, M G Petterson, F McEvoy and M H Stephenson (eds), *Sustainable Minerals Operations in the Developing World* (Geological Society, 2005) 61

Eskridge, William N, *The Case for Same-Sex Marriage: From Sexual Liberty to Civilized Commitment* (Free Press, 1996)

Esmeir, Samera, 'The Violence of Non-Violence: Law and War in Iraq' (2007) 34 *Journal of Law and Society* 99

Ewald, Francois, 'A Power Without an Exterior' in Timothy J Armstrong (ed), *Michel Foucault Philosopher: Essays Translated from the French and German* (Harvester Wheatsheaf, 1992) 169

Fawthrop, Tom and Helen Jarvis, *Getting Away with Genocide? Elusive Justice and the Khmer Rouge Tribunal* (University of New South Wales Press, 2005)

Ferguson, James, *Global Shadows: Africa in the Neoliberal World Order* (Duke University Press, 2006)

Ferguson, James and Akhil Gupta, 'Spatializing States: Toward an Ethnography of Neoliberal Governmentality' (2002) 29 *American Ethnologist* 981

Ferguson, Roderick A, 'Of Our Normative Strivings: African American Studies and the Histories of Sexuality' (2005) 23(3–4) *Social Text* 85

Foucault, Michel, *The History of Sexuality: An Introduction* (Robert Hurley trans, Vintage, first published 1976, 1990 edn) vol 1

———, *Seksualitetens Historie I: Viljen til Viten* (Espen Schaaning trans, Pax, first published 1976, 1999 edn) [trans of: *Histoire de la sexualité 1: La volonté de savoir*]

———, 'Politics and the Study of Discourse' in Graham Burchell, Colin Gordon and Peter Miller (eds), *The Foucault Effect: Studies in Governmentality* (University of Chicago Press, 1991) 53

———, 'Governmentality' (Pasquale Pasquino trans) in Graham Burchell, Colin Gordon and Peter Miller (eds), *The Foucault Effect: Studies in Governmentality with Two Lectures by and an Interview with Michel Foucault* (University of Chicago Press, 1991) 87

Franke, Katherine, 'Dating the State: The Moral Hazards of Winning Gay Rights' (2012) 44 *Columbia Human Rights Law Review* 1

Franklin, Sarah and Susan McKinnon, 'New Directions in Kinship Study: A Core Concept Revisited' (2000) 41 *Current Anthropology* 275

Gallagher, Julia, 'Can Melanie Klein Help Us Understand Morality in IR? Suggestions for a Psychoanalytic Interpretation of Why and How States Do Good' (2009) 38 *Millennium: Journal of International Studies* 295

Gandhi, Leela, *Affective Communities: Anticolonial Thought, Fin-de-Siècle Radicalism, and the Politics of Friendship* (Duke University Press, 2006)

———, 'A Case of Radical Kinship: Edward Carpenter and the Politics of Anti-Colonial Sexual Dissidence' in Brinda Bose and Subhabrata Bhattacharyya (eds), *The Phobic and the Erotic: The Politics of Sexualities in Contemporary India* (Seagull Books, 2007) 92

Gerber, Paula and Joel Gory, 'The UN Human Rights Committee and LGBT Rights: What Is It Doing? What Could It Be Doing?' (2014) 14 *Human Rights Law Review* 403

Giles, Geoffrey J, 'The Institutionalization of Homosexual Panic in the Third Reich' in Robert Gellately and Nathan Stoltzfus (eds), *Social Outsiders in Nazi Germany* (Princeton University Press, 2001) 233

Gill, Nick, 'Whose "No Borders"? Achieving Border Liberalization for the Right Reasons' (2009) 26(2) *Refuge* 107

Gilmore, Stephen, 'The Legal Status of Transsexual and Transgender Persons in England and Wales' in Jens M Scherpe (ed), *The Legal Status of Transsexual and Transgender Persons* (Intersentia, 2015) 183

Girard, Françoise, 'Negotiating Sexual Rights and Sexual Orientation at the UN' in Richard Parker, Rosalind Petchesky and Robert Sember (eds), *Sex Politics: Reports from the Front Lines* (Sexual Policy Watch) 311

Goldberg, Jonathan, *Sodometries: Renaissance Texts, Modern Sexualities* (Stanford University Press, 1992)

———, 'Introduction' in Jonathan Goldberg (ed), *Reclaiming Sodom* (Routledge, 1994) 1

Goldsmith, Jack and Tim Wu, *Who Controls the Internet?: Illusions of a Borderless World* (Oxford University Press, 2008)

Gopinath, Gayatri, *Impossible Desires: Queer Diasporas and South Asian Public Cultures* (Duke University Press, 2005)

Gordon, Avery F, *Ghostly Matters: Haunting and the Sociological Imagination* (University of Minnesota Press, 1997)

Gordon, Colin, 'Governmental Rationality: An Introduction' in Graham Burchell, Colin Gordon and Peter Miller (eds), *The Foucault Effect: Studies in Governmentality* (University of Chicago Press, 1991) 1

Gray, Mary L, *Out in the Country: Youth, Media, and Queer Visibility in Rural America* (New York University Press, 2009)

Gross, Aeyal, 'Between the Homosocial and the Homoerotic: Gays/Military in Comparative and International Law' in A-Ch Kiss and Johann G Lammers (eds), *Hague Yearbook of International Law* (Martinus Nijhoff, 2001) vol 13, 86

———, 'Queer Theory and International Human Rights Law: Does Each Person Have a Sexual Orientation?' (2007) 101 *American Society of International Law Proceedings* 129

———, 'Post/Colonial Queer Globalisation and International Human Rights: Images of LGBT Rights' (2013) 4(2) *Jindal Global Law Review* 98

———, 'The Politics of LGBT Rights in Israel and beyond: Nationality, Normativity, and Queer Politics' (2015) 46 *Columbia Human Rights Law Review* 81

———, 'Gay Governance: A Queer Critique' in Janet Halley et al (eds), *Governance Feminism: A Reader* (University of Minnesota Press, forthcoming 2017)

Habermas, Jürgen, *The Theory of Communicative Action* (Thomas McCarthy trans, Beacon Press, 1984) vols 1, 2

Halley, Janet, *Split Decisions: How and Why to Take a Break from Feminism* (Princeton University Press, 2006)

Halley, Janet, Prabha Kotiswaran, Hila Shamir and Chantal Thomas, 'From the International to the Local in Feminist Legal Responses to Rape, Prostitution/Sex Work and Sex Trafficking: Four Studies in Contemporary Governance Feminism' (2006) 29 *Harvard Journal of Law and Gender* 335

Halperin, David M, *One Hundred Years of Homosexuality: And Other Essays on Greek Love* (Routledge, 1990)

———, *Saint Foucault: Towards a Gay Hagiography* (Oxford University Press, 1995)

Hamzić, Vanja, 'The Case of "Queer Muslims": Sexual Orientation and Gender Identity in International Human Rights Law and Muslim Legal and Social Ethos' (2011) 11 *Human Rights Law Review* 237

———, 'Unlearning Human Rights and False Grand Dichotomies: Indonesian Archipelagic Selves beyond Sexual/Gender Universality' (2012) 4(1) *Jindal Global Law Review* 157

———, *Sexual and Gender Diversity in the Muslim World: History, Law and Vernacular Knowledge* (I B Tauris, 2016)

———, 'Alegality: Outside and beyond the Legal Logic of Late Capitalism' in Honor Brabazon (ed), *Neoliberal Legality: Understanding the Role of Law in the Neoliberal Project* (Routledge, 2016) 192

Han, Enze and Joseph O'Mahoney, 'British Colonialism and the Criminalization of Homosexuality' (2014) 27 *Cambridge Review of International Affairs* 268

Hanke, Lewis, *Aristotle and the American Indians: A Study in Race Prejudice in the Modern World* (Indiana University Press, 1975)

Harrison, Peter, 'Curiosity, Forbidden Knowledge, and the Reformation of Natural Philosophy in Early Modern England' (2001) 92 *Isis* 265

Hathaway, James C and Jason Pobjoy, 'Queer Cases Make Bad Law' (2012) 44 *New York University Journal of International Law and Politics* 315

Hayter, Teresa, *Open Borders: The Case Against Immigration Controls* (Pluto Press, 2000)

Heathcote, Gina, 'Naming and Shaming: Human Rights Accountability in Security Council Resolution 1960 (2010) on Women, Peace and Security' (2012) 4 *Journal of Human Rights Practice* 82

———, 'Feminist Perspectives on the Law on the Use of Force' in Marc Weller (ed), *The Oxford Handbook of the Use of Force in International Law* (Oxford University Press, 2015) 114

Heinze, Eric, 'Sexual Orientation and International Law: A Study in the Manufacture of Cross-Cultural "Sensitivity"' (2001) 22 *Michigan Journal of International Law* 283

Hellum, Anne, 'Vern mot Diskriminering på grunnlag av seksuell legning, kjønnsidentitet og kjønnsuttrykk – religiøse kjønnsdogmer i møte med internasjonal og norsk rett' in Reidun Førde, Morten Kjelland and Ulf Stridbeck (eds), *Festskrift til Aslak Syse 70 år* (Gyldendal, 2016) 191

Henry, Nicola, 'The Fixation on Wartime Rape: Feminist Critique and International Criminal Law' (2014) 23 *Social & Legal Studies* 93

Hilson, Gavin, 'Small-Scale Mining, Poverty and Economic Development in Sub-Saharan Africa: An Overview' (2009) 34(1–2) *Resources Policy* 1

Hilson, Gavin and Angélique Gatsinzi, 'A Rocky Road Ahead? Critical Reflections on the Futures of Small-Scale Mining in sub-Saharan Africa' (2014) 62(A) *Futures* 1

Hilson, Gavin and James McQuilken, 'Four Decades of Support for Artisanal and Small-Scale Mining in sub-Saharan Africa: A Critical Review' (2014) 1 *Extractive Industries and Society* 104

Ho, S Iimay and Megan E Rolfe, 'Same-Sex Partner Immigration and the Civil Rights Frame: A Comparative Study of Australia, Israel, and the USA' (2011) 52 *International Journal of Comparative Sociology* 390

Hoad, Neville, 'Arrested Development or the Queerness of Savages: Resisting Evolutionary Narratives of Difference' (2000) 3 *Postcolonial Studies* 133

Hodgson, Dorothy L and Sheryl A McCurdy (eds), *'Wicked' Women and the Reconfiguration of Gender in Africa* (Heinemann, 2001)

Hoefinger, Heidi, Pisey Ly and Srorn Srun, 'Sex Politics and Moral Panics: LGBT Communities, Sex/Entertainment Workers and Sexually Active Youth in Cambodia' in Katherine Brickell and Simon Springer (eds), *The Handbook of Contemporary Cambodia* (Routledge, 2016) 315

Holtmaat, Rikki and Paul Post, 'Enhancing LGBTI Rights by Changing the Interpretation of the Convention on the Elimination of All Forms of Discrimination against Women?' in Anne Hellum (ed), *Human Rights, Sexual Orientation, and Gender Identity* (Routledge, 2017) 319

Hook, Derek, 'White Privilege, Psychoanalytic Ethics, and the Limitations of Political Silence' (2011) 30 *South African Journal of Philosophy* 494

Horswell, J, *Decolonizing the Sodomite: Queer Tropes of Sexuality in Colonial Andean Culture* (University of Texas, 2005)

Hoskote, Ranjit, *I, Lalla: The Poems of Lal Dĕd* (Ranjit Hoskote trans, Penguin, 2012)

Huggins, Chris, Doris Buss and Blair Rutherford, 'A "Cartography of Concern": Place-Making Practices and Gender in the Artisanal Mining Sector in Africa' (2016) 74 *Geoforum* 182

Irigaray, Luce, 'Toward a Divine in the Feminine' in Gillian Howie and J'annine Jobling (eds), *Women and the Divine: Touching Transcendence* (Palgrave Macmillan, 2009)

Jansen, Sabine, 'Fleeing Homophobia, Asylum Claims Related to Sexual Orientation and Gender Identity in Europe' in Thomas Spijkerboer (ed), *Fleeing Homophobia: Sexual Orientation, Gender Identity and Asylum* (Taylor & Francis, 2013) 1

Johnson, Crystal, 'Napanangka: The True Power of Being Proud' in Dino Hodge (ed), *Colouring the Rainbow: Blak Queer and Trans Perspectives – Life Stories and Essays by First Nations People of Australia* (Wakefield Press, 2015) 21

Johnson, Janet Elise and Aino Saarinen, 'Twenty-First-Century Feminisms under Repression: Gender Regime Change and the Women's Crisis Center Movement in Russia' (2013) 38 *Signs: Journal of Women in Culture and Society* 543

Johnstone, Ian, 'Security Council Deliberations: The Power of the Better Argument' (2003) 14 *European Journal of International Law* 437

Jordaan, Eduard, 'The Challenge of Adopting Sexual Orientation Resolutions at the UN Human Rights Council' (2016) 8 *Journal of Human Rights Practice* 298

Jordan, Mark D, *The Invention of Sodomy in Christian Theology* (University of Chicago Press, 1997)

Kak Odin, Jaishree, *To the Other Shore: Lalla's Life and Poetry* (Vitasta, 1999)

———, 'Introduction' in *Mystical Verses of Lallā: A Journey of Self Realisation* (Jaishree Kak trans, Motilal Banarsidass Publishers, 2007)

Kapur, Ratna, *Makeshift Migrants and Law: Gender, Belonging and Postcolonial Anxieties* (Routledge, 2010)

———, 'De-Radicalising the Rights Claims of Sexual Subalterns through "Tolerance"' in Robert Leckey and Kim Brooks (eds), *Queer Theory: Law, Culture, Empire* (Routledge, 2010) 37

———, 'Gender, Sovereignty, and the Rise of a Sexual Security Regime in International Law and Postcolonial India' (2013) 14 *Melbourne Journal of International Law* 317

Karaian, Lara, 'Pregnant Men: Repronormativity, Critical Trans Theory and the Re(conceive)ing of Sex and Pregnancy in Law' (2013) 22 *Social & Legal Studies* 211

Kasumi, Nakagawa, *Gender-Based Violence During the Khmer Rouge Regime: Stories of Survivors from the Democratic Kampuchea (1975–1979)* (GBV Under the Khmer Rouge, 2nd edn, 2008)

Katyal, Sonya, 'Exporting Identity' (2002) 14 *Yale Journal of Law and Feminism* 97

Kaufman, Will, 'On the Psychology of Slavery Reparation: A Kleinian Reading' (2007) 4 *Atlantic Studies* 267

Kennedy, David, 'Primitive Legal Scholarship' (1986) 27 *Harvard International Law Journal* 1

Kirby, Michael, 'The Sodomy Offence: England's Least Lovely Criminal Law Export?' in Corinne Lennox and Matthew Waites (eds), *Human Rights, Sexual Orientation and Gender Identity in the Commonwealth: Struggles for Decriminalisation and Change* (Institute of Commonwealth Studies, 2013) 61

Kosinski, Michal, David Stillwell and Thore Graepel, 'Private Traits and Attributes Are Predictable from Digital Records of Human Behavior' (2013) 110 *Proceedings of the National Academy of Sciences* 5802

Koskiennemi, Martti, 'International Law and Raison D'état: Rethinking the Prehistory of International Law' in Benedict Kingsbury and Benjamin Straumann (eds), *The Roman Foundations of the Law of Nations: Alberico Gentili and the Justice of Empire* (Oxford University Press, 2010) 297

Kretz, Adam J, 'Aid Conditionality as (Partial) Answer to Antigay Legislation: An Analysis of British and American Foreign Aid Policies Designed to Protect Sexual Minorities' (2013) 7 *Vienna Online Journal on International Constitutional Law* 476

Kristó-Nagy, István T, 'Violence, Our Inherent Heritage' in Robert Gleave and István T Kristó-Nagy (eds), *Violence in Islamic Thought from the Qur'ān to the Mongols* (Edinburgh University Press, 2015) 2

Lahiri-Dutt, Kuntala, '"May God Give Us Chaos, So That We Can Plunder": A Critique of "Resource Curse" and Conflict Theories' (2006) 49(3) *Development* 14

———, 'Digging Women: Towards a New Agenda for Feminist Critiques of Mining' (2012) 19 *Journal of Feminist Geography* 193

de Langis, Theresa, 'A Missed Opportunity, a Last Hope? Prosecuting Sexual Crimes under the Khmer Rouge Regime' (2014) 2 *Cambodia Law and Policy Journal* 39

———, '"This is Now the Most Important Trial in the World": A New Reading of Code #6, the Rule against Immoral Offenses under the Khmer Rouge Regime' (2014) 3 *Cambodia Law and Policy Journal* 61

Laub, Dori, 'Bearing Witness, or the Vicissitudes of Listening' in Shoshana Felman and Dori Laub, *Testimony: Crises of Witnessing in Literature, Psychoanalysis and History* (Taylor & Francis, 2013) 57

LaViolette, Nicole and Sandra Whitworth, 'No Safe Haven: Sexuality as a Universal Human Right and Gay and Lesbian Activism in International Politics' (1994) 23 *Millennium: Journal of International Studies* 563

Lenin, Vladimir Ilyich, 'What Is to Be Done?' in Vladimir Ilyich Lenin, *Essential Works of Lenin: 'What Is to Be Done?' and Other Writings* (BN Publishing, 2009) 53

Lennox, Corinne and Matthew Waites, 'Human Rights, Sexual Orientation and Gender Identity in the Commonwealth: From History and Law to Developing Activism and Transnational Dialogues' in Corinne Lennox and Matthew Waites (eds), *Human Rights, Sexual Orientation and Gender Identity in the Commonwealth: Struggles for Decriminalisation and Change* (Institute of Commonwealth Studies, 2013) 1

Levidow, Les and Kevin Robins, *Cyborg Worlds: The Military Information Society* (Free Association Books, 1989)

Lewis, Rachel, 'Lesbians under Surveillance: Same-Sex Immigration Reform, Gay Rights, and the Problem of Queer Liberalism' (2010) 37(1) *Social Justice* 90

———, 'Deportable Subjects: Lesbians and Political Asylum' (2013) 25(2) *Feminist Formations* 174

———, '"Gay? Prove it": The Politics of Queer Anti-Deportation Activism' (2014) 17 *Sexualities* 958

Lilja, Mona, *Gender in a Global/Local World: Resisting Gendered Norms: Civil Society, the Juridical and Political Space in Cambodia* (Ashgate, 2013)

Lindahl, Hans, 'A-Legality: Postnationalism and the Question of Legal Boundaries' (2010) 73 *Modern Law Review* 30

Lively, Scott and Kevin Abrams, *The Pink Swastika: Homosexuality in the Nazi Party* (Veritas Aeterna Press, 4th edn, 2002)

Lowe, Vaughan, Adam Roberts, Jennifer Welsh and Dominik Zaum, 'Introduction' in Vaughan Lowe, Adam Roberts, Jennifer Welsh and Dominik Zaum (eds), *The United Nations Security Council and War: The Evolution of Thought and Practice since 1945* (Oxford University Press, 2008) 1

Luibhéid, Eithne and Lionel Cantú Jr (eds), *Queer Migrations: Sexuality, US Citizenship, and Border Crossings* (University of Minnesota Press, 2005)

MacLean, Don, *Internet Governance: A Grand Collaboration: An Edited Collection of Papers Contributed to the United Nations ICT Task Force Global Forum on Internet Governance, New York, March 25–26, 2004* (UN Publications, 2004)

Malkki, Liisa H, 'Refugees and Exile: From "Refugee Studies" to the National Order of Things' (1995) 24 *Annual Review of Anthropology* 495

Marvel, Stu, 'Polymorphous Reproductivity and the Critique of Futurity: Toward a Queer Legal Analytic for Fertility Law' (2013) 2(4) *Jindal Global Law Review* 298

Massad, Joseph, 'Re-orienting Desire: The Gay International and the Arab World' (2002) 14 *Public Culture* 361

———, *Desiring Arabs* (University of Chicago Press, 2007)

Maxwell, Richard, *Herbert Schiller* (Rowman & Littlefield, 2003)

McAdam, Jane, 'An Intellectual History of Freedom of Movement in International Law: The Right to Leave as Personal Liberty' (2011) 12 *Melbourne Journal of International Law* 1

McClintock, *Anne, Imperial Leather: Race, Gender, and Sexuality in the Colonial Contest* (Routledge, 1995)

McEwan, Ian, *Atonement* (Vintage, 2002)

McGill, Jena, 'SOGI . . . So What?: Sexual Orientation, Gender Identity and Human Rights Discourse at the United Nations' (2014) 3 *Canadian Journal of Human Rights* 1

McGregor, Sue, 'Neoliberalism and Health Care' (2001) 25 *International Journal of Consumer Studies* 82

McGuinness, Sheelagh and Amel Alghrani, 'Gender and Parenthood: The Case for Realignment' (2008) 16 *Medical Law Review* 261

McLennan, Sharon J, 'Techno-Optimism or Information Imperialism: Paradoxes in Online Networking, Social Media and Development' (2016) 22 *Information Technology for Development* 380

McNulty, Tracy, *Hostess: Hospitality, Femininity, and the Expropriation of Identity* (University of Minnesota Press, 2006)

Medeiros, John, 'Immigration after DOMA: How Equal Is Marriage Equality?' (2014) 35 *Hamline Journal of Public Law & Policy* 196

Mendelson, M H, 'Diminutive States in the United Nations' (1972) 21 *International and Comparative Law Quarterly* 609

Merry, Sally Engle, 'New Legal Realism and the Ethnography of Transnational Law' (2006) 31 *Law & Social Inquiry* 975

Mertens, Charlotte and Maree Pardy, '"Sexurity" and Its Effects in Eastern Democratic Republic of Congo' (2017) 38 *Third World Quarterly* 956

Miéville, China, *Between Equal Rights: A Marxist Theory of International Law* (Brill, 2005)

Millbank, Jenni, 'The Right of Lesbians and Gay Men to Live Freely, Openly, and on Equal Terms Is Not Bad Law: A Reply to Hathaway and Pobjoy' (2012) 44 *New York University Journal of International Law and Politics* 497

———, 'Sexual Orientation and Refugee Status Determination over the Past 20 Years: Unsteady Progress through Standard Sequences?' in Thomas Spijkerboer (ed), *Fleeing Homophobia: Sexual Orientation, Gender Identity and Asylum* (Taylor & Francis, 2013) 32

Miller, Alice M and Mindy J Roseman, 'Sexual and Reproductive Rights at the United Nations: Frustration or Fulfilment?' (2011) 19(38) *Reproductive Health Matters* 102

Mirrlees, Tanner, 'US Empire and Communications Today: Revisiting Herbert I Schiller' (2015) 3(2) *The Political Economy of Communication* 3

Moodie, T Dunbar, 'Migrancy and Male Sexuality on the South African Gold Mines' (1988) 14 *Journal of Southern African Studies* 228

Moran, Leslie J, *The Homosexual(ity) of Law* (Routledge, 1996)

Morgan, Wayne, 'Queering International Human Rights Law' in Carl Stychin and Didi Herman (eds), *Law and Sexuality: The Global Arena* (University of Minnesota Press, 2001) 208

Mosco, Vincent, *The Political Economy of Communication: Rethinking and Renewal* (Sage, 1996)

Mueller, Milton L, *Networks and States: The Global Politics of Internet Governance* (MIT Press, 2010)

Munkholm, Natalie Videbæk, 'Legal Status of Transsexual and Transgender Persons in Denmark' in Jens M Scherpe (ed), *The Legal Status of Transsexual and Transgender Persons* (Intersentia, 2015) 147

Muñoz, José Esteban, *Cruising Utopia: The Then and There of Queer Futurity* (New York University Press, 2009)

Musiani, Francesca, Derrick L Cogburn, Laura DeNardis and Nanette S Levinson (eds), *The Turn to Infrastructure in Internet Governance* (Palgrave Macmillan, 2015)

Mutua, Makau, 'Savages, Victims, and Saviors: The Metaphor of Human Rights' (2001) 42 *Harvard International Law Journal* 201

Narrain, Arvind and Gautam Bhan (eds), *Because I Have a Voice: Queer Politics in India* (Yoda Press, 2005)

Neff, Stephen C, *Justice Among Nations: A History of International Law* (Harvard University Press, 2014)

Nussbaum, Arthur, *A Concise History of the Law of Nations* (Macmillan, 1947)

Nyers, Peter, 'Forms of Irregular Citizenship' in Vicki Squires (ed), *The Contested Politics of Mobility: Borderzones and Irregularity* (Routledge, 2011) 184

O'Flaherty, Michael, 'The Yogyakarta Principles at Ten' in Anne Hellum (ed), *Human Rights, Sexual Orientation, and Gender Identity* (Routledge, 2017) 280

Ong, Aihwa, *Flexible Citizenship: The Cultural Logics of Transnationality* (Duke University Press, 1999)

Ong, Aihwa and Stephen J Collier (eds), *Global Assemblages: Technology, Politics, and Ethics as Anthropological Problems* (Wiley-Blackwell, 2008)

Opsahl, Torkel, *Internasjonale Menneskerettigheter: En Innføring* (Institutt for Menneskerettigheter, 2nd edn, 1996)

Osiander, Andreas, *The States System of Europe 1640–1990: Peacemaking and the Conditions of International Stability* (Oxford University Press, 1994)

Österdahl, Inger, *Threat to the Peace: The Interpretation by the Security Council of Article 39 of the UN Charter* (Iustus, 1998)

Otto, Dianne, 'The Sexual Tensions of UN Peace Support Operations: A Plea for "Sexual Positivity"' (2007) 18 *Finnish Yearbook of International Law* 33

———, 'Power and Danger: Feminist Engagement with International Law through the UN Security Council' (2010) 32 *Australian Feminist Law Journal* 99

———, 'International Human Rights Law: Towards Rethinking Sex/Gender Dualism' in Margaret Davies and Vanessa Munro (eds), *A Research Companion to Feminist Legal Theory* (Ashgate Companion Series, 2013) 197

———, 'Transnational Homo-Assemblages: Reading "Gender" in Counter-Terrorism Discourses' (2013) 4(2) *Jindal Global Law Review* 79

———, 'Between Pleasure and Danger: Lesbian Human Rights' (2014) (6) *European Human Rights Law Review* 618

———, 'Beyond Stories of Victory and Danger: Resisting Feminism's Amenability to Serving Security Council Politics' in Gina Heathcote and Dianne Otto (eds), *Rethinking Peacekeeping, Gender Equality and Collective Security* (Palgrave Macmillan, 2014) 157

———, 'Decoding Crisis in International Law: A Queer Feminist Perspective' in Barbara Stark (ed), *International Law and Its Discontents: Confronting Crises* (Cambridge University Press, 2015) 115

———, 'Queering Gender [Identity] in International Law' (2015) 33 *Nordic Journal of Human Rights* 299

———, 'Contesting Feminism's Institutional Doubles: Troubling the Security Council's Women Peace and Security Agenda' in Janet Halley et al (eds), *Governance Feminism: A Reader* (University of Minnesota Press, forthcoming 2017)

———, 'Queering Gender [Identity] in International Law' in Anne Hellum (ed), *Human Rights, Sexual Orientation, and Gender Identity* (Routledge, 2017) 299

Otto, Dianne and Gina Heathcote, 'Rethinking Peacekeeping, Gender Equality and Collective Security: An Introduction' in Dianne Otto and Gina Heathcote (eds), *Rethinking Peacekeeping, Gender Equality and Collective Security* (Palgrave Macmillan, 2014) 1

Pagden, Anthony, *The Fall of Natural Man: The American Indian and the Origins of Comparative Ethnology* (Cambridge University Press, 1982)

———, *The Uncertainties of Empire: Essays in Iberian and Ibero-American Intellectual History* (Ashgate, 1994)

Pagden, Anthony and Jeremy Lawrance (eds), *Vitoria: Political Writings* (Cambridge University Press, 1991)

Paternotte, David, Manon Tremblay and Carol Johnson (eds), *The Lesbian and Gay Movement and the State: Comparative Insights into a Transformed Relationship* (Ashgate, 2011)

Phillips, Oliver, 'Zimbabwean Law and the Production of a White Man's Disease' (1997) 6 *Social & Legal Studies* 471

Pickard, Daniel, 'When Does Crime Become a Threat to International Peace and Security?' (1998) 12 *Florida Journal of International Law* 1

du Plessis, Max, 'Historical Injustice and International Law: An Exploratory Discussion of Reparation for Slavery' (2003) 25 *Human Rights Quarterly* 624

Porras, Illena M, 'Constructing International Law in the East Indian Seas: Property, Sovereignty, Commerce and War in Hugo Grotius' *De Iure Praedae* – The Law of Prize and Booty, or "On How to Distinguish Merchants from Pirates"' (2006) 31 *Brooklyn Journal of International Law* 741

Powers, Shawn M and Michael Jablonski, *The Real Cyber War: The Political Economy of Internet Freedom* (University of Illinois Press, 2015)

Puar, Jasbir, *Terrorist Assemblages: Homonationalism in Queer Times* (Duke University Press, 2007)

———, 'Rethinking Homonationalism' (2013) 45 *International Journal of Middle East Studies* 336

Rahman, Momin, *Homosexualities, Muslim Cultures and Modernity* (Palgrave MacMillan, 2014)

Raj, Senthorun, 'Affective Displacements: Understanding Emotions and Sexualities in Refugee Law' (2011) 36 *Alternative Law Journal* 177

Rao, Rahul, *Third World Protest: Between Home and the World* (Oxford University Press, 2010)

———, 'Queer Questions' (2014) 16 *International Feminist Journal of Politics* 199

———, 'Global Homocapitalism' (2015) 194 *Radical Philosophy* <https://www.radicalphilosophy.com/article/global-homocapitalism>

Rawls, John, *The Law of Peoples: With, the Idea of Public Reason Revisited* (Harvard University Press, 2001)

Rich, Adrienne, 'Compulsory Heterosexuality and Lesbian Existence' (1980) 5 *Signs: Journal of Women in Culture and Society* 631

Rifkin, Mark, *When Did Indians Become Straight? Kinship, the History of Sexuality, and Native Sovereignty* (Oxford University Press, 2011)

Rosaldo, Renato, 'Cultural Citizenship, Inequality, and Multiculturalism' in Rodolfo D Torres, Louis F Mirón and Jonathan Xavier Inda (eds), *Race, Identity, and Citizenship: A Reader* (Blackwell Publishers, 1999) 253

Rose, Nikolas and Mariana Valverde, 'Governed by Law?' (1998) 7 *Social and Legal Studies* 541

Ross, Fiona C, 'On Having Voice and Being Heard: Some After-Effects of Testifying before the South African Truth and Reconciliation Commission' (2003) 3 *Anthropological Theory* 325

Rubin, Gayle, 'Thinking Sex: Notes for a Radical Theory of the Politics of Sexuality' in Carole S Vance (ed), *Pleasure and Danger: Exploring Female Sexuality* (Routledge, 1984) 267

———, 'Thinking Sex: Notes for a Radical Theory of the Politics of Sexuality' in Henry Abelove, Michèle Aina Barale and David M Halperin (eds), *The Lesbian and Gay Studies Reader* (Routledge, 1993) 3

Ruskola, Teemu, 'Law, Sexual Morality, and Gender Equality in Qing and Communist China' (1994) 103 *Yale Law Journal* 2531

———, 'Raping like a State' (2010) 57 *UCLA Law Review* 1477

———, *Legal Orientalism: China, the United States, and Modern Law* (Harvard University Press, 2013)

Rutherford, Blair, *Farm Labor Struggles in Zimbabwe: The Ground of Politics* (Indiana University Press, forthcoming 2017)

Sachs, Jeffrey D and Andrew M Warner, 'The Curse of Natural Resources' (2001) 45(4–6) *European Economic Review* 827

Said, Edward, *Orientalism* (Penguin, 1979)

Saiz, Ignacio, 'Bracketing Sexuality: Human Rights and Sexual Orientation: A Decade of Development and Denial at the UN' (2004) 7 *Health and Human Rights* 48

Sanders, Douglas, 'Getting Lesbian and Gay Issues on the International Human Rights Agenda' (1996) 18 *Human Rights Quarterly* 67

Sankey, Diana, 'Recognition of Gendered Experiences of Harm at the Extraordinary Chambers in the Courts of Cambodia: The Promise and the Pitfalls' (2016) 24 *Feminist Legal Studies* 7

Sarat, Austin and Thomas R Kearns, 'Introduction' in Austin Sarat and Thomas R Kearns (eds), *Law's Violence* (University of Michigan Press, 1995) 1

———, 'Making Peace with Violence: Robert Cover on Law and Legal Theory' in Austin Sarat and Thomas R Kearns (eds), *Law's Violence* (University of Michigan Press, 1995) 211

Sartre, Jean-Paul, 'Préface' in Frantz Fanon, *Les damnés de la terre* (François Maspero, 1961) 17

———, 'Preface' in Frantz Fanon, *The Wretched of the Earth* (R Philcox trans, Grove Press, 2004) xliii

Sassen, Saskia, 'Two Stops in Today's New Global Geographies: Shaping Novel Labor Supplies and Employment Regimes' (2008) 52 *American Behavioral Scientist* 457

Scavone, Heather, 'Queer Evidence: The Peculiar Evidentiary Burden Faced by Asylum Applicants with Cases Based on Sexual Orientation and Identity' (2013) 5 *Elon Law Review* 389

Scheffer, David, *All the Missing Souls, A Personal History of the War Crimes Tribunals* (Princeton University Press, 2012)

Schiller, Dan, 'The Militarization of US Communications' in Janet Wasko, Graham Murdock and Helen Sousa (eds), *The Handbook of Political Economy of Communications* (Wiley-Blackwell, 2014) 262

Schiller, Herbert I, *Culture Inc: The Corporate Takeover of Public Expression* (Oxford University Press, 1991)

———, *Mass Communications and American Empire* (Westview Press, 2nd edn, 1992)

Schrover, Marlou, Joanne van der Leun, Leo Lucassen and Chris Quispel (eds), *Illegal Migration and Gender in a Global and Historical Perspective* (Amsterdam University Press, 2008)

Schulman, Sarah, *Israel/Palestine and the Queer International* (Duke University Press, 2012)

Schulze, Matthias, 'Patterns of Surveillance Legitimization: The German Discourse on the NSA Scandal' (2015) 13 *Surveillance & Society* 197

Scott, James C, *Seeing Like a State: How Certain Schemes to Improve the Human Condition Have Failed* (Yale University Press, 1998)

Scott, Joan Wallach, 'Gender: A Useful Category of Historical Analysis' in *Gender and the Politics of History* (Columbia University Press, revised edn, 1999) 28

Scoular, Jane, 'What's Law Got to Do with It? How and Why Law Matters in the Regulation of Sex Work' (2010) 37 *Journal of Law and Society* 12

Sedgwick, Eve Kosofsky, *Epistemology of the Closet* (University of California Press, first published 1990, 2008 edn)

———, *Touching Feeling: Affect, Pedagogy, Performativity* (Duke University Press, 2003)

———, 'How to Bring Your Kids Up Gay: The War on Effeminate Boys' in Steven Bruhm and Natasha Hurley (eds), *Curioser: On the Queerness of Children* (University of Minnesota Press, 2004) 139

Segal, Hanna, *Introduction to the Work of Melanie Klein* (Karnac Books, 1988)

Seglow, Jonathan, 'The Ethics of Immigration' (2005) 3 *Political Studies Review* 317

Seuffert, Nan, 'Haunting National Boundaries LBGTI Asylum Seekers' (2013) 22 *Griffith Law Review* 752

Shachar, Ayelet, *The Birthright Lottery: Citizenship and Global Inequality* (Harvard University Press, 2009)

Shalakany, Amr, 'On a Certain Queer Discomfort with Orientalism' (2007) 101 *American Society of International Law Proceedings* 125

Sharma, Nandita, 'No Borders Movement and the Rejection of Left Nationalism' (2003) 37(3) *Canadian Dimension* 37

———, 'Anti-Trafficking Rhetoric and the Making of a Global Apartheid' (2005) 17(3) *NSWA Journal* 88

Sharpe A, *Transgender Jurisprudence: Dysphoric Bodies of Law* (Cavendish, 2002)

———, *Foucault's Monsters and the Challenge of Law* (Routledge, 2010)

Shepherd, Laura J and Laura Sjoberg, 'Trans- Bodies in/of War(s): Cisprivilege and Contemporary Security Strategy' (2012) 101 *Feminist Review* 5

Shepherd, Verene A, 'Slavery, Shame and Pride: Debates over the Marking of the Bicentennial of the Abolition of the British Trans-Atlantic Trade in Africans in 2007' (2010) 56(1–2) *Caribbean Quarterly* 1

Sherwood, Yvonne, 'Francisco de Vitoria's More Excellent Way: How the Bible of Empire Discovered the Tricks of [the Argument from] Trade' (2013) 21 *Biblical Interpretation* 215

Shuman, Amy and Carol Bohmer, 'Gender and Cultural Silences in the Political Asylum Process' (2014) 17 *Sexualities* 939

Shuman, Amy and Wendy S Hesford, 'Getting Out: Political Asylum, Sexual Minorities, and Privileged Visibility' (2014) 17 *Sexualities* 1016

Simpson, Gerry, *Law, War and Crime: War Crimes Trials and the Reinvention of International Law* (Polity Press, 2007)

Sivakumaran, Sandesh, 'Male/Male Rape and the "Taint" of Homosexuality' (2005) 27 *Human Rights Quarterly* 1274

Sørlie, Anniken, 'Rettighetssubjekter i Endring: Den Fødende Mannen' in Ingunn Ikdahl and Vibeke Blaker Strand (eds), *Rettigheter i Velferdsstaten: Begreper, Trender, Teorier* (Gyldendal, 2016) 227

———, 'Legal Gender Meets Reality: A Socio-Legal Children's Perspective' in Anne Hellum (ed), *Human Rights, Sexual Orientation, and Gender Identity* (Routledge, 2017) 353

Soyer, François, *Ambiguous Gender in Early Modern Spain and Portugal: Inquisitors, Doctors and the Transgression of Gender Norms* (Brill, 2012)

Srikantiah, Jayashri, 'Perfect Victims and Real Survivors: The Iconic Victim in Domestic Human Trafficking Laws' (2007) 87 *Buffalo University Law Review* 157

Standing, Guy, *The Precariat: The New Dangerous Class* (Bloomsbury Academic, 2011)

Stiklestad, Sigrun Saur, 'Det biologiske prinsipps skiftende anvendelse' (2007) 24 *Nytt Norsk Tidsskrift* 138

Stoler, Ann Laura, *Race and the Education of Desire: Foucault's History of Sexuality and the Colonial Order of Things* (Duke University Press, 1995)

Stover, Eric, Mychelle Balthazard and Alexa K Koenig, 'Confronting Duch: Civil Party Participation in *Case 001* at the Extraordinary Chambers in the Courts of Cambodia' (2011) 93(882) *International Review of the Red Cross* 502

Strassberg, Maura I, 'Distinctions of Form or Substance: Monogamy, Polygamy and Same-Sex Marriage' (1997) 75 *North Carolina Law Review* 1501

Stychin, Carl F, 'Same-Sex Sexualities and the Globalization of Human Rights Discourse' (2004) 49 *McGill Law Journal* 951

Swink, Arwen, 'Queer Refuge: A Review of the Role of Country Condition Analysis in Asylum Adjudications for Members of Sexual Minorities' (2006) 29 *Hastings International and Comparative Law Review* 251

Tal, Kali, *Worlds of Hurt: Reading the Literatures of Trauma* (Cambridge University Press, 1996)

Thomas, Chantal, 'What Does the Emerging International Law of Migration Mean for Sovereignty?' (2013) 14 *Melbourne Journal of International Law* 1

Thompson, Janna, 'Apology, Justice, and Respect: A Critical Defense of Political Apology' in Mark Gibney, Rhoda E Howard-Hassmann, Jean-Marc Coicaud and Niklaus Steiner (eds), *The Age of Apology: Facing Up to the Past* (University of Pennsylvania Press, 2008) 31

Thussu, Daya Kishan, *International Communication: Continuity and Change* (Bloomsbury Academic, 2nd edn, 2006)

Tindall, Natalie T J and Richard D Waters, *Coming out of the Closet: Exploring LGBT Issues in Strategic Communication with Theory and Research* (Peter Lang, 2013)

Tomlins, Christopher, *Freedom Bound: Law, Labor, and Civic Identity in Colonizing English America, 1580–1865* (Cambridge University Press, 2010)

Torpey, John, *The Invention of the Passport: Surveillance, Citizenship and the State* (Cambridge University Press, 2000)

Utas, Mats, 'Victimcy, Girlfriending, Soldiering: Tactic Agency in a Young Woman's Social Navigation of the Liberian War Zone' (2005) 78 *Anthropological Quarterly* 403

Vance, Carole S (ed), *Pleasure and Danger: Exploring Female Sexuality* (Routledge and Kegan Paul, 1984)

de Vattel, Emmerich, *The Law of Nations; or Principles of Natural Law, Applied to the Conduct and Affairs of Nations and Sovereigns* (first published 1758, 1844 edn)

de Victoria, Franciscus, 'De Indis et de ivre belli relectiones' in James Brown Scott and Ernest Nys (eds), *The Classics of International Law* (John Pawley Bate trans, Carnegie Institution, 1917)

Wagner, Ben, 'Algorithmic Regulation and the Global Default: Shifting Norms in Internet Technology' (2016) 10(1) *Etikk i praksis – Nordic Journal of Applied Ethics* 5

———, *Global Free Expression – Governing the Boundaries of Internet Content* (Springer, 2016)

Waites, Matthew, 'Critique of "Sexual Orientation" and "Gender Identity" in Human Rights Discourse: Global Queer Politics beyond the Yogakarta Principles' (2009) 15 *Contemporary Politics* 137

Walker, Kristen L, 'Capitalism, Gay Identity, and International Human Rights Law' (2000) 9 *Australasian Gay and Lesbian Law Journal* 58

Walsh, P G, 'Making a Drama Out of a Crisis: Livy on the Bacchanalia' (1996) 43 *Greece & Rome* 188

Walters, William, 'Some Critical Notes on "Governance"' (2004) 73(1) *Studies in Political Economy* 27

Warner, Michael, 'Beyond Gay Marriage' in Wendy Brown and Janet Halley (eds), *Left Legalism/Left Critique* (Duke University Press, 2002) 259

Waterton, Emma, 'Humiliated Silence: Multiculturalism, Blame, and the Trope of "Moving On"' (2010) 8 *Museum and Society* 128

Weber, Cynthia, *Queer International Relations: Sovereignty, Sexuality and the Will to Knowledge* (Oxford University Press, 2016)

Weiner, Myron, 'Ethics, National Sovereignty and the Control of Immigration' (1996) 30 *International Migration Review* 171

Werthmann, Katja, 'Working in a Boom-Town: Female Perspectives on Gold-Mining in Burkina Faso' (2009) 34 *Resources Policy* 18

West, Harry G and Todd Sanders (eds), *Transparency and Conspiracy: Ethnographies of Suspicion in the New World Order* (Duke University Press, 2003)

White, Melissa Autumn, 'Documenting the Undocumented: Toward a Queer Politics of No Borders' (2014) 17 *Sexualities* 976

Wiegman, Robyn and Elizabeth A Wilson, 'Introduction: Antinormativity's Queer Conventions' (2015) 26(1) *Differences: A Journal of Feminist Cultural Studies* 1

Williams, Robert A, *The American Indian in Western Legal Thought: The Discourses of Conquest* (Oxford University Press, 1990)
Wimmer, Andreas and Nina Glick Schiller, 'Methodological Nationalism and Beyond: Nation-State Building, Migration and the Social Sciences' (2002) 2 *Global Networks* 301
Winer, Anthony S, 'Levels of Generality and the Protection of LGBT Rights before the United Nations General Assembly' (2015) 41 *William Mitchell Law Review* 80
Wintemute, Robert, 'From "Sex Rights" to "Love Rights": Partnership Rights as Human Rights' in Nicholas Bamforth (ed), *Sex Rights: The Oxford Amnesty Lectures* (Oxford University Press, 2005) 186
Yamin, Alicia Ely, 'Power, Suffering and Courts: Reflections on Promoting Health Rights through Judicialization' in Alicia Ely Yamin and Siri Gloppen (eds), *Litigating Health Rights: Can Courts Bring More Justice to Health?* (Harvard University Press, 2011) 340
Youyou, Wu, Michal Kosinski and David Stillwell, 'Computer-Based Personality Judgments Are More Accurate than Those Made by Humans' (2015) 112 *Proceedings of the National Academy of Sciences* 1036
Yue, Audrey, 'Same-Sex Migration in Australia: from Interdependency to Intimacy' (2008) 14 *Journal of Lesbian and Gay Studies* 239
Žarkov, Dubravka, *The Body of War: Media, Ethnicity, and Gender in the Break-Up of Yugoslavia* (Duke University Press, 2007)
Žižek, Slavoj, *Violence: Six Sideways Reflections* (Profile Books, 2008)

Index

For Product Safety Concerns and Information please contact our EU representative GPSR@taylorandfrancis.com
Taylor & Francis Verlag GmbH, Kaufingerstraße 24, 80331 München, Germany

www.ingramcontent.com/pod-product-compliance
Ingram Content Group UK Ltd.
Pitfield, Milton Keynes, MK11 3LW, UK
UKHW022013180926
475701UK00003B/345

* 9 7 8 0 3 6 7 8 8 6 3 7 0 *